HOW WE GOT TO THE MOON

The Story of the German Space Pioneers

HOW WE GOT TO THE MOON

The Story of the German Space Pioneers

Marsha Freeman

21st Century Science Associates
Washington, D.C.
1993

Contents

This book is dedicated to my father, Joseph Osofsky, whose love for science and contributions to the space program have always inspired me.

ISBN: 0-9628134-1-9

Library of Congress Catalog Card Number 93-061553

On the cover: Astronaut David R. Scott salutes the American flag, with the lunar mountain Hadley Delta in the background. Scott was the commander of the Apollo 15 mission to the Moon in July-August 1971. (Courtesy of the National Aeronautics and Space Administration)

Project editor: Christina N. Huth
Book design: World Composition Services, Inc., Sterling, Virginia

Please direct all inquiries to the publisher:
21st Century Science Associates
P.O. Box 16285, Washington, D.C. 20041
(703) 777-7473
TCB 93-001

Preface

History will undoubtedly record that man's most magnificent accomplishment of the twentieth century was his first landing on the Moon. This ancient dream—to visit new worlds and explore the reaches of space—could only be fulfilled in this century, when the science and the technologies enabling such a feat had been developed. This dream became reality as a result of the dogged efforts of a relative handful of men.

Certainly, the world's space pioneers were not all German. But the unique group of German scientists who came to the United States after World War II had a view of mankind's role in space that had been nourished by the philosophical world view of Nicholas of Cusa, Gottfried Leibniz, and Friedrich Schiller. German classical culture had produced not only giants in mathematics and the natural sciences, but a Bach, a Mozart, and a Beethoven. In this century, the legacy of German classical culture produced a Hermann Oberth, a Wernher von Braun, and a Krafft Ehricke.

This is the story of the German pioneers of space. Their accomplishments were the fruit of five decades of unwavering determination to take man to the Moon and then farther into space. From the backyard experiments of the 1920s and early 1930s, through the launch of Apollo 11 to the Moon in 1969, these pioneers never lost sight of their goal. They persevered through the economic depression and moral collapse following World War I, the Nazi degradation of Germany and World War II, and a fifteen-year detour working for the U.S. Army.

Although their story has been told before, in books, articles, and even movie and television presentations, much of the history is being forgotten. In the United States, the dream of spaceflight has been replaced on center stage by scare stories and hoaxes, with no regard for scientific truth. In Germany, pessimism and despair among young people have replaced the optimism that flows from a grounding in the classics and science, leading to the proliferation of antisocial, anomic, and terrorist acts.

Not only have the stellar accomplishments of the German space pioneers begun to fade from the past and present history of the space program, but these men have had to suffer the indignity in their later years of having the motivations of their entire lives' work questioned. Regardless of the corruption of today's society and its institutions, what the German space pioneers accomplished is an historical fact. Through their ability to look far into the future, they have left blueprints for mankind's ventures into space well into the 21st century. What will ultimately keep the history of the German space pioneers alive will be the recommitment of nations to permanently place mankind where he rightfully belongs—among the stars.

This book has benefitted from the generous help given in the form of documents, encouragement, time, and critical analysis by numerous people. The author would particularly like to acknowledge the contributions of Robert Allen, Mitchell R. Sharpe, Dr. Walter Haüssermann, Gen. John Medaris and Mrs. Francis Medaris, Dr. Rudolf Hermann, Prof. H.H. Koelle, Dr. Harry Ruppe, Dr. Erna Roth-Oberth, Karl Heinz Rohrwild at the Hermann Oberth Museum, Konrad Dannenberg, Dieter Huzel, Mr. and Mrs. Arthur Rudolph, Dr. Gerhard Reisig, Michael Wright at the Marshall Space Flight Center, Ms. Nancy Stillson at the Redstone Technical Information Center, and the staffs of the Space & Rocket Center in Huntsville, the History Office at NASA headquarters, and the Archives Division of the National Air and Space Museum in Washington, D.C.

Long-time friend and colleague Geoffrey Steinherz, at Böttiger Verlag in Wiesbaden, Germany, provided ideas, enthusiasm, and encouragement for this book, and is now preparing a translation that will be published in German.

Acknowledgement also goes to a patient editor, Christina Nelson Huth.

All of these people made this book better than it would have been without their help. One person made it possible—my husband, William Cuthbert Jones. It was his idea to prepare a book, based on a series of articles I had published in 1985 and on the fact that I had the privilege of knowing some of the principal subjects personally. He translated material from original German sources into English, contributed his knowledge of European history, participated in the interviews conducted in Germany and Huntsville, and helped formulate some of the most complex and difficult concepts in the present work. Most important, this book benefits greatly from his understanding that it is history that created the present, and that history written today will help create the future.

—Marsha Freeman
October 19, 1993
Leesburg, Virginia

Prologue

Much has been written about the several hundred German and Austrian scientists, engineers, and technicians who came to America right after World War II in a U.S. government operation code named Operation Paperclip. They were brought over under short-term contracts to transfer to their American colleagues technologies that had been developed in Germany during the war, particularly at the rocket development center at Peenemünde. Their knowledge and experience were of interest to the Department of Defense, American industry, universities, and other organizations.

In this book, Marsha Freeman relates the story of what is probably the best-known group that emigrated during Operation Paperclip, the Wernher von Braun rocket team. This group was specifically invited by the U.S. Army to assist in the assembly, checkout, and launching of about 100 V-2 rockets, which had been shipped from Germany to the army's White Sands Proving Ground in New Mexico. The purpose was to demonstrate the operations, handling, and final launch of large ballistic missiles. Most team members were also extensively interviewed by American engineers and scientists to build up this country's knowledge of design concepts, requirements, and operations of large liquid-propelled missiles.

After expiration of the initial half-year contract several extensions were granted, until eventually a permanent stay in the country and the acquisition of citizenship were offered. A few members returned at that time to Germany and Austria. Some others joined private industry and subsequently made major contributions to the

aerodynamics, guidance, control, and engine design of ballistic and
guided missiles.

This book describes the beginning of rocketry in Germany,
documenting that the goal and intent of all participants was to
design and develop the means for space travel. The early rocket
amateurs soon discovered that the development of large launch
vehicles requires huge test and fabrication facilities and therefore,
tremendous amounts of funding that cannot be obtained by amateurs. This was the reason behind Wernher von Braun's decision
to join the German army as a civilian employee; it was the only
way to secure facilities and funding for large-scale development of
rockets.

The Soviet Sputnik launch had a dramatic impact on America.
The United States was to be embarrassed by more Soviet "firsts" in
the race for space. Soon, the U.S. military and general public were
demanding greater emphasis on our own efforts, thus getting the
"Missile Race" under way. The German missile team was able to
contribute greatly to the national desire to catch up with Russian
technology. The "Old Reliable" Redstone missile launched the first
American satellite January 31, 1958, and shortly thereafter launched
Alan Shepard and Gus Grissom—the first Americans in space.

The high point of all these priority efforts was the daring venture to send three people to the Moon and have two of them walk
on this heavenly body. This feat will remain the greatest technical
and management achievement of this century. It was principally
the product of the "Wernher von Braun Rocket Team," enhanced
by many American engineers, contractors, and supporting personnel. The only Soviet rocket to match the performance of Apollo is
the Energia, but it was developed 25 years later and has flown only
twice.

As a participant in these developments from the early days in
Peenemünde, I am still interested in the continuing progress of
space exploration. I am still lecturing to our young people at the
United States Space Camp and the Space Academy in Huntsville,
Alabama. I follow all space developments closely, and am disappointed that such missions as a lunar base and manned Mars exploration have been cancelled.

I am chagrined by today's negative attitudes toward space exploration and by the diminution of the contributions of the "rocket
team." Members of the press corps unfortunately do not have all

their facts straight and continue to report faulty stories. Peenemünde is often referred to as "Hitler's Weapons Factory," and it is erroneously reported that concentration camp labor was used by the army. Marsha Freeman's book attempts to correct this error.

Only when Hitler's war fortunes collapsed did he assign highest priority to the development of the V-2. He did not trust the army and he delegated this task to Reichsführer Heinrich Himmler, who was put in charge of V-2 mass production in the Mittelwerk underground factory in central Germany, using concentration camp labor.

It is unfortunate that original developments of reaction systems had to be conducted under military funding and oversight, in Germany as well as in this and many other countries. But, as a result of the shortsightedness of politicians, this has historically been the best way to fund a launch vehicle development program for the exploration and study of space.

Marsha Freeman has extensively researched existing literature and has conducted interviews with many of the quoted individuals. Her book aims to correct false information and present the unbiased facts on the development of rockets, guided missiles, and launch vehicles.

The vision of Hermann Oberth, Wernher von Braun, and Krafft Ehricke got us to where we are today. I hope that, in their memory, we can revive the space program and fulfill all of their dreams. Ambitious programs will set meaningful goals for our youth. They will emphasize the need for education, and they will eventually elevate living standards around the globe. We must soon implement "The Extraterrestrial Imperative." *Ad Astra!*

—Konrad K. Dannenberg

Mr. Dannenberg is a veteran of Peenemünde and was a member of the von Braun rocket team. He is retired from NASA's Marshall Space Flight Center.

Hermann Oberth: The Father of Space Travel

CHAPTER I

From the time that the ancients looked up at the heavens at night to the nearby Moon and the distant twinkling dots of light, man has imagined what it might be like to travel to and explore these celestial bodies. Tales about travels to the Moon and beyond have appeared in literature for millennia, based almost entirely on the writers' creative imagination. With the invention of the telescope, the observer of the heavens became better informed as to what might be found on such a journey, but the question of *how* man could actually travel into space remained in the realm of the imagination.

At the end of the American Civil War, the visionary French author Jules Verne made the first serious attempt to propose a technology for lofting men into space. Although the huge cannon in his story, fired not far from what is today the Kennedy Space Center, could not have actually performed its assigned task, the scientific concepts and mathematical detail that informed his story fired the imagination of many young men.

Just after the turn of the century, one such youth who read Verne's 1865 book, *From the Earth to the Moon,* would take pencil to paper, determine what would and would not work in reality, and begin to devise his own ideas on how man could travel into space: Hermann Oberth.

Oberth's work and contributions to space travel span the entire history of the Space Age. In the 1920s, he solved the theoretical problems of rocketry and designed the first practical applications of these concepts to rocket vehicles. He was the teacher and inspira-

National Air and Space Museum, Smithsonian Institution, 20325
Hermann Oberth, the father of space travel, 1894–1989.

tion to a group of young German students and engineers who later
developed the technology for spaceflight. He battled a skeptical
scientific community to establish the new science of astronautics,
and he personally brought these new ideas to the public through
the written word, teaching, lectures, demonstrations, and even film.
Because of this work, and because of his determination to see his
ideas brought into practical reality, Oberth is, without question,
the father of space travel.

The theoretical work of Oberth and his students in Germany
continued the hydrodynamic tradition in German science from
Gottfried Wilhelm Leibniz (1646–1716) through Karl Gauss
(1777–1855) and Bernhard Riemann (1826–1866). With the help
of Ludwig Prandtl and aerodynamicists like Adolf Busemann, they
carried that scientific method and tradition into the 20th century.

Previously, rockets were small and solid-fueled, or "powder

rockets." They were used primarily as flares, fireworks, and ship "rescue rockets," which could carry a rescue rope over a few kilometers to a ship in distress. In the United States, unbeknownst to Oberth, Robert Goddard had proven in his paper, "A Method of Reaching Extreme Altitudes," published in 1919, that liquid-fuel rockets would be superior to solid-fuel powder rockets. Oberth read this paper in 1922 while preparing his first book on rockets.

In the Soviet Union, two decades before Oberth, the theorist Konstantin Tsiolkovsky had written that only liquid fuels would have the necessary energy to carry man's machines outside the atmosphere. But in both these cases, lack of government funding, or any other support, doomed the research to a somnolent birth.

Going beyond Tsiolkovsky and Goddard's theoretical work and experiments, Oberth put *man* into space. To Oberth, rockets were the means to an end, which was spaceflight. Throughout his life Oberth worked on designing the technologies for spaceflight vehicles, space stations, lunar exploration, and missions to Mars. Although he did not participate directly in the development of the world's first guided rocket at Peenemünde, nor in the Apollo program that took men to the Moon, he witnessed both as an honored guest and neither would have been possible without him. He saw the flights of the first reusable spacecraft, the Space Shuttle, and died in his 95th year, in 1989.

It will still take the Space Age decades to catch up to the concepts and plans of Hermann Oberth.

Hermann Julius Oberth was born on June 25, 1894 in the town of Hermannstadt in the Transylvanian region of Romania, which was then part of the Austro-Hungarian empire. His parents were part of the historically German-speaking Saxon community, and his father, Julius, was a prominent physician and assistant surgeon at the Franz Joseph Municipal Hospital. When Hermann was two years old, his father became director and chief surgeon in the County Hospital in Schässburg, Transylvania, and the family moved there.

Oberth reports in a short autobiography that Schässburg was then a town of 11,000 inhabitants. "It wasn't until 1902 that Schässburg acquired water supply mains and electric lights. In 1904, the telephone became available, with only 37 subscribers reported to the telephone service in the first three years." In the 1930s, the town still had no centralized sewer installation, and "cesspools in

Marsha Freeman

Hermann Oberth's parents, Julius Gotthold and Valerie Oberth, in a portrait hanging in the study of his daughter, Dr. Erna Roth-Oberth, in Feucht, Germany.

the houses were emptied by gypsies and discharged into the river 'Kockel' flowing past the town." In 1904, Oberth saw his first automobile.

But this isolated little village had a railway station, which "was about the only thing linking our town with the big world of industry and engineering," he reported. As a youngster, he designed "fantastic projects for locomotives, airplanes, and space ships . . . the quicker, the better" (Oberth 1967, pp. 113–114).

Hermann Oberth's daughter, Dr. Erna Roth-Oberth, in an interview in her home in December 1992, explained that, although living in a community isolated from the mainstream of science and culture, "the Germans in Romania kept close contact with Germany or Austria, so [we] had access to German culture. We had many scientific journals and magazines" (Roth-Oberth 1992).

According to his biographer, Hans Barth, Oberth's interest and love for science were kindled early by his maternal grandfather, Friedrich Krasser, who was a noted intellectual and poet, as well as a practicing physician. Krasser, well known in Social Democratic circles in Hungary, Austria, and Germany, best gives expression to his own philosophy in one of his verses: "The hero, which in the future will break your chains, is science with its light." Barth reports that Krasser himself would often tell his wife: "In a hundred years, man will fly to the Moon. Our grandchildren will yet experience it" (Barth 1991, p. 17).

Erna Roth-Oberth described Dr. Julius Oberth, Hermann Oberth's father, as someone who "knew almost every kind of literature. He liked to recite. He recited often passages of poetry." Every morning, he would come to Erna's room and from Goethe, "offer the passage, 'Noble is man, helpful and good' " and "after this, his day's work would begin."

Like his father, Hermann Oberth learned poetry, and into his nineties could recite the prologue to Goethe's "Faust" by heart. "He knew a lot of literature by heart," Dr. Roth-Oberth explained. "He had a fantastic memory. He occupied himself with incredibly many subjects and knew a lot about biology, chemistry, even theology, which he had studied, and medicine. He had a very broad knowledge of many branches of science."

Oberth found that in his own education, and later in the response to his revolutionary ideas about rocketry and space travel, education was too much influenced by the conceptions, if not prejudices, of the past. "He expressed it in the following way," his daughter said: " 'Our educational system is like an automobile which has strong rear lights, brightly illuminating the past. But looking forward things are barely discernible.' "

"He saw the future very clearly," Dr. Roth-Oberth explained. "It's true, he didn't have much patience for the banalities of everyday life. He actually always lived in the future. My father, even in his early years, as a child, had realized that in his thinking he was quite different from other people. And often he had to admit that his thinking was more rigorous, more elaborated. He developed an allergy toward those who told him, 'Other people have already

William Jones

The author with Dr. Erna Roth-Oberth at her home in Germany, in December 1992. In the background is a portrait of her father, Hermann Oberth.

known this before you, and have always done things *this* way, and *this* is the only way you can do it. It is the correct way.' Often in his life he found that the 'accepted way' of doing things was not as correct as the way he did it."

Many descriptions of Hermann Oberth paint him as an eccentric genius who worked alone and had no use for other people. Even in his youth, Dr. Roth-Oberth said, her father challenged what would today be called the politically correct ideas of the scientific establishment:

He was always skeptical of any collaborators, even the well-meaning ones, who thought that they could help him. He had the experience that this "help" often was only a hindrance and an impediment to his work. He was a very conscientious worker. Actually, he worked his entire life on these matters, and he felt himself somewhat annoyed by social commitments or by requests to hold lectures or to make an appearance somewhere.

He was insensitive to praise as well as to censure. In that way, he got the reputation of being unapproachable. On the contrary, he was very open to young people who wanted to venture into space, and he had infinite patience in explaining everything to them.

This was clearly borne out by the role Oberth played with the scientists and engineers who would later take man into space and to the Moon.

Possessing great confidence in his own mind and his ability to think, reason, and create, Hermann Oberth never kowtowed to authority and was neither impressed by titles nor cowed by academic criticism. John Elder, who interviewed Oberth, points out that at times, "He seemed to enjoy getting into hot water, just to prove his independence of mind" (Elder 1991, p. 24). For example, Oberth himself described what he thought when the University of Heidelberg rejected the thesis he submitted for a doctoral degree in 1922: "I refrained from writing another one, thinking to myself: Never mind, I will prove that I am able to become a greater scientist than some of you, even without the title of a doctor." He continued: "In the United States, I am often addressed as a doctor. I should like to point out, however, that I am not such and shall never think of becoming one" (Oberth 1967, p. 118).

For Oberth, space travel was not just a series of mathematical formulas and technological tests but also represented a philosophical outlook on life. The last paragraph of Oberth's 1957 book, *Man Into Space,* reads: "This is the goal: To make available for life every place where life is possible. To make inhabitable all worlds as yet uninhabitable, and all life purposeful" (Oberth 1957, p. 167).

According to his own account in a 1959 article for *Astronautics* magazine (reprinted in 1967), and another account in the essay, "My Contributions to Astronautics" (presented in 1967 and published in 1974), Oberth was set on the path of his life's work at the age of 11, when his mother gave him a copy of Jules Verne's book *From*

the Earth to the Moon, which, he says, "I read at least five or six
times and, finally, knew by heart" (Oberth 1967, p. 114).

Verne starts his intrepid space travelers on their way by shooting them out of a huge cannon (hence, the term space "shot").
Checking the book's calculations, Oberth found that Verne's estimate, that a velocity of 11,000 meters per second would take a
space capsule outside of the Earth's gravitational pull, was within
the limits of his own calculations. As he explains, his method was
constrained by a "deficient knowledge of mathematics," in that he
had no knowledge of infinitesimal calculus. But, "our young and
clever teacher in physics, Ludwig Fabini, managed to make us understand that the attraction of gravity exerted by the Earth would
decrease in proportion to the square of the distance from the Earth's
center," he writes.

"So I divided the trajectory of the missile up to the Moon into
sections—smaller ones down toward the Earth and larger ones up
toward the Moon—assuming for the gravitational acceleration in
each section a mean value." Like Verne, his calculations led to a
necessary escape velocity of about 11,000 meters per second. He
also found that Verne's time of flight for his travelers to the Moon
was correct, "if it is assumed that the projectile was traveling at
minimum velocity" (Oberth 1967, p. 115).

But spaceflight via cannon was physiologically impossible, Oberth reasoned. He calculated that at Verne's 11,000 meter per second velocity, at a distance of only 300 meters, the passengers would
be subjected to a pressure, measured in multiples of the force of
gravity, equal to 20,000 times their own weight. Oberth recognized,
at the age of 12, that the travelers inside the missile would be
crushed by the enormous gravitational acceleration. "Against this
handicap," he writes, "Jules Verne proposed a water buffer; and he
succeeded with it, too—on paper, at least! Actually, this solution
would be worthless, since man's internal organs could not tolerate
this acceleration. Therefore, shooting someone into space with a
gun would not work, and I had to look for different kinds of space
ships" (Oberth 1974, p. 129).

At the age of 14, after careful analysis, Oberth rejected the idea
that a vacuum tunnel with magnets on runners surrounded by an
electric coil (similar to today's rail guns) could be used to launch
large spacecraft into Earth orbit. He calculated that huge magnets
and a 10,000-kilometer tunnel would be needed. Next, he consid-

ered airplane designs, but rejected them as too heavy. Finally, he also rejected the idea of a wheel lifted into space by centrifugal force.

Oberth saw no way other than rocket propulsion technologies, although he was concerned about the danger of explosions. Rockets had made their appearance in Verne's book, as well. Verne envisioned small rockets to retard the fall of manned projectiles onto the surface of the Moon, what in today's parlance are called retrorockets. The question then posed to Oberth—a question that was to be a matter of contention in the scientific community—was whether or not a rocket operating in airless space, such as on the Moon, could provide propulsive force.

Oberth had envisioned the reaction from propulsion in space as similar to the recoil of firing a gun. However, the argument was made that in a vacuum there would be no air for the gas escaping from the rocket engine to "push against." Oberth wondered whether Jules Verne had erred in his use of rockets to slow his spacecraft approaching the Moon, as he had erred regarding the effects of the force of acceleration on takeoff (Oberth 1967, p. 129).

To answer this question, Oberth conducted a series of experiments to simulate the resistanceless vacuum of space (Hartl 1958, p. 43). He rowed a small boat out into a bay and then, approaching the shore, went to the front of the boat and jumped out. As he did, the boat slid backward, away from the shore, in reaction to his forward motion, even though the boat had nothing to "push against," because water provides little resistance.

In a second experiment, Oberth stowed some large stones in the boat and then threw each one overboard in the open bay. As he did, the boat moved in the direction opposite to the throw of the stones. The phenomenon of recoil, therefore, functions even without resistance, he reasoned, and the way to move forward is to throw matter out of a rocket, in the opposite direction.

In the same way, Oberth proposed, if one were in space, free from the drag of the Earth's atmosphere, and threw pieces of matter backward, one would be pushed forward. If the pieces were small and moved slowly, the speed would be increased less than if the pieces thrown backward were large and moving at higher speed. But it would also be possible to increase speed by expelling a large number of small, high-speed particles, like gas molecules.

Oberth reports that in 1910–1912, while he was at the Bischof-

Teutsch-Gymnasium in Schässburg, he learned infinitesimal calculus, although he describes the school as "more humanistic than scientific in nature." He also bought the book *Mathematik für Jedermann* (Mathematics for Everyone) by August Shuster, "which covered differential calculus and helped me overcome a certain lack of training." As he had no access to a laboratory and could not do experiments, he "pondered the theoretical problems of rocket technology and space travel, and attempted to solve some of them. . ." (Oberth 1974, p. 130).

"No one of whom I had knowledge had done so thoroughly," he wrote. "Dr. Goddard, in 1919, for instance, wrote that it would be impossible to express for a rocket trajectory the interactions of the propellant consumption, exhaust velocity, air drag, influence of gravity, etc. in closed numerical equations. In 1910 I had begun to investigate these mathematical relations and to derive the equations; these investigations were completed by 1929."

In 1909, at the age of 15, Oberth completed his first plan for a rocket to carry several people. "The engine was to have been provided with moistened gun cotton in the manner of a machine gun, with the gas flowing laterally at the top," Oberth writes in an appendix to his 1923 book, *The Rocket into Interplanetary Space.* "The design of the nozzles was still rather incomplete. . . . Despite all its shortcomings, a machine of this type would have been able to leave the ground" (Oberth 1923, p. 100).

His first design for an oxygen-hydrogen rocket came three years later, and by 1918 his calculations for a small multistage model with a first stage using alcohol fuel had the exhaust gases flowing out the bottom of the rocket.

One of the major problems to be solved before any rocket could reach airless space was to calculate "the optimum speed at which air drag and gravity are reduced to a minimum." Oberth determined that if a rocket rises too slowly, it "has to fight against its own weight for a longer time," against the Earth's gravitational force. If it rises too quickly, it encounters the atmospheric drag that is increasing with the square of the velocity (Oberth 1974, p. 130).

One of the difficulties with the rockets that had been built before 1920, Oberth explained, is that they were too small and flew too fast, "for there is a kind of competition between the weight of the rocket and the air density." Although intuitively it would seem

FIGURE 1.1
THE OPTIMUM ROCKET FLIGHT PATH
In order to attain orbit, a rocket must "fight against its own weight," the result of gravity, and also must "fight against" the drag from the atmosphere. Oberth considered the complex relationship between these and other factors, and calculated the best trade-offs to gain the optimal performance for the rocket.

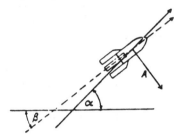

Source: Hermann Oberth, *Ways to Spaceflight* (Munich, Germany: R. Oldenbourg, 1929).

that the smaller the rocket the less atmospheric and gravitational drag, Oberth explained that the rocket must be large enough to carry adequate amounts of fuel to overcome both the gravitational force and the atmospheric drag it encounters, which is greatest at the beginning of the flight. (Figure 1.1)

"The more propellant the better," he wrote, because "the propellant will be the more effective, the higher the exhaust velocity it can produce and the more of it that be carried compared to the rest of the rocket mass. . . . If the rocket carries enough propellant, the rocket can leave the Earth and even escape the Earth's field of gravitation.

"Later on," Oberth wrote, "the requirement for stages developed out of these formulas. If there is a small rocket on top of a big one, and if the big one is jettisoned and the small one is ignited, then their speeds are added," because in space, the velocity is additive (Oberth 1974, p. 131). Without drag, each propulsive impulse increases the speed of the rocket. It would be similar to driving a car on a road without any friction. If your foot were kept steady on the gas pedal, the speed of the car would keep increasing, until you ran out of fuel. The more fuel you carried, the higher speed you could obtain.

While at the Schässburg Gymnasium, Oberth performed simple experiments making use of the swimming pool there, such as examining the behavior of liquids in zero gravity. He jumped off the diving board holding small glass vials filled one-third to one-half with different liquids. He observed them when he was at the peak of the jump and not yet descending, and found that they formed spheres and floated freely inside while weightless. "I recognized that a human being could most assuredly endure this condition for one or two seconds. It was clear to me that he could endure weightlessness for days, physically" (Oberth 1974, p. 132).

In addition to the physiological implications, this question of the behavior of liquids in space would also be important for determining how a rocket motor using liquid fuel would have to be designed to function in space in the absence of gravity.

During his student years, Oberth conducted experiments on himself, as well as on liquids, to study the effects of weightlessness. In 1911, he observed that, under water in the swimming pool (which simulates gravity-free space), he became disoriented when the combination of the cold water and the increase in the carbon dioxide in his blood had desensitized his equilibrium sensors. Space travelers would have to adjust to this lack of normal sensory functioning, he correctly assumed.

In June 1912, Oberth graduated from the gymnasium, receiving a prize in mathematics. The next year, he went to the University of Munich to study medicine, but his studies were interrupted by World War I. After being wounded, Oberth was transferred to a medical unit, where for three years he had access to various drugs at a hospital and military pharmacological supply station. There, he continued his medical experimentation, using drugs to numb the sensory receptors in his muscles and skin "so that by floating under water with my eyes closed; and by using an airhose wound around my body, I could extend the psychological experience of weightlessness for hours" (Oberth 1974, p. 132).

Reflecting on these early experiments, Oberth observed in 1959 that,

during an actual spaceflight, a rendezvous maneuver does not take more than a couple of hours; and during the rest of the flight, gravitation can be produced by rotation and by centrifugal force. I do not believe in the need of exposing man to unnatural conditions. In my opinion, it is the aim of technology to provide man with conditions in space which correspond to

NASA

One of Hermann Oberth's greatest contributions was the education and encouragement of young colleagues interested in rocket research in Germany. Here he is seen with his most famous student, Wernher von Braun. On Oct. 10, 1961, von Braun received the Hermann Oberth Award of the American Rocket Society, from Hermann Oberth himself.

his nature. I have been of this opinion since I was young . . . [Oberth 1974, p. 132].

Oberth often said that although it was a disappointment to his father, one of the most important things he learned in his years at the military medical facility is that he did not want to be a doctor.

During the war, Oberth had tried to interest the military in his rocket ideas. In 1917, he made a presentation to the German Ministry of Armaments, proposing the development of an ethyl alcohol, water, liquid oxygen rocket, "somewhat similar to the V–2, only bigger and not so complicated" (Oberth 1974, p. 131). In the spring of the next year, his manuscript was returned with the comment, "Experience teaches us that these rockets cannot fly farther than 7 km., and taking into account the proverbial Prussian thoroughness with which this missile post operates, it cannot be expected that this distance can be considerably surpassed" (Barth 1991, p. 61). Across the Atlantic, Robert Goddard had encountered the same lack of vision in the U.S. military.

In 1918, Hermann Oberth married Mathilde Hummel, and a year later he returned to the University of Munich, having changed his field of study from medicine to physics. He was soon forced to transfer to the University at Göttingen, because of his lack of a residence permit in Bavaria.

During 1920, at Göttingen, Oberth had the opportunity to study aerodynamics under one of the most notable scientists of that time, Ludwig Prandtl. According to Barth, Oberth took his work to Prandtl to elicit comments. "After looking over the work, Prandtl pointed out a few small errors and recommended to Oberth some pertinent reference books. 'You've got something in you,' said Prandtl, by way of farewell. 'Don't get discouraged by anything!' " (Barth 1991, p. 68).

Historian Michael J. Neufeld has tried to explain how German culture produced a Hermann Oberth and why his ideas found such fertile ground in the Germany of the 1920s. Although he attempts to explain the German fascination with rocketry in the 1920s separately from the vision of space travel, describing it as a "fad" rather than as the precursor to the Space Age, Neufeld does recognize that there was a "pervasive pride in German technological achievements displayed in the Weimar media" (Neufeld 1990, p. 745). However, he fails to see whence this belief in technological progress arose.

John Elder writes in a 1991 paper that Oberth, "was also lucky to be born into German culture. . . . Germany had a tradition of science and technology; German books and journals were far more likely to be read, translated, and circulated throughout Europe. . ." (Elder 1991, p. 6). Elder points out that, between 1901 and 1922, 20 out of the 66 Nobel Prizes awarded in science went to Germans. The period from the middle of the 19th century to the time that Hermann Oberth undertook his university studies in Munich, Göttingen, and Heidelberg was the greatest period of German scientific development, producing many of the breakthroughs that have created our modern technology and economy.

Fritz Haber, who was the head of the Institute for Physical

Chemistry and Electrochemistry at the Kaiser Wilhelm Institute in the 1920s, was a 1918 Nobel laureate in chemistry for the synthesis of ammonia, which laid the basis for modern agricultural fertilizers and a revolution in food production worldwide. Haber observed in 1926, "The last quarter of a century has been a great time for scientific research despite wars and human misery. The researches of the nineteenth century were like the oases in the desert. The last quarter-century has shown these oases can be united" (Goran 1967, p. 141).

This was the twilight of an era of great German science, which would see many of the best minds in Europe emigrate to the United States. Wilhelm Konrad Roentgen, winner of the first Nobel Prize in physics in 1901 for the discovery of X-rays, was professor of experimental physics in Munich. Max Planck, who won the Nobel Prize in 1918 for the quantum theory of light, was president of the Kaiser Wilhelm Institute in Berlin. One of his assistants, Lise Meitner, working later with Otto Hahn, would successfully split the atom, opening this century to the use of nuclear energy. In 1915, Albert Einstein, director of theoretical physics at the Kaiser Wilhelm Institute, published his general theory of relativity. In Berlin were physicist Werner Heisenberg and Hans Geiger, the inventor of the radioactivity-sensing instrument that bears his name.

The greatest concentration of the great minds of science was at Göttingen University. Ludwig Prandtl taught at its Institute for Applied Mechanics. At the Mathematical Institute, Felix Klein was transforming the home of the most brilliant mathematical minds of the 19th century—Karl Gauss, Lejeune Dirichlet, and Bernhard Riemann—into the foremost institute of mathematics in the world. Many of the leading thinkers of 20th century mathematics and physics were gathered at Göttingen during the first quarter of this century: David Hilbert, Herman Minkowski, Hermann Weyl, Max Born, Ernst Zermelo, Richard Courant, Edmund Landau, and James Franck. (Reid 1986.)

During the first two decades of this century, Oberth saw the world of technology around him transformed, largely as a result of the breakthroughs that had been made in German science and mathematics. Oberth had the opportunity to study with scientists making fundamental contributions to the future. This is the cultural environment that creates a belief in the possibility to accomplish great projects through technological progress.

At Heidelberg University, Oberth's dissertation on rocketry was rejected. Getting no serious hearing from the scientific community, he decided that he had to turn toward interesting the public in space travel.

In order to make space travel accessible to the nonscientist, Oberth began investigating solutions to the technological problems of spaceflight so the ideas could be made practical. Oberth experimentally demonstrated a propulsion system with an exhaust velocity of 3,900 meters per second. For these experiments he used gaseous rather than liquid fuels because, he wrote, "in Transylvania I could neither obtain them in liquid form nor find a means to liquefy them."

As he described in 1967: "I wrote about this to some friends in Vienna; whereupon a professor of the Vienna Technical University [Dr. Karl Wolf] answered that I must be a fraud." As Oberth writes in his 1929 book, *Ways to Spaceflight,* Wolf had calculated that the hydrogen and oxygen fuel could not provide more than 2,000 meters per second exhaust velocity because the water vapor produced cannot be hotter than 3,000 degrees, "on account of dissociation" (Oberth 1929, p. 49). As Oberth points out, the professor had ignored the fact that excess hydrogen and cold temperature rendered dissociation practically zero. He remarked: "Actually, I was able to achieve 3,800–4,000 meters per second with a machine far from perfect" (Oberth 1974, p. 134).

Continuing his work on practical problems, Oberth proposed that parachutes be used for landing, that electricity (which was just becoming commercially available at the time) be used to control the valves regulating the flow of fuel, and that a centrifuge be built with a 35-meter arm to examine the effects of high accelerations for selection and training of astronauts.

By spring 1921, Oberth had completed his design of a two-stage rocket using alcohol and liquid oxygen, the theoretical calculations for which were the content of his doctoral thesis completed at Heidelberg University. As noted above, his thesis was not accepted, even though Councillor Max Wolf gave him a certificate saying the work was "scientifically correct and ingenious" (Oberth 1974, p. 136). After six publishers turned him down, Oberth borrowed the money from his wife to publish his doctoral thesis as a small pamphlet in 1923, under the title *Die Rakete zu den Planetenräumen* (*The Rocket into Interplanetary Space*).

At a time when men were just beginning to master the new

Hermann Oberth's 1923 book, The Rocket into Interplanetary Space *not only developed the theoretical framework for rocketry, but also outlined future practical applications of rockets, including manned spaceflight.*

science and technology of flight, this pamphlet of less than 100 pages solved the theoretical problems of rocketry and presented designs of rockets for manned spaceflight. It started a whirlwind of activity and a series of debates in the German scientific community, which spread internationally. Its appearance encouraged dozens of other scientists and visionaries to publish their own work and ideas on space travel. It started many young space pioneers, including Wernher von Braun, on their life-long study of space exploration.

The Rocket into Interplanetary Space also created a flood of criticism. One mathematician who reviewed it the year after it was published pompously opined: ". . . it will not be possible to travel around in space because of the enormous wear of material. We think that the time has not yet come to deal with this problem, and probably it will never arrive" (Oberth 1967, p. 119).

The most important attack by far was from Privy Councillor Professor Dr. Hans Lorenz of Danzig, who published a series of articles attacking Oberth's book in the prestigious journal of the Society of German Engineers (VDI). Privy Councillor Lorenz "proved" that Oberth's spaceship could not attain the approximately 7-miles-per-second velocity needed to escape the Earth's atmosphere. Lorenz argued that using then-known fuels, the spaceship would have to weigh 34 times as much fueled as empty, and that it was therefore impossible.

Oberth wrote a reply, as did VDI member Walter Hohmann, but neither was printed. Although the reason given was lack of space, space writer Willy Ley wrote that he was told years later in a personal conversation that the real reason was, "We cannot permit people half his age to contradict the privy councillor!" Ley also reported that the society relented and published a reply—in 1950 (Ley 1957a, p. 118).

Oberth was, however, given an opportunity to state his case. In June 1928, the Scientific Society for Aeronautics sponsored a debate between Oberth and Lorenz at its annual meeting in Danzig. Hans Barth reports that, in his rebuttal, Oberth pointed out that Lorenz had not even read his book! "Privy Councillor Lorenz, as is generally assumed," Oberth stated, "has not arrived at his present position of rejecting my work by means of a thorough examination of my proposed constructions, but rather a priori." Oberth expressed the hope that Lorenz would give serious consideration to his work, so he would be able to bring to bear his "mathematical power and his sagacity" along a "more fruitful track" (Barth 1991, p. 101).

Ley summarizes Oberth's argument: He agreed that if one had followed the arguments laid out by Lorenz, one would indeed arrive at a ratio of 34:1 for the fueled versus the empty spaceship. However, Oberth had made use of a factor more advantageous than the privy councillor had considered, which lowered the ratio to 20:1—as the privy councillor would have known had he finished reading Oberth's book. "Oberth could not help it if the privy councillor refused to believe that it is possible to build an aluminum pot into which one could pour enough water so that the full pot would weigh 20 times as much as the empty pot" (Ley 1957a, p. 119).

Well-known aerodynamicist Theodore von Karman describes this incident in his autobiographical book, *The Wind and Beyond.* He recounts:

In the 1920s I attended a conference ... in Danzig at which professor Hermann Oberth, one of the pioneers of German rocketry, gave an enthusiastic lecture on the possibilities of escaping from the Earth.

Following that futuristic talk, a distinguished German professor named Lorenz read a long paper "showing" why it was impossible for man to escape the Earth's gravitational pull. He said that Oberth's space ship would not acquire the escape velocity of 7 miles per second because to acquire that high a velocity a rocket would need an enormous amount of energy—in fact, he said, if it used the best fuel of the time the rocket would have to contain so much fuel it would weigh 34 times as much fueled as empty. Lorenz concluded that this was beyond engineering capability and should be forgotten.

I felt he was wrong on principle. I stood up and defended Oberth. "If we calculate the energy in a pound of kerosene, or other hydrocarbon, and transform this into mechanical work," I said, "we would find that there is more than enough energy available to us to send that pound into space." So theoretically it was possible to escape from the Earth, and I didn't think that we should reject the entire idea because it was not practical to implement it with the machinery of the time [Von Karman, 1967 pp. 236–237].

Privy Councillor Lorenz never wrote about rockets again.

The 1923 publication of Oberth's *The Rocket Into Interplanetary Space* spurred the appearance of many other now-classical works in Germany. These included Walter Hohmann's *The Attainability of the Celestial Bodies* in 1925, which laid the basis for interplanetary flight dynamics and trajectory calculations; space writer Willy Ley's more popular *Travel in Space,* published in 1926; and Max Valier's pamphlet *The Assault on Cosmic Space,* which appeared in 1924. By 1928, more than 80 books on spaceflight had been published in German, either of a fictional or more rigorous, scientific nature.

Oberth's small volume also had an important effect on the work of one of the other early space pioneers. Biographer Barth reports that Oberth's publication led to a revival in Russia of the work of Konstantin Tsiolkovsky, which had been all but ignored until that point. Oberth's work was acknowledged in the foreword to the collection of Tsiolkovsky's writings. Its editor, A. Tschiyevski, wrote,

Only after the book of Hermann Oberth about "The Rocket into Interplanetary Space" had created some excitement in Germany, and notice of this was able to penetrate the official Russian press, were we Russians reminded that about thirty years ago an astronautical theoretician, Mr. K. E. Tsiolkovsky had presented to the public a quite detailed and mathematically based work on a recoil vehicle [Barth 1991, p. 80].

Oberth began his 1923 book with these assertions:

(1) Given the present state of science and technology, it is possible to build machines that can climb higher than the limits of the atmosphere of the Earth.

(2) With refinements, these devices will be able to attain such velocities that, left to themselves in space, they need not fall back to the Earth's surface, and they may even leave the Earth's gravitational field.

(3) Such machines can be built so that human beings, apparently without danger to their health, can go up in them.

(4) Given certain economic conditions, the construction of such devices may even become profitable. Such conditions may prevail within a few decades (Oberth 1923, p. 7).

Oberth concluded his introduction:

I make no secret of the fact that I consider some of the provisions, in their present form, as by no means being definitive solutions. As I worked out my plans and computations, I naturally had to consider every detail. In so doing, I could at least determine that there were no insurmountable technical difficulties. At the same time, however, it was clear to me that many questions could be solved only after the most thorough individual study and experimentation lasting perhaps years, in order to achieve the optimum solutions [Oberth 1923, p. 8].

In the 1923 book, Oberth uses the first half to tackle theoretical questions regarding spaceflight. These include an examination of various kinds of possible fuels, their combustion properties and exhaust velocities; the optimal angle, altitude, and latitude from which to launch space vehicles; the effect of weightlessness on liquid fuels in the rocket; the aerodynamic shape of the rocket; and generally, "the relationships among time, mass, force, distance, air pressure, and most favorable velocity" (Oberth 1923, p. 13).

Crucial to Oberth's calculations was the work by Adolf Busemann and others on designs to minimize aerodynamic drag and obtain "least action" to determine the optimal velocity for a spaceship taking off to orbit the Earth. If you fly too fast, the ship encounters maximal aerodynamic drag, because air resistance increases as the square of the velocity, while the operating efficiency of the fuels increases only as the first power of the velocity. A compromise is required between going slower to lower resistance and traveling faster to overcome gravity.

This can be compared to finding the optimum speed of an automobile, at which one moderates speed to achieve better fuel efficiency but increases speed to minimize the amount of travel time. Oberth showed that the science of rocketry entails a constant challenge to find the path of least action within a highly complex set of boundary conditions.

As had Tsiolkovsky and Goddard, Oberth posed the idea of "staging" rockets; that is, designing them with one motor placed on top of the other, with the second one starting when the first finished burning. He also described "tapeworm" rockets, which would jettison empty fuel tanks to get rid of dead weight.

The advantage here, misunderstood by many scientists, was that because there is no air or gravitational resistance once in space,

---

FIGURE 1.2
THE MODEL B ROCKET
In his 1923 book, Oberth included a detailed study of the
multistage Model B Rocket. The auxiliary, or first stage,
booster is an alcohol-fueled liquid rocket, while the second,
or upper, stage uses liquid hydrogen. This combination, he
determined, would be energetic enough to carry the rocket
into Earth orbit.

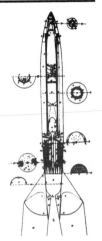

Source: Hermann Oberth, *Die Rakete zu den Planetenräumen* (Munich, Germany: R. Oldenbourg, 1923).

---

the velocity of the rocket becomes additive. For example, if the
spacecraft is traveling at 10 kilometers per second when the first
engine reaches *Brennschluss,* or burnout, if a second motor is
started with a propulsion velocity of 5 kilometers per second, this
increases the speed of the spacecraft to 15 kilometers per second.
In this way the required orbital velocity of about 8 kilometers per
second is achieved, as well as the escape velocity of about 11
kilometers per second required to go beyond Earth orbit.

Oberth is often accused of being a theoretician uninterested
in the engineering needed to accomplish his dreams. However, after
outlining the principal requirements for rocket flight, he ends the
first part of *The Rocket into Interplanetary Space,* stating: "These
requirements frequently contradict each other. The construction
task is to find an optimum combination of these" (Oberth 1923, p.
47).

With the Model B Rocket (Figure 1.2) Oberth applied his solutions to the equations from his theoretical work to a practical rocket
design that later became the starting point for years of experimental
research. The second section of *The Rocket into Interplanetary
Space* describes, in words and drawings, the Model B Rocket, which
consists of an auxiliary, or first-stage, booster rocket, an alcohol-
fueled liquid rocket, and a liquid hydrogen upper stage. "The pur-

pose of Model B," Oberth explained, "is to investigate the height, composition, and temperature of the Earth's atmosphere, to determine the curve for 'resistance' more exactly [which depends upon the speed and shape of the rocket], and to confirm and improve our calculation of exhaust velocity, temperature, pressure, etc. (particularly for the hydrogen rocket)" (Oberth 1923, p. 48).

The Model B, consisting of the alcohol and hydrogen rockets, is 5 meters long, 55.6 centimeters in diameter, and weighs 544 kilograms. Of this total, the highly energetic hydrogen upper stage weighs a mere 6.9 kilograms. Oberth calculated the exhaust velocity of the alcohol first stage at 1,800 meters per second. The rocket has a complement of four fins fastened to the engine, to stabilize and guide the rocket. Oberth proposes that they be moved to fold in front of the rocket upon descent, to make a parachute unnecessary.

Oberth counsels that the rocket should be recovered, because the emptied fuel tank can be used to collect samples of air in the various layers of the atmosphere. The point of launch for the booster and alcohol rockets should be chosen so that the rockets can fall into a body of water and be recovered.

The hydrogen rocket on top would produce an exhaust velocity that Oberth estimated conservatively at 3,400 meters per second. He projected that the rocket could attain a height of nearly 2,000 kilometers. But when the velocities produced by all three stages are added together, the velocity obtained by the Model B rocket in its full configuration would not only be able to carry instruments on the hydrogen upper stage to study the Earth's atmosphere, but also could go into Earth orbit! As Oberth states almost casually, "my vehicles could therefore very probably attain cosmic velocity" (Oberth 1923, p. 75).

The "engineering features" section of *The Rocket into Interplanetary Space* is a manual for a years-long program to engineer, design, fabricate, and test the most important technologies of the proposed rocket system. These include designs for engine diffusers and nozzles, new materials needed to handle liquid hydrogen a few degrees above absolute zero, and the designs of combustion chambers, fuel pumps, gyroscopes, and other components.

The final section of Oberth's historic work, modestly titled "Purpose and Prospects," begins with the bombshell: "The rockets described on page 65 can be built so powerfully that they would be capable of carrying a man aloft." Thus, he did what Goddard and Tsiolkovsky did not dare: He proved that his rockets could work and put man into space.

From a young age, equipped with the knowledge transmitted by his father, Oberth was concerned about the effects of changes in gravity on living things. In his 1929 book, *Ways to Spaceflight,* he speculated that since gravity is lower, for example, on Mars, there would be less of a strain on plants and animals. "Our man could stand on his big toe like a ballet dancer ... [and] according to [the scientist Karl] Gauss, the animals could grow three times as large without getting too plump" (Oberth 1929, p. 117).

In his first book, however, Oberth is most concerned with the effect on men of the increased gravitational force at launch and the effect of weightlessness during flight. First Oberth asks the question, "How much pressure [force] can a man withstand? I know of a case in which a fireman jumped from a height of 25 meters," he recounts, "landing in a prone position in a rescue net, which he depressed to a depth of 1 meter, without incurring any damage. The pressure [or force] to which he was subjected upon striking the net certainly rose to more than 240 meters per second squared. Of course, this represents an exceptional case" (Oberth 1923, p. 70).

After describing the effect of jumping into water from a height of 8 meters, Oberth concludes that

the human can withstand greater force from the head to the feet than in the opposite direction. The human can withstand the greatest amount of force in the transversal or sagittal direction [prone]. Because of the fact that, in this direction, tensile and compressive stresses are least for a given force, nature gave the human body the greatest pressure resistance in the transversal direction. Nature could also have just as well attempted to save material and allowed tissues to be somewhat weaker in this direction. This probably did not occur for practical reasons. We often slip and fall sideways, and we would be unable to survive if internal injuries resulted each time, as would occur with a greater force" [Figure 1.3] [Oberth 1923, p. 70].

Adding a bit from his own experience, Oberth states, "I recall having slipped while jumping into the water from a six-meter board

FIGURE 1.3
THE BEST WAY TO WITHSTAND 'COUNTER-PRESSURE'
From the beginning of his investigations, Hermann Oberth was always concerned with the medical effects of spaceflight on humans. He performed experiments, using himself as a volunteer, to determine how the body can best sustain increased gravitational force, which he termed "counter-pressure." His determination that the horizontal position was superior led to his suggestion that astronauts lie on their backs during orbital ascent.

Source: Hermann Oberth, *Ways to Space Flight* (Munich, Germany: R. Oldenbourg, 1929).

and fell on my side. I experienced not the slightest bit of physical damage as a result of the force of the fall" (Oberth 1923, p. 71). He concludes that the human body can safely withstand the force of 60 meters per second squared acceleration in the direction from head to feet, and up to 90 meters per second squared in the transverse, or prone direction.

One question, however, is whether or not a human can withstand this pressure for a period of the 200 to 600 seconds a spacecraft might be accelerating. Another question Oberth addresses is whether the absence of gravitational force (weightlessness) will cause any untoward effects: "The mere fact that all important life processes can take place either in a prone or a standing position proves that we are not dependent upon a certain force of gravity in any particular direction" (Oberth 1923, p. 72). This, it turns out, is not as simple as it seems, and even by the time of his 1929 work, Oberth questions the condition of muscles and bones after extended stays in space without gravity.

At the end of his discussion of the physiological effects of spaceflight, Oberth solicits ideas from his readers:

Our knowledge concerning the psychological and physiological effects of abnormal gravitational force is still rather incom-

plete. I would therefore be grateful to receive any reports
relating to this subject. . . . I only wanted to show that prepara-
tory work in this area is possible [Oberth 1923, p. 79].

Finally, Oberth reviews his thoughts on the prospects that his
rockets will ever be built:

I don't want to predict that this will happen within the next
10 years, but I should like to show the value of such devices
and what their cost would be in order to draw some conclusions
as to whether they will actually ever be built. . . . Other than
the described [scientific] measurements . . . this model would
be of no practical use. However, the usefulness of a scientific
discovery cannot be judged in advance. Often enough, things
which seemed to have no relation to daily life, later prove to
be of the greatest practical value. (I am reminded here of
electricity.) [Oberth 1923, p. 84].

However, Oberth asserts, once man can go into space, various
practical uses will attract the public interest. Men will be able to
leave their spacecraft using "diving suits" and will be able to do
work in space, provided they stay attached to lines connected to
the ship. Uses will include:

experiments which can only be conducted in a large airless
space; during free flight, the vehicle moves in a state of weightlessness. Therefore, many physical and physiological experiments would be possible which cannot be carried out on Earth
because of gravity; In space, telescopes of any size could be
used, for the stars would not flicker. . .; Since the sky is dark,
masking of the solar disc would suffice to observe the Sun
at will; Certain investigations of radiated energy cannot be
conducted on Earth because the atmosphere absorbs short-
wave light rays: . . . Finally, such a rocket, if given an initial
velocity of 11 kilometers per second could circle the Moon
and explore the unknown side [Oberth 1923, p. 86].

If these scientific investigations are not enough to whet the
appetite and loosen the public purse-strings, Oberth proposes that
rockets this size, traveling around the Earth as a "miniature moon,"

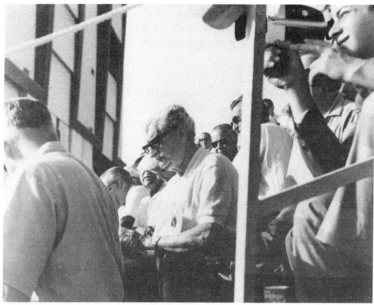

National Air and Space Museum, Smithsonian Institution, 83-297
Hermann Oberth in the VIP stand at Cape Canaveral for the July 16,
1969 launch of Apollo 11. Although Oberth did not participate directly
in the development or first launch of either the war-time V-2 or the Saturn
V rocket that took men to the Moon, he was an honored guest at both
events.

or space station, could perform navigational and communications
functions, early warning for impending natural disasters, or even
provide news service, anticipating the use of today's communications satellites.

   Here, Oberth first describes his concept for an Earth-orbital
mirror, which could collect the energy of the Sun and reflect it to
places on the surface of the Earth (described in depth in his later
books.) These ideas were extended in scope and detail by German
space visionary Krafft Ehricke.

   With all of the practical applications Hermann Oberth could see
for his rockets in the future, he ends *The Rocket into Interplanetary
Space* with a vision of the future: "Visits to other celestial bodies
would certainly be of great scientific value" (Oberth 1923, p. 89).

   In the 1920s, Hermann Oberth developed many of the concepts
that have been the foundation for the U.S. space program. In all

modesty, he remarked in 1959 that he was "rather surprised that
so many of my former suggestions have been adopted in modern
rocket development." Those that should be mentioned, he suggested, were:

> regenerative cooling, reinforcing [fuel] tanks by internal pres-
> sure, liquid fuels such as alcohol containing water and liquid
> oxygen, directional control by means of elastically suspended
> weights, speed control by generating an electrical current pro-
> portional to the acceleration and flowing through an ammeter,
> cut-off velocity control by closing automatically the fuel valves
> when reaching the rated speed, and finally, the use of liquid
> hydrogen as a fuel in upper stages [Oberth 1967, p. 118].

Hermann Oberth's ideas, laid out extensively in the 1920s,
became the organizing principle around which the scientific concepts and practical applications of rocketry would be developed.

The Battle of the Formulae

W illy Ley has described the years following the 1923 publication of Hermann Oberth's *The Rocket into Interplanetary Space* as "the battle of the formulae" (Ley 1957a, p. 108) because of the public fight that ensued in the scientific community. Oberth was determined to see his ideas realized. He took them out to the public, responded to the criticisms and prejudices of a staid scientific establishment, and sought ways to engage others in his research. The educational and experimental activities of the German Society for Space Travel, formed in 1927, spawned similar organizations and experiments all over Europe, and in the United States, and fledgling groups in Asia and Latin America.

The amateur rocket experimenters in Germany tell us in their own accounts that they had little in the way of money or equipment, but they did have unbounded optimism. This optimism, rooted in the method and tradition of German science and culture, couldn't be destroyed, even by the rapid collapse of Germany's economy and the rise of Hitler.

The year that Hermann Oberth's book was published was a political watershed for Germany. The postwar Versailles Treaty had dictated a settlement that intended to irreversibly crush Germany as a European economic power. This attempt to deindustrialize Germany—the goal of British geopolitics since the last quarter of the 19th century—could never lead to a lasting peace. This became clear with the events of 1923.

The Versailles Treaty removed 7 million inhabitants and 25,000 square miles of territory from Germany, including the coal-mining

FIGURE 2.1
TERRITORIAL PROVISIONS OF THE TREATY OF VERSAILLES
The 1919 Treaty of Versailles not only forced draconian reparations payments on
Germany After World War I, but also removed some of the most economically
important regions from German control. More than 25,000 square miles of territory
and nearly 7 million inhabitants were lost, laying the basis for the economic catastrophe of the 1920s and the rise of the Nazis.

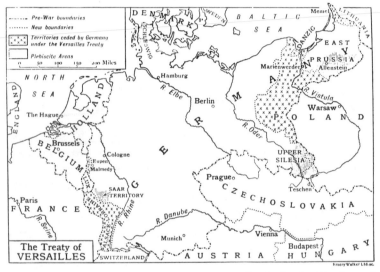

Source: E.H. Carr, *International Relations Since the Peace Treaties* (London: Macmillan and
Co., Limited, 1943).

region of the Saar, which was to be administered by the League of
Nations while its mines were transferred to French ownership. The
densely populated industrial region of Upper Silesia, rich in coal
and iron, was divided with Poland (Figure 2.1). The Versailles Treaty
obliged Germany to "accept the responsibility of Germany and her
allies for causing all the loss and damage to which the Allied and
Associated Governments and their nations have been subjected as
a consequence of the war imposed upon them by the aggression
of Germany and her allies."

This policy, to extract as much wealth as possible through
financial and material means, no matter what the impact on Germany's population, was unprecedented. The Reparations Commission
established at Versailles assessed Germany £1 billion to be paid by
May 1, 1921, and determined total liability at £6.6 billion. The

schedule of payments was £100 million per year plus one quarter of the value of Germany's exports. If this were not accepted, Germany was threatened with Allied troops occupying the Ruhr Valley, seat of more than 80 percent of Germany's production of coal, iron, and steel.

In addition to having lost all of the coal mined from the Saar region to France, Germany was mandated to deliver 7 million tons of coal per year to France, for 10 years. Belgium would be allocated 8 million tons of coal per annum, and Italy, a lesser amount.

In order to make the financial payments without the industrial base to generate the surplus wealth, the German government printed more marks, leading to the onset of a currency crisis by 1921. In December 1922, Germany failed by a small margin to meet the agreed payment, and the French used this excuse to send troops into the industrial Ruhr region to secure payment in kind, called "productive guarantees." The occupation of the Ruhr completed Germany's economic ruin. Stripped of most of its mining and industrial capability, severe austerity and hyperinflation were the only way it could even attempt to meet reparations payments.

This situation was clearly untenable, and the Allies agreed that Germany's finances needed an overhaul. The Dawes Plan, implemented in 1924, made Germany a hostage of international finance, by establishing a complex system of international loans for the reparations payments. This orgy of debt produced a deceptive few years of "prosperity," until the 1929 U.S. stock market crash closed off the credit spigot. By then, every democratic political party and elected government in Germany had discredited itself by having been associated with one or another aspect of the post-Versailles looting of their country.

So the German space enthusiasts, challenged by the ideas and visions of Oberth, started their quest to develop the possibilities of space travel at the same time that their nation was being occupied by foreign troops, suffering tremendous political and economic upheaval.

A most vocal spokesman for the emerging field of astronautics was science writer Willy Ley, born in 1906. Like many other young people, Ley read books about spaceflight in the early 1920s. Ley was inspired to make this new field more accessible to the general public than Oberth's scholarly 1923 book had done. The same thought had occurred to rocket enthusiast Max Valier, who had been traveling in Europe giving lectures. Valier contacted R. Oldenbourg, the publisher of Oberth's *The Rocket into Interplanetary Space,* with a proposal for a popular rendition. Oldenbourg then wrote to Oberth for his opinion.

In a letter to Oldenbourg dated January 12, 1924, Oberth thanked Oldenbourg for letting him know about Valier's plan and proposed that Valier, "send me a copy of his manuscript, when he has come that far, and I will then add to it whatever I think useful from my work, and, at the same time, make him aware of those things which appear to me inappropriate" (Barth 1984, Vol. 1, p. 12). Oberth was planning to write his own popularized version of *The Rocket,* but thought the two projects would complement each other.

Although Oberth helped Valier with calculations that he was unable to do himself, Valier's book, *Der Vorstoss in den Weltenraum* (*Thrust into Space*), published in 1924, had many flaws. Ley states, "When I read Valier's book I perceived immediately that it was not popular, and sat down to simplify Valier's book in turn. Then, I saw that he had not even interpreted Oberth correctly all the time— that way I wrote my own book which was published in 1926" (Ley 1943, p. 67).

Ley explained his motivation in writing a popular book: "While German scientists ... battled merrily and sometimes mistakenly about details, there was clearly a need for some writing which let the general public in on the concepts about which a high-tension battle of equations was going on. . . . The idea had to leave the study and enter the laboratory and later the workshop" (Ley 1957a, pp. 114–15).

In the same year that Valier's book was published, Hermann Oberth moved to Würzburg, Germany, as he wrote: "at the invitation of a banker who wanted to finance my rocket project. However, it turned out that he was awaiting an opinion of the value of this project from a professor at the Berlin Technical University. Finally, after six months, the opinion arrived, by which time the money I had saved for experiments had been used for my support" (Clarke 1967, p. 119).

The "opinion" of the professor was predictable—he advised the banker not to fund the project—and financially ruined, Oberth left to resume his teaching position at the Schässburg high school in Romania.

But in the meantime, Willy Ley, not even 20 years of age, sat down and wrote *Die Fahrt ins Weltall (Journey to the Cosmos)*, which appeared in 1926. This 68-page nontechnical and readable work begins with a survey of the preconditions for life, posing the question, could human beings live on other worlds? Ley answers with a cautious, "yes" and describes the technical means that would be available to protect man against the cold, lack of air, and other hostile conditions in space.

He amusingly presents the "enemies of space travel" that must be overcome, most notably, gravitational force, and outlines from Oberth's concepts how that can be achieved. "The victor is the rocket," he proclaims, giving the details on rocket design, the use of different fuels, parachutes for landing, and other necessary technologies.

Ley outlines how one might use a crater on the Moon to build a habitat and how this base would be an economical depot from which to depart to other planets because of the Moon's lower gravitational force than on the surface of the Earth. He proposes the use of the small Martian moons, Phobos and Deimos, as space stations for Mars exploration.

Ley concludes: "Prophetically, however, we could say, on the day the first manned rocket leaves the Earth's atmosphere, mankind, which physically and spiritually dominates the Earth, has taken the first step into a new age—the age of dominion over space" (Ley 1926, p. 68).

Ley became a recognized spokesman for and promoter of space travel. His small book sold 6,000 copies over the next six years, and he reports that, "for that reason I was invited to join the Verein für Raumschiffahrt e.V. [VfR] a year later" (Ley 1943, p. 67).

In the back room of a tavern in Breslau on July 5, 1927, a handful of space enthusiasts, including two clergymen, met to establish the Verein für Raumschiffahrt, (VfR), the German Society for Space Travel (Winter 1983, p. 35).

The charter of the new organization stated that "the purpose of the union will be that, out of small projects, large spacecraft can be developed which, when secure and obedient to the slightest command of the pilot, can carry us to the stars." The program of the society was "to interest as many people as possible, to collect membership dues and extra contributions, and to create a fund for experimental work." An early slogan of the society was, "Help create the spaceship!" (Winter 1983, p. 36).

One of the originators of the idea of establishing such a society was Max Valier. He had successfully toured Europe lecturing on spaceflight and wrote to Willy Ley in 1927, suggesting that an organization be established to raise money to finance Hermann Oberth's rocket experiments.

Ley, a founding member of the society though unable to be present at that first meeting, related later that he and his colleagues had difficulty registering the new organization, because the word "space-travel" (*Raumschiffahrt*) did not yet exist in German!

The society's leading members were Johannes Winkler and Max Valier. Winkler had studied mathematics and physics, and later religious history, and was employed as a church administrator at the time of the founding of the VfR. Winkler became president of the new society, but was less of an organizer than either Valier or Ley and put most of his effort into work at the Junkers Airplane Works in Dessau to develop powder rockets as assists for airplanes. Ley and Valier assembled a list of internationally notable figures to invite to join the society, and letters were sent to Oberth, Walter Hohmann, Willy Ley, and leading international scientific figures including Guido von Pirquet (Vienna), Prof. Nikolai Rynin (U.S.S.R.), and Robert Esnault-Pelterie (France), who all joined.

Donations for the VfR came from Poland, Czechoslovakia, Russia, France, Denmark, Spain, South America, and a group of German scientists working in Southwest Africa.

The most important activity of the VfR for its first two years, and the major way it spread its ideas and enthusiasm, was through the publication of a monthly journal, *Die Rakete,* edited by Winkler with assistance from Ley. In it appeared the latest concepts of the leading proponents and experts in rocketry. From June 1927 to the end of 1929, *Die Rakete* combined on-the-spot reports of debates and public presentations on space travel by VfR members with more technical articles on astronautics and the physics of spaceflight.

These included a serialized edition of Esnault-Pelterie's largely mathematical treatise, *Astronautics and Relativity,* a series by Guido von Pirquet on flight paths to various planets in the Solar System, and a series by Winkler titled "An Introduction to Space Flight." Less technical articles included the serialization of popular novels by Max Valier, Otto Willi Gail, and Walter Vollmer.

The first issue of Die Rakete announced the goal of the newly
formed German Society for Space
Travel on its cover—to place a
spacecraft into Earth orbit. For two
years, the monthly journal communicated the latest concepts in
astronautics to the society's far-
flung membership, laying the basis
for amateur rocket societies
around the world.

National Air and Space Museum, Smithsonian Insitution, A-4315H

Die Rakete was a leading educational and organizing tool for
the worldwide amateur rocket movement. It reported on developments in the emerging field of rocketry, which at that time consisted
mainly of experiments with rocket-propelled sleds and seaplanes,
rocket-propelled airplanes, and the famous rocket-driven cars of
Fritz von Opel and Max Valier. Each issue informed members of
upcoming events, such as Winkler's October 1928 radio lecture on
"The Rocket as a Motor." The journal even included poems and
jokes.

Book reviews included a May 1929 review by Konstantin Tsiolkovsky of a new book in Russian, *Interplanetary Travel,* by J.J.
Perlmann.

While the VfR was becoming internationally known as the leading organization promoting space travel, other, smaller groups of
enthusiasts were forming around Germany and throughout Europe.

One important battle within the emerging space community
was over the type of fuel necessary for spaceflight.

Until the rocket experiments of the 1920s, "rockets" meant

mainly firecrackerlike devices using combustible powder for fuel. Oberth, Goddard, and Tsiolkovksy had each recognized independently that in order to produce enough thrust to escape the gravitational force of the Earth, more powerful liquid propellants would have to be developed. Oberth also stated that continuous and smooth-burning liquid propellants would be necessary, in contrast to the solid powder rockets of the 1920s, which did not burn smoothly but in bursts. This jerky motion, he stated, would be unacceptable for human space travelers.

The key parameter for judging the effectiveness of a rocket fuel is called specific impulse which is a measure of the amount of thrust produced, or force per unit mass of the fuel consumed per unit time. Measured in seconds, specific impulse is equivalent to the effective exhaust velocity of the material expelled from the combustion of the propellants, divided by the constant of gravitational acceleration.

The higher the specific impulse, the more thrust produced for each kilogram of propellants consumed. For the same propellant mixture, a higher specific impulse indicates a more efficient engine. Higher specific impulse, in terms of thrust produced per kilogram of propellant, thus lowers the weight the rocket must carry in propellants, increasing the amount of useful payload the rocket can carry.

Higher specific impulse, indicating a higher exhaust velocity, increases the speed the rocket can attain. To orbit the Earth a velocity of nearly 8 kilometers per second is required. To escape the Earth's gravitational force to head for the Moon or farther reaches, a rocket must attain a velocity of about 11 kilometers per second.

The solid-propellant rocket motors used to launch the Space Shuttle produce a specific impulse of 250 seconds. The liquid hydrogen Space Shuttle main engines, by comparison, have a specific impulse in the near-vacuum of space of 453 seconds. The second and third stages of the Apollo Saturn V engine, which also used liquid hydrogen fuel as the Shuttle main engines do, reached a specific impulse of only 425 seconds, indicating the improvements in efficiency of liquid hydrogen engines made between the 1960s Saturn V and the Space Shuttle.

In his 1923 book, Oberth had already carefully calculated the velocities that must be obtained by a spacecraft for ballistic trajectories (from one location on the Earth to another), orbital trajectories (around the Earth), and trips outside of the Earth's gravitational sphere. He proved theoretically that the speed a spacecraft could obtain with solid (or powder) fuels could not achieve the velocities required for space travel.

Oberth determined that, with either petroleum-based fuels or alcohol, one could obtain ballistic flight. For Earth orbit, gasoline-derivative fuels are required. The first small satellites, the first intercontinental ballistic missile, and the first stages of the huge Saturn V used these chemical fuels.

To throw a scientific payload to the other planets from Earth orbit, or to hurl man and his heavy payloads to the Moon, a more energetic liquid fuel than gasoline is required. Oberth proposed liquid hydrogen for these purposes. But not every rocket experimenter in Germany took the route laid out by Oberth.

Although instrumental in establishing the VfR to promote Oberth's research on liquid-fuel rockets, Max Valier, who had become a flamboyant advocate of rocket development, insisted upon working on various schemes using solid propellant, or powder, rockets. He believed that rocket technology could be demonstrated first on cars, then airplanes, and finally on spacecraft.

Willy Ley reports that at the very time of the debate in Danzig in June 1928 between Professor Oberth and Privy Councillor Hans Lorenz over precisely the possibility of liquid-fuel rockets (described in Chapter I), newspapers all over Europe carried headlines about "the successful trial run of the world's first rocket-propelled vehicle," referring to Max Valier's rocket car (Ley 1957a, p. 119).

Valier had been successful in "convincing" car manufacturer Fritz von Opel to pay for his experiments and began to develop solid-rocket-propelled cars. The first test run of the rocket car was on April 11, 1928; and although the first few trials were not totally successful, von Opel garnered the publicity he hoped (and paid) for through these dramatic demonstrations.

Members of the VfR were furious. Ley explains: "After the VfR had worked itself to exhaustion explaining the difference between liquid and solid fuels, after pointing out scores upon scores of times that rockets could never be efficient unless they moved at a velocity which was a large percentage of their exhaust velocity ... one of the founders of the VfR had gone and played around with solid-fuel rockets of commercial manufacture to pave the way for what we considered a cheap publicity stunt. Valier came close to being expelled from the VfR" (Ley 1957a, p. 122).

In a letter to Fritz von Opel on May 2, 1928, Oberth politely

Deutsches Museum, München

Dr. Paul Heylandt (left) with Max Valier beside a liquid-fuelled rocket car near Berlin. It was a failed experiment testing a liquid rocket engine designed by Valier and his assistant Walter Riedel which took Valier's life on May 17, 1930.

congratulated the car manufacturer on the car rocket, and then added with considerable personal pique: "At the same time, I consider it my responsibility to warn you about Valier. . . . I must bring to your attention that Valier is not the expert he makes himself out to be. . . . Fifteen months ago I broke off my correspondence with Valier, mainly because I had come to the conclusion, that he is an incorrigible charlatan."

Two years later, in April 1930, Valier told Willy Ley that he had "said good-by to powder rockets" and was experimenting with liquid fuels (Ley 1957a, p. 135). Valier was now going to do experimental work at the firm of Dr. Paul Heylandt—the Association for the Utilization of Industrial Gases—which produced compressed and liquid gases, including liquid oxygen, for German industry.

In May 1930, Valier and his assistants Walter Riedel and Arthur Rudolph were testing engines for liquid-propellant car rockets. Rudolph had come to work at the Heylandt plant on May 1. During a tour of the plant, "we walked through the halls and also the machine shop, and I was not very impressed with that, because I had seen better ones before," Rudolph later recalled. "But finally we went into the backyard and there I saw a strange contraption. " 'What is that?' " Rudolph asked a fellow worker. " 'That is the test stand of Max Valier,' " the fellow replied. "And when he said 'Max Valier,' my ears picked up." The next day, Rudolph met Valier in the yard of the Heylandt plant and he eagerly volunteered to help with the rocket car experiments (Rudolph 1992).

But during a rocket motor test on Saturday, May 17, 1930, there was a terrific explosion—Valier was struck and killed by a piece of flying metal from the rocket. Luckily Riedel and Rudolph were unharmed. After Valier died, Dr. Heylandt made a speech, Rudolph recalled, "half in German and half in English (as it happens to me sometimes) because he came from the United States, just recently re-imported, and so mixed the two languages up" (Rudolph 1992). Heylandt stated that he was committed to continue the experiments, despite Valier's death.

Arthur Rudolph was determined to redesign the injection system of the rocket motor. Valier and Riedel's motor used a "sprinkling can" type of injection system, where the fuel was delivered through small holes. The holes were difficult to drill, according to Rudolph, which led to an uneven distribution of propellant, and uneven combustion. The liquid oxygen flowed along the walls of the combustion chamber, but inlet areas were not well controlled. The rocket overheated and red glowing spots and burn-throughs developed on the wall of the chamber. This caused spikes in pressure, which in turn created severe explosive jolts.

The Rudolph motor design replaced the "sprinkling can" with a lampshade-type injection of fuel and oxygen through ring slots, which could be more easily manufactured (See Figure 2.2). The propellant distribution was very even, and the fuel and oxygen inlets were adjustable. Rudolph was able to obtain a smooth, controlled burn with the new design (Rudolph 1992).

Willy Ley observed: "Valier's death was especially tragic in view of the fact that nothing had ever happened to him during all his dangerous and useless experiments with powder rockets. He died while engaged in his first really useful experiment, although the idea of mounting his motor in a car was, of course, ridiculous" (Ley 1957a, p. 136).

Valier's assistant, Walter Riedel, later became the chief designer at Peenemünde. Arthur Rudolph began to work under an army

FIGURE 2.2
ARTHUR RUDOLPH'S 1930 ROCKET ENGINE DESIGN
The Reidel-Valier liquid rocket engine used a "sprinkling can" type of injection system which produced uneven fuel distribution. This led to local overheating, often resulting in a burn-through of the engine and pressure spikes which produced explosive jolts. Arthur Rudolph's improved design used a "lamp shade" type of injection system which was easier to manufacture precisely, leading to a more even distribution of fuel. Liquid oxygen flowed away from the wall towards the center of the combustion chamber, and the fuel and oxygen inlet areas were well controlled and adjustable. This design was adopted for the first rocket engines developed by the German army.

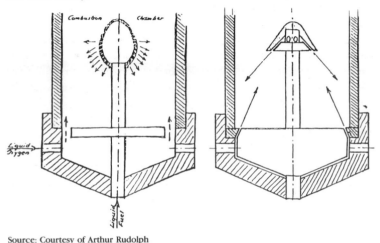

Source: Courtesy of Arthur Rudolph

contract at the Company for Industrial Gas Utilization (Aktiengesellschaft für Industriegasverwertung), and later would join Wernher von Braun in the army rocket program.

Other amateur rocket groups in Germany also were the training ground for what would later become the large-scale military rocket program. In November 1931, an enthusiastic young man named Albert Püllenberg established the Society for Rocket Research in Hanover (Gesellschaft für Raketenforschung-Hannover). He was 18 years old, working at the Hanover Airport. Konrad Dannenberg reports that Max Valier's talks in Hanover and a June 1928 test by Fritz von Opel of a rocket-driven railroad car had aroused his and his friends' interest in rocketry.

More serious study of Hermann Oberth's books and the works of the other German writers prepared them for some preliminary

rocket experiments (Dannenberg 1991, p. 5). Püllenberg and his
assistants, including Dannenberg, tested liquid-fuel rockets at a former ammunition storage bunker on an army base near Hanover.
"In conducting these early firings, we found that all the formulas
and performance data given in the available literature were probably
suitable for future space flights," Dannenberg reports, "but they did
not help us in the design and construction of our early and primitive
rockets. . . . We encountered many blow-ups and explosions" (Dannenberg 1991, p. 6).

In 1934, therefore, Dannenberg entered the Technical University at Hanover to prepare himself for more serious rocket work.
In 1939, Püllenberg, and others in the group transferred to Peenemünde. Before getting to the rocket program, Dannenberg relates,
"In 1940, first I went on foot through all of France, and that was
enough for me." The company he had worked for was able to get
him out of the army, and "after I was out of the army, then it was
possible [to get to] Peenemünde, not as a military man, but as a
reserve soldier" (Dannenberg 1992).

While the most prominent experts in spaceflight had joined
the new VfR in 1927, Willy Ley realized its real job was to reach
out to a wider audience. He began planning the next educational
and organizing initiatives for the German Society for Space Travel.

He decided after the founding of the VfR to: "first, get all the
people who had contributed ideas together and make them write
a book in collaboration. A readable book which would convince a
great number of people, not precisely the man in the street, maybe,
but engineers, teachers, the higher-ups in the civil service, and so
on. Then get the readers to join the now-incorporated society. . . .
Make them pay dues. And give the money to Oberth for experimental work" (Ley 1943, p. 68).

Ley was able to enlist the participation of the leading members
of the VfR—including Oberth, Walter Hohmann, and Franz von
Hoefft in Austria—and they began writing their sections. "I planned
to get Robert Goddard, too, as a contributor," Ley reports, "but he
did not answer" (Ley 1943, p. 68).

The book, *Die Möglichkeit der Weltraumfahrt* (*The Possibility
of Space Travel*), appeared in 1928, and the timing was perfect.
Copies were available at the June debate between Privy Councillor
Lorenz and Oberth, at the meeting of the Scientific Society for
Aeronautics held in Danzig.

In the introduction, Ley states:

> The thought first occurred to me when somebody asked me
> to give them a compendium of all the serious books and writings
> about space travel, adding the comment that these shouldn't
> comprise things which were difficult to understand. That, how-
> ever, is not so easy to accomplish. Since those things which
> are easy to understand were not (and are not) of fundamental
> importance, and those things which are of fundamental impor-
> tance are not so easy to understand.
> There are still no comprehensive works in existence. The
> whole field is too new for that. Our field also lacks the type of
> book, which other sciences more or less do possess—one
> which is both easy to grasp, and yet as comprehensive as possi-
> ble. My idea then was to bring together all the German-speaking
> authors, who had publicly endorsed the feasibility of space-
> flight, in order to compile, as much as possible, a comprehensive
> rocket book, which was at the same time understandable for
> the broadest circle of readers—since we space people more
> than any other technical or scientific branch—are dependent
> upon the interest of the general public. ... My present hope
> is that the book will help awaken the general interest not only
> intellectually, but also financially, so that from this German
> rocket book a German space ship will emerge [Ley 1928, pp.
> iii–iv].

The book covers all of the principal theoretical questions of
rockets and proposes Earth-orbiting space stations, as well as Dr.
Hohmann's precise formulations of travel times, trajectories, and
even landing possibilities on other planets.

One contribution by Dr. Franz von Hoefft, a chemist from
Austria, continued a disagreement he was carrying on with Hermann
Oberth through the pages of *Die Rakete*. Hoefft's chapter, "From
Air Ship to Space Ship," proposed, as had Valier, to apply rocket
technology to airplanes first, and rockets later.

Then, toward the end of 1928, there was a dramatic turn of
events. The VfR and Hermann Oberth's liquid rockets were offered
the chance of a lifetime: to capture the imagination of an entire
generation of youth through the medium of film.

World-renowned film director Fritz Lang was one of the many people reading books about space travel in the 1920s. In 1928, he contacted Oberth in Romania and asked him to come to Berlin to be the technical adviser on what was to become the last great German silent film, *Frau im Mond* (*The Woman in the Moon*, or *By Rocket to the Moon*, as it was called when it ran in America). The book and movie script were written by Lang's former wife, Thea von Harbou, and his wife, Gerda Maurus, played the leading role. In 1930 Maurus became a member of the VfR.

In that period, Ley reports: "In the popular mind, 'the movies' and Fritz Lang were the same. It is almost impossible to convey what magic that name had in Germany at that time" (Ley 1957a, p. 124). So in the fall of 1928 Hermann Oberth traveled to Berlin.

Otto Folberth, cultural historian, writer, and rector of the Stefan Ludwig Roth Gymnasium in Mediasch, reported in an article published in 1930 that one evening in Mediasch, he and three friends

> got together to hear from Oberth about the latest developments in rocketry. . . . He [Oberth] was surprised by the offer of Ufa to be an adviser for the rocket film *Frau im Mond*. The idea of space travel had certainly spread widely since the publication of his ground-breaking work. . . . A dozen novels á la Jules Verne suddenly saw the light of day. In Neubabelsberg near Berlin, the German film *Babel* producers picked up the scent of the hundred percent sensational nature of the material. . . . Oberth had to overcome a number of misgivings before he decided to accept the offer. For the newspapers, magazines, novels, comic strips had already significantly compromised the scientific rigor of the idea. . . [Folberth 1930, pp. 41–45].

Indeed, according to Ley, who met with Oberth when he arrived in Berlin, the professor stubbornly insisted that he would sacrifice no scientific accuracy for the sake of filmmaking. Of course, for dramatic effect, some license was necessary. How could one present a love story taking place on the Moon and have the lead characters talk to each other and hold hands through space suits? So the airless Moon was presented as having an atmosphere (as well as water), and other compromises were made for the sake of drama (Ley 1943, p. 70).

But Ley and also Oberth realized that there could be even more

Hermann Oberth on the set at the Ufa studio in Berlin during the production of the Frau im Mond. *Oberth was the technical director of* The Woman in the Moon, *which inspired many young people to pursue careers in space exploration.*

advantage to the film than introducing the public to the possibility of spaceflight. Ley suggested to Oberth that he ask Lang for money for experimental work to create a *real* rocket, which he did. Lang agreed and he motivated the requested rocket expenditure to Ufa, saying it would be used as an advertisement for the film. Meeting considerable skepticism from the board, Lang promised to commit his own funds to the effort, which he suggested the advertising budget match.

Faced with the task of producing a flight-ready, liquid-fuel rocket in about 12 weeks, Oberth sought assistants and placed a newspaper ad. One that he hired from the ad was Rudolf Nebel, who would later become an active member of the VfR, and to most members, the bane of that organization's existence.

Oberth began a series of tests he hoped would lead to the development of a launchable liquid-fuel rocket for the premier of the film. For what became called "the Oberth Rocket," he designed an ideal combustion chamber shaped like a cone, or in German,

Kegeldüse. He did preliminary tests on the burning characteristics of the gasoline fuel and liquid oxygen, suffering injuries from an explosion during one test that nearly cost him his sight in one eye.

An interesting footnote is that when Oberth was searching for an uninhabited place from which to test-launch his rocket, he decided on Greifswalder Oie in the Baltic Sea. Objections were raised by the local authorities that such tests could possibly damage a lighthouse on the island, and the seashore resort of Horst was chosen instead. Aside from the fact that, as Ley reports, no rocket launched from there could have hit the lighthouse, less than 10 years later, the army would conduct its first rocket experiments there and its major research facility at Peenemünde would be located within view of the Greifswalder Oie.

While Oberth began designing and experimenting, the Ufa film company began advertising that the grand "Oberth rocket" would be launched the day the movie premiered. Considering that virtually no experimentation with rocket motors had yet been tried in Germany, Oberth embarked on a clearly over-ambitious project—to produce an operating liquid-fuel rocket 7 feet tall, holding 2 gallons of propellant, obtaining a 25-mile altitude.

In a 1969 article, Franz Storch described the film company's "unparalleled advertising campaign" to promote *The Woman in the Moon.* The Ufa film company "rented all available telescopes and had them placed at well-trafficked places in order to give passers-by the possibility of seeing the Moon closer up than ever before" (Storch 1969, p. 52). A landscape of the Moon was designed,

> and a sea of electric stars was set blinking against a dark background, and somewhere between them Oberth's rocket would flit back and forth. The same [art work] was reproduced on postcards, stickers, and posters; in the market place you could find rocketlike kaleidoscopes through which peephole you could see "the woman in the Moon," with bare arms reaching for the stars.
>
> Lectures titled, "From Kepler to the Woman in the Moon" were held in order to certify the ostensibly rigorous scientific character of the much-too-fantastic story.

As the time of the movie premier neared, it became clear that the "Oberth Rocket" would never be ready to accompany it. A less

This 1929 portrait of Hermann Oberth was produced by the Ufa film company as part of its extensive promotional effort before the release of the film Frau im Mond *that year. Oberth was to develop and launch an actual rocket for the opening of the film.*

ambitious design, using solid carbon surrounded by liquid oxygen, was tried without success. Finally, shortly before opening day, completely frustrated by the undertaking, Oberth abruptly left town. Ufa made excuses to the press for the absence of the live rocket launch (perhaps the first cancellation due to inclement weather), and Oberth reappeared for the premier on October 15, 1929.

In the November/December 1929 issue of the VfR journal *Die Rakete,* Willy Ley described the scene at the premier: "And then came the big night. The front of the Ufa Palace is transformed into a star-filled sky; a silver rocket sped with thunderous noise between the Earth and the Moon. Lines of cars, a wall of people, guests in smoking [jackets] and fancy evening dresses were pushing their way through.... Prominent people were jostled about.... From [Alfred] Hugenberg to [Albert] Einstein, you could, paradoxically speaking, see no one who wasn't there."

The most dramatic scene in the film was the lift-off of the rocket to the Moon. As Ley described it: "There is without question no other scene, either on Earth or on the Moon, that would have ruffled the poise of this cool, reserved, expert audience—these journalists, scholars, diplomats, men of affluence, and film stars. In the face of these outstanding technical achievements, the audience exploded. Electrified, carried away. The fiery jets of this film rocket swept away their carefully prepared skepticism, indifference, and satiety with the same speed with which the rocket raced across the screen, giving their minds a small glimpse of the tremendous possibilities."

The audience was indeed overwhelmed. Oberth relates in a letter to Romanian film historian Tudor Caranfil on February 19, 1980, "I was also present at the premier at the Ufa Palace at the Zoo and I was twice obliged to give a curtain call" (Barth 1984, p. 275).

Krafft Ehricke relates that a member of Ufa interviewed the American ambassador in Berlin, Dr. Shurman, who stated: "As far as Professor Oberth's long-range rocket is concerned, it can, and certainly will, become an important means of human progress, and I sincerely wish that his work will be successful. America is certainly most interested in Oberth's work" (Ehricke 1960b, p. 17).

The ambassador took this quite seriously, adding that, at the point Oberth were to inform the American Embassy that he was prepared to launch his postal rocket to the United States: "the Embassy would inform the State Department in Washington by cable. From there, the issue would immediately be put before President Hoover, and within the shortest period of time, a cabinet meeting would be called in which particularly the secretary of the navy and the secretary of war would have to be represented. Only such a cabinet meeting would be able to determine the conditions for giving permission to Professor Oberth" (*Die Rakete* Oct. 15, 1929, p. 118).

Frau im Mond is one of the most remarkable films ever made. More than 30 years later, Krafft Ehricke, who watched this marvelous production a dozen times in 1929, reported that, when the Apollo 11 astronauts landed on the Moon on July 20, 1969, and mankind saw this strange world up close for the first time, the thought that crossed his mind was, "It's just like Oberth's movie!" Ehricke said that Oberth's participation as scientific adviser for the film is the

National Air and Space Museum, Smithsonian Institution, A-3543
Pictured here is the scene from Frau im Mond *in which the Moon-bound spaceship emerges from the assembly building toward the launch pad. The scene is most reminiscent of the Saturn V rocket, or today's Space Shuttle, as it leaves the huge Vehicle Assembly Building at the Kennedy Space Center.*

"reason this film was more realistic and technically correct than many other space films, including those of today" (Ehricke 1960b, p. 17).

Watching the film today, the most striking aspect is the preparation and launch of the spaceship. The huge craft is prepared standing upright in a facility similar to the Vehicle Assembly Building at NASA's Kennedy Space Center. It is "rolled out" to the launch pad extremely slowly, along a track, reminiscent of the procedure used with the mobile launch vehicle since Apollo.

There are other similarities. The spaceship is launched resting in a pool of water, to protect its "delicate material" from the violence of the firing of the engines. In 1981, NASA also decided that a flood of water surrounding the Space Shuttle was necessary to protect it, after the shock waves produced by the ignition of the solid rocket boosters and liquid engines had damaged the orbiter Columbia. For dramatic suspense, the crew aboard the lunar spacecraft in the film counts down the launch clock to zero. This has been done in every space launch since then. The similarities are hardly surprising. Hermann Oberth designed the launch in the movie, and his students later designed the launches at the Kennedy Space Center.

Young men like Krafft Ehricke sat in a movie theater in 1929, watched this film about the future of spaceflight, and decided to devote their lives to turning the fantastic journey into reality.

To Oberth the whole episode was personally quite humiliating. He had failed in his effort to produce a real rocket launch and had fled, only to reappear at the premier. He later described the Ufa affair as "disgraceful." But he learned that his strength was in the realm of the scientific and theoretical, and that it would be the job of engineers to turn his ideas into the technologies that would actually take man to the Moon.

The members of the VfR salvaged the test stand and other equipment used for the film's Oberth rocket project. They now had the basis to begin their own, more serious, experimentation effort.

The publication and circulation of *Die Rakete* and the *Frau im Mond* had a welcome effect: The German Society for Space Travel was growing by leaps and bounds. One year after its founding in 1927, it had more than 500 members; by 1929, 870; and membership rose to about 1,000 before the depths of the Depression.

As soon as Oberth's *The Rocket into Interplanetary Space* was published in 1923, the characteristically uninformed criticisms from the scientific community began to pour in. Oberth committed the next six years both to refuting the incorrect notions about rockets and spaceflight from the technical establishment, and to expanding his work to interest the nontechnical but educated person in this new science and technology of astronautics.

Oberth dedicated his book, *Ways to Spaceflight,* written in September 1928, to Fritz Lang and Thea von Harbou. In the introduction, he writes, "I tried to make this edition somewhat more easily comprehensible. ... I chose this somewhat popular version (1) in order to make my book more easily grasped by a wider circle of readers. When I wrote the first edition, I did not believe that the material would find interest in such broad circles. (2) But I also feel inclined to prepare this popular version by the circumstances that, as I will soon show, even the professional journals have in many instances misunderstood my book" (Oberth 1929, p. vii).

It is surely a testament to the level of education and intellectual rigor of that time that this 400-plus page work, which includes its share of mathematical formulae to prove Oberth's groundbreaking scientific concepts, was considered by the author to be a "popular" work.

In his June 1928 debate with Hans Lorenz, Oberth outlined some of the practical applications of his rocket technology. He suggested, for a start, that small rockets with automatic guidance systems could be built, that could cover distances of 1,000 to 2,000 kilometers, carrying a payload of between 10 and 20 kilograms. Such rockets would be suitable for transporting urgent mail over long distances; for example, to deliver letters from Berlin to New York in a half hour.

In *Ways to Spaceflight,* Oberth further outlines uses for his Model B rocket, which today would be described as a sounding rocket: "Since the rocket can better be sent where one wishes than a meteorological balloon, unanswered questions in connection with the formation of thunderstorms, the occurrence of barometric maxima and minima, and the like could be investigated with the use of rockets. Naturally," he cautions, "it cannot be predicted today whether this research will also lead to control of the respective natural phenomena, but it is probable" (Oberth 1929, pp. 367–68).

The Model B rocket could also be equipped with a motion-picture camera and used for reconnaissance, Oberth states. A photographic camera could be outfitted for a geographical rocket that could photograph less accessible areas of the world.

Although the first orbital rocket was still decades away, Oberth detailed his design for the more advanced "Model E rocket" to provide the guidelines for the technology to open space to man.

How would man travel and live outside the Earth's atmosphere? Oberth states that "space vehicles on the largest scale can be put in orbit around the Earth. Then they represent a small moon, so to speak. They no longer have to be able to land. Communication between them and the Earth can be maintained by means of smaller vehicles so that these large rockets (we will call them observer stations) can be progressively rebuilt for their actual purpose while aloft" (Oberth 1929, p. 478).

One purpose of such stations would be as platforms to base telescopes for studying the Earth's atmosphere and to do space science. An orbiting station could also be used as a fueling station for ships that would be coming and going on their travels from Earth to far parts of the Solar System.

One of Oberth's major ideas, filled out in substantial detail by Krafft Ehricke in later years, was the design and construction of Earth-orbital mirrors. Oberth's orbital reflector, described in Figure

FIGURE 2.3
OBERTH'S ORBITAL MIRROR
This drawing illustrates the basic concept of Oberth's space mirror. It would be in polar orbit, (north to south) covering the surface of the Earth as the Earth turned underneath it (west to east). The sunlight would be reflected by the mirror and as seen in the lower right side of this drawing, could be used to light up a part of the night-time Earth.

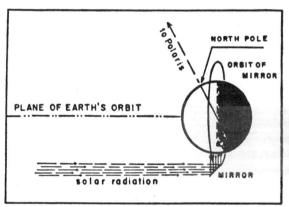

Source: Willy Ley, *Rockets, Missiles, and Space Travel* (New York: The Viking Press, 1957).

2.3, would concentrate sunlight on a series of surfaces tilted 45 degrees, which could all be pointed at a specific region of the Earth or spread out over wider areas. If the reflector were 1,000 kilometers wide, the light could be concentrated, Oberth calculated, on an area of 78 square kilometers on Earth.

Oberth observed that the reflecting surfaces could be of any size, so various applications were possible. Although precise calculations of dispersion and diffusion of light through the Earth's atmosphere could not be made at that time, Oberth made imaginative proposals for use of the orbital mirrors. He also proposed that the ocean route to the Arctic island of Spitzbergen or to the ports of northern Siberia could be kept ice-free during the winter by such concentrated solar rays. He estimated that if the reflector were 100 kilometers in diameter, wide stretches of land in northern latitudes could be made habitable through the dispersed light. And in more moderate climates, "the feared sudden drops in temperature could be prevented, thus saving fruit and vegetable crops of entire provinces."

Oberth proposes putting the mirror in a polar, rather than

FIGURE 2.4
THE SPACE DIVER ON AN EVA
In order for an astronaut to work outside his ship in space, Oberth designed the
equipment for a "space diver," seen in this figure. An oxygen tank (P) is attached
to the space suit and with hooks and claws the astronaut is able to negotiate along
the outside of a spacecraft. A tether (F) connects the space diver to the mother
ship.

Source: Hermann Oberth *Ways to Space Flight* (Munich, Germany: R. Oldenbourg, 1929).

equatorial orbit, so each region of the Earth would pass underneath
it as the Earth turned. In this way, it could perform many tasks at
once.

More than four decades before the first U.S. astronaut left his
spaceship for what is called EVA, or extravehicular activity, Oberth
described a space walk. He described in great detail how a wire
mesh frame could be brought up in the rocket, unwound, and the
mirror's sodium surface prepared by what he called "space divers."
In order to work outside the ship, he showed that "claws" could
be attached to the divers' suits and hooks to their feet. These effects
would anchor the astronauts in free space (Figure 2.4).

It would not be practical to supply air from the cabin of the
spacecraft, he proposed. Instead, the men would "carry compressed
air in a cylinder" mounted on their backs. This is the way EVAs
have been done since 1965. The "diver" would be connected to
the crew cabin and stay in communication with the pilot by a cable,
which he proposed be telephone wires. Oberth creatively suggested
that exhaled air be expelled and used as thrust for the astronaut to

FIGURE 2.5
OBERTH'S GRAVITY ASSIST PROBLEM
In his 1929 book, Oberth posed the problem to readers of the most efficient way
to reach a fixed star 1 quadrillion miles away from an asteroid, which is situated at
A'. As he proves, the best solution is not to leave the asteroid immediately, but wait
a few centuries until you are at point X in the orbit of the asteroid. From that point,
the spacecraft would swing around the Sun (in the center) moving in the opposite
direction to the fixed star, and obtain a velocity increase through a gravity assist.
The spacecraft would follow path D'-D and arrive at point B near the fixed star in
one-half to one-tenth the time it would take on a more "direct" route.

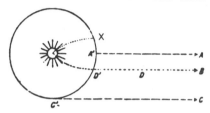

Source: Hermann Oberth *Ways to Space Flight* (Munich, Germany: R. Oldenbourg, 1929).

maneuver around. The cabin would have to include an air lock, he
stated, to prevent the air in the cabin from escaping when the space
walkers egressed, which is common practice today.

But Oberth envisioned that there would also be places where
man could not immediately go, so he set for himself the task of
calculating the best possible ways for reaching faraway celestial
bodies with unmanned probes, not so much as a practical question
but in order to challenge readers to learn how to solve the complex
problems of astronautics. Oberth posed the problem seen in Figure
2.5. If you were on an asteroid and wanted to reach a fixed star
one quadrillion miles away, and if your space ship had an ideal
propulsion of 6 kilometers per second, when should you leave, and
what path should you follow to get there?

The first intuitive response would be that you should start
immediately, and head straight for the star. On this path, the ship
would get there in 5,555,600 years.

The second option might be to wait 20,000 years, until you
have completed three-quarters of an orbit around the Earth, starting
on your trip when you are aiming exactly at the star. If the rocket
starts on line C'C, and the asteroid you are on has a velocity of 1
kilometer per second, the velocity of the asteroid is added to your
fuel velocity and you will get there in 4,780,000 years.

The best solution, however, is to start a few centuries after

point A', with a velocity exactly opposite to the velocity of your
home asteroid. The propelling force of 1 kilometer per second will
put you into an orbit shaped like an elongated ellipse, which takes
you around the Sun. At the point of perihelion, the point closest to
the Sun, you would have attained a velocity of 500 kilometers
per second. This is a gravitational "push" that you would get by
approaching the Sun.

The final velocity obtained on the path D'B is 70.9 kilometers
per second, and the trip time would be 470,000 years, or one-half
to one-tenth the other trip times (Oberth 1929, pp. 198–200). This
concept, today called a "gravity assist," is the method that was used
in the 1970s to get the U.S. Voyager spacecraft on its way to Jupiter,
Saturn, Uranus, and Neptune. It was the only way one spacecraft
could fly by all of the outer planets.

By the time of the publication in 1929 of *Ways to Spaceflight,*
the new science of astronautics was an internationally recognized
field of serious study. In 1928, French banker André Hirsch and
Robert Esnault-Pelterie founded an Annual Award for Astronautics,
which became popularly known as the REP-Hirsch prize. A sum of
500 francs was set aside "to be given to the author or experimenter
who had done the most to further the idea of space travel during
that year" (Ley 1957a, p. 123).

In 1928, Hermann Oberth received the first REP-Hirsch prize
for *Ways to Spaceflight.* As a recognition of the importance of the
work, the amount of the prize money was doubled.

The rocket enthusiasts of the 1920s, who became the amateur
experimenters of the 1930s, the core of the German rocket program
during the war, and the group that took America to the Moon in
the 1960s, had cut their teeth on Hermann Oberth's *The Rocket
into Interplanetary Space* and *Ways to Spaceflight,* Willy Ley's writings, and the material in *Die Rakete,* all made sensuous by the
fabulous *Frau im Mond.*

Now they were ready to begin serious rocket experiments.

CHAPTER
III

From Theory to Experimentation

A t the end of 1929, the German Society for Space Travel moved from Breslau to Berlin and decided to concentrate on enlisting support and procuring facilities for rocket development. Johannes Winkler, the editor of *Die Rakete,* was largely involved in experiments in industry, outside the activity of the VfR, and had resigned as president. Hermann Oberth became president and Willy Ley vice president. The scarcity of funds led the spaceflight activists to cease publication of the journal and raise funds for experimentation. They substituted a mimeographed bulletin to keep in touch with their rapidly growing membership. In early 1930, engineer Klaus Riedel and Rudolf Nebel, Oberth's assistant on *The Woman in the Moon,* joined the VfR's inner circle.

On April 11, 1930, the VfR made its debut in Berlin, sponsoring a public lecture in the auditorium of the General Post Office. The post office had previously purchased articles by Willy Ley for publication in a magazine produced for its employees, and the VfR was hoping it would take up Oberth's suggestion and buy small rockets for mail delivery. In addition to listening to a lecture by Johannes Winkler, the audience viewed the model of the Oberth rocket, hung from the ceiling on a parachute.

To attract more public attention, a display was set up in the basement of the Wertheim department store. It included the rocket, parachute, rocket performance diagrams, gears and motors, photographs and books on astronautics, a display of the wireless telegraphy used to report the position of the rocket in flight, and other equipment. University student Wernher von Braun helped Oberth

FIGURE 3.1
HERMANN OBERTH'S KEGELDÜSE
For the rocket for the 1929 film *Frau im Mond,* Hermann
Oberth designed a rocket motor combustion chamber
he called a "Kegeldüse" or cone. It was made of steel
with a heavy copper lining and was fabricated in two
parts and bolted together.

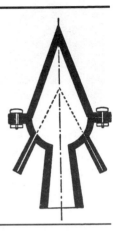

Source: Willy Ley *Rockets, Missiles, and Space Travel* (New
York: The Viking Press 1957.

set up the display and gave public explanations of the equipment
and future flights to the Moon.

For the film, Oberth had designed an ideal rocket motor combustion chamber, which he called a *Kegeldüse,* from the German
word for "cone." This chamber (Figure 3.1), made of steel and lined
with copper, was designed to burn liquid oxygen and methane.

Oberth's plan was to continue development of the Kegeldüse,
and flight-test it in the large Oberth rocket that had been designed
for the film, to show the superiority of liquid-fuel rockets once and
for all. But other members of the VfR disagreed. As Ley relates, "the
rest of us felt that a small rocket which worked was greatly to be
preferred to a large one that didn't" (Ley 1957a, p. 133). Rudolf
Nebel and engineer Klaus Riedel designed and built a smaller Mini-
mumrakete, or Mirak, for preliminary tests.

The next step was to secure funding for development. Ley
states that "the unsuccessful treasure hunt yielded an unexpected
result" when Dr. Franz Ritter from the Chemisch-Technische Reichs-
anstalt, a government institute similar to the National Bureau of
Standards, agreed to witness and record the results of a test. Oberth,
Nebel, and Riedel worked for three weeks at the institute to prepare
for the test, and on July 23, 1930, a successful Kegeldüse motor
test was performed.

Ley provides a description: "It was a miracle it worked at all.
All through the test it poured, it had poured 24 hours before. I have
never been so wet in my life—not even when swimming" (Ley

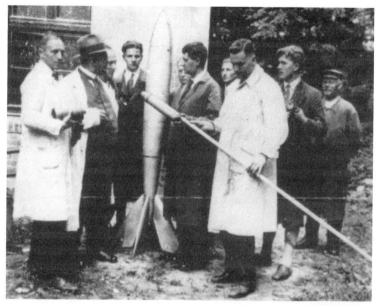

NASA, Marshall Space Flight Center

Soon after the successful test of a "Kegeldüse" rocket motor, leading members of the VfR posed for this photograph. At left is Rudolf Nebel, Oberth's assistant on the project. To his left is Dr. Franz Ritter from the Chemistry Institute. Directly to the right of the "Oberth rocket" designed for the film is Hermann Oberth. To Oberth's left is Klaus Riedel, and behind Riedel in knickers is Wernher von Braun.

1943, p. 77). "The photographers ruined their cameras in the rain, the editors, their notebooks. The scientists, with but few exceptions, caught cold" (Ley 1937a, p. 61).

Although Dr. Ritter could not offer financial help, he did officially certify that a Kegeldüse had performed for 90 seconds, consuming 6 kilograms of liquid oxygen and 1 kilogram of gasoline, delivering a constant thrust of about 7 kilograms. With no funding, but with the certificate from the institute in his pocket, Oberth quietly left for home in Romania to return to his teaching responsibilities.

The young VfR members were not deterred. With some confidence that the little motor worked, Ley and company decided to start testing a Mirak rocket in the countryside on a farm owned by Riedel's grandparents. The death of Max Valier in May had created justifiable fear of rocket explosions so experiments were moved away from populated areas. During the summer, tests on the small rocket motor were successful.

In 1959, Wernher von Braun looked back on those early attempts: "I'll never forget those groping experiments in the summer of 1930, where we had to fire off a combustion chamber filled with alcohol and liquid oxygen with a dagger mounted on a long pole. However rudimentary those experiments may seem to us today, they were just as essential for the success of rocket technology as were the experiments of Otto Lilienthal and the Wright brothers for modern air travel" (von Braun, 1959a).

But on September 7, 1930, Ley received a report from Riedel: "The Mirak has exploded, no harm done; we'll come back and build a new one" (Ley 1957a, p. 136).

As Ley relates, "When we put these reports into the mimeographed bulletins by means of which we held the VfR together, two members saw fit to reveal that they were wealthy." One was Hugo A. Hueckel, who produced aluminum and also manufactured hats. Hueckel, who was also supporting Winkler's rocket research, sent what would be equivalent to $100 and promised $150 per month, strictly for experimental expenses. Ley also mentions that "an engineer named Dilthey ... donated approximately $1,000 in cash in two installments" (Ley 1957a, p. 136).

What was needed was a true test site. After an exhaustive search throughout the Berlin area, on September 27, 1930, a facility secured by Nebel opened in an abandoned army garrison at the Berlin suburb of Reinickendorf. Nebel named it "Raketenflugplatz," meaning literally "Rocket Airport." The site had buildings housing a police garrison that had been used by the army during World War I. It was leased to the rocket enthusiasts for what would have been equivalent to $4 per year.

Historian Frank Winter reports in a recent publication (Winter 1992, p. 98) that a colleague, Michael Neufeld, recently discovered a document in Germany that shows that Col. Karl Becker financed and arranged for the establishment of the VfR facility at Reinickendorf. This would certainly coincide with the army's increased attention to rocketry and seems logical, as well as fortunate.

Nebel and Riedel, both bachelors, set up house there, and von Braun visited when he could take time off from school. A month later, Helmut Zoike, then 15 years old, arrived at Raketenflugplatz.

"My interest in space travel was inspired by reading Prof. Hermann Oberth's book, *Ways to Spaceflight*," he related later:

> A friend of our family at Siemens & Halske, Dr. Weingraber ... discussed my opinion and impressions about this book with me, and fostered my great interest in this subject. He told me about the Raketenflugplatz Berlin activity. ...
>
> After a sleepless night, I drove from Siemensstadt ... to Rein-ickendorf on my bicycle and met with Messrs. Rudolf Nebel and Klaus Riedel and the other members of the Raketenflug-platz. They assigned me to help and making [sic] missile parts, particularly valves and rocket motor parts of all kinds. I was at this time an apprentice at Siemens & Halske, and could talk my superior and teacher into letting me do the parts during my worktime and I brought them in the evenings and on the weekends to Raketenflugplatz where I also participated in the experimental firings [Zoike 1978].

By March 1931, the group had completed a Mirak test stand, a larger test stand originally built for the Oberth rocket, and a portable test stand, which was used for small-scale tests of new rocket motor concepts, brought by numerous people to the Raket-enflugplatz. At the new Raketenflugplatz, Nebel and Riedel contin-ued their work on the Mirak, seen in Figure 3.2(a). It was basically a head and a "guiding stick," similar to the designs for powder rockets. The head was made of cast aluminum and looked like an artillery shell. It was removed to put in the liquid oxygen. The "guiding stick" was an aluminum tube, which was the gasoline tank. At the bottom of the oxygen tank was a small combustion chamber, modeled on Oberth's Kegeldüse.

The liquid oxygen was supposed to cool the motor, and the motor's heat would evaporate some of the liquid oxygen, creating the pressure to pump fuel into the combustion chamber. The second Mirak tested in the spring of 1931 also exploded as the heat of combustion burned through the casing, demonstrating that the cir-culation of the fuel was not sufficient cooling for the motor. A redesign was clearly necessary.

A new engine was developed for a third Mirak, with the motor below the bottom of the oxygen tank. Instead of having only one tail off to the side, it would have two, placed symmetrically, with

FIGURE 3.2
ROCKET ENGINES TESTED AT THE RAKETENFLUGPLATZ
(a) A cross section of the "head" of the Mirak No. 2. The combustion chamber, modelled on Oberth's Kegeldüse, is placed inside the liquid oxygen tank. The guiding stick to the left is the fuel tank.
(b) The "head" of a later Repulsor. The motor is placed within a jacket which is filled with cooling water. The two symmetrical "sticks" supply liquid fuel and liquid oxygen to the motor.

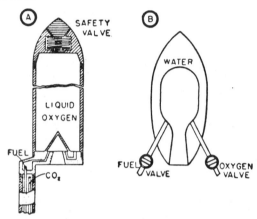

Source: Willy Ley *Rockets, Missiles, and Space Travel* (New York: The Viking Press 1957).

the second containing compressed nitrogen to pressure-feed the fuel and liquid oxygen to the motor. The motor would not be a Kegeldüse made of steel, but one made of aluminum, cooled with water.

A test stand was built to try out the new design. When American Interplanetary Society president G. Edward Pendray and his wife visited the Raketenflugplatz in April 1931, this was the motor they saw demonstrated on the test stand. In the meantime, VfR founding member Winkler had successfully fired Europe's first liquid-fuel rocket on March 14 in Dessau, which encouraged the experimenters.

But the Mirak 3 rocket was never built. When Nebel was off at an exhibition in Kiel, Riedel and Ley redesigned the rocket so the liquid oxygen and fuel would come in from two different sides to the combustion chamber, [Figure 3.2(b)], and Riedel designed a water-cooled jacket.

The first "flight test" of this new motor was accidental, when on May 10, 1931, it broke free from the heavy struts holding it to the test stand and rose approximately 20 meters. Four days later, the same rocket, which had now been dubbed the "Repulsor," was launched and flew up to about 60 meters before crashing.

Ley called their new design a "Repulsor" to avoid using the word "rocket," which implied powdered propellant at that time. He took the name from the novel by Kurt Lasswitz, *Auf Zwei Planeten* (*On Two Planets*), in which Lasswitz invented "repulsit" as his substance for propulsion (Ley 1957a, p. 148).

On May 23, Repulsor No. 2 climbed to about 60 meters but turned sideways, and as the experimenters watched in horror, it headed clear out of the grounds of the Raketenflugplatz! Luckily, it did no damage.

Ley has stressed that the developments at the Raketenflugplatz were not one man's inventions but an effort that resulted from discussion among the group of experimenters, and that any experiment contained parts either used elsewhere or already patented. He relays the story of a "legal experiment" conducted by Oberth, which, he says, proves this point nicely:

> Oberth was beset by "inventors" with enormous ideas. They were all two centuries old—the ideas; the inventors behaved like babies—and they were all expected to yield at least a half a million [dollars]. Oberth had a lot of very practical moments and in one of them he sat down and drew up a patent for a spaceship, complete with air purifiers, water regenerators, and everything. It involved a lot of detailed research, a stack of drawings, and a long description. The German Patent Office rejected the application after some time with an even longer write-up, proving point for point that all the equipment of a spaceship ... was either in actual use somewhere—mostly in power plants, airplanes, and submarines—or had been patented or published before. They were ready to grant patents on some parts, if and when designed in a specific shape for that specific use [Ley 1943, p. 62].

Repulsor model 4 was a redesign, termed a "one-stick Repulsor", where the fuel and oxidizer tanks were one behind the other and the guide stick was along the center line of the rocket. In letters to G. Edward Pendray, Ley described the new design,

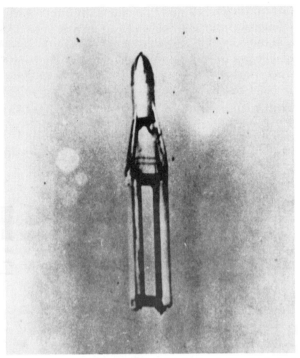

National Air and Space Museum, Rolf Engel Collection, Smithsonian Institution, A-3919
A flight of a four-stick Repulsor.

stating that from an aerodynamics point of view, the whole one-stick repulsor was an arrow, and that this should help solve stability problems (Ley 1931a and b). During one test, the Repulsor rose to an altitude of about 1 kilometer and crashed into a shack owned by the police while the Ufa studio was filming the test launch for the newsreels.

"The police descended on the Raketenflugplatz like an invading army," Ley reports, "and any further experimentation was forbidden then and there" (Ley 1957a, p. 151). Hearings were held and the stop order was withdrawn, but a list of restrictions was drawn up and imposed on future rocket tests.

News of these dramatic tests spread internationally. They were covered in the *Bulletin* of the American Interplanetary Society, headquartered in New York. Society president G. Edward Pendray, who earlier that spring had visited the Raketenflugplatz, expectantly wrote in the *Bulletin* that, "whatever the future may bring in the way of additional changes of design, it is clear that for the first time we have, in the one-stick Repulsor, a rocket that could be made in large size, able to carry scientific instruments into the stratosphere or into space, or able to transmit mail, freight, and even passengers from one point to another on the Earth" (Williams and Epstein 1955, p. 166).

Public enthusiasm in Germany was tremendous. Ley reports that during 1931, "every magazine in existence ran at least one article about our activities" (Ley 1943, p. 58). In the middle of December 1931, knowing he would be visiting his family in Königsberg for about a week in January or February, he wrote to a VfR member there and volunteered to give a lecture while visiting. "My week then looked as follows," he reports: "Sunday, radio; Monday, Engineering Society; Tuesday, free; Wednesday, University, Geographical Seminary; Thursday, Merchant's League; Friday, University, Department of Physics; Saturday, free; Sunday, radio again" (Ley 1943, p. 59). The VfR got half the proceeds from these events.

Albert Einstein's son-in-law, Dimitri Marianoff, recounted in a biography of the famous scientist that he had talked often with "Captain" [sic] Nebel and in 1932 had gone to visit the Raketenflugplatz. "The rocket airdrome consisted of a few starkly simple barracks and many workshops. The impression you took away with you was the frenzied devotion of Nebel's men to their work. Most of them were [like] officers living under military discipline. Later, I learned that he and his staff lived like hermits. Not one of these men was married, none of them smoked or drank. They belong exclusively to a world dominated by one single wholehearted idea" (Marianoff 1944, p. 115).

But Ley states that the Ufa "newsreel and the victory over the police were our last triumphs. What followed afterwards was a hopeless struggle against political tension and economic misery. It was a hard winter climatically. And it was the fatal winter under Chancellor Bruening when Adolf Hitler suddenly assumed prominence" (Ley 1957a, p. 152).

Engineer Herbert Schaefer, who joined the VfR in the spring of 1932, described the conditions at the Raketenflugplatz: They received some money from a public-works-type government welfare office, and got their food from a soup kitchen run by charitable women. About 15 draftsmen, electricians, and mechanics had joined

An early photo of Willy Ley, founding member of the VfR.

the rocket group to have a free place to live, while being able to keep up their skills.

As the economic situation worsened, the roster of the VfR shrank to 300; letters came in from members saying they could no longer pay dues. Industrialist Hugo Hueckel wrote saying he could not contribute any longer; finances to continue rocket experiments dried up.

Ley and other leading VfR members were constantly trying to raise money to continue their rocket experiments, and they solicited funds wherever they could. A letter was even sent to the president of Noyes Buick Sales in Boston, Massachusetts, on October 6, 1931, for example, offering to send him "rocket shows" for a fee of $500 (Winter 1983, p. 36).

But the worldwide depression was grinding economic activity to a halt. Ley wrote a letter to Pendray (in his halting English), from Königsberg, explaining that "our work at the Raketenflugplatz will be continued in February and March, during January we collect money. I know, the economic situation in U.S.A. is also not as good as it was long years, but I hope, that the world has reached the end of the financial crisis in a short time. (Short, that means 1 or 2 years)" (Ley 1932b).

The hyperinflation crisis of 1923, caused by the impossibility of meeting the reparations payments, had been curbed by an orgy of borrowing through the Dawes Plan. The Bank for International Settlements was established to collect and distribute the reparations payments. Between 1924 and 1929, Germany received the equivalent of £900 million in foreign loans and credits, mainly from the United States. Of that, £500 million went to pay reparations. The rest went for federal and municipal programs that produced prosperity but shackled the German economy to international financial institutions—similar to the plight of developing nations today in their relationship to the International Monetary Fund.

The 1929 stock market crash in the United States led to a cessation of American loans to Europe and a deflationary collapse, bringing world trade to a standstill. The bankruptcy of the Austrian Kredit-Anstalt bank in 1931 started a panic throughout Europe and created despair in Germany. In 1929, German exports were equivalent to £630 million pounds. By 1932, this had dropped to £280 million. Unemployment had soared from 2 million to more than 6 million.

The National Socialist Party won 107 seats in the Reichstag in the September 1930 elections, and a majority two years later. Its major campaign plank was a repudiation of the Versailles Treaty.

Cognizant of the economic and political crisis around him, but hopeful that the situation would improve, Ley left for a lecture tour in East Prussia in 1931 to try to raise some funds for a program that could give the world optimistic goals for the future.

Back in Berlin at the Raketenflugplatz, Riedel continued work on rocket engine improvements. Even with his water-cooling jacket, there were still motor burn-outs. He and Ley decided to try to mix the cooling water directly with the fuel rather than have a separate jacket, which meant a switch from gasoline to alcohol fuel.

Ley and Riedel also knew that it took 3.5 pounds of liquid oxygen to burn 1 pound of gasoline, but only 2 pounds of precious liquid oxygen for 1 pound of alcohol. Oberth had recommended using alcohol fuel as the first step to eventually using liquid hydrogen fuel needed for manned spaceflights.

As things grew financially desperate, Nebel wrote to the army to ask for support for the VfR rocket experiments. In April 1932, Professor Colonel Karl Becker, the chief of ballistics and ammunition for the army; his ammunition expert, Major von Horstig; and Captain Walter Dornberger, visited the Raketenflugplatz. More impressed with Wernher von Braun than the primitive facilities and test results, the army gave the team 1,000 marks to prepare a demonstration of their Repulsor rocket at the army proving grounds at Kummersdorf, 17 miles from Berlin.

Three months later, without informing the other directors of the VfR, Nebel, Riedel, and von Braun took the rocket and auxiliary equipment and went to meet Dornberger in a field near Kummersdorf. As von Braun describes it, "Dornberger guided us to an isolated spot on the artillery range where were set up a formidable array of phototheodolites, ballistic cameras, and chronographs—instruments of whose very existence we had theretofore been unaware. . . . At the signal, the Mirak II soared upward for a distance of some 200 feet. Here, however, its trajectory became almost horizontal so that the rocket crashed before the parachute could open" (Ordway and Sharpe 1979, p. 19).

Writing in the 1950s, Dornberger recalls that "the failure of this demonstration brought home to us in the Army Weapons Department how many scientific and technical questions needed answering before we could hope to construct a rocket that could fly efficiently" (Dornberger 1952, p. 43).

After the demonstration, Nebel kept trying to convince the army to fund their work, but they were not interested in the amateur rocket experiments at the Raketenflugplatz. Finally, Wernher von Braun met personally with Colonel Becker. "We are greatly interested in rocketry," von Braun later recalls Becker as saying, "but there are a number of defects in the manner in which your organization is going about its development. For our purposes, there is far too much showmanship. You would do better to concentrate on scientific data than to fire toy rockets" (von Braun 1956, p. 130).

Of course, von Braun explained that the shows were necessary to raise funds for the experiments. Becker offered "some degree of financial support providing that we were prepared to do our work in the anonymity assured by the walls of some army enclave. There'd be no military rocketry at Reinickendorf."

Nebel's reaction to the idea of working for the army was totally negative, and Klaus Riedel, who later would become the head of testing at Peenemünde, told von Braun that he thought private enterprise could produce the necessary finances to continue their research and that he was unwilling to go with von Braun to the army test facility at Kummersdorf.

Shortly after the VfR demonstration for Dornberger, and before the rise of Hitler to power, von Braun was hired as the first civilian to work for the army on liquid-propellant rocket development.

Nebel tried to raise money through a variety of wild and unscrupulous schemes and finally went off on his own, separating from the VfR. The rocket society was in any case falling apart. By Christmas 1933, Ley relates, "everybody's hands were tightly tied by a ruthless totalitarian regime. During that winter the VfR collapsed during a stormy session, and while I pretended to try to reorganize it under another name, I quietly took the first steps toward leaving Germany" (Ley 1957a, p. 161).

It was not at all clear that Ley could easily leave Germany at that time. Willy Ley and many other rocketeers had been in touch with VfR members and spaceflight enthusiasts all over the world and, probably most disturbing to the Nazi regime, with Russian scientists.

In 1932, for example, Ley had written a letter to Oberth, stating: "Yesterday evening I got together with a Russian professor (a physicist) who is a close friend of the Supreme Government Commissar. . . . The Russians are prepared, without any remunerative considerations . . . to build a research laboratory according to my specifications, in a large Russian city of my choosing. [It would include] German, or at least German-speaking workers and craftsman, as well as scientific collaborators. [It would involve] six-day work weeks of six to seven hours a day, and we would reach an understanding as to wages . . . of which 50 percent could be sent home. . . . No obligation for political activity . . . a contract could be signed for 1–2 years" (Ley 1932a).

Neither Ley nor Oberth ever took up the offer, but by the time the Nazis were consolidating power, anyone doing research as sensitive as rocket research who was in touch with foreigners, was under suspicion. Rocket enthusiast Rolf Engel and his assistant Heinz Springer, who had worked with Johannes Winkler, were arrested on April 4, 1933, by two Gestapo agents and charged with "high treason." Their material was confiscated, and the Gestapo opened proceedings against them in the Reichsgericht (Supreme Court). Engel was threatened quite severely should he continue contact with foreign scientists, and it took six weeks for him to be released from prison (Päch 1980, p. 232).

Ley could see the handwriting on the wall. In addition to the crisis from the political right in Germany, there was also another threat. As he wrote to Pendray on June 30, 1932, "Men, hurry, you are the hope of the world and if you will be down long enough, Bolshewism [sic] will eat us all together!" (Ley 1932b).

At the end of 1934, Ley planned a trip, ostensibly to write articles for various German newspapers. His private agenda was to go to London to visit with Phil Cleator, the head of the British Interplanetary Society, and then go permanently to America. In letters to Pendray in New York, he laid out his plans to arrive in the United States in February 1935.

Ley expressed concern for his family in Germany, and asked that the American Rocket Society not publish anything about his trip. By the end of January he was able to write that he had obtained his visa and would leave Berlin and go to London. "An old dream of mine becomes true with this trip and I have to thank you for it," he wrote to ARS head Pendray (Ley 1935a).

Oberth resigned from the VfR, and Riedel, Hans Hueter, Herbert Schaefer, and Helmut Zoike found jobs at the Siemens Company. On April 7, 1936, Schaefer joined Ley in America.

Amateur rocketry was coming to an end in Germany. Von Braun was starting work on the next-generation larger rockets with Captain Dornberger at Kummersdorf. Many of his friends from Raketenflug-platz and members of other rocket societies in Germany would join him five years later at Peenemünde.

When Wernher von Braun started working for the army it was still led by the traditional Prussian officer corps. Throughout the turmoil in Germany, from the late 1920s through the end of the war, attempts persisted on the part of some of the upper-echelon army officers to keep the military out of politics and to keep the Nazis out of the activities of the army, although with diminishing effect. The last major act in this regard was the attempt on Hitler's life in July 1944, which involved a good number of leading figures in the Wehrmacht.

Through the early years of the war, the Army Ordnance Division kept strict control over the rocket program. Hitler expressed little interest in the program and a great deal of skepticism about the prospects for its success. When, in the desperate final phases of the war, Hitler rushed to utilize rocket technology as a "wonder weapon," the SS attempted to gain control over the program. It finally succeeded, after the Peenemünde facilities were bombed by the British in August 1943.

Because the Nazi party apparatus, in the form of the SS, was finally able to get significant control over the German rocket program in the last year and a half of the war, Wernher von Braun's motivations for joining Captain Dornberger's rocket program have been questioned. Krafft Ehricke had a straightforward explanation: "It is the historic merit of Wernher von Braun to have first recognized clearly the hopelessness of private efforts to advance beyond a very modest state of the art in just one limited sector of rocket development, namely, the propulsion system. Dr. von Braun thus raised the whole question of the future rocket development above the level of the backyard inventor, the hero of many science-fiction novels at that time who 'invented' and built the space ship in his garage and surprised his neighborhood with a sudden take-off to the Moon.

"He felt that only large industrial or governmental resources could possibly provide the necessary financial support, laboratories, equipment, and professional manpower commensurate with the magnitude of the task." All attempts at private support had failed. "Balancing visionary enthusiasm," Ehricke continued, "with sober realism, bold leadership with recognition of the facts of life, Wernher von Braun opened the era of modern rocket development (1934–1945)" (Ehricke 1960b, p. 20).

Looking back on the brief but fruitful experimental work of the VfR, Ley wrote in the dark days of 1943 that by 1934, "experimentation had reached a state where continuation would have been too expensive for any [amateur] society, except a millionaires club. ... On the Raketenflugplatz we did everything that could be done on a small scale ... we were about ready for the first design of meteorological rockets when the Nazis marched in ... *but*—we probably could not have paid for it, not under the most favorable of [political] assumptions" (Ley 1943, p. 73).

Ley had considerable, justified pride in the accomplishments of the VfR: Between August 1929 and June 1933, the group made 490 rocket-motor ground tests, using four test stands, and about

95 rocket flights. In 1943, living in America and unaware of the secret developments at Peenemünde, Ley wrote that he saw no way the rocket work would continue during the war, but assured the reader that, "I have never for a moment stopped believing in the ultimate goal: the spaceship" (Ley 1943, p. 73).

In Germany, the amateur rocket societies led directly to the large-scale military program that produced the world's first guided missile and laid the basis for much of the U.S. civilian space program. The publications of the VfR, its public activities to garner financial support through publicity, and most important, the efforts of its members to spread the excitement about space travel far and wide, encouraged young people around the globe to try their hands at rocket experiments and excited the public about their possibilities.

Even in the two other nations that can also proudly claim founding fathers of space—the United States, and the Soviet Union—it was the work of Hermann Oberth and the VfR that spurred young rocket enthusiasts. Space historian Frank Winter remarks in his 1990 book, *Rockets into Space,* that although Tsiolkovsky and Goddard wrote earlier than Oberth, Oberth's "book was, in fact, the cornerstone of the Space Age" (Winter 1990, p. xii). "[B]y virtue of his thoroughness and the fact that his ideas were openly published and sparked a worldwide movement, Oberth alone deserves the title, 'Father of the Space Age' " (Winter 1990, p. 25).

On April 4, 1930, a small group of space enthusiasts, mainly science fiction writers, gathered in the New York home of writers G. Edward Pendray and his wife, Lee Gregory, to form the American Interplanetary Society (AIS). Four days later, member David Lasser wrote to Robert Goddard asking him to give a presentation for the society, but "he politely declined" (Winter 1983, p. 74). Three weeks later, the new society held its first public meeting.

In June of that year, the group started to publish the *Bulletin,* edited by Lasser, later to become *Astronautics,* then *Jet Propulsion.* The *Bulletin* published translated papers and reports from Europe and communications with the VfR. The November/December 1930 issue included a letter from Willy Ley, reporting that the VfR had found a place to do rocket experiments, referring to the Raketenflugplatz, and that Nebel and Riedel were working on problems of ignition, stabilization, and the design of parachutes. Ley promised that "details about these experiments will be given in our next bulletin" (Williams and Epstein 1955, p. 173).

The first *Bulletin* of 1931 announced that French aviation pioneer Robert Esnault-Pelterie would be speaking at the society's meeting, and preparations were begun to host one of Europe's most well-known space enthusiasts. Placards announcing the meeting were placed around New York City, and "owing to the newspaper connections of some of the Society's charter members, it received considerable advance publicity as well" (Pendray 1955, p. 587). As a result of ill health, Esnault-Peltiere had to cancel his appearance, but when the members arrived at the American Museum of Natural History meeting hall, there were more than 2,000 people there. Esnault-Peltiere's speech was read by Pendray, and the portion of *Frau im Mond* with Oberth's rocket was shown. The program had to be repeated to accommodate those who had waited outside for two hours to hear about space travel.

In April 1931, the Pendrays made a trip to Europe and met Willy Ley at the Raketenflugplatz. They witnessed a Mirak static motor firing and made formal arrangements for the two societies to exchange information. The Pendrays were struck by the openness of the German experimenters, especially compared to the response from Robert Goddard.

On the evening of May 1, Pendray briefed the AIS members on this trip, and the December 1931 issue of the *Bulletin* carried his report, titled "Recent Worldwide Advances in Rocketry." Pendray stated:

> To understand fully what the developments mean and whence they have originated we must return briefly to the work of the German Interplanetary Society's engineers at the Raketenflugplatz, Berlin. ... Despite the fact that engineering interest in the possibilities of rockets first appeared in this country through the researches of Dr. Goddard, the Germans appear to have been the first to think constructively along those lines and to sacrifice any great amount of time and money. Whatever the reason, it appears that the Raketenflugplatz at Berlin is today the well of inspiration from which all rocket experiments, with one or two possible exceptions, have drawn.
>
> This is partly due, no doubt, to the fact that the German engineers have never undertaken concealment on the designs

G. Edward Pendray, a founding member of the American Interplanetary Society in 1930, visited the Raketenflugplatz in April of that year. Here he is being shown the equipment for the VfR's Mirak rocket engine tests. On the left, facing the camera, is Klaus Riedel.

or discoveries. They do not give out veiled statements about secret fuels or designs. They have offered the results of their discoveries freely to other experimenters, and the inevitable consequence of this is that rocketry has been greatly advanced by their efforts [Williams and Epstein 1955, pp. 179–180].

In 1931, the society's membership had grown to about 100. David Lasser's book, *The Conquest of Space,* appeared, which was the first book about space travel written in English. It was published in a run of 5,000 copies, thanks to the financial contributions of members of the society (Winter 1983, p. 80).

Spurred on by the reports of developments in Germany, society member Hugh Franklin Pierce, an unemployed engineer who was then working for the New York City subway system, suggested that the AIS build a rocket, a plan for which was announced in December. The German-style two-stick Repulsor, designed by Pierce and Pendray, was shown to the society's members in February 1932.

In 1962, Pendray described the beginning of the AIS's experimental program: "When Goddard in his desert fastness in New Mexico proved uncommunicative, those of us who wanted to do our part in launching the space age turned to what appeared the next best source of light: the Verein Für Raumschiffahrt—the German Interplanetary Society [sic]—in Berlin" (Emme 1964, p. 19).

This first American German-style rocket has been described as "no feat of engineering but a model of thrift and ingenuity," costing $49.40. It had a body made of tin sheet and wooden fins, an aluminum jacket for water cooling which started life as a cocktail shaker, a holder for a parachute made from an aluminum saucepan, and a "silk pongee parachute bought in a department store" (Winter 1990, p. 39).

On November 12, 1932, this motor, using liquid oxygen and gasoline, was static fired near Stockton, New Jersey, and registered 60 pounds of thrust for 20 or so seconds. The first rocket flight attempted by the AIS was with a vehicle designed by Bernard Smith. On May 14, 1933, it had reached an altitude of 250 feet, when the liquid oxygen tank burst. This flight also generated some newspaper coverage (Williams and Epstein 1955, pp. 184–185).

The third AIS rocket, which had fueling problems caused by the design, was, nonetheless, later exhibited at the 1939 New York World's Fair. In the fall of 1934, the society carried out its last flight test; its rocket reached a distance of 1,338 feet, and a speed of 1,000 feet per second. From then until the beginning of the war, the society concentrated on engine designs and static testing in order better to develop the major component that would be needed for rockets. The name of the organization was changed to the American Rocket Society.

Although the VfR had now reached its end in Germany, optimism still characterized the work of the AIS in the United States. In the July 1934 issue of *Scientific American,* AIS President Pendray

National Air and Space Museum, Smithsonian Institution, 83-298
During the early 1930s the American Interplanetary Society tested rockets
in Staten Island, New York and in New Jersey. Here, G. Edward Pendray
(standing on the barrel) with rocket launch equipment.

writes: "There is plenty of theoretical ground and some evidence for
the belief that, given power enough, money enough, and sufficient
experimental data, we could shoot a rocket to the Moon or Venus
or Mars and return. ... Patient mathematicians have even gone so
far as to solve navigational problems relating to space flight and
to indicate how instruments may be constructed to render such
navigation possible" (Pendray 1934, p. 10). He adds, however, that
"rapid advancement today is being much delayed by lack of finances"
(Pendray 1934, p. 12).

After Willy Ley arrived in New York in 1935, he was in contact
with his new American colleagues and worked with other society
members to design a rocket-powered glider designed to deliver
mail. At the same time, he continued to fire the imagination of
people just becoming acquainted with the new field of astronautics,
through a constant flow of popular material published largely in
the science fiction magazines of the day.

An extraordinary development was the establishment of a Committee on Biological Research by the AIS, in June 1932. Members Laurence Manning and Thomas Norton reported results from tests on two guinea pigs, whom they subjected to about 30 g's of force in a centrifugal drum rotating at 600 revolutions per minute (Winter 1983, p. 80). Little did they know that college student Wernher von Braun and his colleague Constantine Generales were doing similar experiments with mice near Zurich.

In 1936, Alfred Africano, an unemployed mechanical engineer who had joined the AIS in 1932, had the honor of receiving the REP-Hirsch prize, shared with the society, for his rocket design. In 1942, he did rocket defense work at the National Defense Research Committee and after the war, joined the Curtiss-Wright Corporation. He later worked for the Missile Division of the Chrysler Corporation at the Redstone Arsenal in Huntsville, and for North American Rockwell's Space Divison on the Apollo program. He also did some preliminary work on the Space Shuttle before he retired (Winter 1983, p. 16).

The society also attempted to interest the U.S. Weather Bureau in a sounding rocket for practical applications, pointing to the limitations, largely bad weather, of the balloons and airplanes the bureau was then using.

The October 1937 issue of *Astronautics* outlined the requirements for such a rocket: It should reach an altitude of 3 miles, be able to carry a package of instruments weighing 2 pounds, be simple and safe to operate and able to be launched by only one or two men, cost approximately $20 per flight, be easily located on descent and retrieved, suffer little damage on landing to be used repeatedly, and land within half a mile of the launch site. To achieve these goals, the rocket should obtain vertical flight with a deviation of less than 10 degrees, and descend slowly, not exceeding 1,000 feet per minute, or 10 miles per hour (Williams and Epstein 1955, pp. 192–193).

The Technical Committee of the ARS translated documents and articles from various languages. Subcommittees on aeronautics, chemistry, physics, astronomy, mechanical engineering, electrical engineering, and the effects of space on living creatures were created, as the society attracted members with expertise in these fields who were anxious to apply their knowledge to the new field of space.

James Wyld, who joined the National Advisory Committee on

Aeronautics at Langley Field, Virginia, in 1940 (the predecessor to NASA), designed a motor using regenerative cooling he had read about in a paper by Eugen Sänger, which he translated from the German. In 1941, the Navy offered Wyld a $5,000 six-month contract to produce a series of experimental motors from 100 to 1,000 pounds of thrust. He and three other ARS members formed Reaction Motors, Inc., and the Navy used their motors for assisted take-off systems for their PBM flying boats. In 1946, Reaction Motors built a four-motor unit that drove Bell Aircraft's X-1 and was later used in the Viking rocket. Reaction Motors became a division of Thiokol Chemical Corporation, which today makes the solid-fuel boosters for the Space Shuttle and other vehicles.

Frank Winter has described the American Interplanetary Society and its successors as "second to the VfR in importance" (Winter 1990, p. 39). Although their activities did not lead to the impressive wartime effort to develop guided rockets as it did in Germany, many of the people trained through their experiments went on to pursue careers in the burgeoning military, and later, civilian, space programs after the war. The society also inspired the formation of smaller, regional rocket clubs in the United States and coordinated activities with them.

One of the most successful was the Cleveland Rocket Society, described in detail by Frank Winter (Winter 1983, pp. 97–104). It was founded by German Ernst Loebell, who had moved to America in 1929. In 1933, the Cleveland Engineering Society asked Loebell to make a presentation on space, which led to the establishment of the CRS. Loebell designed a regeneratively cooled engine system, actually predating James Wyld's design by three years. By 1935, however, funds were drying up for the Cleveland Rocket Society, and although they had done some static engine tests, the more advanced rocket was never fired.

In April 1937, the French Ministry of Commerce and Industry asked the Cleveland Rocket Society to participate in the Paris International Exposition, and the society sent a rocket model to exhibit. By the summer of that year, out of funds, the society "ceased to exist for all practical purposes," according to Winter (Winter 1983, p. 102). Ernst Loebell went on to work for William Lear, the originator of the Learjet, for 26 years.

The second world power that would appear on the rocket scene was the Soviet Union. Similar to the situation in Germany, by the mid-1930s Russia had a government-funded military rocket effort. Amateur rocket societies sprang up in the U.S.S.R. soon after the publication of Oberth's small 1923 book. As reported in Chapter I, the republication of Tsiolkovksy's own 1903 book took place in 1924 in response to the publication of Oberth's work.

The world's first amateur rocket society was started in 1924 by Fridrik A. Tsander, who had read Tsiolkovsky as a child. According to Winter, Tsander made the proposal that a society be formed during a presentation he delivered in January 1924 before the Technical Section of the Moscow Society of Amateur Astronomers (Winter 1983, p. 27). In April a group was indeed established, as part of the Military Science Divison of the N.E. Zhukovsky Air Force Academy, and a month later this was reorganized into the Society for the Study of Interplanetary Communication (OIMS).

A journal was planned and a host of activities announced, including a competition to produce a small rocket. Presentations were made and membership swelled to 150, but the society fell apart before the year 1924 was over. Winter points out that lack of finances and the chaotic state of the Soviet Union contributed to the society's early demise.

One of the most interesting aspects of the earliest activities of the amateur rocket groups is their organization of and participation in international expositions, representing the newest exciting field of science, technology, and industry. In 1927 the Interplanetary Section of the Association of Inventors sent out an appeal for international participation in an "exhibition which will be held on 10 February 1927 at the Association of Inventors Building, 68, Tverskaya, Moscow. This is the world's first exhibition of models and mechanisms of interplanetary vehicles constructed by inventors of different countries" (Winter, 1983, p. 29).

The exhibition was held between April and June of that year, although media attention seems to have been nil outside of Moscow. Displays included exhibits on the cannon launcher of Jules Verne and on work by Goddard, Tsiolkovksy, Oberth, and Valier, describing nuclear propulsion, space suits, and a space station (Winter 1983, p. 30).

At that time, a few loosely knit rocket groups existed in the U.S.S.R. One, headed by the prestigious Professor Nikolai A. Rynin, did modest rocket experiments but did not attempt larger activities.

The Gas Dynamics Laboratory was established in Leningrad in 1928. The next year, one of the younger staff members, Valentin

Marsha Freeman
The Gas Dynamics Laboratory was established in 1928 and was supported by the Soviet military. Today the laboratory is a museum of early Soviet space history in St. Petersburg. The display seen here is of an early experimental rocket.

Glushko, suggested that the powder rocket, or solid propellant, research of the laboratory, incorporate a subdivision for liquid rocket engines. In 1932 the laboratory came under the supervision of Marshal Mikhail Tukhachevsky, the Soviet Armaments Minister and vice chairman of the U.S.S.R. Revolutionary War Council, who, for a number of years, had promoted rocket research. As Soviet space expert James Oberg reports, "Under the patronage of Tukhachevsky, rocket research flourished."

    In 1931, two other rocket organizations were started in the Soviet Union: the Group for the Study of Reaction Motors (GIRD) in Moscow and a similarly named group in Leningrad. These and other rocket groups were begun by space enthusiasts, many of whom later became the founders of the Soviet space program, such as famed spacecraft designer Sergei Korolev. There was international recognition of their activities (Winter 1983, p. 57) but they were short-lived as amateur rocket groups because they were quickly funded by the military and vectored toward military research, similar to the situation at the time in Germany.

As the work progressed, the political situation in the Soviet Union worsened. On June 10, 1937, Marshal Tukhachevsky was arrested and "his whole staff followed him into prison and to their deaths" (Oberg 1981, p. 18). Tukhachevsky was executed with seven other generals, and eventually the Stalin purges killed or cashiered 35,000 Red Army officers. In an eerie parallel to what Wernher von Braun later faced under the Nazi regime, Soviet chief spacecraft designer Korolev himself was arrested (Winter 1983, p. 64).

Many of the details of the technical accomplishments of rocket scientists and engineers in the Soviet Union from the mid-1930s forward have been difficult to obtain because they have virtually all been military efforts. It is possible, however, to trace the most recognized experts in the later Soviet programs to these early amateur efforts, where the excitement and enthusiasm for manned spaceflight caught hold, just as it had in the rest of Europe and in the United States.

A markedly different response to rocket and space developments was encountered in Great Britain. There, in 1933, Phillip Ellaby Cleator founded the British Interplanetary Society (BIS). But not only did the government oppose any efforts for experimental rocket research, it is reported that Cleator "found no public interest" either (Winter 1983, p. 97).

Cleator met with Willy Ley in Berlin in 1934. But by then the VfR had collapsed and Ley could offer little assistance. The British Interplanetary Society was never able to raise enough money for an experimental program and was hampered by very restrictive legal codes regarding the use of gunpowder, which date back to the 17th century and are still in effect today. The British Interplanetary Society, therefore, concentrated on publishing its *Journal.*

A second British group, the Manchester Interplanetary Society, was founded by 16-year-old Eric Burgess in 1937. After World War II, Burgess became one of the most prolific popular writers about space travel.

Numerous small groups proliferated. One of the oddest space

Hans Kaiser was the founder of the Society for the Exploration of Space in Breslau in 1937. The most famous member of this amateur rocket society was Krafft A. Ehricke, who became its director during World War II. Kaiser, like Ehricke, later worked at the Peenemünde Army research center during the war.

National Air and Space Museum, Andrew G. Haley Collection, Smithsonian Institution, 80-1270

societies of the 1920s was the Austrian Society for High-Altitude Exploration (Oesterreichische Wissenschaftliche Gesellschaft für Hohenforschung), founded in Vienna in 1926 by Franz von Hoefft and Baron Guido von Pirquet. Max Valier was opposed to starting it but later joined, whereas Hermann Oberth was never even invited and seems to have been purposely excluded. Austrian rocket pioneer Eugen Sänger offered to work with the new society and even met with Pirquet to discuss experiments, but no experiments ever materialized because the Austrian society did not have enough money. Most of the leadership of the society joined the VfR when it was founded a year later.

The Society for the Exploration of Space, or Gesellschafft für Weltraumforschung e.V. (GfW), was founded in 1937 in Breslau, after the ban on rocket experiments. Amateur rocket work had been practically outlawed in Germany, and there are reports that the word "rocket" could not be used in any publication. Hans Kaiser, an astronomer and physicist, had given talks on spaceflight in 1934–1935 to try to reinvigorate interest after the end of the VfR, and on August 18, 1937, with 11 others, he founded the GfW.

The purpose was educational, Kaiser recounted in 1949, including the founding of a scientific library. In 1939, the GfW started to publish the magazine *Weltraum,* (*Space*). The government allowed the publication of *Space* and affiliated groups formed in Berlin and Cologne. In 1940, as members were conscripted into the military, the GfW temporarily halted its activities; but young people kept joining and it started up again a year later.

The most prominent member of the GfW was Krafft A. Ehricke, who later, like Kaiser, joined the army rocket program at Peenemünde. Remarkably, Ehricke became president of the GfW in 1944, while at Peenemünde, and continued to write for *Space* throughout the war. The magazine, Kaiser states, ceased publication in 1943, because of a lack of paper. It "wasn't allowed to appear" (Kaiser 1949, p. 50).

Around the globe, rocket and space activities proliferated. In 1932, a chemistry student at the University of Buenos Aires, Argentina, started an astronautical magazine. Ezio Matarazzo, who had translated some technical papers from German, corresponded with Herbert Schaefer of the VfR until 1936. The first foreign edition of Ley's 1944 classic work, later titled *Rockets, Missiles and Space Travel,* was published in Buenos Aires in 1947.

The Australian Rocket Society was formed in 1936, and there are indications of rocket experiments in Japan in the 1930s (Winter 1983, p. 107).

Looking back over the activities of the amateur rocket societies from the late 1920s to World War II, Winter observed that, "the societies used every modern means of communication to proselytize their work and aims—public talks, newspapers, magazines, radio, newsreels, exhibitions, and even nascent television." Regardless of the success each achieved, they all "established a certain public acceptance and infectious enthusiasm for the possibility of spaceflight where none had existed before" (Winter 1983, p. 115).

Mindful of the scale of the task involved, and clearly using the center-stage Apollo program as his frame of reference, American Rocket Society founding member Edward Pendray wrote in 1962 that the early rocket experiments "stirred a large part of the human race to desire the eventual conquest of space—thus generating the broad public support which for any great and costly new project is a vital necessity for success in a democratic society" (Emme 1964, p. 27).

Considering the worldwide economic and political upheavals

from the late 1920s to the beginning of World War II, it is remarkable that throughout that period small groups of people, led by the Germans, stubbornly committed to the idea of developing the technology for spaceflight, laid the theoretical and experimental foundation to begin to make that possible during World War II.

Peenemünde:
A Scientific
Mobilization

Peenemünde-east, where General Walter Dornberger led a team of scientists and engineers in an eight-year effort to develop the A-4 rocket, was a complex of science and engineering laboratories, experimental test stands, and design and manufacturing facilities, built at the mouth of the Peene River on the Baltic Sea in northeast Germany (Figure 4.1).

Before the end of World War II, this army research center would develop rockets, plan upper atmospheric research, and lay the basis for future space exploration. To accomplish this, the scientists at Peenemünde designed and had access to the finest laboratories in the world for technical design, aeroballistics and mathematics, wind tunnel aerodynamics, materials, guidance, control, and telemetry development, fabrication facilities, test laboratories, and a think-tank "special projects" office.

To make the necessary breakthroughs, the scientists and engineers could draw on decades of the most advanced work by Bernhard Riemann, Ludwig Prandtl, and Adolf Busemann in mathematical physics and aerodynamics. They had access to the developments in nuclear science of Marie Curie, Lise Meitner, Ida Noddack, Enrico Fermi, Otto Hahn, and Werner Heisenberg. There existed a body of scientific work, and scientists at work, on upper-atmospheric physics. Dramatic accomplishments could be made in the rocket program at Peenemünde because it was built upon the foundation of the 100 years of European, and especially German, science.

When the army became interested in rockets in 1929, handfuls of amateurs were doing experiments in makeshift facilities without

FIGURE 4.1
THE PEENEMÜNDE EXPERIMENTAL STATION
Located at the mouth of Peene River near its entrance to the Baltic Sea, Peenemünde
provided an isolated site for the design, construction, and testing of rockets. The
major rocket test stands were located on the north-west coast of the island of
Usedom, and the huge Test Stand VII was at the north-west tip.

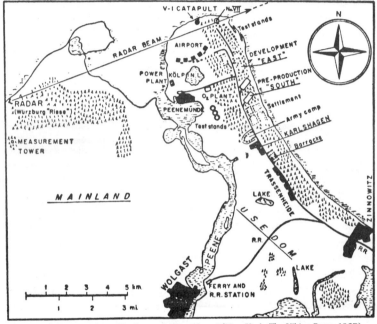

Source: Willy Ley *Rockets, Missiles, and Space Travel* (New York: The Viking Press, 1957).

any money, scientific equipment, or possibility of success. Ten years
later, when Peenemünde was operational, many of the best minds
in German science either were working there or were working on
"consulting contracts" for Peenemünde at their universities or in
industry.

Designing a projectile that would attain and remain stable at
supersonic speeds, traverse the upper layers of the atmosphere
where air-breathing engines could not function, reenter the atmosphere at multiples of the speed of sound, carry along its own
cryogenic oxidizer, and travel unmanned beyond visual ground
control required entirely new concepts in aerodynamics, combustion chemistry, lightweight materials, electronic controls, telemetry,
and communications.

Unlike the wartime U.S. Manhattan Project to develop the atomic bomb—in which, it was revealed after the war, military authorities tried to prevent project scientists from even talking to *each other*—the rocket program at Peenemünde was thrown open to the entire scientific community in Germany to tackle the problems of early spaceflight.

With the outbreak of war in September 1939, security restrictions at Peenemünde were loosened to permit the participation of technical experts from outside the army facility. On September 28–30, 1939, the staff at Peenemünde organized a "Day of Wisdom" (der Tag der Weisheit) conference, and invited a "stellar collection of scientists from the excellent system of institutes of technology" in Germany. There were 36 professors of engineering, physics, and chemistry from the Technische Hochschulen, or Technical Institutes, from the universities at Darmstadt, Dresden, Berlin, and Göttingen (Ordway and Sharpe 1979, p. 35).

Wernher von Braun, Walter Thiel, and Klaus Riedel briefed the scientists—some of whom were their former professors. It was stressed that results would have to be available within two years. The scientists were asked to consider solving problems including trajectory tracking by Doppler shift, gyroscope and radio technology, radiowave propagation in the ionosphere, antenna patterns, new measuring methods for the supersonic wind tunnel, computing machines for flight mechanics.

During his interrogation by U.S. technical personnel on April 21, 1945, Professor Alwin Walter, a mathematician at Darmstadt when he participated in the "Day of Wisdom," stated that "a military atmosphere was completely lacking." Dr. Ernst Steinhoff, in charge of instruments, guidance, and measurements at Peenemünde, had been his student before the war, and Walter had worked with physicist Erich Regener on measuring air temperature at high altitudes (Peenemünde East 1945, p. 98).

This cooperative program continued throughout the war, through symposia and visits. Dr. Walter reports that he visited Peenemünde about twice a year as he worked on trajectory calculations for the A-4 rocket. "Contracts for scientific work were eventually drawn in very broad terms, in order that the institutions be allowed a wide latitude of approach," von Braun notes (Ordway and Sharpe 1979, p. 36).

According to Walter, the professors of the Darmstadt region working on these contracts belonged to what was called a "Vorhaben

Peenemünde" (VP) or "Arbeitsgemeinschaft VP," and there was also
one in Dresden. In addition to mobilizing the scientific community
to meet the challenges of the rocket program, university contracts
protected otherwise vulnerable scientists from the military draft—
and from the SS. Darmstadt was so busy with contracts from Peenemünde, Walter reports, "it could practically guarantee its people
freedom from war service." Walter himself was drafted for one week,
and then returned to the university (Peenemünde East 1945, p.
98).

Before Peenemünde had to be abandoned under the threat of
advancing Russian troops in 1945, its scientists and engineers had
flown the world's first guided missile, launched missiles from sub-
merged submarines, investigated the use of nuclear energy for future
spaceflights, and done the preliminary design work for sounding
rockets, Earth-orbital satellite launchers, and manned spacecraft.
This legacy they brought with them to the United States after the
war.

The only comparable scientific mobilization since Peenemünde
was the Apollo program in the United States to land a man on the
Moon. Not surprisingly, that effort was in large part organized by
the former Peenemünders.

In 1952, when he was working in the United States, Walter
Dornberger looked back at his 15-year involvement in the development of rockets from 1930–1945 in his book, *V-2:*

> Never would any private or public body have devoted hun-
> dreds of millions of marks to the development of long-range
> rockets for purely scientific purposes. ... We tackled one of
> mankind's great tasks, regardless of circumstances and found
> a first practical solution; we opened the gate and pointed the
> way to the future.
>
> By gathering together in one place young, enthusiastic, and
> steadfast scientists, engineers, and technicians in the most var-
> ied fields and providing science and technology installations
> on a generous scale, we successfully tackled, in isolation from
> "the dynamic of events" around us, problems whose solution
> seemed to lie far in the future.
>
> Ignoring the rocket as a weapon of war, its general potentiali-
> ties are enormous. A dream can become a reality, hopes and

theories the space ship. To this our labor, our creation and our success made the first contributions [Dornberger 1952, pp. 254–256].

Walter Dornberger was born in Giessen in 1894. "Custom decided what my career was to be," Dornberger later related. "In German families, the older son inherits the family business, the second son goes into the army, and the third son is free to do as he pleases. I was the second son. So, though I wanted to become an architect, I enlisted in the German Army in August 1914. By November of that year, my world of carefree happiness tumbled," as World War I began (Thomas 1961a, p. 46).

On October 27, 1918, Lt. Dornberger was captured by the second American Marine Division and spent two years as a prisoner of war in southern France, where "attempts to escape earned him solitary confinement for most of the term." Upon release, he was grateful to be able to remain in the 100,000-man army allowed under the Versailles Treaty, since he otherwise would have joined the growing ranks of the unemployed.

The restrictions of the Versailles Treaty left Germany without the capability of even defending itself against foreign invasion, although until 1925 there had been foreign troops on German soil. The army was not to have more than 100,000 men, composed of seven infantry and three cavalry divisions. All munitions, as well as plants intended for manufacturing military materiel, were to be turned over to the Allied High Commission. The German general staff was dissolved.

For this rump military force, the importation of arms, munitions, and war materiel was "strictly prohibited." There were to be no military or naval air forces. Dirigible manufacture was to cease, and the import of aircraft, engines, and engine parts was forbidden.

Like a Third World nation today living under the boot of harsh economic conditionalities dictated by the International Monetary Fund, Germany had to accept these military restrictions in order to remain within the world community defined then by the League of Nations. The rise of Hitler is largely attributable to his willingness to publicly oppose the intolerable economic conditions and dissolution of national sovereignty dictated by the Versailles Treaty, when the other political parties in Germany refused to do so.

Although the Versailles Treaty was very specific regarding the restrictions on the German military, the "new physical principle" of rocketry was not included in it, just as the "new physical principles" of directed energy beam weapons were not included in the 1972 Anti-Ballistic Missile (ABM) Treaty between the United States and the U.S.S.R. In both cases, too little had been developed for the technologies to be considered of military significance.

In the 1920s, the leadership of the German Army was faced with the straightforward task of looking "for new developments in armaments which would increase the fighting power of the few existing troops, without violating the Treaty" (Dornberger 1952, p. 31). "Why should it have been different with the rocket than with atomic energy, with the airplane, or with most other revolutionary technical inventions?" Dornberger would ask later, when describing the army rocket effort (Emme 1964, p. 30).

The project would be led by German artillery officer Karl Emil Becker, who ". . .received the first impulse for this [interest in rocketry] from Hermann Oberth's book *Die Rakete zu den Planetenräumen*. On the basis of this book, work on rocket ballistics and reaction drive had been carried out at the institute of his doctoral professor, Professor [Julius] Cranz" (*Astronautik* 1976, p. 80). In 1926, Becker, studying under Cranz, had helped him to write, *Lehrbuch der Ballistik* (*Textbook of Ballistics*).

In 1929, as chief of the Heereswaffenamt (Army Weapons Board) and chief of the Ballistische und Munitionsabteilung (Department of Ballistics and Munitions), Col. Becker had ordered Captain Ritter von Horstig to carry out a thorough examination of the available literature on rockets, including Robert Goddard's 1919 paper. Von Hoerstig's review "quickly reached a dead end" (Winter 1990, p. 45) in terms of recommending an experimental program.

In the spring of that year, Walter Dornberger was appointed to the Ballistics Council of the Army Weapons Department. He had earned a masters degree in mechanical engineering from the University of Berlin in 1929, and in the tradition of Scharnhorst and Carnot, Dornberger was a military professional trained as an engineer.

On December 17, 1930, Becker and Dornberger met with Colonel Erich Karlewski, and gained a grant of approximately $50,000 from Army Ordnance for a rocket program. This would consist of an experimental program at the Kummersdorf-West station, 27.3 kilometers south of Berlin, and also some small amounts

Major General Walter Dornberger directed rocket research in Germany from the beginning of the army program in 1930 until 1945.

National Air and Space Museum, Smithsonian Institution, A-5347Acm

of money for the existing groups of amateur rocket inventors to see what they could contribute to the program.

The next year, Dornberger contracted with Paul Heylandt's Association for the Utility of Industrial Gases to develop a small liquid-fuel motor with a thrust of 45 pounds, based on those used by Max Valier in his rocket cars. But a fatal explosion in March 1934 ended that line of industrial experiments (Winter 1990, p. 46; Winter 1983, p. 52).

In the early 1930s, rocket "research" was a constant source of frustration for Dornberger. "On the one hand, theorists and university professors quarreled about the sixth decimal behind the comma in the calculation of a flight path to Mars and Venus. On the other, a branch chief of the Board of Ordnance made a written report to his supervisors in 1931 that a liquid fuel rocket could never take off from the ground on its own," he complained (Emme 1964, p. 31). But he also persevered.

In the spring of 1932, Becker, Dornberger, and von Horstig visited the Raketenflugplatz. "Great was our satisfaction when Nebel signed with them a contract for the sum of 1,000 marks, contingent upon a successful firing of the Mirak II [sic] at ... Kummersdorf," von Braun reported (von Braun 1956, p. 129).

The failure of that test in August (see Chapter III), convinced Dornberger that rocketry had to be put on a more rigorous scientific basis than was possible by the amateur rocket experimenters. "The dream of space travel so dominated most of the 'inventors' that they forgot what was practical, of immediate importance, or fundamental" (Klee and Merk 1965, p. 11).

"For two years the [Army Ordnance] Department tried in vain to obtain something to go on," Dornberger reported. "No progress was being made in the work. There was also the danger that thoughtless chatter might result in the department being known as the financial backer of rocket development. We had therefore to take other steps" (Dornberger 1952, p. 32).

Because industry was not anxious to become involved in this fledgling field and secrecy was needed for a weapons effort, Dornberger convinced Becker to create an independent, well-equipped test facility at Kummersdorf, where the best technical expertise would be brought into the army program.

The irrepressible von Braun was determined to garner support for his dreams of space travel. Although the army had refused to extend any support to the VfR, after repeated requests by Nebel, von Braun relates, "I finally decided to beard the lions in their den, and armed with the meager scientific data we had I called upon Col. Becker. He was by no means such as ogre as had been represented by Nebel ... he seemed to be broadminded, warm-hearted, and a scientist through and through" (von Braun 1956, p. 130).

By agreement of a contract dated October 1, 20-year-old Wernher von Braun showed up a month later as a civilian employee to Kummersdorf, charged with the development of liquid rockets. Colonel Becker also provided him with a grant to continue his graduate education in physics at the University of Berlin.

Walter Riedel (not related to Klaus Riedel), who had worked with Max Valier, was working on army projects for the Association for the Utility of Industrial Gases near Berlin. "Papa" Riedel joined the von Braun group when this project was merged with that of Kummersdorf. Early the next year, Arthur Rudolph, who had also worked with Valier, was hired when he showed up with the "complete alcohol-oxygen rocket power-plant" he had designed, "which made two wholly successful static runs at first trial" (von Braun

1956, p. 132). Heinrich Grünow, a "mechanical genius," also joined the small team.

A test stand that could "produce some useful information" was built. Whereas at the Raketenflugplatz only the thrust and duration of engine burn could be measured, at Kummersdorf fuel consumption and flow rate, combustion temperature, and other parameters could be simultaneously measured to begin to put rocketry on a scientific footing (Ley 1957a, p. 200).

The first Kummersdorf combustion motor test on December 21, 1932, exploded and wrecked the test stand. The test stand was rebuilt and the second try, ready in three weeks, "had been working flawlessly for a few seconds," and developed 140 kilograms of thrust, when the aluminum combustion chamber burned through. Dornberger reports, "thus we encountered our first cooling problem" (Dornberger 1952, p. 39).

Undaunted, Dornberger decided not only to continue with the development of a 600-pound-thrust rocket motor, but also to test not just the motor but a complete projectile, in what Apollo program engineers would later call "all-up testing." In this way, progress in rocketry would extend beyond just the development of the motor, to include stability, guidance, and control. The entire assembly was designated A-1, for "Aggregate-1."

In order to ready an A-1 for testing, a year of hard work followed, with engine burn-throughs, redesigns, successes, and failures. Dornberger reports that the motor was constructed and "after breaking down a few times, worked perfectly" (Dornberger 1952, p. 44). The A-1 stood 1.4 meters high, held 85 pounds of propellants, had a take-off weight of 150 kilograms, and was to develop 300 kilograms of thrust for 16 seconds (Schultz 1965, p. 1).

But the A-1 rocket was never flight-tested. One of the problems that had plagued the smallest rockets, as well as the A-1, was guidance and control. Even if the engine worked flawlessly, rockets would careen wildly out of control. Willy Ley later remarked that "what was then known about rocket stability could have been written on a postcard, leaving some blank space" (Ley 1957a, p. 200).

To stabilize the A-1, Dornberger had suggested that the rocket be rotated about its longitudinal axis, or spin-stabilized, as is done today with satellites. This is also how artillery projectiles were stabilized. But only the rocket would rotate, not the fuel tanks. Otherwise, "fuel would rise up on the walls of the tanks as a result

Deutsches Museum, München

The rocket engine designed by Arthur Rudolph was the heart of the A-1, or Aggregate-1, built at the army experimental station in Kummersdorf. This photograph was taken in 1934.

of centrifugal force, and this would make feeding of the propellants difficult" (Dornberger 1952, p. 43).

Therefore, the A-1 was built so the top steel section, which would act as the payload carrier, would rotate on ball bearings, functioning as a gyroscope. This 85-pound rotating section was placed at the nose of the rocket, however, which made the aggregate unstable. Since the center of gravity of the A-1 was too far forward, the A-2 was designed with a gyroscope in the center of the rocket, rather than at the nose. Two years after the start of the army rocket program, in 1934, two A-2s, affectionately named Max and Moritz, were successfully launched before Christmas from the Island of Borkum. Each reached an altitude of approximately 1.5 miles.

While the A-2s were being readied for their tests, the rocket team was working on the development of a much larger engine that could attain a thrust of 1,500 kilograms. This A-3 rocket, however, would need an active stabilization system, since it was to be five times the weight of the A-1 and A-2, with a length of 6.74 meters.

Wernher von Braun had been insisting that models of the A rocket series they were designing would have to be tested in wind tunnels in order to determine the aerodynamic stability of the rocket in flight. On January 6, 1936, he traveled to Aachen University to meet with Dr. Rudolf Hermann. There von Braun showed him a drawing "of a pointed, slender body with fins, to be tested for drag and stability up to our maximum Mach number," as Dr. Hermann describes it (Hermann 1981), and the science of aerodynamics was brought to bear on the rocket program.

Ludwig Prandtl was a professor of applied mechanics at Göttingen University from 1904 to 1953, and had encouraged Hermann Oberth in his work during his year at the university. In 1963, Oberth recalled in a letter to Eugen Sänger that "Prandtl ... raised the objection to me that it didn't matter whether the means of propulsion were placed above or below [on the rocket]; it would not have any influence on the stability of the rocket. That was a fruitful criticism, as well as when he, on another occasion, said that wheels could not achieve a higher boundary velocity than 500 meters per second" (Barth 1984, p. 81). This encouragement came at a time when Oberth's "radical" ideas were the object of ridicule in much of the established scientific community.

When he came to Göttingen, Prandtl built Germany's first sizable wind tunnel. His work on air currents, sparked by a problem encountered when he was an engineer at the Machinenfabrik Augsburg-Nürnberg in 1900, was informed by the research of Bernhard Riemann, whose 1859 paper on shock waves "proved to be most important and influential in the theory of supersonic flight" (Henke 1986, p. 41).

The great mathematician Felix Klein, who promoted the cooperation between university science and engineering, instigated the

API Niels Bohn Library, Lande Collection

Ludwig Prandtl, who built Germany's first sizeable wind tunnel, encouraged Hermann Oberth in his researches while he was studying at Göttingen University.

appointment of Prandtl in 1906 to the engineering committee of the Association for the Study of Motorized Air Ships (Motorluftschiff-Studiengesellschaft), which was developing the Parsifal airship. Prandtl suggested that the company construct a wind tunnel, which was put into service in 1909.

By the next year, Prandtl was considering the behavior of airplane wings and discovered the dependence of lift on the angle of attack of the plane and the aspect ratio. His critical discovery that the boundary layer, or surface of discontinuity, at the surface of an airfoil, (model airplane wing), led to the possibility of mathematically solving "the problems of lift, drag, and all of the aerodynamical problems that are critical to discuss the possibility of flight" (Henke 1986, p. 42). After World War I, with help from the army and navy departments, a larger wind tunnel was built.

One of Ludwig Prandtl's most important students was Adolf Busemann, whose work later made supersonic flight possible. Even

Fusion/Carlos de Hoyos

Dr. Adolf Busemann (at the podium) at a dinner in New York in 1981 sponsored by the Fusion Energy Foundation honoring his accomplishments in aerodynamics. Seated at the dias are (from the left) Krafft A. Ehricke, Ingeborg Ehricke, Dr. Friedwardt Winterberg, and Dr. William Grossman.

before World War I, Busemann was studying the formation of shock waves in a wind tunnel. "This was already Prandtl's main interest at Göttingen," Busemann explained in a 1979 interview in *Fusion* magazine (Busemann 1979, p. 34). "He had lots of people working on high speeds during World War I. After the war was over, Germany wasn't allowed to work on practical airplanes anymore. ... The application for airplanes seemed out of reach or suppressed."

Theoretical studies at Göttingen continued, but in 1931, as Busemann described it, Prandtl "sold" him to a laboratory for applications of aerodynamics for turbine engineering in Dresden. "Because of the economy, Prandtl couldn't keep so many people at his institute," Busemann reported.

In 1936, Busemann moved to Braunschweig. This was after Hitler had announced Germany's abrogation of the restrictions of the Versailles Treaty and there were fewer restrictions on the research of German scientists. There, he built a supersonic and a transonic wind tunnel. Busemann was investigating the formation of shock waves at the speed of sound (responsible for the misnamed "sound barrier"), to inform the design of supersonic airplanes.

Describing his work with the aerodynamicists working on the rocket program at Peenemünde, Busemann mentioned that he also "had to go there a couple of times every month to see what they were doing. Therefore, my problem was at that time not only wind tunnels, but rocketry, too. It was then that I got to know von Braun. We Germans talked to each other so that we didn't spend a million reichsmarks on the same experiment. When they had experience, they told me about it, and when we wanted a new experiment, we told the other" (Busemann 1979, p. 38).

In 1929, Rudolf Hermann was awarded his doctorate of philosophy degree in physics at Leipzig University. In 1934, he became head of the Supersonic Wind Tunnel Division in the Aerodynamics Institute of the Aachen Institute of Technology. This was his post when Wernher von Braun came to see him in 1936. Dr. Hermann's small wind tunnel at the Aerodynamics Institute, with a test section of 10 by 10 centimeters, was capable of reaching 3.3 times the speed of sound. It was operated from 1934–1937, financed by the German Air Force (Luftwaffe).

The requirements for the rocket vehicles being designed included the development of the "optimum aerodynamic shapes for minimum drag" and "aerodynamic stability in both the subsonic and supersonic ranges... but stability must not be too large," or rudder control movements would be too large, Hermann noted. Also considered were the distribution of aerodynamic pressure loading and heating on the rockets (Hermann 1981).

The A-3 design Wernher von Braun brought Dr. Hermann was to incorporate new guidance mechanisms—full-fledged three-dimensional gyroscope control and jet rudders and actuators. Internal fins, placed in the exhaust stream of the engine, could be used to maneuver the rocket in flight. This solution to rocket guidance problems had been suggested by Oberth in his earliest works and was used by Goddard.

The arrangement of the fins for the A-3 proposed by the von Braun drawing, however, would have caused an unstable configuration. "In July 1936, Dr. Hermann brought us unfavorable news of a stability test in the Aachen wind tunnel on the first model of the A-3," Dornberger later reported, "and explained all the difficulties of finding the right form of fin for arrow-stabilized projectiles [without wings] at supersonic speeds" (Dornberger 1952, p. 57).

In September, Dr. Hermann brought back results of improved

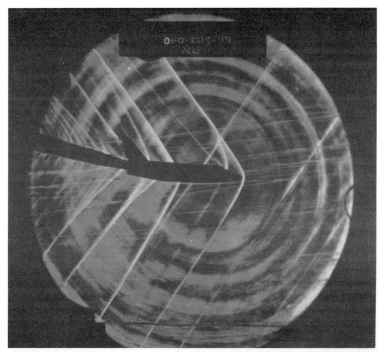

NASA, Ames Research Center
This Schlieren photograph was taken in a wind tunnel at the NASA Ames Research Center in California. Using this photographic technique, the shock waves created when the small Space Shuttle model encounters air flow at supersonic speeds are made visible to the scientist.

stability of the tail fins of the third A-3 model. The A-3 also incorporated a liquid nitrogen pressurization system with a vaporizer to feed the alcohol fuel and liquid oxygen into the motor, and new valves that were operated pneumatically by magnetic servo-valves.

On December 4, 1937, the A-3 performed its first flight test on the tiny (1,100 yards long and 300 yards at its widest) island of Greifswalder Oie in the Baltic—with no lighthouse trouble this time. After a perfect takeoff, the parachute ejected uncontrollably, pulling the rocket to one side. It crashed 300 meters from the launch site, and exploded (Schulze 1965, p. 5).

Believing the parachute to be the culprit after a second A-3 test failure, the experimenters removed it, but the third and fourth tests, all in December, also saw the rocket tumble and crash. It was determined that though the projectile was aerodynamically stable, the "gyro system was too slow and the movements produced by the exhaust jet rudders too small to counteract heavy winds" (Hermann 1981).

The importance of the wind tunnel and A-3 tests was noted after the war by Dr. Fritz Zwicky. He remarked that the tests "furnished the first evidence that missiles could be aerodynamically stabilized by solid fins. Previously rockets were generally somersaulting all over the place" (Zwicky 1945, p. 84).

While the guidance system was being completely redesigned, the experimenters proceeded with the design of a modified A-3. And because of the four failures, "the reputation of the A-3 was by now down to 'absolute zero,' we christened that new bird 'A-5,' " von Braun wrote in 1951. The A-4 designation was left "open to be applied to the more ambitious project which we had hoped would follow A-3" (von Braun 1956, p. 133).

A year before the flight tests of the A-3, however, it was clear that new facilities would be required. Preferably, they would be in an isolated location where rockets could be tested without endangering civilians, which could be made secure, and which provided the ability to put in place a series of observation stations along a 200-mile corridor. "We needed a research and development site fully equipped with all the latest resources of science and technology," Dornberger asserted (Dornberger 1952 p. 49).

In March 1936, "we managed to persuade General [Werner] von Fritsch to visit our experimental station at Kummersdorf," Dornberger reported (Dornberger 1952, p. 48). He witnessed static firings of the 650-pound, 2,200-pound, and 3,500-pound thrust rocket motors, and was supportive. ". . . [A]n increased budget was secured by staging demonstrations to high-ranking officers—causing Dornberger to recall uncomfortably that he had strongly disapproved when rocket experimenters had used the same tactics to try to secure financing from him" (Thomas 1961a, p. 53).

Colonel Wolfram von Richthofen, head of the Development Branch of the Air Ministry (and cousin of the World War I "Red Baron") was also interested in a rocket development facility. A month later, a meeting took place with the director of aircraft construction, General Albert Kesselring, at which Becker, Dornberger, von Braun, and Richthofen explained the "scheme for an 'Army Experimental Station' at Peenemünde," with a range eastward along the Pomeranian coast. Kesselring gave his approval (Dornberger 1952, p. 49).

But the army was not going to finance a large research and development project just for the sake of the science and technology. "The A-3 rocket we were then developing had not been equipped to take a payload," Dornberger reported. "It was a purely experimental missile. As we kept on pestering the army chiefs for money for continued development we were told we should only get it for rockets that would be capable of throwing big payloads over long ranges with a good prospect for hitting the target" (Dornberger 1952, p. 55). This led to the formulation of the design specifications for the future A-4.

To aid in the continued development of the A series rockets, Dr. Hermann agreed to come to Peenemünde in April 1937 to build a wind tunnel 16 times the size of the one at Aachen University, and capable of reaching Mach 5, as well as operating in the subsonic range, "since all rocket-powered vehicles start with zero velocity" (Hermann 1981). The wind tunnel became operational in the summer of 1939, with a staff of 60 people.

Two test sections, each 40 centimeters by 40 centimeters with two measurement sections, worked alternatively. As Dornberger described it, "It was the showpiece of our establishment both artistically and functionally." A quotation engraved on the wall of the building stated, "Technologists, physicists, and engineers are among the pioneers of this world" (Dornberger 1952, p. 114).

A Schlieren-optical system was built for the wind tunnel by Zeiss Optical of Jena. This allowed observation and photography of the flow fields around the rocket models by rendering visible differences in air density caused by pressure or heat. "Shock waves could be clearly seen as they traveled diagonally backwards at a sharp angle and sent their characteristic lines of different degrees of brightness across the black and white pictures," as Dornberger described it (Dornberger 1952, p. 120).

"Outside air was sucked in through large funnels, passed through drying filters, sent through sheet metal straighteners in the tunnel which smoothed the airflow and then accelerated it to the supersonic speed which corresponded to the de Laval nozzle in use" (Dornberger 1952, p. 115).

Typical wind tunnels built up until that time for aircraft and projectiles, produced the essential data of lift, drag, and pitch, but

National Air and Space Museum, Max Planck Society, Smithsonian Institution, 89-19726
Dr. Erich Regener, who designed the instruments and the barrel-shaped "tonna" to sit in the warhead section of the V-2 holding the scientific devices for measuring the upper atmosphere. This photograph was taken after World War I.

this was insufficient for guided missiles. Dr. Hermann and his group developed devices to take oscillation measurements on freely vibrating rocket models in order to determine the center of pressure, which is decisive for rocket stabilization.

The wind tunnel group also did experiments to see if radio signals, needed for telemetry, could be received by the supersonic missile in flight. Dr. Hermann reported to Dornberger: "[T]he experiments were successful. The shock waves occurring at supersonic speed do not stop the sound-waves getting through, providing the sensing instrument has been properly shaped" (Dornberger 1952, p. 119).

The wind tunnel tests on the A-9—a winged version of the A-4—laid the basis for this vehicle to became the first winged craft, to break the "sound barrier," at a speed of 3,000 miles per hour. Dr. Hermann and his team had to find a trade-off between high-lift sweptback wings, to produce the best lift-to-drag ratio (first designed by Adolf Busemann), and tail fins for stability. Through hours of redesign, the wind tunnel team produced data for an A-9a, that flew, a predecessor to today's Space Shuttle,

As early as 1941, the rocket team had begun working on a "super-supersonic wind tunnel," for a speed of Mach 10. This "Project A" was to be used for the largest long-range rocket on the drawing boards—the A-9/A-10. Neither the wind tunnel nor the long-range rocket were built during the war because they could not be justified as potential military rockets.

On November 24, 1988, to celebrate the 50th anniversary of the Max-Planck Institute for the Study of the Upper Atmosphere (Institut für Aeronomie), the institute issued a press release describing the protocol signed on July 8, 1942, "which must be considered the birth date of space exploration." The protocol states: "The A-4 provides the possibility of conducting atmospheric high-altitude measurements by new methods. Carrying out such experiments as quickly as possible is not only in the interest of the Research Institute for Stratospheric Physics (Forschungsstelle für Physik der Stratosphäre) at Friedrichshafen, but also in the interest of the Army Experimental Station (Heeresversuchsanstalt) at Peenemünde, as it relates to gaining data for the calculation of flight paths, questions concerning thermal increases, ballistic tables. etc.' "

The wording of the protocol reflects the confidence of the scientists at Peenemünde—the first successful launch of an A-4 rocket was still three months away.

On July 8, 1942, the day the protocol was signed, Wernher von Braun visited Erich Regener at his Research Institute for Stratospheric Physics of the Kaiser Wilhelm Institute. Along with von Braun came Ernst Steinhoff, who headed the Instruments, Guidance, and Measurements Laboratory at Peenemünde; Gerhard Reisig, who worked on instrumentation to measure atmospheric temperature and pressure; and others (DeVorkin 1992, p. 30). This was one in a number of stops for the Peenemünde scientists, who were on a recruitment "tour" to engage university experts in solving problems for the A-4, which they expected to be flying shortly.

David DeVorkin, in his book on the history of space science, describes Regener as "one of the best known experimental physicists in Germany" at that time (DeVorkin 1992, p. 26). Regener was the director of the Physical Institute of the Technical College in Stuttgart, until he was ousted from that position in October 1937, because he had been a signer of the Heisenberg-Wien-Geiger memorandum denouncing the Aryan physics movement in Germany, and reportedly because he refused to divorce his Jewish wife (DeVorkin

1992, p. 27). DeVorkin describes Regener's institute as a "magnet
for those wishing to learn how to construct and fly balloons that
could carry spectrographs, thermographs, barographs, and a wide
range of cosmic-ray devices into the stratosphere" (DeVorkin 1992,
p. 26).

Throughout the 1930s, scientists flew balloons, that could reach
the stratosphere in order to help answer basic questions about the
Earth's atmosphere. Why did the ionosphere exist, and why did it
interfere with radio and other electromagnetic radiation? How was
the ionosphere created and maintained, and what was the effect of
solar radiation? What were the wind patterns, heat balance, and
electrical characteristics of the atmosphere that produce the
weather? What were the effects of cosmic rays?

Regener had led an extensive program of placing measuring
instruments on balloons, that reached heights of 30 kilometers, and
he had advanced the state-of-the-art in this technology. When he
was ousted from the university in Stuttgart, the Kaiser Wilhlem
Institute, which still had funding independent of the government—
with support from the Air Ministry—established a new Institute
for Stratospheric Physics for Regener in Friedrichshafen (DeVorkin
1992, p. 29).

Regener proposed further study of ozone concentrations in
the atmosphere and their transfer to the lower troposphere, suggesting in 1940 that daily weather forecasts could be improved if
such turbulence were understood. Measurements at higher than
balloon altitudes (45 to 90 kilometers) could produce a complete
picture of this ozone transfer phenomenon, he believed, and for
that rockets would be necessary (DeVorkin 1992, p. 29).

The contract with Peenemünde requested Regener to build
instruments to measure the changes in temperature, pressure, and
density of the atmosphere at various heights. Since the A-4 would
be flying through unknown layers of the atmosphere, questions
concerning the heating of the rocket, stability through winds and
turbulence, and the possibility of maintaining radio communications
with the vehicle all were of import to the rocket specialists.

According to von Braun's minutes of the meeting with Regener,
the contract also stated that Regener was "free to develop additional
instruments for the A-4, but Regener apparently did not do so. . ."
(DeVorkin 1992, p. 30).

During a test flight of an A-4 during the war, Dornberger had

NASA

While there was no possibility that nuclear energy could be developed for rocket propulsion during Krafft Ehricke's initial investigations at Peenemünde, he recognized that in the future the heat of fission could be used to accelerate hydrogen to propel a spacecraft. This became the design concept for NASA's NERVA engine, seen here at the Nuclear Reactor Development Station in Nevada in 1964.

noticed that "zigzags forming in vapor trails [from the exhaust of the rocket] in a matter of seconds had already indicated differences in direction and velocity of the wind in successive air layers. . . . I could imagine," he later related, "the eagerness with which meteorologists, physicists, and astronomers would look forward to their first voyage into the stratosphere and ionosphere. . . . These people were always asking to be allowed to experiment with our missiles" (Dornberger 1952, p. 214).

Dr. Rudolph Hermann

A 1943 inspection at Peenemünde. General Dornberger is speaking. To the right, in the light jacket, is Rudolph Hermann. Wernher von Braun is in the dark suit, looking toward the camera. At the extreme right is Colonel Zanssen.

On July 11, 1942, Regener's institute received a contract worth 25,000 marks from Peenemünde to design and build the apparatus. This included the container (which became known as the Regener tonne, or barrel) to house the measuring instruments that was placed in the nose of the rocket, instead of a warhead (Klee and Merk 1965, p. 111). As DeVorkin states, "If he could lick the problems of instrument integration, explosive separation [of the tonne from the A-4], deployment of the parachute under near-space conditions, stabilized parachute flotation [for water recovery], and safe retrieval, the rest—that is, making the instruments themselves work—was simple" (DeVorkin 1992, p. 30).

An imaginative solution to one of these problems was described in 1988 by Professor H.K. Pätzold, who, as an optics expert, had been recalled from active military duty during the war to work on Regener's project: There was concern that at an altitude of 50 to 60 kilometers, there would not be adequate air pressure to open and support a parachute. "In this case also it was Regener who found a very simple and amusing solution," Professor Pätzold recalled. "The idea was to sew in a parachute about 20 meters in diameter six rubber hoses in lines of six rays going from the center to the perimeter, connected at the perimeter by a rubber ring bounding the rim of the parachute. As soon as the barrel separated from the rocket, a needle would puncture a membrane, so that compressed air from a small bottle carried on the flight would automatically flow into the hosing, inflating it, and by doing so, open the parachute."

The parachute system was tested in January 1945 inside a large hall, from a height of 30 meters. Prof. Pätzold recalled, "It was impressive to see how the great parachute, after falling only 10 meters, had fully opened up."

Through 1944, work continued to develop the precision instruments as well as the tonne. But the technical challenges of designing the instruments so they could operate in space and not interfere with each other, all needed time. The barrel container had to be shaped so it would be aerodynamically efficient, and the instruments had to fit perfectly into the tonne. In 1944, however, the technical staff at Peenemünde was still trying to solve inflight explosions occurring with the rocket itself.

By early 1945, the specialists at Peenemünde, along with Regener and his associates, had run out of time. Plans were being made in January to evacuate. Von Braun ordered Regener's team to leave for Friedrichshafen and the flight test never took place. It was a complex experimental research project with technical problems, DeVorkin states, that "took years to overcome in the United States after the war" (DeVorkin 1992, p. 37).

In explaining the activities at Peenemünde to American scientists at the end of the war, Wernher von Braun reported that the tests were "planned in the spring of 1945 ... from an island near Peenemünde.... The measuring instruments were set in a watertight container capable of floating, which was to have been descended [sic] by parachute. This project, all preparations for which were completed, could not be carried out on account of military events. It could be done in a short time, however, with some of the A-4 rockets still at hand" (1945).

After the war, the Kaiser Wilhelm Institute was restored as the Max-Planck Institute. In 1948, Regener became its vice president. The experiments Regener had planned were later carried out on A-4 (V-2) rockets brought from Germany to White Sands, New Mexico.

It is not surprising that farsighted propulsion researchers at Peenemünde, such as Dr. Walter Thiel, began thinking about the possibilities of using the developments in the new science of nuclear fission for rockets, even though the practical application would be decades away. Most of this new science had been created in continental Europe (Tennenbaum 1991a, 1991b). From 1896 until her death in 1934, Marie Skodowska Curie had worked to create the new science of nuclear chemistry. The year of her death, her daughter, Irene Joliot, and her husband, discovered artificial radioactivity.

Also in 1934, German nuclear chemist Ida Noddack proposed nuclear fission as an explanation for the anomalous experimental results being obtained by Enrico Fermi in Italy. In the same year, Vienna-born physicist Lise Meitner persuaded her colleague at the University of Berlin, chemist Otto Hahn, to embark on an experimental program at the Institute of Chemistry, that led to the demonstration of nuclear fission five years later. Meitner was forced to leave Germany in 1938, only six months before Hahn and Fritz Strassmann published their discovery of the fissioning of uranium.

The understanding of the nuclear fission process at the end of 1938 opened the door, particularly in Germany and in the United States (which had become the safe haven for a group of Europe's leading nuclear scientists), for work on an atomic bomb and other applications for this new form of energy. In Berlin, Nobel Laureate Werner Heisenberg, director of the Institute of Physics, oversaw the German atomic bomb program. In October 1942, Peenemünde commander Colonel Leo Zanssen signed a document "which is a research task entrusted as an urgent project ... to a unit with a cover address hiding nuclear research investigation," according to Klee and Merk (Klee and Merk 1965, p. 102).

The document instructed the Research Institute of the General Post Office "to investigate the possible exploitation of nuclear decay and chain reactions for rocket propulsion" (Klee and Merk 1965, page 125). The next month, Peenemünde propulsion expert Dr. Walter Thiel gave space enthusiast Krafft Ehricke—who had just come to Peenemünde from the Russian front—reports that he had regarding the research in nuclear fission being pursued by Professor Heisenberg.

Ehricke explained in 1984 that he was involved "in an evaluation of the Hahn-Strassman-Fermi fission theory, and the Heisenberg-

Pohl studies of the nuclear generation of steam as a method of propulsion for a spaceship, which, while certainly not needed for Earth-Moon travel, is necessary for interplanetary voyages" (Ehricke 1984b). The designs involved using the heat of disintegrating atoms of uranium to produce heat for a steam turbine.

Among Ehricke's teachers at the Technical University of Berlin before the war was "the famous physicist Hans Geiger, for whom the Geiger counter was named. At the University of Berlin, he heard the world-renowned nuclear physicist Werner Karl Heisenberg," Shirley Thomas reported in her 1960 book, *Men of Space* (Thomas 1960, p. 6). But in terms of the application of nuclear power to rocket propulsion, Ehricke said, "I didn't get very far with it, for the work in Germany was much less developed in the nuclear field than it was in the United States" (Thomas 1960, p. 7).

General Dornberger concurred, stating that "after 1943 we had approached Prof. Heisenberg for information about the practical possibilities. He could give us no firm promises of any description" (Dornberger 1952, p. 277).

In an interview with the authors of *The Rocket Team* in the 1970s, Ehricke recalled:

> My rocket-propulsion recommendations were negative as far as the heavy water moderator or the use of water as a propellant was concerned; but they were positive in recommending the replacement of heavy water by a solid moderator and of water by hydrogen (or at least methane). These were rather far-out recommendations for those days. But Dr. Thiel, who was very forward-looking, concurred.
>
> I saw Heisenberg in late 1944. He was trying to make a heavy water moderated reactor "go critical." He told me, "of course one could build an atomic bomb." But this would require huge isotope separation plants that could not be erected under the situation of Allied air superiority. He thought the most immediate military use of a nuclear reactor would be for submarine propulsion [Ordway and Sharpe 1979, p. 58].

Although he rejected the possibility of using nuclear decay as a heat source to produce steam as a propellant, Ehricke recognized that the heat could be used to accelerate hydrogen, and this became the fundamental design concept of the nuclear-thermal NERVA (Nu-

As an intermediate step be-
tween the A-4 and the secret
A-9 glider, the A-4b, or an A-4
with wings, was built and
flight tested at Peenemünde.
Seen here is the A-4b shortly
before its successful launch
January 24, 1945.
Deutsches Museum, München

clear Engine for Rocket Vehicle Application) successfully developed
by NASA in the 1960s.

   The most exciting work, and the place Wernher von Braun
reportedly enjoyed spending his time, was at the Peenemünde's
Special Projects office. Here, the scientists could plan out their trips
into Earth orbit, to the Moon, and the stars.
   The design of the large A-4 was determined strictly by what it
had to accomplish—to carry a warhead of about 1 ton twice the
distance of the Paris Gun, or about 180 miles. This translated into
a vehicle with about 25 tons of thrust. But the rocket designers
built the large Test Stand VII at Peenemünde with the future beyond
the A-4 in mind. It could handle static tests of rocket engines with
up to at least 100 tons of thrust.
   Before the A-4 ever flew, Ludwig Roth's Special Projects office
was designing the spaceships of von Braun's dreams. The A-9 would
be a winged glider and the step into manned space flight.
   Tests in Dr. Hermann's wind tunnel in 1940 had shown that

Courtesy of Dr. Rudolf Hermann

Dr. Rudolf Hermann in the 1980s in his home in Huntsville, Alabama.

the range of the A-4 could be more than doubled by adding wings. The A-4b, which was an A-4 with wings, was designed and test-flown as an intermediate step toward the transatlantic A-9. The A-9 glider was never intended as a military vehicle, though it has been claimed that it was designed to bomb New York. The only way the range of the A-9 could be extended to double that of the A-4 was to reduce its velocity to below the speed of sound after engine cutoff, letting it glide to a landing. The military value of the A-4 was that its noiseless supersonic approach made defense against it very difficult. As a weapon, the A-9 would have been no more of a surprise than the noisy subsonic V–1 buzz bomb.

In some of the drawings of the A-9, a pressurized cockpit for a crew replaced the warhead; there was also a tricycle landing gear. The A-9 would have been capable of carrying a pilot a distance of more than 300 miles in 17 minutes. It would have taken off vertically, like the A-4, and then landed glider-fashion on a medium-sized airstrip. The next step, envisioned in the Special Projects office, was mating the A-9 winged vehicle to a new, larger booster, the A-10. This rocket would have a thrust of 440,000 pounds, or 10 times the capability of the A-4.

If the manned A-9 were placed atop an A-10 booster, it would be a supersonic transatlantic rocket plane (Figure 4.2). Then, von

---

FIGURE 4.2
MODEL OF THE A-9/A-10
The secret advanced planning work done by the scientists and engineers at Peenemünde included the design of a large booster, the A-10, on top of which would sit
an A-9 piloted glider vehicle. This combination would produce the capability for a
supersonic transatlantic plane. This drawing, with a man in the lower left, gives an
idea of the scale.

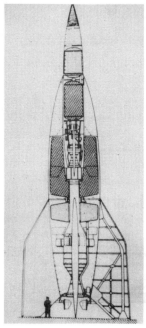

Source: Joachim Engelmann *V-2: Dawn of the Rocket Age* (West Chester, Pa: Schiffer Publishing
Ltd, 1985).

Braun planned, would come the A-11, as the booster for a three-
stage combination. This three-stage A-11/A-10/A-9 spaceship would
be capable of obtaining orbital velocity, and man would be able to
live and work in space for the first time.

When he was interrogated by the American technical/military
representatives after surrendering in 1945, von Braun told them
that the A-10 could also be converted to a winged upper stage; the
A-11 into a second stage; with a gigantic booster—the A-12, with
12,800 tons of thrust. Such a combination would produce a vehicle
that could take not only man, but man plus 30 tons of payload to

Earth orbit. "This would permit the hauling of crews and substantial amounts of material into space. A number of such ships, maintaining a regular shuttle service to the orbit, would permit the building of a space-station there" (von Braun 1956, p. 145).

A recent biography of Wernher von Braun includes a reminiscence by Adolf Thiel, one of Wernher von Braun's early collaborators:

> The A-4b, a single-stage rocket with wings, would have a range of 450 kilometers. A bigger two-stage combination, the A-9/A-10, would have been able to reach 3,000 kilometers. Our investigations dealt, however, only with the aerodynamic aspects; no work was done with regard to propulsion, construction, guidance, thermal analysis, etc. . . .
>
> We tried to see far in the future and announced in 1944 that multistaged rockets would permit the construction of space stations in Earth orbit and that glider rockets returning from space would be able to reduce their kinetic energy over a long flight path and therefore could securely land on Earth. . . . Our studies dealt only with space travel, not with weapons. Von Braun stimulated and encouraged us in our work. He was convinced that they would help realize his hopes of future undertakings in space [Stuhlinger and Ordway 1992, p. 74].

In a conversation in 1983, Rudolf Hermann described the atmosphere at Peenemünde in which these scientific developments took place: "Wernher also had a cello which he played with enthusiasm. On so many evenings you could hear the sounds of a Haydn or Mozart quartet: Wernher playing the cello, Gerhard Reisig on the viola, and Heinrich Ramm and myself on the violins."

"Did you often discuss in those days about rocket flight in space?" Hermann was asked.

"All the time," was his short and convincing answer. "We always were occupied with space. Wernher was full of ideas about flights to the Moon, satellites with telescopes and transmitters, a tremendous space station and a manned mission to Mars. Our giant A-4 rockets were for him only the first step on the road to space rockets of the future. In February 1938 we decided to celebrate Shrove Tuesday and organized a masquerade ball with the theme 'Mardi Gras on Mars' (Stuhlinger and Ordway 1992, p. 79).

"There was a Martian goddess with her court who were visited by spacefarers from Earth. White-bearded 'Prof. emeritus' von Braun informed one and all that he was the Vagrant Viking of Space making a short stopover on the red planet" (Ordway and Liebermann, 1992, p. 113).

"Was there ever at that time [1937–38] anything said about the possibility of war?" Dr. Hermann was asked.

"Never," he answered. "In the years 1937–38 we were not thinking about war, and neither would we have believed in the possibility of a war. When the awful apparition began to reveal its threatening forms, we became increasingly worried. Everybody had the feeling that it was far beyond our abilities to influence such events" (Stuhlinger and Ordway 1992, p. 80).

What were the motivations of the scientists who joined von Braun in the army rocket program? Krafft Ehricke wrote in 1960:

> The claim of conceptual ties between the Peenemünde missile weapon development and lofty space ideals has frequently been doubted after World War II as a pious story invented by the "Peenemünde Group" in the United States. Peenemünde, like every missile team today, had in its ranks many engineers who were not particularly interested in space flight. . . . There is no doubt, however, that Peenemünde contained a hard core of men totally devoted to space flight as the ultimate goal and purpose of missile development.
>
> This author can attest to it, because he was one of them. When he joined Peenemünde, General Dr. Dornberger explained to him that he fully concurred with the ideals of the space flight pioneers, but that the existing situation, beyond control of the Peenemünde team, demanded utmost concentration on the immediate problems, many of which would have to be solved in any case. . . . Many engineers and scientists, engaged in missile weapon systems research and development after 1945, will today take credit for advancing astronautic technology like the Peenemünde team did 17 years ago when, in fall 1942, the first V-2 missile ascended into space [Ehricke 1960b, pp. 35–6].

What was the motivation of the army? From the beginning in 1929, and after Hitler was in power, the army stated clearly—and maintained until the end of the war—that the purpose of long-range rockets was to increase the firepower of an army with a drastically reduced number of troops. That Hitler personally, and leading Nazis, had a completely different idea of the role of the rockets, will be detailed in the next chapter. As the former Peenemünders and honest historians have often enough made clear, "Hitler wasn't even interested" in the A-4 (Ley 1957a, p. 211).

The A-4, Ley explains, "was the one which later was to be publicized as V-2, and which all Allied, or at least all English-written newspapers called, 'Hitler's rocket' with beautiful unanimity." Only after the war, could people "know what a misnomer this was," he wrote.

Dornberger, who had witnessed the ouster of successive upper-echelon independent-thinking army officers by Hitler, including the suicide of General Becker after a "quarrel" with Hitler, states in 1964: "I would like to correct an error . . . namely that the V-2 was Hitler's devilish idea, designed to conquer the world. Up to 1943 Hitler had absolutely nothing to do with the rocket program. . . . Hitler never saw the A-4 except in movies, nor had he ever been in Peenemünde. He simply was not interested" (Emme 1964, p. 32).

Making use of the best minds in German science, and a tradition in scientific method that stretched back centuries, the scientists and engineers at Peenemünde laid out the program to create a new technology—rockets. It was due to their success, during an increasingly irrational war, that Hitler seized on the A-4 rocket as a last-ditch attempt to turn the tide of the coming defeat.

How the A-4 Rocket Became the V-2

In 1943, after 10 years of disinterest and opposition, and at the point that Germany was facing defeat by the Allies, Adolf Hitler decided that the A-4 rocket could be the "retaliation weapon" for the Allied aerial bombings of German cities and could turn the course of the war. He demanded a crash program at the army installation at Peenemünde to bring the experimental rocket into mass production. But by the time the first A-4s, which Hitler re-named V-2s, were launched in the fall of 1944, the Allied invasion at Normandy had already taken place.

The Peenemünde rocket team worked for 10 years under army auspices with little support from the Nazi government apparatus. They constantly battled for resources. When the project finally showed some success, the rocket team was under the threat that the government or SS would seize control of the project and destroy the possibility of future advances in rocketry and space travel.

The impossible political environment within which the rocket team attempted to develop its new technology during the war is epitomized by the experience of Hermann Oberth. From 1930 to 1938, Oberth was teaching in his native Romania, unable to finance the development of his rockets. Despite tremendous frustration, he had never given up hope that his rockets would be developed. He told *The New York Times* on January 30, 1931, "I hope one day, not before 15 years at the earliest, to be able to fly in a rocket, if not to the Moon, to the planet Mars or Jupiter" (Elder 1991, p. 20).

One would assume that Oberth, the inventor of the rocket in Germany, would be one of the first called upon to participate in the army rocket program once it was under way in 1932. Although it is true that Oberth's genius was in the theoretical rather than in the practical engineering realm, the reasons he was kept out of the rocket program until 1941 were more political than technical.

In April 1937, Oberth was invited to Berlin, where he met with Dornberger, von Braun, Busemann, and representatives of the air ministry. Oberth did not know that this meeting was a "debriefing session" as Peenemünde was being established. There was no way at that time that von Braun could openly involve his revered teacher in the secret rocket program (Barth 1991, p. 180). As von Braun explained to Oberth later: "two obstacles have made it impossible for us to bring you to Peenemünde earlier, Professor. On the one hand, the question of your citizenship, where the Gestapo created difficulties. Secondly, a reason which is for you very honorable: You are well known abroad, and we had to fear that your presence would betray what we were up to at Peenemünde to a foreign intelligence agency" (Barth 1991, p. 181).

Oberth described the situation in a letter to Austrian scientist Eugen Sänger, written on April 28, 1948:

> Up until 1938 I was entirely prevented from being called to Germany. Actually, the reasons given for that were completely indefensible, for instance, that I was not of Aryan extraction (my parents were in any case complete Aryans), that I was superficial and careless in my work (you can only make such a claim when the person in question has shown this on some occasion), or that I was not an engineer at all and that I understood as a Balkan German less about technical matters than even a layman in Germany. . . .
>
> When I then drew the consequences from the fact that there was obviously no position for me in Germany and sought employment abroad, I was suddenly called to the Technical High School in Vienna, but only to be more effectively put on ice, as my chief at that time and my assistant, explicitly told me [Barth 1984, p. 145].

Considered by the Nazi state as a man who knew too much about a potential military technology, Oberth was brought to "greater Germany" by the German Air Force to work in Vienna, where he laid out an experimental facility at Felixdorf nearby (Gartmann 1956). Von Braun visited Oberth in Vienna and later described his situation: He had "one miserable test pit, one mechanic. . . . Something Oberth should have realized when the call to Vienna came . . . that he, once he had even one foot on the soil of the Third Reich, was condemned to unconditional collaboration" (Ley 1957a, p. 221).

In a letter to Ley, dated December 24, 1948, Oberth recalled what happened next:

> I explained to Prof. Beck, the director of the Department of Motor Propulsion at the Vienna Technical High School . . . that I had had enough of this type of work and that I would like to return to Siebenbürgen [Romania]. The answer: "We can no longer let you leave the Reich, as long as you are not a German citizen, because, in spite of all the security measures, you already know too much, and we would have no handle whatsoever on you if you wanted to divulge anything. You have only the choice of becoming a German citizen or marching into a concentration camp." The real cruelties perpetrated in the concentration camps were still unknown to me, nevertheless I preferred becoming a German citizen. . . .

Von Braun tried to expedite Oberth's citizenship, so he could bring him to Peenemünde. Oberth recalled:

> I was made a German citizen in July 1941, and in August 1941 I came to Peenemünde, where I remained until December 1943. Here I had to examine all the existing patent applications and ideas in order to see if there was anything in them that would be of value in the rocket technology. . . . In addition, I wrote several reports, for instance, a paper "Concerning The Optimal Division of Multi-Staged Rockets," and a study "Defending Against Enemy Aircraft by means of Remote-Controlled Powder Rockets," in which I proposed an entirely new type of powder rocket [Barth 1984, pp. 152–153].

Although Oberth was at Peenemünde a relatively short time and was not in the mainstream of the work, his presence there made it possible for younger men who knew him only through his books to meet and talk with him. In his work on multistage rockets,

Deutsches Museum, München
An A-4 is prepared for tanking on the launch pad at Test Stand VII.

for example, Oberth worked with Special Projects office head Ludwig Roth.

By the time Oberth arrived at Peenemünde in 1941, the development of the A-4 rocket was largely complete. The father of the liquid-fuel rocket was never allowed to work on the A-4. But Oberth's stay at Peenemünde was marked by more than frustration and disappointment. He was there during the British air raid on the facility on August 17–18, 1943, and two weeks later, his daughter Ilse died in an accident at the Redl-Zipf liquid oxygen facility in Austria.

Von Braun wrote to Oberth on August 31:

I would like to express my heartfelt condolences, my dearly respected colleague, Professor Oberth, for the terrible blow, that you and your family have received by the death of your daughter. There is here a special kind of tragedy in the fact that this young girl, who had the most wonderful years of her life still to look forward to, had to fall in the service of a task that was based on the unique and in the history of technology never-to-be-forgotten pioneer deeds of her father. . . . Her sacrifice entails for us who remain behind a responsibility not to grow weary in our struggle to reach our great goal [Barth 1984, vol. 1, p. 127].

After the August raid on Peenemünde, work that Oberth was doing on multistage rockets, along with other advanced projects, was officially stopped. He then transferred to the Westfalen-Anhalten Explosive Materials Company, (Westpfälisch-Anhaltische Sprengst-off-Aktiengesellshaft) and "was assigned the task of developing a gunpowder rocket for anti-aircraft defense, for which I had submitted a suggestion" (Oberth 1967, p. 121).

When Oberth first saw the A-4 rocket, he was shocked that so much progress had been made. But he said that he thought they were building the wrong rocket! "He said that for military purposes, a powder [solid-fuel] rocket would have been far better and less expensive than these complicated rockets with liquid fuels," Oberth's daughter Erna Roth-Oberth said in an interview. But von Braun and his key circle of collaborators were faithfully building the rocket Oberth had preliminarily designed in the 1920s. It was not designed as a weapon. As Roth-Oberth stated, the rockets von Braun was building at Peenemünde one "would need for the purpose of space travel" (Roth-Oberth 1992).

So while the visionaries among the scientists and engineers were building the rockets they planned one day to launch around the Earth and to the Moon, the army was trying to develop a long-range artillery weapon for attacks on military targets. But the Nazis had a different agenda.

Hitler's plans for the conquest of Europe were based on the "blitzkrieg" (lightning) short war. To him, there was no need for either long-term research and development projects to develop long-range missiles, or even short-range rockets for air defense. In 1938, when to the surprise of many, the British capitulated to further aggression by Hitler at Munich, it seemed as if Hitler's strategy would be a success. When the war started, therefore, "von Braun, like most Germans," Peenemünde veteran Ernst Stuhlinger writes, "did not envision a protracted war and was therefore confident that the A-4 would never be deployed in combat" (Ordway and Libermann 1992, p. 113).

When Hitler came to power in 1933, the German Army, the Wehrmacht, had been reduced to a mere remnant of the prewar institution by the restrictions of the Versailles Treaty. The army had looked to the elderly president of the republic, Marshall Otto von Hindenburg, as the conservator of army values after the abdication of the kaiser in 1919. The old conservative Prussian military leadership presented a potential threat to Hitler, and was least inclined, as those who would pay the greatest price of war, to support the upstart Austrian corporal's expansionist plans.

At the beginning, Hitler did his best to win the army's support, because without the military he could launch no war of conquest. Hitler's destruction of the private Nazi army, the Sturmabteilung (SA) in 1934, led by Ernst Roehm, Hitler's foremost competitor for the leadership of the Nazi movement, was aimed at bringing the Wehrmacht over to his side. Roehm had ambitions of making the SA into *the* military arm of the Third Reich, eventually absorbing most of the functions of the Wehrmacht. Hitler, fearing the political ambitions of Roehm more than the opposition of the Wehrmacht, moved against him.

At the same time, however, Hitler had no intention of allowing an independent-minded military leadership to exist. In the 1934 "Night of the Long Knives," when Hilter decimated the leadership of the SA, he also had Gen. Kurt von Schleicher, von Schleicher's wife, and his adjutant murdered. Von Schleicher had been Hitler's foremost opponent before 1933. As the last chancellor of the Weimar Republic under President Hindenburg, von Schleicher had attempted to implement an economic policy that could undermine the social basis of Hitler's take-over.

The top leaders of the Wehrmacht, Field Marshal Werner von Blomberg and Colonel General Baron Werner von Fritsch, were driven from their positions—von Blomberg under the shadow of having married a woman of "ill repute" and von Fritsch on false charges of homosexuality.

As Ley later described it: "The Nazi Party ... found that there were a few old established groups which followed their own traditions and did not change much, or as fast, as desired. The Catholic Church was a prime example, and the German Army also remained something apart in the body politic, simply by failing to develop political attitudes, not to mention enthusiasm" (Ley 1957a, p. 223).

In 1938, General Ludwig Beck, the chief of the German general staff, considered leading a military coup against Hitler, having failed to convince him of the folly of moving into Czechoslovakia. Beck assumed that the other nations of Europe would be prepared to go to war rather than permit Hitler further aggression, and had sought support from the British and the French for an attempt to organize a coup. In spite of numerous exchanges between the German opposition to Hitler and the British and Americans, through Vatican and other channels, the decision was made by the British to deny support. By 1941, British Prime Minister Winston Churchill had given orders to the foreign office to meet any peace-feelers from any opposition with "absolute silence."

British Prime Minister Neville Chamberlain's capitulation at Munich to military moves into Czechoslovakia considerably strengthened Hitler's hand domestically and undermined the coup plan of Beck and his collaborators. Those on the general staff like Beck, who had warned that war would immediately ensue were Hitler to move into Czechoslovakia, were portrayed as "defeatist." A military coup attempt under these conditions would have been doomed to failure. Beck resigned from the army in protest of the invasion of Czechoslovakia.

With the German invasion of Poland on September 1, 1939, World War II began, and Germany's industrial resources were focused on the production of conventional weapons to fight only "short" wars. Army Field Marshal Walter von Brauchitsch, however, gave the army rocket installation at Peenemünde highest priority and reduced the time to finish construction of the laboratories and housing facilities, recognizing the possibility that it would not be a "short war."

Over the three years from 1939 to 1942, however, the priority status of the rocket program changed unpredictably, as various centers of power vied for control of war policy. Just two months after the construction at Peenemünde was accelerated, the project's steel allotment was cut back in order to supply the armaments industry; the project had lost its top priority.

"Hitler had lost interest in rockets after the lightning victory

Deutsches Museum, München

Gen. Erich Fellgiebel, head of the Army Information Services, congratulating members of the Peenemünde team for the first successful launch of an A-4 rocket on October 3, 1942. At the left is Gen. Leo Zanssen, the commander of Peenemünde and next to him is Gen. Walter Dornberger. Wernher von Braun is seen behind Gen. Dornberger. Dr. Rudolf Hermann is in the light-colored suit smiling, and to the right of Dr. Hermann is Dr. Gerhard Reisig. By the time of this first successful launch, all of the top brass of the German Army which had supported the rocket program had been replaced more than once.

against Poland, and the high costs of the Experimental Station at Peenemünde had suddenly become a thorn in his side," according to an article about General Becker. "Although the commander in chief of the army, Field Marshal von Brauchitsch had given Peenemünde in September 1939 the army's 'highest priority' designation, Hitler eliminated half of the materials allocations ... on Nov. 23,

1939. 'I will need no rockets in this war, and besides, you know my skepticism about these experiments,' were his words. He then began to shower sharp criticism on General Becker" (*Astronautik* 1976, p. 80).

Hitler was distrustful of the army from the beginning. As early as 1940, he had decided to set up a weapons production system in parallel to, and purposely in competition with, the military. An "argument" with Hitler over the loss of army control over how to fight the war led ballistics expert General Emil Becker to commit suicide in the spring of that year.

At the end of 1941, the Peenemünde rocket team lost its second supporter in the top command of the army. Field Marshal von Brauchitsch was "relieved" of his position because of differences with Hitler over the Russian campaign. In 1940, when "our best men were being called up and we faced complete suspension, the field marshal, at my suggestion and without Hitler's knowledge, had allowed us to draw from the fighting troops 4,000 technically qualified men, engineers, and laborers, for work at Peenemünde," Dornberger relates (Dornberger 1952, p. 74). In 1941, Germany lost the Battle of Britain, and the limits of air power were clear; Peenemünde temporarily regained top-priority status.

This was also an opportunity for some of the rest of the scientific community. "Raw materials, in particular steel, were again [at Peenemünde's] disposal—a factor of decisive importance for research and development work. ... While [von Braun was] visiting the Kaiser Wilhelm Institute for Physics in Heidelberg, the director of the institute, Dr. Walther Bothe, showed him some of the components of a cyclotron, the first of its kind in Germany. Construction had come to a standstill, since Bothe was not able to get the necessary authorization for purchase of the necessary steel. Von Braun soon sent a couple of tons of the steel allocated for Peenemünde to Heidelberg, and construction of the cyclotron at Bothe's institute could continue" (Stuhlinger and Ordway 1992, p. 81).

Then, in March 1942, when the A-4 was nearly ready for flight testing, priorities shifted to the invasion of the Soviet Union, and the rocket program once more was off the priority list. Finally, after 10 years of development, on October 3, 1942, the A-4 had its first successful test flight. But as Dornberger predicted at the time, success only made the situation worse.

By then, "our requirements far exceeded the supplies our army superiors could allocate on the home front. They extended to the field of administration of the Ministry of Munitions and needed the consent of Adolf Hitler" (Dornberger 1952, p. 75). Dornberger decided to appeal to Albert Speer, the minister of munitions, for support to complete experimental work on the A-4. Previously the armaments industry had been directed by the Army Weapons Department. Speer's Ministry of Munitions was formed as an independent coequal to try to control the military.

On January 8, 1943, Dornberger and von Braun met with Speer, only to be told that, "the Führer cannot give your project higher priority yet. He is still not convinced that your plan will succeed" (Dornberger 1952, p. 78). After the meeting, Speer approached Hitler again about the rocket program, and Dornberger soon received a message from Speer: "The Führer has dreamed that no A-4 will ever reach England" (Dornberger 1952, p. 93).

To help with procuring material needed from industry for A-4 production at Peenemünde, Speer sent Dornberger Gerhard Degenkolb, who had been chairman of the Locomotives Special Committee and was known for his ruthlessness. Dornberger soon realized "with a shock that Degenkolb's name had been linked in the spring of 1940 with the suicide of General Becker." Degenkolb had made clear in a speech shortly before Becker's death, "his bitter hatred of the Army Weapons Department and its officers" (Dornberger 1952, p. 81).

Degenkolb put together an impossible plan for the immediate production of 300 A-4s per month by October 1943, rising to 900 rockets per month by December. Speer's move to put production in the hands of "industry" was the first serious attempt to take the project out of the hands of the army. It caused a near-mutiny by the scientists, who knew that the rocket production schedule was impossible.

Later, Speer would write: "The whole notion [of producing 900 V-2s a month] was absurd. The fleets of enemy bombers in 1944 were dropping an average of 3,000 tons of bombs a day over a span of several months. And Hitler wanted to retaliate with 30 rockets that would have carried 24 tons of explosives to England daily. . . . I not only went along with this decision on Hitler's part but also supported it. This was probably one of my most serious mistakes" (Speer 1970, p. 249).

To meet the unrealistic production schedule, Reich SS Leader

Heinrich Himmler "volunteered" the use of "foreign labor" under the SS's control, to accelerate the project. Hitler rejected this suggestion at that time, because of concerns with possible sabotage. Dornberger was therefore supposed to ready the rocket for production without any additional manpower; he could not obtain more German workers because the program still did not have top priority.

Then, on July 7, 1943, Hitler decided to give Peenemünde top priority in the German armaments program. That day Dornberger, von Braun, and Ernst Steinhoff were summoned to a meeting at Hitler's headquarters, because Hitler would never come to Peenemünde. "I could never account for this except on the grounds of fear of his own soldiers," Dornberger said later (Dornberger 1952, p. 101).

At the meeting, Hitler viewed a film of an A-4 launch and was shown models of the rocket. "What I want is an annihilation—annihilating effect!" Hitler raved. Dornberger responded, "Please discourage the propaganda that is starting about the decisive effect these 'all-annihilating wonder-weapons' are going to have on the war. It can lead to nothing but disappointment for the country. Our aim was to increase the range of heavy artillery" (Dornberger 1952, p. 105).

According to Dornberger, he tried again to convince Hitler of the folly of a "wonder-weapon," and said, " 'When we started our development we were not thinking of an all-annihilating effect. We—' Hitler swung round in a rage and shouted at me: 'You! No, you didn't think of it, I know. But I did—' " (Dornberger 1952, p. 106). The A-4 was renamed the V-2, for "Vergeltung" or "retaliation," as Hitler's response to the massive carpet bombing that was destroying German cities (Figure 5.1).

Now, with Hitler's final support, the Ministry of Munitions decided that 2,000 V-2s should be produced per month. To meet this impossible production schedule, construction started on a "new emergency factory" called the Nordhausen Mittelwerk (Central Works), built underground in tunnels near the Hartz Mountains (Dornberger 1952, p. 110).

After the success of the A-4 test on October 3, 1942, another major player started to make his move to grab control of the rocket program.

In March 1943, as Munitions Minister Albert Speer was trying to implement his fantastic plan for A-4 production, Heinrich Himmler

FIGURE 5.1
DIAGRAM OF THE A-4 ROCKET
This drawing is a cross section of the A-4 rocket on its firing table. The instrument section beneath the warhead housed the guidance and control equipment. This technology had not been developed and tested adequately enough to allow the A-4 to be accurately pointed at a target. Hence its only use during the war was as Hitler's "annihilating" weapon used primarily for the area bombing of Allied cities in retaliation for the saturation bombing of German cities.

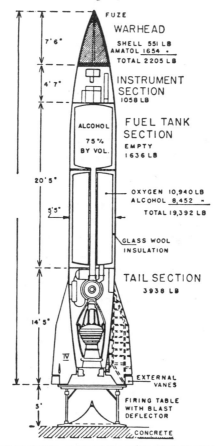

Source: Willy Ley, *Rockets, Missiles, and Space Travel* (New York: The Viking Press, 1957).

prepared a trip to Peenemünde. He showed up in April with army Generals Emil Leeb and Friedrich Fromm, who had replaced Generals Becker and von Brauchitsch. Himmler said that since the rocket research was now "in the limelight," he wanted to see it.

Greatly impressed with the A-4 program, Himmler made the incredible announcement to Dornberger and the army brass: "I am here to protect you against sabotage and treason." Turning pale at the thought of the SS in control of Peenemünde, Dornberger turned to his army superiors for support, and Generals Fromm and Leeb quickly stated that since Peenemünde was an army facility, the army would take care of internal security (Dornberger 1952, p. 172).

But Himmler had his eye on Peenemünde. A week after Himmler's visit, Dornberger reports, "one of my group leaders back from Brünn . . . told me that SS officers there were openly saying that I was the brake on rocket development in Germany. . . . The loudest voice had been that of SS Captain Engel, who had earlier worked for a short time at the rocket airfield in Berlin [the VfR's Raketenflugplatz], and was in charge of an SS rocket research station . . . near Danzig" (Dornberger 1952, p. 172).

To counterattack, Dornberger invited Engel and others for a visit to Peenemünde to ask them about these reports. He also prepared a paper, "Rocket Development: The Achievement of the Army Weapons Department, 1930–1943," in self defense (Dornberger 1952, p. 174).

Not having given up the idea of an SS takeover of Peenemünde, Himmler returned alone, without army escort, for a two-day visit on June 28. During a demonstration a V-2 crashed only 300 feet from an air force runway at Peenemünde, destroying three parked aircraft. Himmler is reported to have quipped, " 'Now I can return to Berlin and order the production of close-combat weapons with an easy conscience!' " (Irving 1965, p. 73). But Himmler kept a close eye on the rocket project.

The role of the SS in the rocket program changed dramatically on August 17, 1943 when Air Marshal Arthur "Bomber" Harris sent more than 600 bombers from the British Royal Air Force on a mission to "kill the scientists" at Peenemünde. More than 3 million pounds of explosives and incendiary bombs were dropped on Peenemünde and surrounding housing facilities. Although about 735 people died in the raid, including propulsion expert Dr. Thiel and his family, only 210 Germans, mostly women and children,

Deutsches Museum, München

Although 60 out of 100 buildings at Peenemünde were hit during the British raid, most suffered only minor damage. Here, workers clear the debris in the assembly building. A-4 rockets can be seen against the back wall of the building.

died. The majority of the casualties were foreign prisoners (Emme 1964, p. 40).

What British military analysts have had to say about the raid, and about the V-2, is most instructive. British author David Collier, who dedicates his book, *The Battle of the V-Weapons,* to Air Marshal Roderic Hill, the organizer of the British defense against the V-1, reports: the "V-2 [was] not accurate enough, at the stage reached in 1944, to hit a target as large as Norwich once in 43 rounds, even when fired by a crack [field] unit." Therefore, he says, it could only be used "when Hitler ordered 'terror attacks of a retaliatory nature,'" against the British "area attacks" on Berlin, Essen, Munich, Hamburg, and Cologne (Collier 1965, pp. 140–41).

Was the British raid on Peenemünde in August 1943 worth the loss of 40 aircraft?, Collier asks. "It was a striking demonstration of the extravagance of bombing, for many of those killed [on the ground] were impressed foreign workers whose deaths were of no benefit to the Allies and were, indeed, regretted by the organizers of the raid" (Collier 1965, p. 143).

Prime Minister Winston Churchill's son-in-law Duncan Sandys, who headed the investigation ordered by the war cabinet into the German rocket weapons, had convinced Sir Arthur "Bomber" Harris that one of the targets of the raid should be the housing facilities of the Peenemünde scientists. (It was a radar error that landed the bulk of the bombs 2 miles south of the target, on the housing complex of the foreign workers at the nearby town of Trassenheide.)

Some 26 years later, on the day after the first Americans landed on the Moon, Member of Parliament Duncan Sandys sent a telegram to Wernher von Braun that read: "Warmest congratulations on your great contribution to this historic achievement. I am thankful that your illustrious career was not cut short in the bombing raid at Peenemünde 26 years ago" (*The Washington Post* 1969).

Although 60 out of the 100 buildings at Peenemünde were hit, most suffered only minor damage. The critical liquid oxygen plant that produced the oxidizer for the rockets and the huge power plant needed for all the operations were untouched. The work at Peenemünde was delayed for about six weeks, according to all knowledgeable accounts. For that reason, David Irving has described the "Operation Crossbow" raid on Peenemünde as "a qualified failure" (Irving 1965, p. 309).

In fact, the most serious outcome of the raid was not the damage to the physical facilities or the scientists but that it took the production of the rockets out of the hands of the army and placed it in the hands of the SS.

Wernher von Braun described how the SS finally grabbed control of part of the rocket program in a 1966 letter to the editors of *Paris-Match,* written in response to accusations by former Dora camp inmates claiming that he was responsible for their suffering:

After we had made some progress with our research and development, and having achieved a number of successful flights with the new V-2, the decision was made by Speer's Ministry for Armaments and Munitions in Berlin to begin mass production of the V-2. According to the original plan of the ministry, production lines were to be put into operation in three or four different places in Germany and Austria—all of them in existing above-ground factories. (The thousands of parts, out of which the rocket was to be assembled, were allocated to numerous factories in all of Germany.) While the assembly factories were being equipped, within a two-week period, all four installations had suffered severe damage as a result of bomb attacks. . . . .

After that Hitler himself gave the order to place the final assembly of the V-2 underground. The installations and equipment in the three or four factories were transported to an underground oil depot in the vicinity of Nordhausen, south of the Hartz mountains. . . . SS-General Kammler was assigned by Hitler and Himmler to get as many educated and uneducated forced laborers as were necessary in order to fulfill the production goals of the ministry. The prisoners were chosen from various concentration camps and transported to Dora, a camp surrounded by barbed wire in the vicinity of one of the entrances of the former underground depot. . . .

As developers of the rockets it was our responsibility to see that our sketches and specifications were observed by the hundreds of firms which took part in the mass production. This functioned in the following manner: We had representatives from Peenemünde, for the purpose of quality control, at all the bigger firms which participated in the V-2 program, including Mittelwerk. These representatives could inform us about any deviation from the specifications and about any flaws in the fabrication or production that would impair the precise functioning of the rocket or any of its parts.

It should hardly be surprising that the attempt to force the mass production of a still not fully developed prototype of a fundamentally new weapon like the V-2 rocket created a vast amount of technical difficulties. While Speer's ministry pressed the Mittelwerk management for a rapid increase in the rate of production, the experimental prototypes of the rockets were still exploding, both in tests at Peenemünde and in the military units where they were used for training. They either failed in midflight, or they veered off their flight paths because of a faulty steering system. This situation forced me to make numerous trips to the production installations everywhere in Germany, which provided Mittelwerk with faulty parts for assembly, as well as some trips to Mittelwerk itself" [Stuhlinger and Ordway 1992, pp. 114–15].

One month after the raid on Peenemünde, Himmler appointed SS Brigadier General Hans Kammler to take charge of the construction of the Mittelwerk underground factory for the Ministry of Munitions, although he reported directly to Himmler rather than to Speer. Kammler had already been making a name for himself in the SS hierarchy.

"Kammler's ambition was abnormal even by SS standards; he would build gas chambers in Auschwitz or launching ramps for the flying bombs with equal attention to detail" (Höhne 1969, p. 461). When he came to Peenemünde, Kammler "was already well known in the Nazi hierarchy for his involvement in the design and construction of the crematoria at Auschwitz and the destruction of the Warsaw Ghetto during the previous summer" (Kennedy 1983, p. 24).

Kammler's slave laborers were "housed in tents in a work camp code-named 'Dora,' which was a sub-camp of the infamous Buchenwald extermination camp," and their "wages" were paid to the SS, which operated the camp (Kennedy 1983, p. 23). Most of the work to dig out the underground tunnels was done by hand. Thousands of prisoners died during the construction.

On December 10, 1943, Albert Speer and members of his staff visited Mittelwerk. Speer's own description is graphic: "The conditions for these prisoners were in fact barbarous. ... The sanitary conditions were inadequate, disease rampant; the prisoners were quartered right there in the damp caves, and as a result the mortality among them was extraordinarily high" (Speer 1970, p. 474).

Speer relates an interesting incident from the summer of 1944: "I recall a tour through the Linz steelworks ... where prisoners were moving about freely among other workers. They stood at the machines in the lofty workshops, served as helpers to trained workers, and talked unconstrainedly with the free workers. It was not the SS but army soldiers who were guarding them. ... In contrast to the people in the caves at the Central Works, who were obviously wasting away, these prisoners were well fed" (Speer 1970, p. 479).

The conditions the SS enforced at Mittelwerk and the attempts

Deutsches Museum, München

The raid on Peenemünde finally gave Heinrich Himmler control of part of the rocket program. Production of the V-2 and other equipment was moved into underground tunnels in a complex known as Mittelwerk. The SS used slave laborers to dig the tunnels, killing thousands. In this photo a piece of equipment is being inspected inside a tunnel.

of the Peenemünde specialists to improve them have been described by two of the people who were there:

It was axiomatic that every visitor to Mittelwerk was sworn to strict silence, but, nevertheless, von Braun shared his experience with some of his closer collaborators and friends. "It's hellish," he said. "My first reaction was to speak with one of the SS posts. He responded with unmistakable gruffness that I should mind my own business or I would end up in the same prison attire. I would never have believed that men would have been able to sink so low. But I knew that any attempt to persuade them with arguments about humane considerations would have been totally senseless. These individuals had become so distant from the most fundamental principles of human morality that they were completely unmoved by this showplace of indescribable suffering.

"So I picked up an item, went up to one of the higher SS officers and explained to him that we simply couldn't accept such shoddy work. 'How could you expect a better quality of work,' I said, 'if you don't make sure that your workers remain at least halfway healthy? Our ability to produce workable A-4 rockets depends totally on the work of these people. If they don't get better living and working conditions, we will never attain a better quality of work than we have now. ... The engineers and scientists who are training the prisoners cannot do more than they are already doing. It is your responsibility to improve the physical and mental capabilities of the workers!... If you cannot produce a better product, then your entire project is a failure! Give your workers better conditions and you will achieve better results!' " [Stuhlinger and Ordway 1992, pp. 104–105].

A few weeks after the August raid, long-time von Braun collaborator Arthur Rudolph was sent from Peenemünde to Mittelwerk to organize production of the V-2. As he recalled: "I had the overpowering, awful feeling that I was trapped in a cage like an animal, and that I was caught in the claws of the SS system" (Franklin 1987, p. 76).

Later, Rudolph described the conditions in Mittelwerk:

When I first saw what was going on, I was totally shocked. I tried immediately to speak with one of the SS overseers, but he interrupted me saying, "That's got nothing to do with you. You either keep quiet or you'll be wearing the same uniform." Somewhat later I tried again with a higher-ranking SS guard. "Just take a look at this," I said and showed him some manufactured articles. "This work is not good enough. This equipment does not correspond in the least with our [required] tolerances. It's certainly not ill intent or even sabotage, but simply that the people are over-fatigued and weak. If we don't see to it that the workers remain physically able to work, we will not get an acceptable product and we won't be able to make our quota!"

The results were modest. Conditions were improved slightly

for the prisoners who were working under my direction on the A-4. I don't know if any improvements had been made in other production areas, in particular, for the unfortunate prisoners who had to work in the areas where they were dynamiting" [Stuhlinger and Ordway 1992, p. 104].

The attempts by Rudolph and other technical specialists from Peenemünde to try to improve the conditions of the forced workers on the assembly lines at Mittelwerk have been amply documented by recent statements from former Dora inmates. The media, however, have dishonestly confused the issue of the thousands of forced laborers who died building the Mittelwerk tunnels under Heinrich Himmler's SS, and those whom Arthur Rudolph and the engineers supervised in the tunnel factories.

Although recent writers have ridiculed Arthur Rudolph's statements that he suffered food deprivation as did the prisoners, recently his wife told this author that during the time that he worked underground at Mittelwerk, Arthur Rudolph lost 60 pounds, going from 180 to 120 pounds. She was afraid, she said, that if he had continued to work in the tunnels, he would have died.

The experience of Lt. Milton Hochmuth, an American, is perhaps more "objective" than the recent media accounts. "I was the first intelligence officer to get to the Mittelwerk (V-2 assembly plant)," in 1945, Hochmuth wrote in a letter to Sen. Sam Nunn 40 years later. "I interviewed the head of V-2 assembly—a man named Sawatzki. . . . [Arthur] Rudolph was the *engineer* in charge, and of V-2s only. . . . I was surprised at seeing numbers of apparently well-fed, healthy 'Häftlinge' (slave laborers) and even took the time to talk to one at some length. . . . The next day, I went to a small village where there was a large ammunition loading plant where V-2 warheads were loaded with high explosive. The labor in this plant was also forced labor and I was the first American in the village—troops of neither side had been through.

"These people were quite healthy, robust enough to start looting and strong enough to carry sewing machines, etc. which they were liberating. This confirms the fact that you do not use horrible methods to exact work that requires care and precision."

In regard to the motivation for the case brought against Rudolph by the U.S. Justice Department regarding his activity at the Mittelwerk plant, Hochmuth aptly states: "The Russians never could accept the fact that the von Braun team offered themselves to the United States and refused their very generous offers. It is well within the realm of probability that the Russians are amusing themselves while at the same time punishing a member of the "Paperclip" exodus by planting false information that cannot be substantiated or easily refuted" (Hochmuth 1985).

Not satisfied with having the mass production of the rockets under the control of the SS, Himmler moved to wrest control of *all* rocket activities from the army, most important the research work at Peenemünde. In order to do this, he had to get rid of General Dornberger. On February 21, 1944, Wernher von Braun was called to come to meet personally with Himmler. The SS chief "offered" to give the leader of the rocket team, "vastly more effective support than can those hidebound generals" if he would leave the army and work for the SS.

Von Braun responded: "Herr Reichsführer, I couldn't ask for a better chief than General Dornberger. ... The V-2 is rather like a little flower. In order to flourish, it needs sunshine, a well-proportioned quantity of fertilizer, and a gentle gardener. What I fear you're planning is a big jet of liquid manure! You know that might kill our little flower!" (von Braun 1956, p. 143).

In a 1960s memo for author David Irving to answer Irving's questions about the role of the SS in the rocket program, von Braun stated that Himmler "never dreamed of giving me a free hand. I rather believe that he would have turned me over to Kammler who was his protégé, and Kammler would have used the next opportunity to break my back. ... Himmler was first trying to break up the 'Dornberger-von Braun front,' thus getting Dornberger out first, then taking care of me separately."

Himmler had his own "weapons of retaliation" against the recalcitrant rocket specialists. On March 5, von Braun and a number of colleagues were relaxing at a party in nearby Zinnowitz where the conversation typically turned to space travel. "We worked at least 16 hours a day," Gerhard Reisig recalls, "seven or eight days a week. Sometimes you had to relax. There was a big party and of course we found a way to have some alcohol, thank God, and we got pretty loose with our tongues. 'We want to go into space, and the hell with all this military stuff,' and things like that. There was a Gestapo spy in this party, a lady [dentist], and then it happened" (Reisig 1992).

Ten days later, von Braun, Klaus Riedel, and Helmut Gröttrup were arrested by the Gestapo, and taken to the prison in Stettin. After two weeks, as von Braun later described: "a court of SS officers charged me with statements to the effect that the A-4 was not intended as a weapon of war, that I had space-travel in mind when it was developed, and that I regretted its imminent operational use! That sort of attitude was rather common at Peenemünde, so I felt relatively safe, were that the only accusation with which they could confront me. But they went further and maintained that I kept an aeroplane in readiness to fly to England with important rocket data!" (von Braun 1956, p. 143). The prisoners were only released through threats by Dornberger that without von Braun there would be no A-4 and through the personal intervention of Albert Speer.

There was other retaliation. On August 4, 1944, rocket pioneer Klaus Riedel died in a car accident at Peenemünde. The following is an excerpt of an interview with his wife Irmgard Riedel, which was conducted by Karl Wenzel Guenzel and appears in his 1988 biography of Riedel:

Guenzel: Do you want to tell me something about the death of your husband?

Frau Riedel: Why not? In the evening there was a discussion in the officer's club that one of us would be transferred to Paris. When I woke up at sunrise, Klaus was not there. I called to the plant, but nobody gave me any information. Hans Hueter came and said: "Klaus is at the hospital, he ran into a tree with his car in the restricted area—he is dead." Magnus von Braun [Wernher's brother] tried to calm me down and told me: "You should not speak of murder. That could cost you dearly." ... I only later referred to it as an accident, but only out of fear of making a wrong step. We were, as families of the engineers, always surrounded by Gestapo informers, but none of us knew who they were.

Guenzel: Willy Genthe, the administrative director of the Army Experimental Station at Peenemünde, said under oath on May 12, 1952, that the right axle of the car had been sawed through and that he had seen the sawed place himself.

Frau Riedel: I knew Willy Genthe and his wife very well. Why should such an honorable person lie? Naturally, it was known at the installation that Klaus now and then made remarks against the Nazis and against the SS [Guenzel 1988, p. 113].

On June 6, 1944, the Allied invasion at Normandy signaled the coming German defeat. Hitler increased the pressure to get the V-2 "retaliation weapon." Numerous deadlines were set, followed by numerous delays.

On July 20, 1944, officers of the German Army, including members of the German General Staff, attempted to assassinate Adolf Hitler by placing a bomb in his bunker during a briefing. The bomb exploded, but failed to kill him. The failure of their attempt led to a sweeping purge by Hitler of the German Wehrmacht and murderous retaliation against all oppositional elements. As a result, the SS was given almost complete control over all of the business of the Third Reich.

The 1943 insistence by the Allies that they would accept only an "unconditional surrender" by the Germans, had left little leeway for the German resistance to rally domestic support for a move against Hitler. The roots of that Allied policy are most clearly indicated by the contents of an internal memo written by John Wheeler-Bennett of the British Foreign Office Political Intelligence Department, after the execution of the coup plotters: "We are better off than if the plot of July 20th had succeeded and Hitler had been assassinated ... the present purge is presumably removing from the scene numerous individuals which might have caused us difficulty ... after the defeat of a Nazi Germany. ...

"The Gestapo and the SS have done us an appreciable service in removing a selection of those who would undoubtedly have posed as 'good' Germans after the war. It is to our advantage, therefore, that the purge should continue, since the killing of Germans by Germans will save us from future embarrassments of many kinds" (Kanter 1993, pp. 56–57).

On August 8, 1944, less than one month after the failed attempt on Hitler's life, Kammler was made general commissioner for the A-4 program. "Since 20th July the army departments at home, right up to the Armed Forces High Command itself, had been cowering before the SS and Himmler. Reluctant they might have been, but they yielded," Dornberger stated (Dornberger 1952, p. 222–3). Two weeks before the assassination attempt, Kammler had described Dornberger as a public danger, "who should be court-martialed for

FIGURE 5.2

THE A-4 PRIMER, OR FIBEL

Faced with the task of quickly teaching field troops how to ready, fuel, and launch finicky rockets, Krafft Ehricke found an entertaining method of presentation for the field manual. Eye-catching cartoons were used to illustrate the basic concepts. Here, the description of how a guide beam keeps the missile on track and aimed at the target is illustrated.

Motto : Der Spur des Mädchens folgt der Kanonier.
Der Leitstrahlspur folgt willig das A 4.

Leitstrahl-Bordanlage

Der Jagdhund folgt der Fährte des Wildes. Er weicht nicht rechts und links davon ab.

Das A 4 folgt der Fährte des Leitstrahls. Es weicht von dieser Fährte auch nicht nach rechts oder links ab.

Durch die Leitstrahl-Bodenanlage wird eine elektrische Fährte gelegt:

Die Leitstrahl-Ebene;
sie führt über die Feuerstellung zum Ziel.

Die Leitstrahl-Bordanlage stellt fest, ob sich das A 4 rechts oder links von der Leitstrahlebene befindet.

Sie ruft dann Ruderausschläge hervor; die das A 4 wieder in die Leitstrahlbahn zurückholen.

Dadurch fliegt das A 4 viel genauer auf das Ziel zu, und die seitlichen Abweichungen im Ziel werden geringer.
Auf die Schußweite hat der Leitstrahl keinen Einfluß

Sehr wichtig : Das Leitstrahlverfahren wird nur bei einem Teil der Abschüsse angewandt. Nur in diesen Fällen hast Du die Anlage betriebsbereit zu machen.

Deine Aufgabe ist, die Leitstrahl-Bordanlage zu prüfen, ohne daß der Sender der Leitstrahl-Bodenanlage in Betrieb genommen wird.

Sonst — könnte Dich der Feind anpeilen.
Du verwendest deshalb einen Modellsender, der im B-Gestell des Prüfwagens untergebracht ist.

Source: A4-Fibel, August 1944.

weakening Germany's war effort with a hopeless project" (Irving 1965, p. 238).

On August 31, 1944, Kammler took control over all V-2 deployment. "Dornberger was to continue to be responsible for improving the weapon but . . . was to have no say in combat planning" (Ordway and Sharpe 1979, p. 193). Dornberger, von Braun, and the Peenemünde team knew the V-2 had not been ready for mass production, nor was it now ready for field deployment.

The first V-2s were launched toward Paris on September 6, 1944, but both failed. Three did reach land two days later. But for months, about 10 percent failed and dropped back on the launch pad. An additional 20 percent exploded while ascending, and about 40 percent exploded 2 to 3 miles up. It was later decided that these inflight failures were caused by a weakness in the rocket's structure. Because of their incomplete development, Dornberger described

NASA, Marshall Space Flight Center

V-2 rockets were camouflaged in the field and hidden in tunnels or temporary structures out of the sight of airplane reconnaissance. They were erected upright for firing and had to be fueled with liquid oxygen on site, requiring an entourage of vehicles and equipment—not an ideal technology for a weapon, as Hermann Oberth pointed out when he arrived at Peenemünde.

the V-2s as "flying laboratories," rather than feared weapons of war (Emme 1964, p. 42).

The military effectiveness of the V-2 has been greatly exaggerated. Air Chief Marshal Sir Philip Joubert described the V-2 assault as not a rain "but a drizzle of rockets" (Joubert 1957, p. 114). According to Joubert, the British and American Air Forces lost 450 aircraft and approximately 2,900 pilots and aircrew in the raids on Peenemünde to try to stop the V-2. A lesser number of English civilians—approximately 2,700—lost their lives due to the V-2, from 1,115 rockets, over a period of seven months (Joubert 1957, p. 171). In contrast, Sir Arthur Harris's bombing of Hamburg in July 1943 killed 40,000 civilians over nine days (Irving 1965, p. 88). Peenemünde veteran Gerhard Reisig stated recently: "I was in Dresden when the bombing attack occurred. For me it's a marvel that

I am still walking around. I was in Russia at the front, and it was not half as terrible as what I saw in Dresden" (Reisig 1992).

During the war, 1,675 V-2s fell on Continental Europe. The vast majority of all of the V-2s, 88 percent, were not aimed at London but at the port city of Antwerp, which was key to the logistics supply of the Allies.

In October 1944, von Braun visited his father, who told him of the coming Yalta plan to divide up Germany after the war. The rocket scientists began preparing their flight from the advancing Russian troops and their surrender to the Americans. Chaos reigned. In January 1945, von Braun later reported, "I had ten orders on my desk. Five promised death by firing squad if we moved, and five said I'd be shot if we didn't move" out of Peenemünde (Ordway and Sharpe 1979, p. 254).

To most of the rocket team, there was never any doubt as to what to do after the war. As Dornberger stated: "[B]y far the majority of our scientists and other men were educated with a Western flavor and culture. We loved that. We didn't fit, as Germans, into the slavish picture of the Russians. Our decision to go West had nothing to do with the economy. It was the cultural aspect that was the decisive factor" (Thomas 1961a, p. 59).

On February 17, the first train left Peenemünde with 525 people aboard. A major question for the scientists was what to do with their 10 years of technical data. As Peenemünde engineer Dieter Huzel explained, this was "a treasure trove of documents containing the sum and substance of the whole German rocket development effort. ... These documents were of inestimable value. Whoever inherited them would be able to start in rocketry at that point at which we had left off, with the benefit not only of our accomplishments, but of our mistakes as well—the real ingredients of experience. They represented years of intensive effort in a brand new technology, one which all of us were still convinced, would play a profound role in the future course of human events" (Huzel 1962, p. 151).

Von Braun had been ordered to destroy all classified material. Instead, he instructed Huzel and Bernhard Tessmann, chief designer of Peenemünde's test facilities, to load up trucks with the 14 tons of precious documents, and bury them in an appropriate place, to be retrieved later. This material was later brought to the United States.

Never losing sight of the real aim of their endeavors, artist Gerd de Beek painted the rocket scientists' heroine, The Woman in the Moon, *on the side of an A-4 rocket.*
Deutsches Museum, München

Overall, the A-4 was never the "retaliation weapon" Hitler madly hoped it would be. As Dornberger well knew, there was no chance the V-2 could alter the course of the war.

On the evening of June 12, 1942, just hours before the first A-4 was to be flight tested, Walter Dornberger stated to the team: "The rocket now offers the possibility of using space above the Earth and the atmosphere as a path for travel between the continents. The Peenemünde project is a first step in the direction of the spaceship which will inevitably come" (Klee and Merk 1965, p. 110).

As the rocket scientists, military representatives, and government dignitaries anxiously watched the first flight test of an A-4, however, "the motor ignited with a terrifying roar and the missile rose majestically for about 1 second—until the fuel-feed malfunctioned and allowed it to settle back on its fins. Lacking sufficient stiffness to withstand the shock, the fins crumpled and the A-4 toppled over to disintegrate in a huge explosion" (von Braun 1956, p. 139).

On August 16, the scientists were ready for a second try.

Though the rocket "passed through the dreaded sonic barrier without incident, to the great relief of the engineering staff, for many
aerodynamicists had predicted that the missile would be torn to
pieces by 'transonic phenomena,' it began to oscillate and broke
apart in midair due to a weakness in the hull section."

After this section had been reinforced, the third test took place
on October 3. The rocket left the pad, reached a height of 85
kilometers and a range of 190 kilometers, and the engine cut off at
the programmed 63 seconds. On the front of the A-4, artist Gerd
de Beek had painted the team's mascot—*The Woman in the Moon.*

In a television interview in the early 1980s, Krafft Ehricke
stated:

Those were the "Wild West" days of rocketry and space flight.
You didn't have to be miles away—you could almost stand
beside the rocket. And I was on the roof of one of those high
risers, actually looking down on the launch complex. ... We
all screamed with delight [when the rocket lifted off]. It is hard
to describe what you feel when you stand on the threshold of
a whole new age ... like Columbus or Magellan must have felt.
... This is the feeling many of us had and in me it was absolutely
overwhelming. I almost fell off the roof, I was so excited. ...
We knew the space age had begun.

Dornberger recalled that after the flight, he "saw hurrying towards me Professor Oberth, the originator of modern rocket theory.
... As he shook hands and congratulated me, I could only say that
the day on which we had been privileged to take the first steps into
space must also be a day of success and rejoicing for him, and that
the congratulations should go to him for showing us the way"
(Dornberger 1952, p. 28).

That evening Dornberger spoke to his "small band of intimate
colleagues," and recalls stating: "We have invaded space with our
rocket and for the first time ... have used space as a bridge between
two points on the Earth; we have proved rocket propulsion practicable for space travel. To land, sea, and air may now be added infinite
space as a medium for future intercontinental traffic. This 3rd day
October, 1942, is the first of a new era in transportation, that of
space travel."

Throughout World War II, Wernher von Braun's former ama-

Deutsches Museum, München

The successful launch of an A-4 rocket from Test Stand VII at the northwest corner of Peenemünde. The Baltic Sea is visible in the background.

teur rocket colleague Willy Ley was in New York, having escaped from Nazi Germany in early 1935. He had no access to special or secret information, but he did have years of experience and knowledge about rockets and the people who were building them, and he had a keen political understanding of what must be going on inside Nazi Germany. What others could not understand about the V-2, even with high-level "intelligence sources," he could put together from what he knew—and what he could imagine.

In the 1950s, British space enthusiast Arthur Clarke described to German colleagues his reaction during the war when V-2s started to fall on London: The members of the British Interplanetary Society were excited because they knew that the rocket had been developed, that would open the Space Age when the war ended.

In the spring of 1945, Willy Ley wrote:

> Like Arthur Clarke of the British Interplanetary Society, I found myself torn between two wishes. As far as the war was concerned . . . the better hope was to discount all the German propaganda stories as propaganda. But as far as the future of

Marsha Freeman

There is a model of Test Stand VII at the small museum at Peenemünde. In the center is the assembly building, and to the right is an A-4 rocket on the launch pad.

rocket research was concerned, a 20-ton rocket with a range of 100 miles or better, would be a definite trump card. One would be able to point at that weapon and to say: "See, it can be done. But you didn't believe it!"

That it is not an effective war weapon goes almost without saying. A weapon which lands "at widely scattered points" is only a terror weapon but nothing which can decide a war.

"They must have invented a lightweight, high-capacity fuel pump," Ley surmised. "With such fuel pumps you can . . . even build a spaceship! As a matter of fact, this is no longer in the future, the first spaceship has been built already, only it is not used as such. Yes, we might as well admit it, the V-2 is the first spaceship."

Very perceptively, Ley recognized the political vice his former rocket friends were caught in, though he was a bit more pessimistic than future events would dictate: "It will probably be necessary to re-create V-2 after the war. . . . We cannot hope to take Peenemünde. . . . The Nazis will see to it that everything will be utterly destroyed before we get there. And Himmler, I am sure, has lists of all those who know a good deal about this work. If they escape future Allied bombings, they will be shot by the Gestapo. . . . But the re-creation of these things can be undertaken with confidence after the war, because Peenemünde proved that it can be done" (Ley 1945, p. 122).

Recently, in September 1991, Jan Heitmann, reporting for the British magazine *After the Battle,* visited Peenemünde along with other press and television people, and more than 200 scientists, engineers, technicians, and other former Peenemünde employees, who took advantage of the first opening of some of the grounds to the public, after German reunification.

The Russians had arrived at Peenemünde in May 1945 and proceeded to carry off or destroy what they could of the facilities. Today only the electric power plant, used until 1990 for the East German electric grid, remains intact. Although the Russians tried to blast it out of existence, the basic structure of the critical liquid oxygen plant still stands.

Heitmann called Peenemünde the "cradle of modern rocketry," and he described the willingness with which the scientists at the 1991 reunion discussed their scientific work. He described their wartime work as "being forced upon them by events beyond their control," and stated quite hopefully that, "in October 1992, the survivors of the Peenemünde rocket team will return to commemorate the 50th anniversary of their greatest wartime triumph: the first successful launching of a rocket, which opened the door to space" (Heitmann 1991, p. 25).

Unfortunately, the October 3, 1992, celebration, planned by the Peenemünde veterans to commemorate the first successful flight of a rocket into space, became an international political battle. *The Washington Post* reported four days before the planned celebration that "Germany's aerospace and arms industries and government bowed to foreign demands and dropped plans for a celebration of the 50th anniversary of the first launch of Adolf Hiter's 'wonder weapon,' the V-2 rocket." Marc Fisher, reporting for the paper from Bonn, continued, "The German decision to cancel the event contrasts sharply with the British reaction to a similar controversy last May. Britain then ignored German charges of insensitivity and erected a statue in memory of Arthur 'Bomber' Harris, inventor of the saturation or carpet bombing technique used to level Dresden, killing an estimated 135,000 people" (Fisher 1992).

Reporting from London for *The New York Times,* William E. Schmidt more accurately described the British pique at the Peenemünde celebration as an expression of an "anti-German" campaign being waged in the British press over the economic potential of the reunified Germany (Schmidt 1992).

Capitulating to pressure from the British, the German government withdrew its support for the celebration. Nonetheless, the now-elderly former Peenemünders from Germany, other European nations, and the United States traveled to a place on the Baltic they had not seen for nearly 50 years, and commemorated the beginning of the Space Age.

As Krafft Ehricke wrote many years earlier, "The heritage of Peenemünde is not the war rocket, but the invaluable treasure of basic knowledge about the first steps toward man's keenest adventure—flight to other worlds" (Ehricke 1950, p. 87).

To conquer space was still their goal as the war was ending and the German space pioneers started their journey to America.

CHAPTER VI

Coming to America— Operation Paperclip

On May 2, 1945, Wernher von Braun's younger brother, Magnus, took a bicycle and pedaled down the Kuehgund mountains from Oberjoch in the Tyrol to look for the nearby Americans. In halting English, he explained to Private First Class Frederick Schneikert that he "wanted to see Ike" [General Dwight Eisenhower]. He told the astonished serviceman—an interpreter in the 44th Infantry Division—that he and a group of his compatriots had built the V-2 rocket and wanted to surrender to the Americans. As Schneikert recalled in 1977, "You know what they were doing, don't you? Treason, because Germany was still at war!" (*Herald-Times-Reporter* 1977, p. 6).

Magnus returned to the small group of Peenemünders, with instructions to bring them to the Austrian town of Schattwald later that day. In the group, in addition to the von Braun brothers, were Major General Walter Dornberger, Bernhard Tessmann, Lieutenant Colonel Herbert Axter from Dornberger's staff, Hans Lindberg, and Dieter Huzel. They were taken to Reutte, where they found a few other Peenemünders, and later to the resort area at Garmisch-Partenkirchen, where eventually about 500 men from the rocket program and some of their dependents were gathered and held for interrogation.

While the group was waiting for contracts to be offered to them to go to America to continue their work, the American military was trying to figure out what to do with them. More than a year before, all of the Allied powers knew that the fruits of German science and engineering would likely be the only booty for the victors. But what to do with the specialists—to take the best advan-

NASA, Marshall Space Flight Center

The early May 1945 surrender to the U.S. Army of Wernher von Braun and a small, top-level group from Peenemünde. On the left is Charles L. Stewart from the Army Counterintelligence Corps. Next to him is Lt. Col. Herbert Axter, followed by Dieter Huzel, Wernher von Braun, Magnus von Braun, and Hans Lindberg. Gen. Dornberger was also in this group.

tage of what they knew and what they had developed before and during the war—was not so clear.

Before American troops even entered Germany, teams of scientists had been "drafted" by the armed forces to scour each nation liberated from the Nazis. Their mission was to locate prominent scientists, examine their facilities, and interrogate them for critical information, such as the progress of the German atomic bomb project. A new concept of "intellectual reparations" emerged.

During the war, as Clarence Lasby stated, "Hitler had at his disposal a reservoir of ability unequaled anywhere in the world. During the 20th century, German universities had been the exciting centers of research; German scientists had been the most frequent recipients of the Nobel Prize; and on the very verge of war, German physicists had pioneered the discovery of nuclear fission" (Lasby 1975, p. 12).

Between May 1945 and December 1952, the United States

government imported 642 foreign scientists, engineers, and technicians under several different programs, which all became known
as "Operation Paperclip" (Lasby 1975, p. 5). Of these, the most
well-known group, which insisted that it be kept together as a
team, was made up of the rocket specialists under the leadership
of Wernher von Braun.

When the Allies opened the Western front in March 1945,
more than 3,000 experts followed close behind the troops. However, "almost momentarily the optimistic plans of Washington and
London, which described exploitation with such adjectives as 'or-
derly' and 'systematic' gave way before the realities in the field."
Investigators came to refer to CIOS (the Combined Intelligence
Objectives Subcommittee) as "CHAOS" (Lasby 1975, p. 23). The
British and Americans were racing around Europe to find German
scientists, and the Russians were doing the same.
    In April 1945, using the excuse that dispersing the 450 Peene-
münde refugees from Bleicherode near Nordhausen would make
them less vulnerable to Allied bombing raids, von Braun managed
to remove the technical people from the clutches of Hans Kammler
and the SS. He, Dornberger, and a small group were waiting for the
Americans in Oberjoch.
    Once they arrived at Garmisch-Partenkirchen, von Braun, Dorn-
berger, and other top Peenemünders were interviewed and interrogated numerous times by various specialists, who, for the most part,
had "little or no appreciation of what their captives really knew"
(Ordway and Sharpe 1979, p. 273). At the same time, Major Robert
Staver, a 28-year-old mechanical engineer, was in a race against
time—before the British and then the Russians arrived—to find the
still-dispersed rocket specialists, the V-2 components that had been
left in the Mittelwerk facility, and the tons of technical documents
he knew were hidden.
    To the U.S. scientists, including Jewish Hungarian aerodynami-
cist Theodore von Karman and California Institute of Technology
physicist Fritz Zwicky, there was no doubt as to the value of what
the Germans from Peenemünde were offering. One of the first things
that was decided at the end of May 1945, was to move the Peenemünde wind tunnel in Kochel, with 20 specialists, to the United
States. Von Karman, among others, had recommended to the U.S.

Navy that a small group of the aerodynamicists be brought across the Atlantic.

Dr. Fritz Zwicky participated in the examination of facilities and debriefing of scientists in Europe from April 25 to July 28, 1945. He describes his "extensive work over a two-month period at the Peenemünde supersonic wind tunnel located at Kochel": "Although the SS had given orders that all documents at Kochel be destroyed and the equipment blown up, these orders were not executed. . . . During my whole stay at Kochel the Germans worked for us with great efficiency and in an unusual spirit of cooperation, which was most surprising in view of the fact that, because of procurement difficulties, our team was most of the time unable to deliver to them the lunches which we had promised them as the only compensation for their efforts" (Zwicky 1945).

Zwicky suggested that 50 German experts be taken to the United States along with the wind tunnel: "The author estimates that several years of work could be saved if the services of the German personnel were exploited" (Zwicky 1945, p. 76). When he left Kochel, the Mach 4.4 wind tunnel, built by Dr. Hermann, was being packed up and made ready for shipment (Figure 6.1(a) and 6.1(b).

Zwicky was most excited about "Project A," the Mach 7 to 10 "super-supersonic" wind tunnel the scientists had been planning next. The design was for a 1 meter by 1 meter working section, with power requirements of 57,000 kilowatts, and air fed through 11 compressors. Zwicky wrote in his evaluation that Project A "would have represented a very flexible arrangement inasmuch as various combinations of stages of the compressors could have been used to operate simultaneously different working sections."

He summarizes: "The author *highly recommends* that this Project A be thoroughly studied and that a tunnel of this kind, or one similar, be built in the U.S.A., preferably with the help of the Peenemünde engineers; such a plan, under the present circumstances, would represent a considerable gain in time" (Zwicky 1945, p. 5).

At Garmisch, the process of interrogation was chaotic. Dr. Zwicky reported after his three-month stay in Germany that "there were too many technical teams, both British and American, the members of which conducted interviews helter-skelter without any coordination with others and with little regard to what had been

FIGURE 6.1a
EXPERIMENTAL RESULTS FROM DR. HERMANN'S WIND TUNNEL
During his interrogation by Dr. Zwicky and a team of U.S. scientists, Dr. Rudolf
Hermann shared the results he had obtained during tests in the supersonic wind
tunnel at Peenemünde. These results of aerodynamic tests of rocket models at
supersonic speeds were combined with new research, as the cream of the crop of
the German aerodynamics scientists came to the United States.

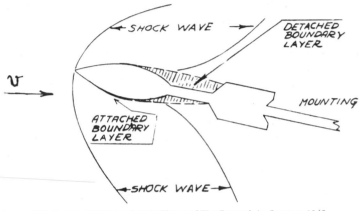

Source: Fritz Zwicky *Report on Certain Phases of War Research in Germany* 1945

FIGURE 6.1b

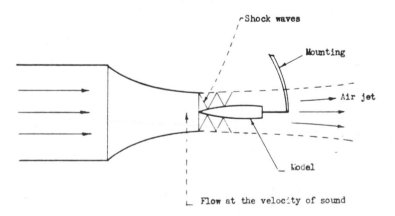

Source: Fritz Zwicky *Report on Certain Phases of War Research in Germany* 1945

previously done. General Dornberger, a very energetic and astute man, and his collaborators on the V-2 ... watched the unexpected and disorderly procedures of the British and American teams with discerning eyes and it became apparent that they considered our missions pretty much of a farce" (Zwicky 1945, p. 174).

It appears that the most useful information obtained was from reports some of the rocket team members were asked to put down on paper. In a document titled "Survey of the Development of Liquid Rockets in Germany and Their Future Prospects," von Braun laid out the vision for the future of a wholly new technology, that would change world history.

> We consider the A-4 stratospheric rocket developed by us (known to the public as V-2) as an intermediate solution conditioned by this war, as a solution which still has certain inherent shortcomings.
>
> We are convinced that a complete mastery of the art of rockets will change conditions in the world in much the same way as did the mastery of aeronautics and that this change will apply both to the civilian and the military aspects of their use. We know on the other hand from our past experience that a complete mastery of the art is only possible if large sums of money are expended on its development and that setbacks and sacrifices will occur, such as was the case in the development of aircraft.

"The development of the 'A-4' required a great number of preliminary scientific investigations," von Braun stressed, including wind tunnel tests "at all ranges of air speeds between 0 and 1,500 meters per second ... test bed investigations on the combustion chamber of the rocket, and on the complete propulsion unit"; development of mechanisms for steering the rocket, and the use of simulators; measuring methods for "plotting the complete flight path of the rocket;" and the investigation of "wireless communication between rocket and ground, etc."

After summarizing the history of the German rocket work before and during Peenemünde, von Braun discussed the "more distant future" for rockets, laying out the work for the next 30 years of the Space Age.

[T]he development of liquid rockets offers in our opinion the following possibilities, some of which are of tremendous significance:

Development of long-range commercial planes and long-range bombers for ultra high speeds. . . .

Construction of multistage piloted rockets, which would reach a maximum speed of over 7,500 meters per second outside the Earth's atmosphere. At such speeds the rocket would not return to Earth, as gravity and centrifugal force would balance each other out. In such a case the rocket would fly along a gravitational trajectory, without any power, around the Earth in the same way as the Moon. . . . The whole of the Earth's surface could be continuously observed from such a rocket. . . . [The crew] could also carry out physical and astronomical research on problems which could only be tackled at that altitude, due to the absence of the atmosphere. . . .

Instead of having a rocket set up an "observation platform" outside the Earth, it would be possible later on to build a station especially for the purpose, and send the components up into the interstellar spaces by means of rockets, to be erected there. . . . The work would be done by men who would float in space, wearing divers suits, and who could move at will in space by means of small rocket propulsion units. . . .

According to a proposal by the German scientist, Professor Oberth an observation station of this type could be equipped with an enormous mirror. . . . This would enable large towns, for instance, to get sunlight during the evening hours. The weather, too, can be influenced by systematic concentration of the Sun's rays on certain regions. Rain could be induced to fall on regions hit by drought, by concentrating the Sun's rays onto distant lakes and seas, and increasing their evaporation.

Finally, von Braun asserted: "When the art of rockets is developed further, it will be possible to go to other planets, first of all to the Moon. The scientific importance of such trips is obvious. In this connection, we see possibilities in the combination of the work done all over the world in the harnessing of atomic energy together with the development of rockets, the consequence of which cannot yet be fully predicted" (von Braun 1945).

On May 17, Walter Dornberger wrote a report at the request

of the interrogation team, summarizing the rocket work at Peene-münde. "Even tho [sic] the first step of advance into space owes its existence to military commands," he wrote, "yet the proof has been obtained contrary to all opposing theories—that space may be mastered for peaceful purposes, and it is only necessary to make certain that the experience once gained is not lost. That state will be first in space which has first the courage to make a clear decision" (Peenemünde East 1945).

It would be 12 more years before the Soviets launched the satellite Sputnik, demonstrating to the United States that it had been folly to ignore von Braun and Dornberger's challenge to an aggressive space effort. It would be 13 years before the United States would even have a civilian space program. But, in 1945, the German space pioneers had already laid out to the Americans what the future decades in space could be.

In a philosophical sidelight to his report on the German war effort, Zwicky warned that

[I]n winning a war the victor may easily fall into the error of thinking that he is superior to the vanquished in every respect. Such unrealistic thinking is largely prevalent in the United States today. ... It should, however, be stressed that another dictator bent on conquering the world may not make enough mistakes to insure his defeat. Stalin, for one, has demonstrated that, even though his regime be inferior in inventiveness and in the means of developing new inventions and producing them in mass, a dictator may win a war through political astuteness. The democracies of the world cannot expect to win every war because a dictator is necessarily going to make more mistakes than they do" (Zwicky 1945, p. 177).

While the Germans were being debriefed and writing reports, the military commands were still trying to decide what to do. Major Staver had found a treasure trove of V-2 parts in the underground factory at Nordhausen. Colonel Holger Toftoy, who was in Paris as the chief of the Ordnance Department of Intelligence Services, agreed with Staver that the components should be moved and "as many as 100 of [the specialists] be evacuated within 30 days." This,

NASA, Marshall Space Flight Center

The 118 Peenemünde scientists and engineers who came to America under Operation Paperclip, with over 400 tons of V-2 components, gave the United States a head start on the Space Age. Here, a modified V-2 rocket is readied for firing from Cape Canaveral in July 1950.

Staver said, must be done "before such time as the U.S. Navy or the British decide to do the same" (Lasby 1975, p. 43).

Colonel Toftoy deployed Major James P. Hamill of Ordnance Technical Intelligence to oversee the operation. Hamill later described the situation: "We knew about the Nordhausen plant long before we took it. The written orders I received indicated that Nordhausen was to be in the Russian zone and that all plans and equipment were to be left for the Soviet [sic]. These orders originated at a very high level. Unofficially and off the record I was told to remove as much material as I could, without making it obvious that we had looted the place" (Akens and Satterfield 1962, p. 29).

On May 25, 1945, Staver was granted permission to move specialists to the American zone, and on June 20, only days before the region had been scheduled to become part of the Russian zone, Staver evacuated the nearly 1,000 Peenemünde personnel and their families that he had located. Four hundred tons of V-2 components were moved to the port at Antwerp, and eventually to White Sands, New Mexico, where they were later assembled and test-flown for the U.S. Army by the Germans.

It was clear to the American scientists "on the ground" that the only way to make full use of the developments in science they had witnessed during their stay in Germany was to bring the scientists, and as many of their facilities, documents, and plans as possible, with them, to the United States. They also knew that of primary importance to the scientists and engineers was that they be able to continue their work.

One debriefing document stated:

> With regard to the 200 qualified engineers and scientists who remained at divisional headquarters, Garmisch-Parten-kirchen, it is obvious that in the course of two to three weeks, it was quite impossible to extract the full story of the rocket weapons or to go deeply into any of the scientific facets of this work. . . . Although up to now most of the staff have been willing to talk, whether or no [sic] this will continue, will depend upon whether one can foster the confidence that the team will not be dispersed and may have the opportunity of continuing their work even if only on a very much reduced scale.
>
> Should authorities wish to obtain the high altitude data as proposed by Professor von Braun or to launch A-4s and A-9s, much time could be saved and risk to material and life avoided by utilizing the unique experience of this team of workers (Figure 6.2) [Peenemünde East 1945].

Back in Washington, more than 3,000 miles away, an army of bureaucrats and policymakers was battling over what should be done with defeated Germany overall, as well as with the cream of the crop of its scientific capability.

The U.S. Department of State "acted quickly to ban German scientist emigration," Lasby reports, preferring instead that they be kept in Germany where they could be "controlled" (Lasby 1975, p. 56). From the beginning, State Department bureaucrats, none of

FIGURE 6.2
THE PILOTED A-9
One of the designs from the advanced planning department at Peenemünde was
this version of an A-9 which carries a pilot, rather than a warhead, in the forward
section. A tricycle landing gear is visible in front of the pilot. While this design
would be useless for military purposes, von Braun promoted development of this
and other technologies during his debriefings by the army after his surrender, in
the hope that a program for space exploration would be on the agenda when he
and his team moved to America.

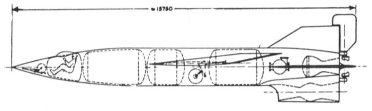

Source: "Peenemünde East Through the Eyes of 500 Detained at Garmish" 1945

whom appears to have met or talked with any of the German scientists, started from the assumption that all German citizens had to
be "de-Nazified," because all Germans shared the "collective guilt"
for the horrors of the Hitler regime.

U.S. Treasury Secretary Henry Morgenthau proposed that Germany be deindustrialized and turned into a "pastoral" agricultural
society. The British attitude toward defeated Germany is epitomized
by a statement by William Malkin, a legal adviser to the British
Foreign Office: "As the war itself has demonstrated, Germany is
an immensely efficient industrial organization, capable of vast and
sustained output. British industry compared miserably with the
German competition. . . . There was no doubt that if German industry
was able to sustain similar efficiency in peacetime, bankrupt Britain
would never recover" (Bower 1987, p. 83).

The U.S. military, still trying to defeat Japan in the Pacific, felt
that time was of the essence if any of the German technology
developed would be useful to end the war and had little patience
for bureaucratic wrangles. The civilian and military scientists and
technical people who were actually debriefing the Germans were
aware of both the contribution they could make, and their disinterest in politics.

Dr. Zwicky observed that "much more valuable work could
have been extracted from the Germans had it not been for our

initial skepticism or outright conviction that as fanatical Nazis they
would not cooperate." The lack of loyalty to any political doctrine
that Zwicky observed, which has been recast recently into a sinister
lack of support for democratic ideals, he attributed to "a severe
lack of education, insight, or even interest of these scientists in
both internal and international politics, sociology, and economics"
(Zwicky 1945, p. 175). This outlook of the Peenemünde scientists
was something perhaps only another scientist could understand.

On June 30, Major General Gladeon M. Barnes, who was chief
of the Technical Division, Office of the Chief of Ordnance in Washington, laid out a plan to transfer a select number of the Peenemünde
group to the United States (Ordway and Sharpe 1979, p. 287). The
War Department decided to back up the technical and military
people, and on July 6, project "Overcast" was established by the
War Department General Staff to make use of "chosen, rare minds."
Overcast was announced on July 20, 1945, and allowed for the
entry of 350 people, "to assist in shortening the Japanese war and
to aid our postwar military research." It stated that "no known or
alleged war criminals should be brought to the United States" and
that the exploitation of the scientists would be "temporary" (Lasby
1975, p. 77).

Colonel Toftoy went to the Pentagon for discussions about his
rocket team, which was still waiting at Garmisch-Partenkirchen. He
asked for 300 rocket experts and received permission to choose
100 to come to America, initially as a "privileged group of prisoners
of war" (Lasby 1975, p. 153).

Meanwhile, the 400 or so German Peenemünde veterans were
still waiting at Garmisch. Dieter Huzel describes what they did to
keep themselves busy while bureaucrats in Washington were trying
to keep them out of the United States, worried that they might be
"war criminals." They put together a lecture series, "at the university
level" which included talks on "thermodynamics, astronomy, nuclear physics, mathematics, ballistics, meteorology, guidance, and
several other topics, even the art of chess playing, followed in due
course by the inevitable chess tournament" (Huzel 1962, p. 192).

"A small orchestra soon formed and gave modest evening con-
certs in the auditorium. ... A theatrical group was formed which
eventually 'produced' four plays, to which everyone had to bring
his own chair." Magnus von Braun and a former soldier adapted
Oscar Wilde's play *The Importance of Being Ernest* to a musical

show, which was enjoyed by the Germans and Americans alike (Ordway and Sharpe 1979, p. 275).

The Peenemünde group held "mass meetings," in which everyone participated. These were addressed by German and American spokesmen, and they all voted on any decisions to be made. Having the opportunity at Garmisch to reflect back on the experience of the war for the first time, Huzel relates, "We realized that there had been a kind of detachment at Peenemünde. The war wasn't real. . . . It was a nuisance somewhere else, a devil conjured up to make an already tough technical task all the more impossible, and which only occasionally brought its wrath down on us.

"What was real were the day-to-day tasks and the long-term engineering goals toward which we built. Looking back from now, 1962, I realize that the Peenemünde engineers' view of the V-2 was little different from the Convair engineer's view of the Atlas, or the Douglas engineer's view of the Thor [two U.S. Intercontinental Ballistic Missiles] today" (Huzel 1962, p. 194).

To prepare for his new life in America, Arthur Rudolph turned to the task of learning English. "There was just one English-German dictionary . . . among all of the 500 people who were in that camp." he said. "The problem was that I could get it only at six o'clock in the morning, and then for only half an hour" (Franklin 1987, p. 96.) So Rudolph set about the job of making his own dictionary, which had 18,000 words in it by the end of his stay at Garmisch.

Finally, in July, Colonel Toftoy joined Major Staver and Dr. Richard Porter from the General Electric Company to decide with von Braun which Germans should be offered six-month contracts in the United States. Toftoy came up with a list of 127 men.

The decision was also announced on July 21 that a select group would be "surrendered" to the British for "Operation Backfire," to launch V-2s in the British zone at Cuxhaven. In mid-August, coincident with Operation Backfire, Dornberger was escorted to London, "for what was alleged to be an interrogation." He was taken to the British War Crimes Investigation unit and told by its commander Lieutenant Colonel Andrew P. Scotland that "since the British could not find Obergruppenfuehrer Kammler for trial at Nuremberg, they were willing to settle on him as a surrogate 'lamb for sacrifice' " (Ordway and Sharpe 1979, p. 303).

Writing his report on the development of the V-2 at Garmisch in 1945, Dornberger stated that, "even tho [sic] the development could be considered as no means closed and I objected to immediate introduction of the weapon, total responsibility and the time of introduction were placed in the hands of the SS after events of 20 July 1944. I was left in the position of technical adviser and in charge of home organization" (Peenemünde East 1945).

"I spent two years after World War II as a prisoner of war in England," Dornberger later related. "They intended at first to hang me for firing missiles on the open city of London. But I did not fire them—Kammler did. I was in charge of manufacturing them and sending them to the front. If they hanged me for that, anyone who developed any war weapon would be risking a similar fate" (Thomas 1961a, p. 59).

The reaction to Operation Backfire was immediate. "The United States was outraged. It had long suspected that Britain was out to scuttle Overcast, which was spiriting away to America scientists whom the British coveted" (Ashman and Wagman 1988, p. 217). After his internment, Dornberger was invited to come to the United States as a consultant to the Air Force and spent two years at Wright-Patterson Air Development Center in Dayton, "where I wrote about 150 reports concerning the future of missiles and rocketry" (Ashman and Wagman 1988, p. 60).

Finally, on September 6, 1945, while at Cuxhaven, Dieter Huzel received a message from Wernher von Braun, that he was on "List 1" of the people to go to the United States. Von Braun, who would be in America himself three weeks later, also stated, "May I take this opportunity to point out that the term 'dependents' in connection with certain rights in the forthcoming work contracts does not include fiancees. If your previously expressed intention to marry are as serious as I obtained the impression they are, I would urge you to make the matter legal prior to your departure.

"Expecting to see you as a well-established husband in America, I remain with best regards" (Huzel 1962, p. 202).

On January 21, 1946, Dieter Huzel sailed for New York with the third group of Peenemünders to head for their new world. Some 20 had decided for personal reasons to remain for the time being in Germany. Dr. Walter Haüssermann told the author, for example, that he was interviewed in 1945 by Dr. John von Neumann in Darmstadt. "At that time I said I was definitely interested to go to the States," he said, "but there was one shortcoming. My wife was, at that time, so sick mainly because of starvation," that before he could leave, he said she "has to spend so much time at the hospital, I am sorry, I cannot accept it. But I'm glad that you came here today and when my wife is in a better situation, if you give me another invitation, I will probably accept it" (Haüssermann 1992).

He was invited again to come to the United States, and arrived in New York on January 2, 1948. In later years, while attending technical meetings with Russian counterparts, Dr. Haüssermann reports that "the Russians asked me often how I came to the States, whether I was forced, or so. For me it was always fun to say, 'I'm the best example that I could say, No, and it was accepted, and when I later said, Yes, it was accepted, too.' They hardly would believe it" (Haüssermann 1992).

Nor was Krafft Ehricke ready to leave for the United States. He hoped that his wife, Ingeborg, was somewhere in Berlin and he traveled on foot from Bavaria to Berlin, where they were reunited. Later, he rejoined the Peenemünde group at Fort Bliss, Texas.

Many of the 20 specialists who were invited to come to the United States but remained in Germany were under contract with the U.S. government there. The rest were in America by January 1946.

As Krafft Ehricke described their situation at Fort Bliss, the German rocket specialists were "prisoners of peace." No provision, only a promise, had been made for their families to join them in their new land. They had been offered no visa that could lead to citizenship, and only a six-month work contract. They were surrounded by military guards and not allowed to go out alone. Similar situations existed for the scientists at Wright Field in Ohio, where the group of aerodynamicists had been relocated. There, the discontent was reaching serious proportions.

As Lasby comments, compared to the army air corps and navy Germans: "The [army] rocket experts were more content. . . . They had arranged their capture and sold their talents to the Americans for a definite purpose: They wanted to continue their exploration of outer space. . . . Their future, as they saw it, was in the United States" (Lasby, 1975, p. 124).

By February 1946, it was clear a new government policy was needed. The vast majority of the Germans had no desire to return to Germany but wanted to become citizens of the United States. Although the war with Japan was over, military and political analysts could see that the end of the war had not produced a lasting peace, but new tensions with the Soviet Union. They also knew that the Russians were in a no-holds-barred competition with the Americans for "intellectual reparations."

A new policy was promulgated that month, to replace Operation Overcast, and a new name was chosen because the code name had been compromised. "Army ordnance offers proposed a substitute. They recalled that when they were selecting rocket experts at Witzenhausen, they had attached a paperclip to the folders of those whom they wished to employ. In this manner, Operation Paperclip became the secret designation of the new program, and the symbol of a new purpose and a new hope" (Lasby 1975, p. 155).

Operation Paperclip increased the quota to 1,000, provided for the transfer of families, and "made an implicit offer of citizenship." As the situation in Europe had changed, it also "took cognizance" of the importance of denying German expertise to the Russians. The Commerce Department promulgated a plan called "National Interest," which called for 50 Paperclip specialists to be brought into U.S. industry and nonprofit institutions of learning and research (Lasby 1975, p. 9).

In early 1946, 165 German scientists had arrived in America, out of the 350 maximum that had been allowed under Project Overcast. More than 100 of those were the rocket specialists. For the next few months, battles raged in the offices of the military commands, the Department of State, the Department of Commerce, the Department of Justice, and the White House as to the constraints that would be placed on the arrival of more Germans, and the offer of citizenship to those already at work in the United States.

In a compromise with the State Department, which was concerned about war crimes and criminals and complained that not enough security precautions were being taken, Paperclip required that the United States "would not employ ardent Nazis, but neither would it discriminate against those who had been 'nominal' party members or who had received awards or honors under the Nazi regime" (Lasby 1975, p. 177).

Few voices had been raised in protest, and very few knew, when German experts were brought to America. The war continued, and their stay was to be temporary. With Operation Paperclip, and the promise and hope to remain and bring their families to their

FIGURE 6.3
**PART OF THE TREASURE TROVE OF DOCUMENTS BROUGHT
FROM GERMANY**
In 1946, U.S. Army personnel at the Ordnance Research and Development Center
at the Aberdeen Proving Grounds in Maryland, with help from Paperclip specialists,
produced an English translation of the February 1945 Peenemünde manual for the
A-4 rocket. It includes a full inventory of the engineering specifications for the
rocket, such as these schematic drawings of the access openings of the missile.

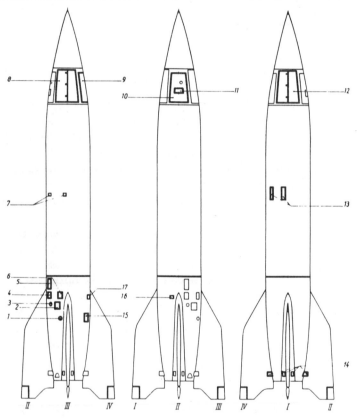

1 Klappe fur Z-Spulventil
2 Klappe z. Druckkontakt u. T-Spulventil
3 Klappe fur Z-Entluftung
4 Klappe fur Z-Betankung
5 Klappe fur A u T-Betankung
6 Klappe fur Druckminderer

7 Entlufterklappen
8 Gerateraumklappe III
9 Gerateraumklappe IV
10 Gerateraumklappe II
11 Federklappe fur Abwurfstecker
12 Gerateraumklappe I

13 Ladeklappen
14 Rudermaschinenklappen
15 Einstiegklappe
16 Klappe fur Zwischenverteiler
17 Klappe z. Durchgreifen d. Pumpe
   u. Einbau d. Schnellschlussreglers

Vom 1. 2. 45

Abb. 28

Source: Manual A-4

new homeland, the project necessarily became more public and both opposition and support were voiced for the first time.

As early as February 1946, the Americans knew that the Russians had a significant rocket program under way. They had resumed the operation of installations in their zone of East Germany, and were moving other "recruited" experts to Russia (Lasby 1975, p. 152). The Americans naively were observing the regulations that had been promulgated earlier, such as the November 1944 Joint Chiefs of Staff Directive 1067, which had imposed a complete ban on scientific research in the U.S. zone, in line with Treasury Secretary Morgenthau's deindustrialization plan. Allied Law Number 25 ordered a complete dismantling and destruction of all German wartime research (Bower 1987, pp. 146–7).

On October 11, 1946, the Soviet Union announced that all scientists in its zone must register with the military government (Bower 1987, p. 147). Late in the night of October 21, 1946, "Russian secret police had surrounded the homes of thousands of scientists and technicians in East Germany. Taking advantage of the helpless sense of terror that thrives in darkness, they roused the inhabitants of each house and told them they were leaving at once for the Soviet Union" (Lasby 1975, p. 178). Estimates vary on how many people were "spirited" away that night, from 15,000 to 40,000. Ninety-two trains were loaded by the Russians (Bar-Zohar 1967, p. 152). More than 400 persons were removed, from Berlin alone.

General Clay "reminded" the Soviets that Gauleiter Fritz Sauckel was hanged at Nuremberg for deportation of civilians for use as forced labor, but this failed to impress them (Lasby 1975, p. 182). Finally, General Eisenhower authorized the reopening of some of the German research centers, largely to prevent the unemployed and displaced scientists in the American zone from taking up the generous offers of the Soviets (Bower 1987, p. 147).

In response to charges that "this country let Russia and Great Britain skim off the cream of Germany's scientific brains and experience" (Huzel 1962, p. 220), the U.S. Army decided on December 4, 1946, to release some information to the press about the Germans settling in America. Some members of the von Braun team were introduced to reporters. That month there was an article in *The El Paso Herald-Post* based on interviews with the scientisits. Its headline read, "German Scientists Plan Re-Fueling Station in Sky en Route to Moon."

By the beginning of 1947, however, the tenor of the coverage was quite different. The liberal press began to give voice to a relatively small but loud opposition. Lasby describes the opposition as "relatively short-lived" and "almost exclusively an outbreak of American liberalism" (Lasby 1975, p. 191). *The Daily Worker,* newspaper of the Communist Party, U.S.A., predictably described the Germans as "back at their old game" of designing weapons. The paper studiously neglected to mention how the other superpower was employing the Germans it had kidnapped.

At the end of December 1946, a group of 40 individuals, including Albert Einstein, A. Philip Randolph, and Rabbi Stephen S. Wise, sent a telegram to President Truman to register their "profound concern" over the character of the German scientists. The letter, released to the press, read in part:

> We hold these individuals to be potentially dangerous carriers of racial and religious hatred. Their former eminence as Nazi Party members and supporters raises the issue of their fitness to become American citizens or hold key positions in American industrial, scientific, and educational institutions. If it is deemed imperative to utilize these individuals in this country we earnestly petition you to make sure that they will not be granted permanent residence or citizenship in the United States with the opportunity which that would afford of inculcating those antidemocratic doctrines which seek to undermine and destroy our national unity [(Lasby 1975, p. 193].

Did any of these 40 prominent individuals meet with and talk with any of the rocket specialists—the group most identified with Operation Paperclip? No. Was there any documentation to support their opinion that these scientists were "eminent" Nazi Party members, or "carriers of racial and religious hatred"? No. These accusations echoed the "concerns" of some State Department employees, which had somehow been leaked to the public.

Some time later, the liberal *New Republic* magazine published an article by Seymour Nagan, denouncing the German scientists as a "great and growing threat to national security" because U.S. military secrets would be made available "to the eyes and ears of Nazis." The article also quoted two physicists who advised that the Germans

Alabama Space & Rocket Center

That concerns by scientists and others in the United States that the German space pioneers would be "dangerous carriers of racial and religious hatred," were unfounded is confirmed by the activities of the Germans who settled in Huntsville, Alabama. This is an aerial view of the Space and Rocket Center in Huntsville, which was lobbied for by Wernher von Braun.

"were equivalent to high-class radio hams, or at best clever military engineers" (Lasby 1975, p. 194).

The Society for the Prevention of World War III added its voice to the protest. This group of "several thousand members" had been formed in 1944, and was dedicated to preventing all future wars by "whittling down Germany's war potential in all fields of activity" (Lasby 1975, p. 195). The society started from the premise, as did the Department of State, "that there was no distinction between 'Nazis' and 'the German people'." This group of self-appointed "peacemakers" jumped into the fray over the German scientists in 1947. They ignored the possibility that World War III might be caused not by Nazis but by the Soviet Union's taking over Eastern Europe under the Yalta plan.

The so-called National Conference on the German Problem, whose membership overlapped the Society for the Prevention of World War III included Henry Morgenthau, Jr. and "liberal internationalists" such as Edgar Ansel Mowrer, active in the United Nations. The group met in New York in the spring of 1947 at the invitation of Eleanor Roosevelt. It also lobbied for crippling the German economy and "punishing a great mass of war criminals" (Lasby 1975, p. 196).

Rabbi Stephen Wise, the president of the American Jewish Congress, was examining the records and pasts not only of some of the German specialists but also of their wives and families. A few of the specific cases documented might have warranted some investigation. But in an April 1947 study of Paperclip by the American Jewish Congress for Senator Homer Ferguson of Michigan, the sweeping statement was made that "all of these men actively participated in the Nazi war effort" and that "all have been exposed to the un-American propositions of 'master race' and 'Aryan superiority' which they have absorbed in varying degrees' " (Lasby 1975, p. 197).

As Lasby documents, a "variety of other organizations, each with its particular interest in the civil rights or civil liberties field, supported the general effort to wreck Paperclip" (Lasby 1975, p. 197). He concludes, however, that "although these disturbed liberals made known their dislike of Paperclip to the American public and its officials, they exerted little influence on either" (Lasby 1975, p. 198).

The most powerful opposition to Operation Paperclip came from sections of the scientific community. The leading banner was carried by the Federation of American Scientists (FAS). The federation was organized primarily by the nuclear scientists who had participated in the wartime U.S. Manhattan Project drive to develop an atom bomb. They had "still not recovered from the shock of the many thousands killed by the dropping of the atomic bomb over Hiroshima and Nagasaki, for which they felt morally responsible," French writer Michel Bar-Zohar observed in his 1967 book, *The Hunt for German Scientists* (Bar-Zohar 1967, p. 142).

The federation lobbied to establish international control over atomic energy development through the United Nations, on order to prevent any other nations from having access to this new technology. Their unofficial organ, *Bulletin of the Atomic Scientists,* supported international control, even to the extent of "Security Through the Sacrifice of Sovereignty" (Barnard 1946, pp. 30–31). Articles with this viewpoint were printed by New Dark Age advocate Bertrand Russell, anthropologist Gregory Bateson, and nuclear-control diplomat Bernard Baruch.

By early 1947, it was clear that this campaign had failed. The Soviet Union rejected an international nuclear control plan. Lasby reports that "the Soviet action deprived the FAS of a definite program and sense of direction, and led to pessimism, uncertainty, disagreement, and waning enthusiasm among its members" (Lasby 1975, p. 199). The federation then turned its attention to Operation Paperclip. In addition to insisting on the "collective guilt" of all Germans in order to make their case against the scientists, the scientists' work was denigrated as part of the attack.

Writing in 1960, General Curtis LeMay asserted, "It so happened that an effective majority of our scientists didn't want [the Germans] around. Not so unbelievable, as it seems. Frankly, I think that many of our scientists were frightened by their own deficiencies. They didn't welcome any German competition" (Lasby 1975, p. 109).

A letter printed in the January 1947 *Bulletin of the Atomic Scientists* by respected emigré physicist Hans Bethe raised a series of questions about Operation Paperclip, including whether it was prudent to bring the Germans here in light of the fact that "many of them, probably the majority, were die-hard Nazis, or, at least worked whole-heartedly with the Nazis." He asked "whether the war had been fought to "allow Nazi ideology to creep into our educational and scientific institutions by the back door?" He warned against "the exaggerated appraisal of their scientific achievements and abilities," and asserted that "willingly or unwillingly they will be advocates of Nazi methods and ideology" (Bethe and Sack 1947, p. 65).

In a refreshing display of fairness, the *Bulletin* also printed a companion letter by Samuel Goudsmit, who had led the Alsos mission in Europe to look for German nuclear scientists. Goudsmit, whose parents had died under the Nazis, certainly "knew more about the motives and activities of the Germans than any American scientist," and wisely counseled, that "the problem was more com-

Marsha Freeman

Every year thousands of children and young adults come to Space Camp at the Space & Rocket Center to learn the basics of astronautics and try their hand at simulators and training equipment for space missions. The center boasts a complete Space Shuttle assembly, seen here, made up of pieces of flight hardware from the NASA program.

plex than the opponents seemed to realize" (Goudsmit 1947, p. 64).

"It is sad indeed to observe that the few surviving victims of Nazism are mentally and morally starving in Displaced Persons Camps, while these 'Heil' shouting scientists are offered privileged positions in our country," Goudsmit wrote. But if the United States "had made the serious mistake of putting our principal technical efforts upon super rockets instead of radar and nuclear research, we too would have produced a V-2-like weapon and probably lost the war" (Goudsmit 1947, p. 67).

"If these imported scientists are gradually absorbed in places in accordance with their true ability and personality, they can fill a need," he counseled. He concluded that the Germans "on the whole would be quite harmless."

On February 1, 1947, the National Council of the Federation of American Scientists prepared a letter to President Harry Truman asking him to deny citizenship to the Germans. It also complained that during the period of international adjustment after the war, the program would "cast doubt on the nation's sincerity toward the United Nations" (Lasby 1975, p. 201). Federation Executive Secretary William Higinbotham, however, had second thoughts about the entire offensive. At a meeting in May, Higinbotham reported that the majority of the organization's membership "looked upon the statement as a contribution to reviving wartime hatreds and an expression of fear of foreign competition" (Lasby 1975, p. 204). The issue was quietly dropped, as more than a few people noticed that the international political situation was quickly deteriorating and that the security threat to the United States was hardly from German scientists.

One response to the Federation of American Scientists offensive appeared in a newspaper editorial on March 27, requesting that the group first amend its protest to declare that Russia's importation of hundreds of German scientists to work in Soviet laboratories was an affront to the American people" (Huzel 1962, p. 221). Indeed, the sympathy leading members of the federation felt toward the Soviet political system certainly, at best, blinded them to the reality of where the threat of the next war would come from, and what the Soviets were doing to prepare for it.

Secretary of War Robert Patterson's reaction to the federation letter to President Truman, featured the observation that "a great many German scientists had been taken by the Russians, and their protest makes no mention of this fact" (Lasby 1975, p. 206).

There was another important element in the fight over Operation Paperclip, which Lasby states quite clearly: Those in charge of Paperclip

judged each case individually after having sifted the apparent motives for membership and degree of political dedication. They rejected those who were war criminals, ardent believers in National Socialism, and profiteers from and notorious supporters of the Party. They did not reject those who were "nominal" members or who had accepted rewards for their scientific contributions to the war effort.

Most of the opponents, on the other hand, gave no credence to the human dilemma of those who lived under the Nazi dictatorship. They established resistance to Hitler—and possible martyrdom—as the standard of judgment, and denounced those who had failed to meet its requirements as unworthy of American citizenship [Lasby 1975, p. 211].

By these standards, of course, virtually no German citizen would have been allowed to emigrate to the United States, since most of the German resistance fighters had been killed by the Nazis, largely because they received no support from the Allies.

If one deplores the fact that more German citizens were not risking their lives in the resistance, to be honest, one must also apply the same standards to American citizens of today. Supposedly we have learned the lessons of the Holocaust, and we do not live in a police state where the Gestapo can put us in a concentration camp if we oppose the regime in power. Yet how many do nothing to stop the slaughter of innocent millions through starvation and disease in Africa, or how many tolerate American paralysis in dealing with the Serbian genocide in the former Yugoslavia? In both cases, this slaughter is not hidden, but on view every evening on television.

German scientists who took no public stand against Hitler may be criticized as morally flawed or cowardly, but one cannot, therefore, assume that they supported the evil of the regime or were "ardent Nazis." For the most part, the German rocket specialists concentrated on their research in isolation from the horror of the war and considered themselves to be apolitical.

Cornell University Professor Philip Morrison had claimed that the scientific community in the United States would not easily welcome those who "worked for the cause of Himmler and Auschwitz, for the burners of books and the takers of hostages." German Nobel Laureate Max von Laue, whose open opposition to the Nazi regime was well known, rejoined that "if one or other among the German scientists found it possible during the war to avoid being drawn with his work into the maelstrom, it is not allowable that it was so for all" (Lasby 1975, p. 212).

The Department of the Army employed 210 German specialists under Paperclip out of a total of 573 by the time Operation Paperclip ended in 1952, and of that only 132 were located at Fort Bliss in the rocket program. But that team was certainly, as Lasby describes, "a lightning rod for domestic critics" (Lasby 1975, p. 252). This was true because they were the largest group of Germans in any single program, they functioned not as individuals but as a team, and, most important, because under the leadership of Wernher von Braun, they knew why they were here, what they wanted to accomplish, and were perfectly willing to lobby for their space program with anyone who would listen.

Over the past decade, there has been the most dishonest attempt to rewrite history to try to give support to the claims of the U.S. Justice Department's Office of Special Investigations that "ardent Nazis" and war criminals who should never have been allowed to enter the United States came in under Operation Paperclip. These recent histories, including Linda Hunt's book *Secret Agenda* and Tom Bower's *The Paperclip Conspiracy,* not only repeat unsupported allegations but selectively ignore all of the events that nullify their politically motivated arguments.

The allegations and threats leveled against Arthur Rudolph are only the most recent accusations that have been made against the rocket team. There were attempts to discredit the Germans, and specifically Wernher von Braun, as early as the beginning of the 1960s, by East bloc intelligence agents such as scribbler Julius Mader, a retainer of East Germany's Stasi.

It is not surprising that the Soviets, fearing the likelihood that the Americans would beat them in a protracted space race, would circulate wild accusations against the Germans in the early 1960s, claiming these were "Hitler's Nazi scientists." It is, therefore, also not surprising that the legal cases brought against the targets of the Office of Special Investigations have depended, to a large extent, on material from East bloc files and testimony from citizens under the yoke of the Soviets.

Linda Hunt's 1991 book, *Secret Agenda,* is the most recent and most perfidious rendition of Operation Paperclip. Since rocket pioneer Arthur Rudolph is pictured on the cover of Hunt's book with a swastika, one assumes some new information will be revealed regarding his involvement in the wartime production of the V-2 rocket, and that this new evidence will convince the reader, in hindsight, that this man, along with hundreds of his colleagues, should never have been allowed into the United States.

It is undeniable, and not contested here, that a few people with undesirable records were brought into the United States, both for their technical and intelligence expertise and because they would otherwise have ended up—many against their will—working for the Soviets. Hunt dismisses the threat that the Soviets would have captured the scientists as an unserious "excuse" for bringing the Germans here, even though for more than 30 years the Soviet kidnapping of thousands of German scientists has been well known and in the public record.

To put the German space pioneers in the same category as the "Nazi doctors" is quite incredible. In the most inflammatory fallacy of composition, Hunt asks in her book: "Why have we made heroes of men who assisted in one of the greatest evils in modern history? Some were unquestionably highly qualified scientists. Wernher von Braun, for example, was a brilliant man who contributed immeasurably to American missile and space programs. But he was also a Nazi collaborator. What price did we ultimately pay to tap the Germans' knowledge? The most common response is that it got us to the Moon. But how do you balance that against murder," Hunt says, implying Wernher von Braun had been accused of such crimes (Hunt 1991, p. 267).

Unlike Hunt, von Braun had experienced the Nazi regime and had as well an understanding of the communist system. In August 1949, England extended to him "one of the highest tributes to be given a man in his field—he was invited to become an Honorary Fellow of the British Interplanetary Society." Accepting the honor, von Braun likened living under the threat of the Nazi secret police to the plight of the "700 million people [who] are living under communist rule," undoubtedly giving some heartburn to the KGB (Thomas 1960, p. 133).

Hunt makes the incredible claim that Operation Paperclip was a *Soviet* operation to infiltrate Nazis into American society to undermine its democratic ideals! She does not explain, however, why Operation Paperclip and the German-American space pioneers have been under *attack* by the Soviets since the end of the war. But even if one could believe that the Soviets were behind Operation Paperclip (for which Hunt presents no evidence), or that the people who entered the United States were "ardent Nazis," Linda Hunt wrote her book 45 years after the fact. What is the record? Did this devious plan work? Have the Germans been spreading antidemocratic ideology, as the American scientists feared they would at the time and as Linda Hunt today still asserts? What did the Germans do in America?

Actually, they did something much more heinous—from the

Soviet standpoint. In 1950, the majority of the group of more than 100 German space pioneers arrived in Huntsville, Alabama to work for the Army Ballistic Missile Agency. There, they designed and tested the medium-range missiles that were deployed by the North Atlantic Treaty Organization (NATO) to protect Western Europe from an expanding Soviet empire. This is the activity by the Germans that enraged the Soviets and motivated the attacks on them from East bloc intelligence agencies and left-wing groups in the United States.

When the Germans arrived in Huntsville, it had fewer than 15,000 residents. It was known as the watercress capital of the country and most of its residents picked cotton. Today, due largely to the efforts of Wernher von Braun and the Germans, it has the largest space museum in the country, an astronomy observatory, a symphony orchestra, a performing arts theater, an art museum, and the finest rocket research and testing laboratory of any civilian space program in the world, at the NASA Marshall Space Flight Center. This team of scientists and engineers who built the rockets that took American astronauts to the Moon, since 1948 have worked on the programs to take mankind to Mars. "Nazi" ideology? *German,* perhaps, but when did the *Nazis* ever formulate a space program?

To give Hunt the benefit of the doubt, one might suppose that perhaps she had never been to Huntsville, Alabama, or never had the opportunity to meet and talk with any of the German space pioneers. But I personally met her in Huntsville in the spring of 1985 at a press conference, which incident and circumstances she describes in her libelous book, accusing this author, who is Jewish, of being anti-Semitic for defending Arthur Rudolph.

How then does Hunt continue to charge that some of these men were "ardent Nazis?" Her definition is strictly formal—they were early members of the Nazi Party, for example. Of course, this definition would make millions of Germans "ardent Nazis" without cause. Does such a criterion make millions of Communist Party members in the former Soviet Union "communists"? Ms. Hunt does not seem to know very much about living under totalitarian regimes.

Why, Wernher von Braun, himself, she reports, was a major in the SS—hardly a new revelation but a very well-known fact. Hunt neglects to mention, however, the other well-known fact about "SS Major" Wernher von Braun: that he was arrested by the SS and thrown into prison for "sabotaging the war effort." Hunt does not

Marsha Freeman

In March of 1985, the German space pioneers, pictured here, gathered for a reunion in Huntsville, Alabama. They posed before a Saturn V rocket, which they were instrumental in developing, at the Space & Rocket Center. To the left, holding the photograph of von Braun, is Dr. Eberhard Rees who became the director of the Marshall Space Flight Center following Wernher von Braun. To the right, is Konrad Dannenberg, who has played an important role in the Space Camp at the center. Linda Hunt was present for the press conference held during the reunion.

tell us how she would classify someone as an "ardent Nazi" who had been arrested by the SS for sabotage.

It is a serious accusation to say someone is a "Nazi." Most of the chapters of Hunt's book are devoted to recounting in gross detail the horrible human experiments conducted on inmates of concentration camps by medical doctors; and indeed, some of these "Nazi doctors" were brought to the United States after the war. However, none of their photographs appear on the cover of Hunt's book.

Arthur Rudolph's photograph does.

After Wernher von Braun died in mid-1977, the surviving members of the team of German space pioneers became vulnerable targets for "Nazi-scientist" hunters and writers such as Linda Hunt, who had been initially organized by the Soviets and Communist Party, U.S.A. members and "fellow travelers" soon after the war.

The attacks on the Germans come full circle from the 1940s to today—Linda Hunt's first writing on the "Nazi" Arthur Rudolph appeared in the *Bulletin of the Atomic Scientists* in 1985, which had led the campaign against Operation Paperclip nearly 40 years before. In 1982, Arthur Rudolph, who had been the manager for the Pershing intermediate range missile developed by the army and the project manager for NASA's Saturn Moon rocket, was interrogated, without a lawyer present, by attorneys from the Justice Department's Office of Special Investigations.

He was told that the government possessed evidence, as well as witnesses, who could testify to atrocities he supposedly committed while production manager at the war-time underground Nordhausen V-2 plant. He was not aware that the "evidence" and "witnesses" had been provided from KGB and East German Stasi intelligence sources.

In his late 70s, in poor health, and living in retirement in California isolated from most of his colleages still in Huntsville, Rudolph decided that it was better to take the "deal" the OSI was offering—quietly leave the United States and relinquish his American citizenship—rather than stand trial. Thus, the OSI won this "victory" by default.

In order to regain German citizenship, Arthur Rudolph had to undergo a thorough investigation by the German government. After more than a year, the German government announced that it could find no evidence or witnesses that would have made a credible case against the space pioneer, and it granted him German citizenship. Since he had been cleared of any charges against him, Rudolph launched a legal suit in the United States in February 1992 to fight to regain his American citizenship.

The legacy of what the German space pioneers brought to the United States, which included European culture and classical education along with tons of technical documents, and what they built since they have been in America, stands on its own. Out of the Operation Paperclip group, 126 were listed in *American Men of Science* by 1960 (Lasby 1975, p. 288).

The way the Germans themselves viewed the road they had traveled from their wartime rocket research to the United States has been eloquently expressed by Dieter Huzel. When the first

William Jones
Arthur Rudolph with the author in his home in Hamburg, Germany in December 1992. Rudolph is an "American in exile," fighting to regain his American citizenship and return to the United States.

Redstone missile was flight-tested, he wrote, "the ring was closed. It had started in Peenemünde and was now continuing at Cape Canaveral. When later generations look back on this period, they will see the two events, the two locations, as one, just as a distant double star appears as a single light. Indeed, leaving Peenemünde was not the end of a road but, in truth, the beginning of the long, long road to the stars" (Huzel 1962, p. 230).

The Space Age Begins!

By the time the German space pioneers arrived in America, they had faced numerous difficulties. Many had done rocket experiments through an economic depression, the Nazi regime, and a world war. The frustration and delays they met in the United States, however, would be even greater.

When Wernher von Braun and his collaborators arrived in the United States, the country was tired of weapons and war. Military budgets were being cut and military forces demobilized. They spent their first few years reassembling and launching old V-2s from Germany, in a desolate desert area that bore no resemblance, physically or culturally, to their homeland.

The civilian space program did not yet exist. At times, von Braun and the others doubted that they would ever get the resources needed to develop the rocket technologies of the war years and aim for the stars. But they did not despair.

This period of frustration ended in October 1957, when the U.S.S.R. shocked and excited the world with the launching of Sputnik, the first satellite. The official Space Age had begun and the Germans were ready for it.

The first Germans arrived at the U.S. Army White Sands Proving Ground in New Mexico in October 1945. White Sands had been chosen for its desolation and nearby mountains, which were used as sites for radar stations to track rocket launches (Figure 7.1). About 35 members of the Peenemünde group moved to White Sands. The rest lived and worked at Fort Bliss, Texas, 50 miles from the proving ground.

FIGURE 7.1
THE WHITE SANDS PROVING GROUND IN NEW MEXICO
Because it is surrounded by mountains and isloated from population centers, the
U.S. Army chose this site for the Hermes Project to fire captured V-2 missiles. While
some of the team was stationed at White Sands, the bulk of the Germans were at
Fort Bliss near El Paso, Texas.

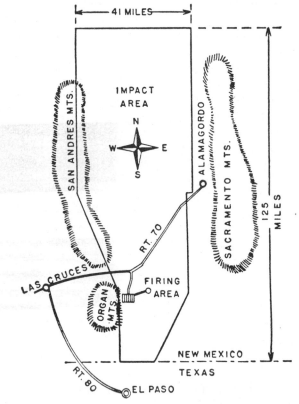

Source: Willy Ley *Rockets, Missiles, and Space Travel* (New York: The Viking Press, 1957).

    To entertain themselves, in December 1945, Wernher's brother
Magnus von Braun "produced a kind of teutonic 'Christmas
Carol....' [which] described an event that would take place in the
distant year 2000—*Man's first flight into space* ... Observing the
hustle and bustle of men and machines around a huge rocket there
in the desert was a curious figure that most people seemed to ignore.
Constantly in the way was an old man, bent with age and supporting

himself shakily on a cane. It was 88-year-old Wernher von Braun, who had lived to see his dream come true" (Ordway and Sharpe 1979, p. 346).

The Germans were brought to White Sands to work on the Hermes Project to launch captured V-2s, which had been initiated on November 15, 1944. But as chief of the rocket branch for Army Ordnance, General Holger Toftoy described the situation: "There was a spirit of unhappiness [at Fort Bliss]. . . . They were separated from their families, who needed food and vitamins." After some wrangling with the bureaucracy, Toftoy arranged for the Germans to send packages to their dependents still in Germany (Henry 1958).

> But . . . they wanted their families with them. So once more I took off for Germany to see what I could do. . . . I got proper living quarters for the families, as well as food, fuel, and medical attention. Finally I got them over here and the German families were reunited.

The Germans were most fortunate that General Toftoy, like Germany's Peenemünde General Walter Dornberger before him and General John Medaris after him, had both a deep appreciation of the talent, creative imagination, and scientific experience of these individuals and a concern for their well-being. Although there was no approved civilian space program, these commanding officers encouraged the creative spirit of the Germans and looked the other way when unapproved "futures" projects were quietly undertaken. They protected the German rocket team from bureaucrats who had little appreciation of their capabilities, were suspicious about their activities, and, worst of all, had no vision of mankind's future.

On May 10, 1946, there was a demonstration of the V-2 rocket for the press, and Willy Ley finally had the opportunity to witness the preparation and launch of the rocket (Ley 1957a, p. 257). Later, he would recount in books what it was like to launch a V-2.

In 1949, North American Aviation began to make copies of V-2 engines for the army's Redstone missile, which closely resembled the V-2. Peenemünde veterans Walter Riedel and Gerhard Heller "spent months at the plant of North American Aviation in California, where they assisted fledgling American propulsion engineers in the fundamentals of rocket engine design and fabrication" (Ordway and Sharpe 1979, p. 351). Later, Dieter Huzel and others were employed

The German space pioneers were quite fortunate that their initial activity in the United States was under the supervision of Gen. Holger Toftoy, seen here holding a rocket model in discussion with Hermann Oberth. To the right of Oberth is Peenemünde veteran Dr. Ernst Stuhlinger.

by North American to "transfer the technology" of the V-2 propulsion systems to the new U.S. aerospace industry (Winter 1990, p. 76). Huzel translated into English technical memoranda on propulsion systems that had been written by propulsion expert Dr. Walter Thiel at Peenemünde, which he brought with him.

This early work on rocket engines at North American, "played an unrecognized but enormous role in the subsequent development of American's next generation of large liquid-fuel rocket engines," (Winter 1990, p. 53). A decade later, North American made the engines for the Saturn V rocket that carried American astronauts to the Moon. In 1955, North American's rocket division was named Rocketdyne. Today, Rocketdyne is a division of Rockwell, the company that builds the engines for the Space Shuttle.

The most gratifying work the Germans did in New Mexico involved a new field of discovery—space science. As reviewed in

Chapter IV, German physicist Erik Regener's work to design and build scientific instruments for upper atmospheric research using the V-2 was known to American scientists during the war. Gerard P. Kuiper, an astronomer at the Yerkes Observatory in Williams Bay, Wisconsin, went to Germany and visited Regener on "several occasions in September and October 1945." Upon his return to the United States, Kuiper wrote a report on Regener's work, which was circulated throughout the American astronomical community. Kuiper was very impressed with the scientific instruments that had been designed and built (DeVorkin 1992, p. 51).

Historian David DeVorkin reports that

at least two of Regener's instruments reached Aberdeen [Proving Ground] in December 1945 and were brought to the attention of prospective American rocket scientists during a meeting at the Naval Research Laboratory on January 16, 1946. ... The very fact of Regener's attempt stimulated some early excitement and proposals, even though specific plans were already afoot in the United States well before details of Regener's instruments became available [DeVorkin 1992, p. 53].

Regener never came to the United States, but his "scientific agenda would be duplicated here at the Naval Research Laboratory and the Applied Physics Laboratory, and by the army at Aberdeen, by the Signal Corps ... and a number of military contractors on university campuses" (DeVorkin 1992, p. 53).

From the beginning of Project Hermes, General Toftoy promoted a five-year research program with the V-2s rather than an approach to launch the limited number of rockets as quickly as possible. Under this project to reconstruct and launch the rockets to enable the transfer of technology to U.S. industry, Toftoy "equated the scientific work with the ballistic missile development" (DeVorkin 1992, p. 123). He organized the program so that the needs of the new space scientists were met, even if this meant delaying launches because instruments were not ready.

Dr. James van Allen was the chairman of the V-2 Rocket Panel, later renamed the Rocket and Satellite Research Panel, which coordinated the experiments on the V-2s. He was energetically supported

NASA, Marshall Space Flight Center

Under Project Hermes, 67 V-2s were launched and the technology trans-
ferred to the American team learning about rockets. Pictured here is a
launch at White Sands on August 22, 1951. This rocket attained a 132-
mile altitude, the highest ever reached by a V-2.

by General Toftoy. In 1961, Shirley Thomas wrote that van Allen,
"has stated that [General] Toftoy is the person most responsible for
establishing this nation's high altitude research effort—adding the
comment that it is somewhat rare for such a proposal to come from
a military man" (Thomas 1961b, p. 223).

DeVorkin draws the parallel between German and American
upper-atmospheric research by stating, "Both the American and
German plans were conducted wholly within a military context
and both were led by civilian scientists . . . instigated by von Braun
at Peenemünde or by Toftoy at the Pentagon" (DeVorkin 1992, p.
345).

"The list of high-altitude experiments conducted in White Sands
on V-2 rockets is impressive," report von Braun's biographers:

In total there were 223 different experiments, 38 which measured cosmic radiation, 32 for observing the Sun, 32 for measuring the ionosphere, 25 for determining the temperature profile of the atmosphere, 25 for measuring its pressure profile, and 19 to investigate its composition. During 18 flights, photographs of the Earth's surface had been taken [Stuhlinger and Ordway 1992, p. 165].

As Ernst Stuhlinger reports,

instrumented V-2s had shed new light on the upper atmosphere and borders of space and had made possible the discovery of solar X-rays, measurements of the Sun's far ultraviolet spectrum, clarification of the nature and origin of various layers of the ionosphere, and accurate measurements of atmospheric composition, temperature, density, and pressure [Ordway and Liebermann 1992, p. 119].

Also performed at White Sands were the first experiments in space biology. On December 17, 1946, a V-2 carried a package of fungus spores, used to determine the effect of cosmic rays on living tissue. Fruit flies, corn seeds, and a mouse were also rocketed into space. In 1949, four Rhesus monkeys, all named Albert, were flown in specially designed pressure capsules, "which were the precursors of the manned cabins used more than two decades later" (Winter 1990, p. 54).

When Project Hermes ended in June 1951, 67 V-2 rockets had been constructed, tested, and launched. The final report on Project Hermes states:

This group was undoubtedly selected with care since it included representatives of almost all phases of German V-2 activities. Among these were scientists, engineers, technicians and manufacturing personnel. . . . [Their] experience was passed on to GE personnel as rapidly as circumstances permitted. The cooperation was excellent [General Electric Company 1952].

The new Space Age was beginning to outgrow the somewhat temporary quarters it had been allocated. Kurt Debus reports that

Since the pace of activities at Fort Bliss cramped the limited facilities such as chemical, material and electronic laboratories, some unidentified miscreants under cover of darkness picked up a quarter mile of fence one night and moved it sufficiently to take in more acreage [Debus 1973, p. 19].

But General Toftoy knew that more than moving a fence would be necessary. In 1948, he urged the consolidation of rocket research under the auspices of the U.S. Army with new facilities made available. Toftoy had more than missiles in mind. In a May 8, 1948, interview with *The Birmingham Post,* he stated:

It is possible this generation will see huge rocket ships carrying passengers that can circle the Moon and return to Earth safely. If work could begin on such a project immediately, and [there were] enough money to finance it in the interests of pure science, it could be done and witnessed by persons who are alive today [Ordway and Sharpe 1979, p. 361].

After he retired from the army in 1960, Toftoy said in an interview that "of all the uses to which satellites can be put, the one I see with the greatest promise—and challenge—is the Space Station" (Thomas 1961b, p. 235). Toftoy saw the station as a necessary transfer point for the exploration of the universe.

Although Gen. Toftoy tried to accommodate the needs and interests of the German pioneers, the years at White Sands were frustrating, especially for Wernher von Braun. Firing old V-2s provided little opportunity to advance rocket science. And where was the space program to take us to the stars?

A personal reminiscence of William F. Winterstein, one of the army superiors of the German scientists at Fort Bliss, comments on von Braun:

It became clear that [von Braun] was close to leaving the organization and looking for employment in industry. At that time [at the end of 1946] it didn't look as if the U.S. government wanted to get involved in the foreseeable future or in any significant way in the area of rocket technology and spaceflight.

The major argument that held him back was the recognition that, at that time, no private company had the necessary means to finance anything like spaceflight. I advised him to hang in there. One day Congress would relent and authorize funding for the research. I explained to him then that he at some point in the future would be recognized as the greatest rocket scientist in the United States, yes, perhaps even in the entire world. Although the immediate outlook was bleak, Wernher decided to endure the difficult times and hope for better days [Stuhlinger and Ordway 1992, p. 159].

The transfer of 120 members of the German team to the new U.S. Army missile program in Huntsville, Alabama, started on April 15, 1950, and was completed in October. When the Germans arrived in Huntsville, many people in this "Watercress Capital" of the nation were picking cotton for $1 per 100 pounds or working as "lint heads" for 28 cents an hour in the nearby cotton mills (Ordway and Sharpe 1979, p. 365). Soon after they were settled in Huntsville and on nearby Monte Sano—more reminiscent of their native Germany than the New Mexico desert had been—the Germans founded the Rocket City Astronomical Association. The association built an observatory with a 53-centimeter mirror, on what was then one of the best telescopes in the South (Ordway and Sharpe 1979, p. 368).

As reported in *The Rocket Team:* "With the arrival of the Germans [the small chamber music group which existed in Huntsville] was amazed to find that many of the scientists and engineers who designed the V-2 missile were also very talented musicians." The scientists helped to found the Huntsville Civic Orchestra, and its first concert took place on December 13, 1955 (Ordway and Sharpe 1979, p. 369).

Not all of the German space pioneers chose to stay in Huntsville, however. Krafft Ehricke joined Walter Dornberger at Bell Aircraft in Buffalo, New York, and later transferred to General Dynamics in California, where he worked on the Atlas missile, along with other former Peenemünders. Dr. Adolph Thiel became the project engineer on the Thor missile, and later vice president of TRW. Dr. Martin Schilling went to work at Raytheon, and Magnus von Braun accepted a position at Chrysler (Ordway and Sharpe 1979, p. 373).

The army established the Ordnance Guided Missile Center at Redstone under Major James Hamill, with von Braun as technical director. Arthur Rudolph was made technical director for the Redstone rocket.

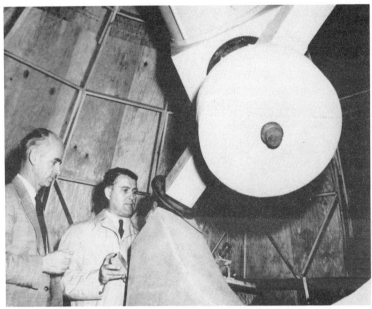

NASA, Marshall Space Flight Center

The Rocket City Astronomical Association, founded by the German space enthusiasts, boasted one of the best telescopes in the south at the time. Here, Ernst Stuhlinger and Wernher von Braun are at the telescope in 1956, at what is today is called the Von Braun Observatory in Monte Sano Park.

During World War II, a portion of the Redstone Arsenal facilities was used for chemical manufacturing and storage. After the war ended, the arsenal was mothballed; more than 7,000 acres were leased to farmers, and buildings were rented or sold. On October 28, 1948, the secretary of the army designated the arsenal as a center for rocket research and development and transferred the Ordnance Research and Development Division Sub-Office (Rocket) at Fort Bliss to the Redstone Arsenal.

The Korean War began on June 25, 1950. In July, with new urgency, the Redstone Arsenal was asked by the army chief of ordnance to perform a feasibility study on a 500-mile-range rocket weapon (von Braun 1964, p. 108). This led to the development of the Redstone missile, a single-stage vehicle with a 400 to 450 mile range. In February 1951, the army increased the payload require-ment to more than 6,900 pounds, to accommodate an atomic war-

NASA, Marshall Space flight Center

The Redstone missile was developed in the 1950s to meet the new urgency in response to the Korean War, which started on June 25, 1950. Here, a Redstone missile is erected in the gantry at the Restone Arsenal on July 23, 1959.

head, which reduced the range to only 50 to 200 miles because of the limited engine power available (Debus 1973, p. 21).

In 1958, the Redstones were deployed as mobile missiles backing up NATO forces in Europe. They were replaced by Jupiter missiles by 1960; the Jupiters were in turn replaced with the solid-propellant Pershing missile in 1963, all built by the Germans (von Braun 1964, p. 110).

The intermediate-range (1,500 mile) Jupiter was authorized in late 1955, and its development required new facilities, which led to the establishment of the Army Ballistic Missile Agency (ABMA). It also created the need for a second wave of German talent to be "imported" to the United States. As Heinz Hermann Koelle explains in a recent interview, "I was a prisoner of war in the United States in 1945 and '46, and then I came back and took up my studies at the Technical University of Stuttgart." In 1948, Koelle reestablished the Society for Space Research (Gesellschaft für Weltraumforschung), which had been "founded by Krafft Ehricke and Hans Kaiser in 1935 in Berlin." Through that activity, he says, "I got in contact with the all the Peenemünde people . . . some in the States, like von Braun" (Koelle 1992).

Koelle recounts:

In 1952 I met an American professor, Professor Pierce—he was the chief advisor of the American Air Force in Wiesbaden—and he got me a research contract from Wright Field, while I was a student. . . . I made projects for the Air Force from 1952 to 1954 on long-range rocket trajectory calculations. [In 1954, von Braun] wrote me a letter which said, more or less, "I know you are interested in things we are going to do very soon. Why don't you come and join us?" That's the way I got in on the Paperclip action, and was one of the first people coming over in that bunch of people in the mid-1950s when it was decided that the United States would build long-range rockets. There was a shortage of engineers for the Atlas, Titan, and intermediate-range ballistic missiles.

I was the one then who got other people to the United States, like Harry Ruppe. . . . He was a student of mine . . . and later became my deputy. At that time, 1955, I became chief of preliminary design. . . . I was a member of the launch crew in January of 1958 [when Explorer 1 was launched] and had some responsibilities like payload and performance and lifetime, with Dr. Stuhlinger [Koelle 1992].

Harry Ruppe recently recalled:

I studied theoretical physics in postwar Germany. Obviously nothing like rockets was permitted under the military laws in Germany. Beside, if it were permitted, it wouldn't have been taught. There were no teachers.

Later on, I had to leave Leipzig, which was in the former Soviet-occupied part of Germany. . . . I went to Berlin and resumed studies there. I had contacted already, some people, amateurs, interested in space. The most important . . . was Heinz Hermann Koelle. . . . He was a professor there.

He was in Stuttgart running an amateur club for the exploration of space, and I joined that club and became the boss of the Berlin [section]. . . . I met, at one of the international astronautical congresses, I think in London, with Wernher von Braun for the first time. . . . I had no doubt that this Peenemünde group was busy working for spaceflight in the United States. I was wrong, but this was my belief.

I gave a paper there and got to talk to Dr. von Braun, and I made it clear that I wanted to join that team. Hermann Koelle was also helpful [Ruppe 1992].

In 1957, Harry Ruppe was invited to join the team in Huntsville. But, he says:

to my utmost disappointment, when I came to Huntsville, there was a contract waiting for me, and . . . it said I was hired as a specialist to assist in wire-guided anti-tank missiles.

Now, I had no inclination to do that at all. . . . So I went to Dr. von Braun with that contract in hand and I told him, "there's a great misunderstanding here; it's not at all what I want. I want to work on space." Wernher grinned at me and said, "Well, sir, I have to write something in the contract that the army agrees [with], and aren't you the expert in wire-guided anti-tank missiles?" There was an immediate understanding of what he wanted and what I wanted, and somehow, I have to say, I never saw in Redstone Arsenal, even *saw*, wire-guided anti-tank missiles! [Ruppe 1992].

The Army Ballistic Missile Agency (ABMA) was activated, and, on February 1, 1956, Brigadier General John Medaris arrived in Huntsville to take command. Employment at the Redstone Arsenal jumped from 1,600 to 5,000. The first multistage rocket, the Jupiter C, was launched on September 20, 1956, and reached an altitude of nearly 700 miles. Von Braun was sure that with a small fourth stage, it could carry a small satellite into Earth orbit.

General Medaris described the ABMA as

NASA, Marshall Space Flight Center

It was under the leadership of Gen. John Medaris that the U.S. Army launched America's first satellite, Explorer I, in January 1958. In this photo, Gen. Medaris is joined by members of the ABMA team. In the light jacket is Arthur Rudolph. Between Rudolph and Medaris is Wernher von Braun. This photograph was taken in 1959, shortly before General Medaris retired from the army.

unique in the annals of the United States Army.... The development team, headed by Dr. Wernher von Braun, which had established such an outstanding reputation through the successful development and flight test of Redstone, became the nucleus around which the Agency was built [Medaris 1956, p. 54].

General Medaris introduced the concept of "concurrent development" for the Jupiter program to ensure maximum progress. Three projects would be under way at the same time: One missile would be "translating" from advanced development to production and field use; a second, "using the momentum of the above as a springboard [would be] translated into hardware development;" while a third project would be developing new components and testing the feasibility for a new weapons system (Medaris 1956, p. 58).

Production capabilities in industry were developed concurrently with the design and testing of the missile system in Huntsville. Medaris explained that "prime contractors and major subcontractors [were] brought into the program from the very beginning to follow the development cycle and take over the production of hardware as soon as any degree of stability [was] established" (Medaris 1956, p. 60).

On October 14, 1958, while the United States was still struggling to perform a successful launch to the Moon, General Medaris told 350 top electronic scientists that despite early difficulties, American military agencies "will contact the Moon, and put men in outer space, and establish space platforms" (*Chicago Tribune* 1958).

Medaris was adamant in the view that there should be no separate civilian space program. On November 29, 1959, in the midst of his tug-of-war with the Department of Defense and the civilian National Aeronautics and Space Administration (NASA) over the fate of the army space program and the von Braun team, Medaris was interviewed on the television program "Meet the Press." He knew, as did the rocket engineers, that for years the new NASA civilian agency would have to depend upon military missiles as launchers. "I cannot feel that any complete effort to divide so-called civilian and military work in the missile and space field will give us our best answers," he said.

Medaris's major concern, transcending his own personal desire that the team stay with the army program, was that a coherent, working group be maintained and that the scientific talent not be divided among different government agencies. Responding to a question from the TV interviewer concerning whether the von Braun group would be transferred to NASA, Medaris said that initially,

there was not a coherent mission in NASA that would have taken all of this group as a whole, and this was, of course, backed up by the fact that they didn't ask for all of them. Now this year the condition is different. The Saturn program has been assigned to NASA, along with the transfer.

When asked about how to make the public more aware of the space program and whether the White House should be criticized

National Air and Space Museum, U.S. Army, Smithsonian institution, A-5258D
General Medaris led a constant lobbying campaign within the army for an aggressive space effort for both military and scientific purposes. He is seen here with Wernher von Braun inspecting a model of a Redstone rocket at the Pentagon on January 20, 1956.

for a lack of leadership, Medaris replied, "Unfortunately in my present environment the answer to that is a little difficult, because I have been more critical of the press for not making the public fully aware" ("Meet the Press" 1959).

Were the German scientists in favor of being transferred to NASA? It seems that there was a division of opinion. Harry Ruppe recalls that

there were some fundamental discussions within the ex-Peenemünde team whether we should stay with the army or go with NASA. Wernher was with flying colors for NASA. He saw his dream of working for space only, fulfilled. He did not convince everybody.

Some of the old-timers, with all their experience, felt there might be more stability in the military. They felt NASA might

lose public support if the climate somehow changed. . . . Some
of the group stayed with the army [Ruppe 1992].

Some, like Arthur Rudolph, who was the project manager of
the new Pershing missile, were considered too crucial to the army
programs to be immediately transferred to NASA. In recognition
for his work in rocketry for the army, Rudolph had received an
honorary doctor of science degree from Rollins College in 1959,
and also the Exceptional Civilian Service Award, which is the highest
award the army gives to civilians (Franklin 1987, pp. 118–119).

Harry Ruppe went to NASA with von Braun and most of the
group. Then, in 1966, he was offered the chair of the newly founded
Astronautics Institute of the Technical University in Munich. He
sought von Braun's advice, and found "he had known about it before
I did! His words settled the matter: 'If the old country calls you,
you go.'" Germany was then just beginning to join the handful of
space-faring nations in the development of space technology.

Hermann Koelle also left the United States about this time. In
1965, he received a call from the Technical University of Berlin
asking him to take over the chair that had been held by Eugen
Sänger until his death. "I can easily try it out," he thought to himself,
"because I can always come back." By then, however, he had realized
there was nothing being planned in the U.S. space program after the
completion of the Apollo flights, "because there were no additional
payloads for Saturn vehicles [being developed], and it takes about
seven years to get new big payloads of this size to be manufactured
and developed." Koelle went back to Berlin, and found that "things
didn't shape up in the States too well after Apollo, so I stayed here"
(Koelle 1992).

As General Medaris was preparing to retire from the military
he did not hesitate to criticize those he felt to blame for the state
of the nation's space program. He went out on a limb in testimony
before the House Space Committee on February 2, 1960, attacking
President Eisenhower's assertion that the United States was not in
a space race with anyone and that civilian and military programs
should be separate (*Washington Star* 1960).

Throughout his life, General Medaris held fast to the idea that
the military, and specifically the army, should run all U.S. space
programs, and he strongly opposed the establishment of the civilian

NASA. He felt that separate programs would lead to duplication and that the military already had the necessary capabilities.

Medaris faced opposition to his proposals for an aggressive space program from within the military as well as the White House. A 1960 article in *Aviation Week* magazine attacked Medaris's "own proposed $13 billion program to initiate military operations on the Moon, [Project Horizon] as well as projects of comparable fantasy periodically suggested by others in the Pentagon" (Morse 1960, p. 118).

A few months later, after he had retired from his military career, Medaris had no kind words for either the other military services, or the Joint Chiefs of Staff. "I honestly believe that if the Joint Chiefs, when confronted by an irreconcilable difference among themselves, would lock the door, toss the coin, and agree to support the decision selected by the coin, we would be better off in the area of military guidance than we are at present," he stated in an article in *Space World* magazine in March 1961 (Rublowsky 1961, p. 56).

While General Medaris was commanding the Army Ordnance Missile Command, the Redstone Arsenal was working on the development not only of the intermediate-range ballistic missiles needed for the defense of Europe, but also on ground-based interceptor rockets, such as the Nike-Zeus, which could protect the United States from nuclear attack. Medaris saw this technology as the key to a positive change in U.S. strategic policy. In the same *Space World* article—titled "Tough-Talking General"—writer John Rublowsky reports that "General Medaris takes a hard look at the whole concept of massive retaliation—a concept that has completely dominated our military thinking." Medaris describes this policy as "sheer, destructive revenge" (Rublowsky 1961, p. 57).

Medaris continued:

> In our preoccupation with "massive retaliation" as the best shield for attack ... we have shoved all our poker chips of human civilization into the middle of the table, but if our bet is called and we must show our hand, there can be no winners—only losers. [Figure 7.2]

In September 1961, Medaris predicted that the Nike-Zeus system could intercept 80 percent of incoming missiles, as long as the attacking forces did not outnumber the defensive missiles (Witkin

FIGURE 7.2
THE MAD TARGETS: 200 MILLION AMERICANS
As early as the 1950s, General Medaris opposed the policy of Mutually Assured
Destruction, which pushed all of humanity's chips into the center of the table. Shown
on this map are the military targets of a Soviet strike (within the small bull's-eyes)
and the major targeted population centers (in the shaded areas). Instead, he proposed
defensive technologies, the idea which years later would become President Reagan's
Strategic Defense Initiative.

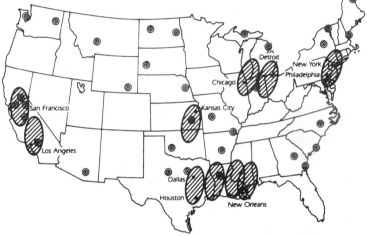

Source: Fusion Energy Foundation, *Beam Defense: An Alternative to Nuclear Destruction* (Fallbrook, Calif: Aero Publishers, 1983).

1961). President Kennedy's Defense Secretary Robert McNamara
had testified in the spring of 1961 to "widespread doubts as to
whether the Nike-Zeus system should ever be deployed," according
to *The New York Times*. Medaris countered that "the development
by either side of any reasonably effective defense against nuclear
missiles would drastically affect the balance of power immediately."
If the Russians developed it first, Medaris said, they would be

> assured of having such an advantage for only a relative time
> ... they would be presented with a fleeting opportunity to try
> for their goal of world domination. We must accept the fact
> that the technology of communism is just about as likely to
> come up with such a defense as is our own [Witkin 1961].

Medaris restated this theme in June 1985 in a presentation to
a memorial conference for Krafft A. Ehricke. "In the present case,"

he told the audience, "it becomes madness not to turn our attention to an effective strategic defense that will make a nuclear holocaust so unsuccessful as to assure that it would not happen" (Schiller Institute 1985, p. 252).

The U.S. policy of massive retaliation was not reversed until March 23, 1983, when President Ronald Reagan announced the Strategic Defense Initiative (SDI). At that time, although he had been retired from military service for more than 20 years, General Medaris's advice and counsel was sought by the new SDI program head, General James Abrahamson.

Few would describe General Medaris as a modest man, but he related one event to the author that indicated the humility of the man who had been a very strict taskmaster during his years in the military. When Medaris arrived late at an SDI advisory committee meeting in Washington, he was astonished to find that the chair at the head of the table had been reserved for him. When he entered the room, all those who were present, regardless of rank, rose in respect. General Medaris said he was somewhat surprised and genuinely honored.

An earlier indication of the respect, but also humor, with which he was treated by his men, is a poem written in 1958 by Ivan Hirschberg, in Huntsville:

In the missile game, we have won great fame.
The world knows our Jupiter C
And what we have done with Explorer One.
Medaris, Von Braun and me.

Explorer Two went off in the blue
On its own self-guided spree.
Number Two kept in tract, and reports back
To Medaris, Von Braun and me.

We will send others to join their brothers
Some will orbit; some will fall in the sea....
Yet, history will toast the men with the most....
Medaris, Von Braun and me.

Just watch our smoke as we go for broke
To solve the Space Mystery.
For we have a thirst to get there first....
Medaris, Von Braun and me.

In our skills we pride, we'll travel wide,
Into space so wild and free.
To the Moon; then Mars, and then to distant Stars. . .
Medaris, Von Braun and me.

When finally they plan a Space Ship that's manned
And they call for brave men—two—three—
To try for the Moon in that metal balloon,
Call Medaris, Von Braun, not me.

On May 16, 1990, the National Space Club in Washington, D.C. hosted a "Salute to U.S. Army Achievements in Space." They presented the inaugural Major General John B. Medaris Award for Army Achievement in Space to General Medaris, Major General Holger Toftoy, Dr. William Pickering, Dr. James van Allen, and the Wernher von Braun team. Also honored was Brigadier General (retired) Ivey O. Drewry, Jr. who had been commander of the Army Sentinel and Safeguard Systems, the world's first ballistic missile defense system. He was project manager when the first intercept of an ICBM with a Nike-Zeus missile took place in July 1962.

In the spring of 1990, while he was gravely ill, General Medaris was elected a fellow of the Aerospace Hall of Fame in San Diego, California. In a press release announcing the honor he is "cited for his tenacity and vision and for his work in inspiring young people to pursue excellence in space and aeronautics."

General Medaris died on July 11, 1990. After winning his first battle with cancer in Huntsville in the 1950s, General Medaris wrote an essay in 1957 titled, "A General Looks at God," which won the Freedoms' Foundation award. He had a bout with bone cancer in 1964, which went into remission. It resurfaced six years later and again went into remission, but reappeared again in 1989. General Medaris entered the clergy in 1970, and when he died, he was an arch-deacon emeritus in the Anglican Catholic Church.

The important work that was accomplished by the German space pioneers in Huntsville for the army was enabled by the support, guidance, and shared vision of General Medaris.

While all of the technical prerequisites for launching a U.S. satellite existed as early as 1954, the lack of recognition by President Eisenhower of the importance of such an initiative led to the Soviet "first" in space.

Marsha Freeman

Although he was a very strict taskmaster and commander, General Medaris was treated with both respect and affection by those who worked under him. In this photo, then-Father Medaris was greeted by old colleagues and friends at a celebration of the 20th anniversary of the first lunar landing in Huntsville, in July 1989.

Three years before Sputnik, not many technical people were talking about satellites. Much more attention was being given to the idea of developing manned space stations. But on May 4, 1954, at the Third Hayden Planetarium Symposium on Space Travel, sponsored by the American Rocket Society, Dr. Harry Wexler of the U.S. Weather Bureau outlined one of the most promising missions for unmanned spacecraft:

It can be stated without question that a satellite vehicle, moving about the Earth at the proper height and manner, would be of inestimable value as a weather patrol for short-range forecasting and as a collector of basic research information for solar and geophysical studies, including long-term weather changes and climatic variations [Ley 1957a, p. 330].

That spring, the Space-Flight Committee of the American Rocket Society, headed by Krafft Ehricke, sent a proposal it developed for a satellite "through various channels" (Ley 1957a, p. 332). On June 23, 1954, Fred Durant, former president of the society and president of the International Astronautical Federation, called Wernher von Braun to invite him to a meeting to discuss satellite proposals in Washington. Two days later, von Braun was at the Naval Research Office with Durant, University of Maryland physicist S. Fred Singer, Harvard astronomer Professor Fred Whipple, Commander George W. Hoover of the U.S. Navy and Amercian Rocket Society, David Young of Aerojet General, and representatives of the Office of Naval Research.

As Willy Ley relates:

I must mention that from about 1950 on the favorite pastime of everybody interested was combining existing rockets on paper to see whether they might reach satellite-carrier velocities. ... If you took a Redstone rocket as the first stage, von Braun explained, and then placed successive clusters of Loki rockets on top, you should add enough velocity to get the top Loki into an orbit around the Earth [Ley 1957a, p. 332].

The Loki was a successor to the Taifun, solid-fuel anti-aircraft rocket under development at Peenemünde.) Von Braun estimated that a small, 5-to-7-pound satellite could be orbited, depending upon the number of Loki rockets used in the upper stages (Ordway and Sharpe 1979, p. 375).

On August 3, 1954, navy representatives visited General Toftoy and von Braun at the Redstone Arsenal to see the available hardware, and Commander George Hoover was assigned as project officer. A tentative firing date was set for the summer of 1957 (Ley 1957a, p. 333). Von Braun wrote a secret report on September 15, "A Minimum Satellite Vehicle Based On Components Available from Missile Development of the Army Ordnance Corps," which he had been put together with the Jet Propulsion Laboratory in California and the Navy. The plan was called "Project Orbiter."

The proposal requested $100,000, "a modest sum indeed for the man who had spent millions of marks to develop the V-2 and who would later spend several billions of dollars to produce the Saturn V." Von Braun states prophetically, that "the establishment of a man-made satellite, no matter how humble. . . would be a scientific achievement of tremendous impact." Warning what the Russians might be doing, with the help of thousands of their captured German engineers, von Braun continued, "Since it is a project that could be realized within a few years with rocket and guided missile experience available *now,* it is only logical to assume that other countries could do the same. *It would be a blow to U.S. prestige if we did not do it first*" (Ordway and Sharpe 1979, p. 376).

On January 20, 1955, a proposal that was based on von Braun's secret report was presented to the assistant secretary of defense for research and development. During the same month, Radio Moscow announced the Soviet Union would launch a satellite during the 1957 International Geophysical Year (Winter 1990, p. 71). During that spring, the U.S. Central Intelligence Agency confirmed the Soviet claim (Ordway and Sharpe 1979, p. 377).

Excitement spread through the ranks of the German rocket team at the possibility of launching the world's first Earth-orbiting satellite. On April 15, 1955, there was a pause in the daily routine as 40 German space pioneers gathered at the Huntsville High School auditorium. There, two federal district judges administered the oath of citizenship. "Some twelve hundred fellow townsmen turned out, and Mayor R.B. 'Spec' Searcy officially declared the occasion to be New Citizen Day (Ordway and Sharpe 1979, pp. 376–77).

Inspired by a Walt Disney television show (see Chapter VIII), President Eisenhower announced through his press secretary on

NASA, Marshall Space Flight Center

On April 15, 1955 a pause was taken in the hectic schedule of the German space pioneers, as 40 gathered in the Huntsville High School auditorium to be administered the oath of citizenship. In this photograph, Martin Schilling, Ernst Stuhlinger, and Wernher von Braun sign their citizenship papers.

July 29, 1955, that the United States would indeed orbit a satellite during the International Geophysical Year. But the program was to be called Vanguard, not Project Orbiter, and it would be developed by the navy, not the army. Eisenhower wanted this new scientific program to be unclassified and nonmilitary. Some also have observed that there were those in Washington who wanted the first U.S. satellite to be launched by "Americans," not "Germans." History would later make the Germans first, nonetheless.

Dr. Stuhlinger recalls that their satellite

work was interrupted since the army in the autumn of 1955 had received orders to end all experiments and all research, development, and construction projects relating to satellites. But the people involved continued that work in their free time so that when the army finally opened the door to the satellite project, the designs were ready. General Toftoy, and after him

Marsha Freeman

The ground-breaking work done at the Redstone Arsenal in the early days of rocketry has been recognized in the designation of the Redstone test stand area at the arsenal as a National Historic Site. This area includes the first blockhouse, seen here, which was fashioned from railraod cars and covered over with mounds of dirt for the protection of the launch crew.

General Medaris, promoted these efforts, since they generously looked the other way, when they visited a laboratory and discovered on a drawing-board a sketch which looked suspiciously like a small satellite [Stuhlinger and Ordway 1992, p. 227].

Looking back on this period in 1960, General Toftoy told *The St. Petersburg [Florida] Times:* "Somebody...decided it wasn't worthwhile to get this first [U.S.] Sputnik into space. In 1954, when I took command of Redstone Arsenal, I asked Washington for permission to fire this satellite. ... We were quite disappointed at the answer we received: 'Sorry, there is no requirement for this sort of thing' " (*Washington Star* 1960).

Although disappointed at the refusal to allow Project Orbiter to begin,

von Braun and his collaborators signaled the Navy repeatedly
that they were prepared to collaborate with the Vanguard team.
They were even prepared to use a Redstone rocket to launch
a Vanguard satellite, all in the name of "Project Vanguard" and
under the supervision of the Vanguard team. But the responsible Navy officers always responded with a decisive "no!" [Stuh-
linger and Ordway 1992, p. 227].

On September 20, 1956, Jupiter rocket No. 27 was fired and
attained a height of 600 miles and range of 3,000 miles. General
Medaris recounted a few years later:

When it was over we knew we had a vehicle that could be
used as a satellite carrier. We didn't need missile No. 29, so
we put it on the shelf with the hope that someday we might
be able to use it to launch a satellite. This was exactly 12 months
and two weeks before Sputnik I was launched [Rublowsky 1961,
p. 56].

It was ABMA's Jupiter Missile No. 29 [Juno I as it was then
called] that boosted Explorer I into Earth orbit in January 1958.
Similarly, von Braun wrote in 1964 that

we at Huntsville could not scrap the satellite idea, and we did
not scrap our satellite-oriented hardware. ... While Project
Vanguard was the approved U.S. satellite program, we at Huntsville knew that our rocket technology was fully capable of
satellite applications and could quickly be implemented [von
Braun 1964, p. 114].

An "interservice rivalry" between the U.S. Army and newly
created U.S. Air Force, over which service would have responsibility
for which missile systems, raged for years. Every branch of the
military wanted the central role in the new field of space, but the
Army/Air Force competition was the most fierce.
As Harry Ruppe explains:

There was always this discussion—if a long-range missile is
rather a gun (army) or an airplane (air force)—or as we at
times respectfully said, "Wind Force." The Peenemünde group

already had some brushes and bruises from the Air Force [during the war, with the Luftwaffe]. So there was a pre-formed hostility toward the Air Force from Peenemünde days, and now they figured that the picture is kind of repeating itself [Ruppe 1992].

During the work on Project Horizon, Ruppe says, "General Medaris took objection to something which I felt was completely unimportant. We used 'missile' and he wanted 'rocket.' Later, I understood he had a point. 'Missile' was the Air Force term, and he wanted not even to use their language!" (Ruppe 1992).

A year later, on November 26, 1956, the army rocket program received another blow. Responding to the fierce rivalry among the military services, Defense Secretary Charles Wilson promulgated a so-called Roles and Missions Directive, which restricted the army to missiles with a 200-mile range. Their new Jupiter missile was turned over to the Air Force for operational use and deployment.

After the announcement, Medaris and von Braun packed their bags and went to Washington, where, they tried—without success— to get permission to launch a satellite. Later, Medaris would comment wryly: "Vanguard proved to be a very expensive toy. With no objective beyond the IGY [International Geophysical Year], it had little growth potential. Its final cost came to over $110,000,000, and five out of six launchings were failures" (Rublowsky 1961, p. 56).

The third Jupiter test launch on August 8, 1957, carried a one-third scale model of an intermediate-range ballistic missile (IRBM) nose cone, to determine what material could withstand the reentry environment. It became the first man-made object to return from space. "A little surprise awaited General Medaris. We had placed a letter addressed to him inside the cone and later presented it to the ABMA Commander as the first rocket-carried mail which traveled over IRBM range," Kurt Debus reported (Debus 1973, p. 36).

While the von Braun team had been stymied in their attempts to forge ahead in space, the Russians had given many indications that they would attempt a satellite launch during 1957. Less than a week before the Russian Sputnik would beep-beep the opening of the Space Age,

Stuhlinger made an urgent appeal to General Medaris: "I am fully convinced that there will soon be a Russian satellite in orbit. Could you not, General, make another attempt with the secretary of defense to ask for the go-ahead for our project? The shock for our country would be tremendous, if they are first in space!"

"Don't be so nervous," Medaris replied. "You know better than anyone how complicated it is to build and to launch a satellite. The Russians will never be in that position! I haven't the slightest evidence from any of my intelligence sources of an imminent satellite launch. As soon as I hear anything, I will act. If we learn anything about their activity, we would still have plenty of time to act. Go back to your lab and relax!"

On October 1, 1957, Radio Moscow gave the transmission frequency of the announced satellite in order for everyone to be able to receive its signal. And less than a week after Stuhlinger's conversation with Medaris, on October 4, 1957, the Soviet Union proudly announced that Sputnik I was in orbit. Anyone with a small radio receiver could hear its small, but enduring, beep every 96 minutes. And on clear nights one could even see this small moon rapidly traverse the heavens.

Von Braun asked Stuhlinger: "Has the General since spoken to you? I would think he owes you an apology!"

"Yes," he retorted. "But all he said was: 'These damned bastards!' " [Stuhlinger and Ordway 1992, p. 228].

In one of the most fortunate coincidences in rocket history, the day that Sputnik was launched, the new defense secretary, Neil McElroy, was visiting the ABMA in Huntsville. Upon the announcement to the dinner gathering that Sputnik was circling the globe, von Braun said, "Today, man has taken his first step towards Mars." To McElroy, von Braun suggested: "When you get back to Washington and all hell breaks loose, tell them we've got the hardware down here to put up a satellite any time" (Ordway and Sharpe 1979, p. 382).

Von Braun told the defense secretary that his team could launch a satellite within 60 days. Preferring to err on the side of caution, General Medaris made the proposal for 90 days.

On November 8, 1957, General Medaris received approval from McElroy to modify two Jupiter C vehicles and attempt a launch by

March (Debus 1973, p. 43). Then, on December 6, in full view of the American public and the world, the Navy's Vanguard dramatically exploded. The von Braun team was taking advantage of this new "go" situation, exploiting the fact that the nation was depending upon a successful army launch to save its pride and prestige. "We knew that no one had been thinking about these problems as long or as thoroughly as Wernher von Braun and some of his people," General Medaris later explained. "So we put a few of the best of them off in a closed room to come up with a 12- or 15-year national space program," to follow what would surely be a successful army satellite launch (Medaris 1960, p. 186).

General Toftoy *publicly* expressed his disgust at the disgrace of being second in space. Speaking at a press conference with Brigadier General John A. Barclay, deputy commander of ABMA, at the 8th Congress of the International Astronautical Federation in Barcelona in the fall of 1957, Toftoy said that when the army had offered to launch a satellite, "We were told that this was not a race." General Barclay stated, a bit more diplomatically "the wisdom of this course of action remains to be evaluated" (*New York Times* 1967).

As *The New York Times* described those events a decade later, "The generals' statements brought prompt reaction from Washington." The next day, the army sent out instructions worldwide that it was inappropriate for anyone to comment on the satellite program.

In mid-December, while readying the launch of Explorer, the ABMA circulated a study in the Defense Department and scientific community on a "Proposal for a National Integrated Missile and Space Vehicle Development Program," based on the development of a booster with 1.5 million pounds of thrust. This would allow an unmanned soft lunar landing by 1960, an Earth-orbital two-man satellite by 1962, a manned circumnavigation of the Moon the same year, a 20-man permanent space station by 1965, a 3-man lunar expedition in 1967, and a 50-man lunar expedition and permanent outpost by early 1971. The total cost was $21 billion over 14 years (Medaris 1960, pp. 187–88).

General Medaris's description of the tribulations of the launch of the Explorer satellite, which put the United States into space on January 31, 1958, has lessons for today. One of the things that most concerned the general was the publicity of the launch. "Two years of close personal observation had convinced me that the chances of success on any important firing effort were in inverse proportion to the number of VIPs present," Medaris said. He was concerned that undue pressure would be placed on Kurt Debus and the launch crew because "there was a very human tendency to decide in marginal cases to go ahead and accept the risk rather than disappoint the visitors" (Freeman 1989b, p. 19).

As a matter of policy, General Medaris was always present at important rocket firings to take personal responsibility for delaying a launch if he felt there was too much pressure on the crew. This was standard operating procedure for a competent commanding officer, Medaris said. In an interview with this author on July 16, 1989, Medaris said:

> It is incredible to believe that, on the morning of the Challenger's disastrous launch, there was *no one* at the launch site who could say, "Shut it down. ..." We never had a launch where, either Wernher von Braun, Kurt Debus, or myself was not present, and any one of the three of us could shut it down any minute we wanted to and say, "That's enough. We're not going to do this one."
>
> "Did that ever happen?" I asked the general. "Oh yes," he replied. "I used to sit in the control house with my earphones on and I could check in on everybody that was working on the stands. ... More than once, I called a halt—delay—simply because I could hear tension in the voices of the men. They were tired and they were beginning to make mistakes, and I'd say, 'I'm calling a two-hour hold. Now get down off of there and go take a break" [Freeman 1989b, p. 19].

While General Medaris went to Cape Canaveral for the January 31, 1958, Explorer launch, Wernher von Braun went to the National Academy of Sciences in Washington to be at a press conference. After the launch, "as the group entered, the newsmen stood, cheered, and applauded. ... As to the nation's reaction ... in effect, it was the reverse of the state of shock induced by Sputnik," Kurt Debus reflected years later. "The ABMA had made good its promise of three years earlier. For the Peenemünde engineers, it was the long-awaited fulfillment of a dream" (Debus 1973, p. 54).

During the general uproar in the United States after the Vanguard launch failure in December 1957 (variously called, "flopnik"

208 HOW WE GOT TO THE MOON

and "kaputnik"), the Select Committee on Astronautics and Space Exploration in the House of Representatives, finding no leadership in the Eisenhower White House, took the initiative to discuss what a space program should be. The chairman of the committee, Rep. John McCormack, a Massachusetts Democrat and majority leader in the House of Representatives, sent out a questionnaire in 1958 to "more than half a hundred" experts in astronautics and rocketry to have their considered opinions on the future possibilities in space.

The committee report, *The Next 10 Years in Space, 1959–1969,* contains the responses to those questionnaires. The letter of transmittal of the report from the staff to the chairman said, "All the plans, programs, and projections these qualified men present will count for little unless the United States decides to meet this challenge with the mobilization of its private industry as well as public facilities, its resources, manpower, materiel, and money, which the national space effort requires. The indications are the Soviet Union is prepared to make such commitments." This view was echoed by President John F. Kennedy as America geared up for the Apollo Moon shot.

Three weeks before the launch of the Explorer satellite, on January 10, 1958, there was a meeting in Huntsville to discuss "Project Man Very High." Out of that meeting came a proposal for a manned, suborbital spaceflight. On May 16, the secretary of the army forwarded this proposal to ARPA. Von Braun made a personal presentation on the proposal three days later, but the decision was made not to fund it (Ordway and Sharpe 1979, pp. 383–4). Happily, another space program was already in the works.

On April 2, President Eisenhower, in a message to Congress, said, "I recommend that aeronautical and space science activities sponsored by the United States be conducted under the direction of a civilian agency, except for those projects primarily associated with military requirements" (Project Horizon, Volume III, p. 62). Eisenhower forwarded to the Congress a bill to create a civilian space agency, which was passed and signed into law on July 29. The National Aeronautics and Space Agency (NASA) began operation on October 1. Within weeks, Project Mercury, to put the first man into space, was approved.

Although the army space program was soon to be eclipsed by

the new civilian agency, the expertise of the German specialists was recognized by those who would inherit them and their work. At NASA's request, von Braun (director, Development Operations Division), H.H. Koelle (chief, Future Projects Design Branch), and Ernst Stuhlinger (director, Research Projects Laboratory), made a presentation to NASA on December 15, 1958, on behalf of the ABMA on "Present and Future Vehicles and Their Capabilities."

In his verbal presentation, von Braun stressed that it was important "how the elements of the various space programs—such as the man-in-space program or the orbital rendezvous capability, cargo capability, and so forth—must dove tail with such programs, as, say, putting a man on the Moon" (ABMA 1958, p. 1). There would be commercial opportunities in space, he said, such as communication satellites, global mail service, orbital transport systems, and "then from the year 2000 on, we could start mining the Moon, or something like that" (ABMA 1958, p. 5).

Von Braun outlined the family of new launch vehicles needed for the next decade in space, concentrating on what was then called the Juno V, with 1.5 million pounds of thrust. It would have multiple engines for safety, similar to airplanes. "For large vehicles like this," he stated, "there is a great difference between aborting the mission and killing the crew" (ABMA 1958, p. 66). Both the man-rated Saturn V and the Space Shuttle were designed on this principle.

Hermann Koelle proposed that by November 1964, the United States could have the first space station in equatorial orbit. Three years later, the first man could be on the Moon, he said, "and we still hope not to have Russian Customs there" (ABMA 1958, p. 35).

The representatives of the ABMA group indicated their willingness to take on an assignment from NASA to look at various options for a lunar landing, studying the required orbital work to prepare the lunar ships, rendezvous maneuvers between vehicles, construction work, and refueling in space (ABMA 1958, p. 122).

Touching the key point of mission objectives, Stuhlinger told the NASA group that

> the objective of the first manned lunar expedition should be carefully studied. Somebody should start thinking about what are we going to do on the Moon once we get there. ... We believe that the program of vehicles as shown and discussed

... will be justified only if it can be matched by an equivalent program of missions and objectives. .... The main objective ... should be man in space; and not only man as a survivor in space, but man as an active scientist [ABMA 1958, p. 129].

The ABMA team concluded, "We would like to request NASA to support these activities of ABMA's in the future, because we believe that we can make a considerable contribution to the NASA space program" (ABMA 1958, p. 149).

Although the future of the German team was clearly to be with the new, civilian agency, General Medaris was not ready to give up the best group of rocket and space specialists in the world without a fight. He doggedly lobbied the army's top brass in Washington, D.C., to keep the German team in the army. On March 20, 1959, Medaris received a directive from the chief of research and development for a study of a manned lunar outpost for the army. As Harry Ruppe relates, General Medaris's view of the army's role was: "The Moon has no water, it has no air, but it has land. That's the army's chance!" (Ruppe 1992).

General Medaris organized a crash effort to carry out the study, which became Project Horizon. Less than three months later, on June 8, the study was completed. On the first page of the study (four of five volumes of which have been declassified), the conclusions are stated:

Military, political and scientific considerations indicate that it is imperative for the United States to establish a lunar outpost at the earliest practicable date. ... Project Horizon represents the earliest feasible capability for the U.S. to establish a lunar outpost [Project Horizon 1959, volume 1, p. 1].

The report also contains the warning that

delayed initiation, followed later by a crash program, which would likely be precipitated by evidence of substantial Soviet progress in a lunar outpost program, will not only lose the advantage and timeliness, but also *will inevitably involve significantly higher costs and lower reliability* [Project Horizon 1959, vol. 1, p. 3].

FIGURE 7.3
THE BASIC LUNAR OUTPOST FOR 12 MEN
In the first phase of establishing a permanent lunar base of operations, a complex of facilities would be constructed as seen here. Four nuclear reactors located off-site would power the base, which would include not only living quarters, but a biological sciences laboratory, medical hospital, and physical sciences laboratory.

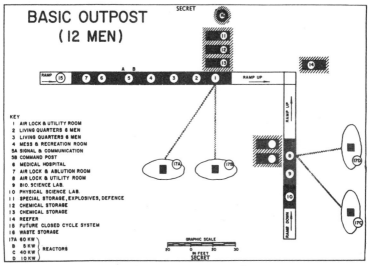

Source: *Project Horizon* (Army Ballistic Missile Agency, 1959)

Project Horizon put forward a fabulous program to develop national space capabilities during the 1960s. It assumes the development of the Saturn family of launch vehicles, with liquid hydrogen upper stages to increase payload capabilities, and the mass-production of vehicles and other hardware as space technology moved into industry. The goal was to perform the first lunar landings in the spring of 1965, have a 9-man construction crew on the surface by July that year, and to establish an initial outpost with a crew of 12 men by late 1966, as seen in Figure 7.3. The total cost was estimated at $6.014 billion over 8.5 years, which, it was pointed out, was less than 2 percent of the 1958 defense budget (Project Horizon 1959, vol. 1, p. 6).

The scale of the program, in contemporary terms, was mind-boggling. By 1967, a total of 252 persons would have left Earth orbit, 42 would have continued on to the Moon, and 26 would

FIGURE 7.4a
EARTH-RETURN VEHICLE ASSEMBLED ON THE MOON
This schematic represents the design of a vehicle which would be assembled from
components brought to the lunar surface from the Earth and used to return to Earth.

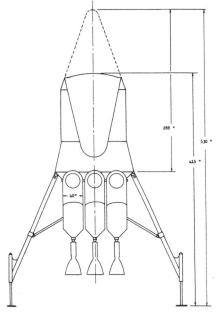

Source: *Project Horizon* (Army Ballistic Missile Agency, 1959).

have already returned to Earth. An Earth-orbital space station would
have a crew of 10 at all times; the station would be in constant use,
mainly as a refueling station for vehicles going to the Moon.

The total number of Saturn vehicles launched with men and
cargo to accomplish this would be 229, requiring 73 recoverable
first-stage boosters, similar to today's reusable Space Shuttle solid
rocket boosters (Project Horizon 1959, vol. 1, p. 30). A fleet of
small space maneuvering vehicles would be used for movement
outside the space station, to position the fuel containers near the
lunar vehicles for fuel transfer operations (Project Horizon 1959,
vol. 2, p. 268).

In a discussion with Hermann Koelle in December 1992, I
asked him about the ambitious launch rate for Project Horizon. He
explained:

FIGURE 7.4b
LUNAR LANDER WITH PROPULSION UNIT
During regular trips to the lunar surface, 6,000-pound propulsion units would be
brought as payload, such as that pictured here, and delivered to the outpost. Three
such propulsion units would then be transferred to an Earth-Return Vehicle seen
in Figure 7.4a to make up the propulsion system for the return trip.

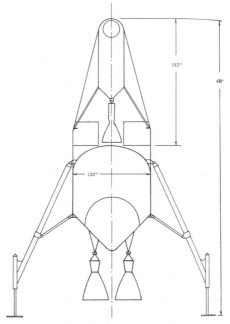

Source: *Project Horizon* (Army Ballistic Missile Agency, 1959)

It was stressing the state of the art. . . . Therefore, we didn't
dare come up with the idea of a bigger [launch] vehicle. If we
had, then you could reduce the number [of launches]. But the
message from Washington was, don't count on a bigger Saturn
vehicle than the Saturn I that we had at that time.

Project Horizon put forward nothing more than what the space
pioneers believed they could accomplish. "It takes a lot of courage
to say that you can do it," Koelle said, "but we were very confident
that it was feasible, and that much we stated, and I think it contributed to the decision to go to the Moon. Certainly, it was the only

systems study available at the time the decision was made" (Koelle 1992).

Why the army? The report cites historical precedents: "Throughout history the military outpost has served as a hub around which evolved the social, economic and political structure of civilization" (Project Horizon 1959, vol. 1, p. 46). Citing the expansion to the American West and the scientific outposts of Antarctica, the report points out, "Where others had failed, the U.S. Army Corps of Engineers and Medical Service conquered the elements of nature to build the Panama Canal." Antarctic explorer Dr. Paul Siple, who had accompanied Admiral Richard Byrd, read and made suggestions for the report (Project Horizon 1959, vol. 1, p. 8).

The army had within it, the report asserted, the research and technical capabilities to carry out such a program. In addition to the premier rocket team in the world—the Germans at Redstone Arsenal—the Army Corps of Engineers, the largest single construction organization in the world, could build the lunar outpost itself, and lead the mapping of the Moon. The U.S. Army Medical Service would train the astronauts, develop the technology for their health, nutrition, and comfort in space, and take care of all medical needs.

The Army Signal Corps would be responsible for communication systems and tracking. The Quartermaster Corps could supply the food, clothing, general supplies (such as tools, repair parts, religious, and recreational supplies), as well as space suits and other materiel. The Transportation Corps would develop lunar surface transport, cargo handling, and launch-site transport for the program.

It was projected that, beginning in fiscal year 1960, a program would be under way to

> adapt conventional foods for use in orbit and on the lunar surface, and [oversee] development of procedures for hydroponic vegetable gardening at the outpost. Beginning in FY62, programs will be initiated to develop procedures for raising poultry and animals on waste material and algae for oxygen and food production [Project Horizon 1959, vol. 2, p. 262].

A series of nuclear reactors would power the base, buried under the lunar soil for shielding. In addition to habitation and supply modules for the crew, the seven-module complex would include a physical sciences laboratory for *in situ* studies of the Moon's characteristics, and a medical laboratory.

There was no support in the army for such a lunar outpost effort. But NASA was looking beyond Project Mercury to the future. Did Project Horizon play a role in the Apollo decision? Hermann Koelle reports:

> I think it contributed to the decision to go to the Moon. Certainly. It was the only systems study available at the time the decision was made. There was no other study at that time of this magnitude of detail to show that you can build a lunar base if you want to. Without that study there would have been no Apollo program [Koelle 1992].

In February 1960, only months before the ABMA team was to be transferred to NASA, the von Braun team produced a book-length study titled *A Lunar Exploration Program Based Upon Saturn-Boosted Systems*. Three chapters were extracted and reproduced in a special publication for distribution to individuals involved in the NASA Lunar Exploration Working Group, set up in 1959. In addition to outlining a full program for the scientific exploration of the Moon, the report included a program for detecting microorganisms on Mars!

On October 21, 1959, President Eisenhower announced the transfer of the von Braun team to NASA, and General Medaris finally lost his tug of war with Washington. NASA's new Marshall Space Flight Center was dedicated by the President on September 8, 1960.

The era of the army's premier role in space exploration was ending. Finally, after three decades, the German space pioneers could concentrate their full effort on what they had committed themselves to do back in the 1920s: to take mankind into space.

CHAPTER VIII

Willy Ley Rallies the Nation for Space

One of the most remarkable men among the German space pioneers chose not to become an engineer or rocket scientist, but a writer and educator. This was Willy Ley, who was born on October 2, 1906, in Berlin and entered the university there in 1924. Ley later attended the University of Königsberg, where he concentrated his studies on paleontology and astronomy. He had to leave after three years of college because of financial strains on his family.

As described in Chapter III, Ley left his compatriots in the German Society for Space Travel and sailed for America, arriving at the beginning of 1935. His friend and fellow writer Sam Moskowitz reported in 1966, "he started writing and publishing as soon as he got to the U.S." (Moskowitz 1966, p. 31).

Working closely with friends, such as G. Edward Pendray of the American Rocket Society, Willy Ley immediately started proselytizing. On March 8, 1935, after he had been in the United States for less than two months, he spoke at an American Rocket Society public meeting at the Museum of Natural History on "Rocketry in Europe" (Figure 8.1).

By 1937, Ley was billed in magazines as "the world's foremost rocket authority." Moskowitz remarks that "Robert Goddard might have legitimately protested ... true to his customary reticence, nothing was heard from him" (Moskowitz 1966, p. 39).

Throughout the 1930s, Ley wrote articles for aviation and flight magazines to explain the new science of rockets. "Few problems connected with modern aviation are so frequently discussed, so often misunderstood, misinterpreted, and misstated

FIGURE 8.1
ROCKETRY IN EUROPE
Less than three months after he arrived in the United States from Germany, Willy Ley was the featured speaker at a public meeting of the American Rocket Society in New York. Thus started his career as a major public spokesman to rally the nation for space.

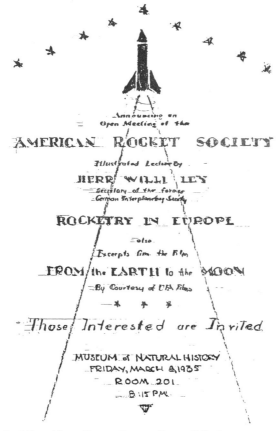

as rocket propulsion," he wrote in *Aviation* magazine (Ley 1936, p. 18).

However, Ley concentrated on writing non-science-fiction articles for science fiction publications. His writing touched on every subject one can imagine that has fascinated scientists and young people alike. "Visitors from the Void," in *Astounding Stories,* was a report on a huge meteor that had struck Siberia. In it, he speculated that such a "visitor from outer space" could have transported life to Earth, in the spore state (Ley 1937c).

Ley pubished an article titled "Stations in Space" in the February 1940 edition of *Amazing Stories,* but this was not about Oberth's Earth-orbiting stations. "Space travel would already exist if we lived on Mars," Ley told his readers. Providing an explanation of the concepts of gravity and escape velocity, he wrote that there is so much less energy needed to go into the orbit of Mars, because of its lower gravity (to reach a velocity of only 3 miles per second) compared to reaching orbit around the Earth (a velocity of 7 miles per second) that surely if we lived on Mars, space travel would already have been accomplished (Ley 1940a, p. 122).

Ley also pointed out that the Martian moons Phobos and Deimos are so small and so near the planet, they are almost irresistible. This "would increase the efforts of Martian rocket enthusiasts considerably and silence the critics at the same time," he proposed. Phobos and Deimos were perfect locations for spacecraft refueling stations, he said.

Ley made clear the moral of the story for Earthlings: Man should build a space station. "The existence of Phobos and Deimos is valuable to us even though we live on Earth," he wrote. "It constitutes an example of what space travel could gain by having near and comparatively small bodies around them." After all, transatlantic pioneers had considered building an artificial (floating) island midway between America and Europe, as "a fuel depot, repair shop, and temporary haven in bad weather" (Ley 1940a, p. 123).

Ley's article "Calling All Martians" appeared in November 1940. After reviewing the myriad theories about life on Mars and ideas of how to communicate with these intelligent beings, including a suggestion by Karl Gauss, Ley considers the development of language and how one would communicate through symbols with beings not familiar with any of our languages. A "letter of introduction" to the Martians should be prepared, he said, to show the expedition's planet of origin, and its relationship to Mars, and to demonstrate basic concepts of geometry and mathematics, which are universal (Ley 1940d, p. 38). Some 30 years later, when scientists were planning the launch of the Pioneer 10 spacecraft to Saturn and Jupiter, they knew that after its planetary fly-bys, it would be the first man-made object to leave the Solar System. Reaching a similar conclusion, they placed aboard a plaque illustrating some of the concepts Ley had specified.

Willy Ley took as his model for communications with extraterrestrial life the "message to the future" contained in a time capsule buried at the site of the New York World's Fair in 1939, to be opened by archaeologists 5,000 years later. "The differences between a message to the future and a message to the Martians are mainly gradual," he wrote (Ley 1940d, p. 39).

In 1940, Ley became science editor of the tabloid *PM,* and the next year published his book *The Lungfish and the Unicorn,* dealing with a subject which was his first love—zoology. During World War II, to explain basic principles of current interest, Ley published titles such as *Bombs and Bombing* and *Shells and Shooting* (Moskowitz 1966, p. 40).

At the same time, Ley's colleagues in the American Rocket Society were also turning out exciting articles about space. In 1940, ARS founder G. Edward Pendray posed the possibility of combining the potentials of the two current frontiers in science in "Rocket Power From Atoms?" Pendray wrote:

> If atomic power were available—in usable form—fuel troubles would be among the least of our worries. . . . Little journeys to the Moon and planets could be undertaken with less fuel than now attends a [rocket] shot of a couple of miles with gasoline and liquid oxygen (Pendray 1940, p. 9).

Pendray alerted American readers to scientific developments in Europe. "About a year ago," he wrote, "Professor Otto Hahn, of Berlin, bombarded uranium with neutrons, and produced such unexpected results that he immediately communicated with colleagues in Europe and the United States who hastened to repeat his experiments," on the possibility of a chain reaction to release energy from nuclei (Pendray 1940, p. 12).

The work of the Detroit Rocket Society after the end of the war also helped to coordinate European advances in rocketry with the fledgling U.S. effort. Boasting Hermann Oberth and Eugen Sänger as "technical directors," the Detroit Rocket Society magazine, *Rocketscience,* published articles on the future of space as well as historical series, such as Krafft Ehricke's on Peenemünde.

With all of his writings on a wide variety of subjects, it was

Chesley Bonestell, courtesy of Fred Durant

This painting of the Moon ship ready to return to Earth by Chesley Bonestell, which appeared in the 1950 book The Conquest of Space *written by Willy Ley, became the model for popular representations of spaceships. It is immediately recognizable as the same basic design as the Peenem-ünde-designed A-9.*

space that would "catapult [Willy Ley] into the limelight during 1944 and 1945," Moskowitz wrote (Moskowitz 1966, p. 40). In his history of space science, David DeVorkin reported that reading Willy Ley's writings after the war spurred many scientists to develop proposals for space experiments, as they learned of the potentials of the new field of rocketry (Moskowitz 1966, p. 52).

An article in 1945 titled "Rocket to the Moon," published in *Mechanix Illustrated,* was the start of a very fruitful collaboration between Ley and artist Chesley Bonestell. Ley wrote the text for Bonestell's astronomical illustrations. Bonestell was born in 1888, and was drawing before he was five years of age. Until the age of 50, his art work centered on architectural drawings and renderings,

FIGURE 8.2
MISS PICKERELL GOES TO MARS. . . .
. . . in a spacecraft which looks hauntingly familiar. In this children's tale, Miss Pickerell comes home from a trip to find that a Mars-bound spacecraft is sitting in her cow pasture. Such optimistic (and humorous) themes were commonplace in the children's literature of the 1950s.

"Don't you dare return to this pasture!"

Source: Ellen MacGregor, *Miss Pickerell Goes to Mars* (New York: Pocket Books, 1951).

but in 1938 he went to Hollywood as a special effects artist for the motion picture industry (Miller 1983, p. 6). At that time, Bonestell's interest in astronomical subjects flowered, and a series of his illustrations appeared in the May 29, 1944, edition of *Life* magazine, depicting Saturn as seen from five of its moons. His astronomical paintings also appeared in *Look* magazine, *Astounding Science Fiction,* and many other magazines.

Bonestell's collaboration with Ley after the war produced spectacular (and realistic) views of the surface and craters of the Moon, Earth-orbiting manned space stations, interplanetary spaceships, and missions to Mars. In 1949, the team produced its first book, *The Conquest of Space,* which included Bonestell's pictorial representation of the spaceship designed by Ley, that would become the model for most popular renderings of the subject (Figure. 8.2).

Perhaps so as not to be mistaken simply for a beautiful picture book, the work opens with tables containing the basic data of the planets of the Solar System and their satellites. Astronomer Robert Richardson read the manuscript of the book for accuracy (Ley 1950, p. 9). Willy Ley also describes in detail, from his eyewitness experience, the exciting launch of a V-2 rocket at White Sands.

In his introduction to *The Conquest of Space,* Ley writes that by 1949, Bonestell had already painted "half a hundred astronomical pictures" (Ley 1950, p. 9). Color reproductions by Bonestell show aerial views of the Earth from space, reminiscent of today's images from remote sensing satellites. A view of the Earth from 2,000 miles is described as "a sight which people will see during the first trip around the Moon" (Ley 1950, p. 39).

The Moon ship, designed by Ley and painted by Bonestell in *The Conquest of Space,* assumes the use of atomic power as fuel, and the renderings of craters, mountains, and lunar mare were surprisingly accurate. In fact, better images of these scenes were not available until years later, when the Apollo astronauts took photographs from a few miles above the lunar surface. The book describes the development of a lunar base requiring weekly transport missions that would be traveling from the Earth to the Moon. For the first time scientifically sensible renderings of what astronauts will do on the Moon appeared in print, accompanied by Ley's discussion of the basics of astronomy, and how the outer planets were discovered.

In a chapter titled "Vermin of the Skies," Ley tells the story of the discovery of the asteroid belt between Mars and Jupiter. In 1801, he relates, the mathematician Karl Gauss performed calculations for Professor Giuseppe Piazza, who had been observing a small "star" in its irregular orbit. Gauss calculated its distance from the Sun as 2.77 astronomical units (an AU measures 93 million miles), and Gauss thought "there was something special about this very figure" (Ley 1950, p. 137). In the 17th century, astronomer Johannes Kepler had determined that the relationship of the radii of the planetary orbits followed the five regular solids of geometry. Ley reports that Kepler wrote simply: "Inter Jovem et Martem planetam interposui— Between Jupiter and Mars I put a planet." Ley then traces the discovery of the major asteroids, reporting that between 1850 and 1870, there were an average of five new discoveries each year (Ley 1950, p. 138).

In 1951, when astronautical congresses were beginning to take place in Europe, Ley had a meeting with Robert Coles, the chairman of the Hayden Planetarium in New York City. Ley was concerned that few Americans could attend the meetings in Europe, and urged that similar events be held in the United States (Ley 1957a, p. 330). Coles approved Ley's proposal to organize a symposium at the planetarium. Ley chose October 12, Columbus Day, or Discovery Day, for the event. Attendance was by invitation, and scientific and government institutions, the press, and armed forces stationed in New York were invited (Ley 1957a, p. 330).

The symposium was a great success. According to Ley, after it was over, "I was stopped by two gentlemen who identified themselves as being representatives of *Collier's* magazine. Our two-minute discussion led to another luncheon, which was the germ of the first *Collier's* symposium on space travel." One of the gentlemen was Cornelius Ryan. The presentations at the *Collier's* symposia were based on the speeches delivered at the planetarium by Willy Ley, Wernher von Braun, and Heinz Haber, in particular (Ley 1957a, p. 331). Out of the symposia, eight articles about space appeared in a series printed in *Collier's* magazine, with the first appearing on March 22, 1952.

The release of the first article was preceded by an elaborate publicity campaign, including "window displays of the *Collier's* art work in the American Express offices in Manhattan and downtown Philadelphia," press releases, kits for use by local radio and newspaper staffs and high schools and colleges, and news photos (Ordway and Liebermann 1992, p. 141). This media offensive was certainly reminiscent of that waged by Fritz Lang before the release of the film *Frau im Mond* in Germany in 1929.

As part of the publicity, von Braun and Cornelius Ryan had speaking engagements in New York and Washington, D.C. Peenemünde artist Gerd de Beek constructed models of the space station and the rockets, which were used on television. It is estimated that 5.5 million people saw von Braun interviewed on television by John Cameron Swayze (Ordway and Liebermann 1992, p. 141).

The *Collier's* articles produced a flood of inquiries to the publisher on how to become an astronaut, which led to articles in 1953 on the human aspects of space travel. The seventh article in the *Collier's* series, published on June 27, 1953, described a "baby space station" with a Rhesus monkey on board and included a proposal to study the medical effects of spaceflight while in orbit for 60 days. Such a station could be ready in five to seven years, von Braun said, as a precursor to a manned station (Ordway and Liebermann 1992, p. 142).

Collier's decided to end the eight-part series in the summer of 1953 with an article about a manned expedition to Mars. But this article had to be delayed because of the large number of requests for information on how to train to be an astronaut, Randy Liebermann reports, but it finally appeared on April 30, 1954. It incorporated von Braun's 1948 idea to build a flotilla of 10 Mars spaceships, to be assembled in Earth orbit. Mars would be home to 70 explorers who would stay for 15 months, having undertaken the most fantastic voyage man could then imagine (Ordway and Liebermann 1992, p. 143). Many men who went on to work in the U.S. space program "attribute their initial spark of interest to the pages of *Collier's*," according to Liebermann (Ordway and Liebermann 1992, p. 142).

The response to the *Collier's* series led to a project to make the material available in a more permanent form. In 1952, Cornelius Ryan edited *Across the Space Frontier*, with illustrations by Chesley Bonestell and others. The book was an expansion of the scientific symposia that appeared in the pages of *Collier's* magazine, as Ryan explained in the introduction:

> This book is a fascinating preview of how man can reach space and establish, 1,075 miles above the Earth, a huge wheel-shaped space station. What you will read here is not a science-fictionist's dream. These chapters embody the latest available scientific data on the many problems which man must face when he travels beyond areas of space. Here is a blueprint of a programme for the conquest of space, prepared by some of the world's best scientific minds on space research. . . .
>
> The claim that huge rocket ships of the type here described can be built, and a space station created, is no longer challenged by any serious scientist. . . . All they need now is time—about 10 years—plus money [about $4 billion] and authority. . . . And when one considers the billions of dollars spent during World War II and on rearmament since the Korean war, such an expenditure would be small compared to the returns [Ryan 1952, p. xii].

In a warning unheeded by the Eisenhower administration, Ryan continued:

> This book is also an urgent warning that the United States should immediately embark on a long-range development programme to secure for the West "space superiority," since a ruthless power established on a space station could actually subjugate the peoples of the world. Sweeping around the Earth in a fixed orbit like a second Moon, this man-made island in the heavens could be used as a platform from which to launch guided missiles. ... We know that the Soviet Union, like the United States, has an extensive guided-missile and rocket programme under way...
>
> We have already learned to our sorrow that Soviet scientists and engineers should never be underestimated. They produced the atomic bomb years earlier than was anticipated. ... We have the scientists and engineers. We have the inventive genius. We have vast industrial superiority. We should begin a space programme immediately, for in the hands of peace-loving nations the space station could be man's guardian in the skies. ... It would be the end of Iron Curtains wherever they might be [Ryan 1952, xiv].

Across the Space Frontier was lavishly illustrated. Wernher von Braun supplied the first chapter, headlined "Prelude to Space Travel," which would make excellent reading for today's congressmen and all policymakers, who urgently need a new sense of what man can accomplish if his sights are set on the stars.

Von Braun described the space station, "which [would] be man's first foothold in space." The huge, new "moon" was to be carried into Earth orbit in pieces, assembled there, and placed in a 1,075-mile polar orbit around the Earth. From that vantage point, the space station was to circle the globe once every two hours, with the Earth turning East-to-West underneath it. In addition to making spectacular observations of the Earth, "from this platform, a trip to the Moon itself will be just a step, as scientists reckon distance in space" (Ryan 1952, p. 12).

Von Braun predicted that "development of the space station is as inevitable as the rising of the Sun; man has already poked his nose into space and he is not likely to pull it back" (Ryan 1952, p.

15). The $4 billion cost, von Braun wrote, was only "about twice the cost of developing the atomic bomb, but less than one-quarter of the price of military materials ordered by the Defense Department during the last half of 1951" (Ryan 1952, p. 19).

Rockets would be built, according to von Braun, able to carry a crew and 30 or 40 tons of cargo to the space station. Such a rocket would stand 265 feet tall, measure 65 feet in diameter, and be equipped with 51 rocket motors capable of delivering 28 million pounds of thrust (Ryan 1952, p. 25). (By comparison, the Saturn V rocket that took Apollo astronauts to the Moon stood 365 feet tall, measured 30 feet in diameter; Saturn V used a cluster of five liquid propellant engines in the first stage and five hydrogen engines in the second stage, which produced 7.5 million pounds of thrust.)

Von Braun estimated that about a dozen flights would be needed to construct the station, including the construction of a space observatory some distance away from the station and telescopes for mapping the Earth and heavens. The illustrations for von Braun's design, executed by Chesley Bonestell, remained a popular image of a space station until the 1984 initiation of President Reagan's Space Station program, when more modern planning and design work replaced it.

When would the United States complete the construction of this outpost on the new frontier? Von Braun estimated that America would establish a permanent manned space station during the year 1963.

The question "Can we survive in space?" is addressed by Dr. Heinz Haber, formerly with the Air Force Department of Space Medicine, who summarized what was then known about the effects on humans of spaceflight.

Ley ended the book on the following optimistic note:

The establishment and subsequent operation of the space station is undeniably a large-size project. But so was the liberation of atomic energy, so were Grand Coulee Dam and Boulder Dam. And so, at an earlier date, were the Panama Canal and the Suez Canal. ... And there is one other thing that should never be forgotten even for a minute. The space station is, or will be, the first step toward the exploration of space. Any first step is said to be difficult. ... But once it has been made the difficulties will diminish at a surprisingly rapid rate and the

FIGURE 8.3
THE ROUND-THE-MOON SHIP
This is the fabulous 1952 design for a ship to take a crew to the Moon which
appeared in *Across the Space Frontier*. The cluster of engines were to burn nitric
acid and hydrazine. The personnel sphere would carry a crew around the Moon,
and then bring it back to dock at the space station. The scale is indicated by the
figure of a man at the bottom right.

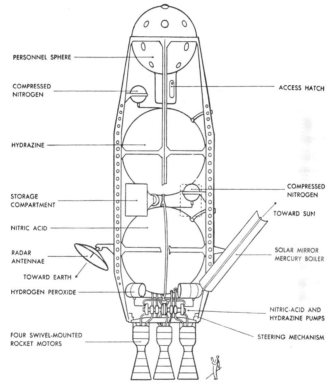

Source: Cornelius Ryan *Across the Space Frontier* (London: Sidgwick and Jackson Limited, 1952).

gate to the Solar System will have been opened [Ryan 1952,
p. 117].

Man on the Moon, which appeared in 1953, was the second
installment of the *Collier's* symposium and magazine series in book
form. It was also edited by Cornelius Ryan, who forecast in his
introduction that after the establishment of a space station, within

FIGURE 8.4
THE LANDING OF THE RETURN VEHICLE
It was assumed from the beginning of spacecraft designing that men would return
to Earth elegantly (and aerodynamically) with a glider, rather than plop into the
ocean as the U.S. spacecraft before the Shuttle did, or crash to the ground, as Soviet
spacecraft still do. The landing vehicle drawn here is the third stage of a multistage
rocket which would land at a slower speed than airliners.

Source: Cornelius Ryan *Across the Space Frontier* (London: Sidgwick and Jackson Limited, 1952).

10 or 15 years, mankind will have gone "another step forward—to
the Moon":

> The ships the explorers will use for the long journey through
> space will bear little resemblance to those depicted by the
> science-fictionists. In fact, their appearance is even more fantas-
> tic. But there is this difference: They work.
>
> The reader may well ask if it isn't rash to attempt a detailed
> technical description of vehicles that are at least a quarter of
> a century away. He may also wonder whether, by the time
> such vehicles are constructed, there may not be better solutions
> to the technical problems than those presented here. The an-
> swer, of course, is yes [Ryan 1953, p. 13].

Using an approach employed a few years earlier by Wernher
von Braun in his description of an even more distant manned mission
to Mars, Ryan wrote:

The purpose of this book, however, is to show that a lunar voyage is possible even now, by applying the basic engineering knowledge and technical ability available to us today. . . .

There have been many books written about journeys to the Moon, but few of the writers seem to know what to do with their explorers once they get them there. The authors of this book have tried to describe definitely both the types of scientists who will go on the expedition and the experiments and investigations they will perform [Ryan 1932, p. 14].

The illustrations in *Man on the Moon* provided the closest look we had at that adventure until man actually got there. "The first men to reach the Moon will discover a world of magnificent dilapidation," Ryan wrote. "Covered with deserts, rugged mountain chains, and without an atmosphere, oceans, or vegetation, the Moon will appear to the visitors as a ghastly heavenly corpse" (Ryan 1953, p. 17). Ryan's description was perhaps a bit melodramatic, but when the Apollo astronauts arrived on the Moon, they sent descriptions back to Earth of an airless, lifeless, lonely, and desolate place.

The scope of the lunar venture described in *Man on the Moon* was truly grandiose. Its only rival was the Project Horizon report, a technical, factual scientific study assembled later by the same group, based on the same concepts and optimism. "Here is how we shall go to the Moon," Chapter 3 opens. "The pioneer expedition of at least 50 scientists and technicians will begin its journey from the space station's orbit in three clumsy-looking but highly efficient rocket ships. . ." (Ryan 1953, p. 25).

To build the Moon ships, 360 flights of three-stage supply rockets will be required to deliver construction material and fuel to the space station. They will "need about three times as much fuel as was consumed in the form of high-octane gasoline during the Berlin Airlift" (Ryan 1953, p. 29). This job will make use of a fleet of 15 ferrying ships, each making about 24 flights over a period of eight months.

Ryan and his collaborators understood the impact such an adventure would have on the public. The authors predicted that the takeoff from the space station to start the journey to the Moon would "be watched by millions. . . . Television cameras on the space station [would] transmit the scene to receivers all over the world" (Figure 8.5) (Ryan 1953, p. 60).

The authors continued to describe a procedure quite similar to that of today's science missions aboard the Space Shuttle:

> Throughout the six weeks of the exploration [on the Moon] a special panel of scientists on Earth will remain in constant session ... they will follow our every move by radio and tele- photo, keeping careful track of our findings and difficulties— as, indeed, the entire world may be expected to do!
>
> At the end of each day, on receipt of the team reports, the scientific-group leaders on the Moon will confer with the panel of experts on the Earth. New developments and new leads will be discussed, and methods devised for trouble-shooting in all phases of our work. ... Sometimes the panel of experts on Earth will request a repetition of an experiment or suggest a revision in our plans. In this way, nearly every branch of science can take full advantage of the exploration [Ryan 1953, p. 107].

Man on the Moon ended with the return of the astronauts to Earth:

> There, the members of the scientific panel which guided us during the Moon's exploration will await us—and, without question, a great crowd of Earthlings, come to see the first men ever to set foot on the ancient, mysterious soil of the Earth's closest neighbour in the heavens. We shall have been the first— but not the last [Ryan 1953, p. 126].

During parts of 1952, 1953, and 1954, while the *Collier's* series and the books based on them were circulating, Willy Ley made an extensive lecture tour, which took him to 40 states and to Canada. In 1957, Ley described the atmosphere of public excitement about space exploration at that time, although he modestly does not say that he played a major role in creating it: "Scientific institutions, public lecture halls, the magazines, the newspapers, the radio waves, and the television channels were full of space-travel and satellite talk" (Ley 1957a, p. 330).

On tour, Ley explained the basics of rocketry and spaceflight: "To a mathematician or astronomer this explanation is 'obvious,' but I have found that it isn't quite that obvious to highway engineers,

FIGURE 8.5

SEQUENCE OF MANEUVERS TO BE CARRIED OUT TO THE MOON
The Moon ship leaves from the surface of the Earth and rendezvous with the space station. From there, the Moon ship departs and its empty fuel tanks are jettisoned. Nearing the Moon, the ship turns to be in position for landing, for which retro-rockets are employed.

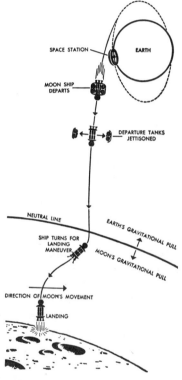

Source: Cornelius Ryan *Man on the Moon* (London: Sidgwick and Jackson Limited, 1953).

judges, medical doctors, and just plain interested laymen" (Ley 1957a, p. 323).

Public excitement about space travel was so great, in fact, that the architects of popular culture joined the bandwagon. "Once before, the history of space travel had been influenced by the motion-picture industry. Soon [after the *Collier's* series] history repeated itself," Ley wrote in 1957 (Ley 1957a, p. 331). Ley related

232   HOW WE GOT TO THE MOON

that he had received a phone call from Walt Disney who proposed
that he make monthly trips to California, to be an adviser for a new
Disney film, *Man in Space.* Ley agreed.

Ward Kimball, a collaborator of Disney beginning in the 1930s,
related that Walt Disney had asked him for ideas for the theme of
his planned Tomorrowland at the new Disneyland Park, then under
construction in California. Kimball replied that he had read some
very interesting articles about spaceflight in *Collier's* and said he
found it "fascinating that such noted scientists believed that we
would actually be moving into space" (Stuhlinger and Ordway 1992,
p. 205).

Kimball studied the *Collier's* article, worked out some ideas
with his layout people, and presented them to Disney on April 17,
1954. As reported in the 1992 biography of von Braun:

> "We wanted to be cautious, however, and to retain, beside
> the more fantastic aspects, the serious aspects as well. . . . Our
> reputation was based on fantasy," explained Kimball, "but here
> we were to offer only a presentation based on solid science.
> People with imagination would come together with men who
> dealt with facts, to combine their resources."
>
> Disney was excited about the preparations made by his col-
> laborators. "When we were finished," Bill Bosché, Disney's
> sketch-man reminiscences, "Walt was beside himself. He ran
> out of the story room, went up to a desk, and tore a blank
> piece of paper out of a notebook. He handed it to Kimball and
> said something that nobody had ever heard him say, ' 'Just tell
> me what you need!' "
>
> With this support from his boss, Kimball set to work. He
> imagined a three-part show: "Man in Space" "Man and the
> Moon," and "Mars and Beyond." But first he needed some rocket
> and space experts. He remembered the *Collier's* series and got
> in touch with Willy Ley, who gladly agreed to cooperate. "Willy
> proved to be a virtual encyclopedia," Bosché recalls. "He could
> address almost every issue. . . . He was a very amusing guy and
> we all had great fun with him!" (Stuhlinger and Ordway 1992,
> p. 205).

Wernher von Braun and Dr. Heinz Haber also consulted on
the television series. In the first show, all three consultants, plus

National Air and Space Museum, Smithsonian Institution, 80-19166

Walt Disney and Willy Ley discuss the space film series at the Disney studio in California. The three television broadcasts introduced millions of viewers to the future of space travel, and encouraged President Eisenhower to commit the United States to launch a satellite during the 1957 International Geophysical Year.

Walt Disney and Ward Kimball, all appeared on the program to explain to the audience what would follow. In all, Disney spent $1 million to produce the three shows.

"Man in Space" was planned for Disney's weekly television show, but was produced on film so it could also be released in movie houses. It was first shown on March 5, 1955, on ABC-TV.

Willy Ley estimates that 42 million people saw the program (Ley 1957a, p. 331), while Randy Liebermann quotes the figure "nearly 100 million" (Ordway and Liebermann 1992, p. 145).

The second show, "Man on the Moon," aired on December 28, 1955. "The scene called for only a circumlunar reconnaissance flight without attempting a landing. The lack of any landing may have disappointed many viewers, but it corresponded to one of Disney's ground rules for the series, that it be "based on solid science" (Stuhlinger and Ordway 1992, p. 206).

The third show, "Mars and Beyond," was seen on television on December 4, 1957, precisely two months after Sputnik. According to an autobiographical account by ion propulsion expert Ernst Stuhlinger:

> [Stuhlinger] suggested a spaceship for the manned flight to Mars, which would produce an electrical current with the help of a nuclear-electric generator system. The thrust would be produced by a stream of ions, which accelerated an electric field to a high exhaust velocity. A propulsion system of this nature had never previously been constructed, but according to the opinion of experts, was a technically feasible principle.
>
> Von Braun had no objections to seeing this used in the project for Mars, especially since the electrical system would allow a significantly greater payload as well as a shorter travel time [Stuhlinger and Ordway 1992, p. 207].

The Disney series had a profound effect on many in the audience, including Dwight D. Eisenhower, the President of the United States. It thereby changed the course of the American space effort. Stuhlinger reported: "Shortly after the first Disney Space show had been presented to the television public, 'President Dwight D. Eisenhower borrowed the show and showed it to high-ranking officials at the Pentagon,' according to David R. Smith, the head of the archives at Walt Disney Productions. Six weeks later, he announced the intention of the United States to put a small unmanned satellite into orbit," during the International Geophysical Year (Stuhlinger and Ordway 1992, p. 206).

During the 1950s, the German space pioneers were engaged in a quick-paced activity to build the popular support for space

NASA, Marshall Space Flight Center

Walt Disney photographed with Wernher von Braun in 1954, with some of the models used in the Disney television series. The films combined imaginative animation of trips to space stations and the Moon and sequences with actors, with appearances by the consulting experts, such as von Braun, to explain the basic concepts of rockets and space travel.

exploration they knew was necessary for a national program. Most ubiquitous was Willy Ley. As Sam Moskowitz describes it:

> Everywhere one turned, Willy Ley's name was on a book, in a magazine, in the newspapers or in a catalogue endorsing a rocket toy. His face peered out from the television screen; his voice, instantly identifiable, seemed always on radio; and posters announced his lectures at major cities across the country [Moskowitz 1966, p. 42].

Although frequently on the road, Ley found time to do a review of science books for children in October 1953, using the works of

Jules Verne as a model. "All of Jules Verne's books had the intent of instructing: as somebody once put it, 'all his heroes had swallowed the encyclopedia and disgorged sections of it with or without provocation,' " Ley wrote.

Ley described his standard for children's books: "A science fiction story, and especially one for young readers, has to pass its science test first. It is not a question of whether the reader is taught a little or a lot, the point is that whatever he is taught must be correct" (Ley 1953, p. 1742). Five years later, Ley himself wrote a series of books for young people, which was published by the Guild Press in Poughkeepsie, New York.

Willy Ley's book *Rockets, Missiles, and Space Travel,* which should be read by every literate person, was first published in May 1944 under the title, *Rockets.* In 1947, an expanded version was titled, *Rockets and Space Travel,* and the final title first appeared in 1951. With almost every new printing, Ley expanded and updated the book. The 1957 version of *Rockets* was published only months before Sputnik. It is a comprehensive history of the concept of space travel from ancient times through modern science, and an on-the-spot account of rocket development from the 1920s on.

In his final chapter, "The Spaceship," Ley credits Hermann Oberth's 1923 book, *The Rocket into Interplanetary Space,* with the first scientifically competent discussion of manned, Earth-orbiting space stations. "This really is much more than the mere germ of an idea," Ley wrote. "It is the whole concept without engineering detail" (Ley 1957a, p. 366).

Ley discussed alternative concepts as well. "It was especially Krafft Ehricke who pointed out that it was *not* necessary for every top [upper] stage to return to the ground. Some, or rather most, of the rockets designed to ferry the space station into orbit could be straight cargo carriers." In this case, they would not need wings to land back on Earth and could be unmanned. "Wernher von Braun accepted this suggestion," Ley reported, "and then went one step further. Manned carriers didn't have to carry cargo then and the size could be drastically reduced" (Ley 1957a, p. 379).

Although after Sputnik, space exploration was the major subject of interest to Ley and his readers, a compilation in book form of the columns he published in *Galaxy Science Fiction Magazine* during the 1950s includes some of the most fascinating topics in the history of science: "Tribes of the Dinosaurs" (with illustrations

National Air and Space Museum, Smithsonian Institution, A-4792C

Willy Ley combined his well-known expertise in rockets and space travel with a broad knowledge and interest in all areas of scientific endeavor. Here he is pictured in undoubtedly one of his favorite New York City spots, at the dinosaur exhibit at the American Museum of Natural History.

by his wife, Olga); "Slow Lightning," about the ball lightning experiments of P.L. Kapitsa in the Soviet Union; "Strange Planet Next Door," which is not about Mars, but the world on the floor of the ocean; "The Early Days of the Metric System;" and "The Observatory on the Moon" (Ley 1957b). Today, if one stayed home and spent time assimilating Willy Ley's articles and books, one would have a better education in science history than can be obtained at most high schools.

After the Sputnik shock, Ley was called upon to explain what the new "space race" was all about. In an article for *The New York Mirror* on January 5, 1958, he responded to queries on the meaning of the phrase "space superiority," which had been used at Senate Preparedness subcommittee hearings:

"Bluntly speaking, it means that the Russians could prevent us from using space if they got there first. It is an equivalent of what has happened in the past—first with the sea and later in the air." Ley then guessed that "probably the most visible expression of space superiority will be the manned space station," and went on to describe some of the technical details of Wernher von Braun's enormous ring-shaped structure and its functions (Ley 1958a).

Two weeks later, Ley continued his explanation:

> While in the long run, the purpose of the space station is peaceful and devoted to research and progress, the immediate and urgent purpose is to establish and maintain space superiority. This is accomplished by careful scrutiny of the ground. With the aid of optical equipment, it will be possible to see objects as small as single airplanes. . . . The fact that very little could be done without being observed is in itself a rather powerful deterrent [Ley 1958b].

At the same time that Willy Ley was saturating the print media and the airwaves, the German-led rocket team in Huntsville established its own "outreach" effort to keep space exploration issues before the public.

In 1957, the magazine *SPACE Journal* was established, as "the official organ of the Rocket City Astronomical Association, a non-profit, non-political, scientific and educational organization" (Stuhlinger 1958). The associate editor was Mitchell Sharpe, who is a historian and chronicler of the Space Age, working today in Huntsville. The board of consultants included Wernher von Braun, Ernst Stuhlinger, and Hermann Oberth.

Oberth had finally come to Huntsville in July 1955, after von Braun had made that possible. He worked for Ernst Stuhlinger in the Research Projects Office of the Army Ballistic Missile Agency (ABMA). After the war, Oberth had been interrogated, arrested, and then released. He worked for two years in Switzerland, and in 1950 went to La Spezia to work for the Italian admiralty on an ammonium rocket project. He returned to his home in Feucht, near Nuremberg, in 1953. But he knew that the future development of his ideas would be in America.

Oberth's contributions to the development of rocketry were well known in Europe, although less appreciated in the United States. In August 1950, Willy List, the grandson of the noted German

political economist and American citizen Friedrich List, wrote a
letter on Oberth's behalf to the commander in chief of U.S. Military
Forces in Germany. In his letter List states that his reason for writing
is that he is "eagerly endeavoured to let the U.S.A. have every
advantage given by the elaborations of scientists." In that spirit, he
reports that "Professor Oberth . . . authorizes me to utilize his new
inventions. Have the kindness to inform yourself of the enclosed
appendix. You will find there that he has got [sic] *results of the
greatest importance for the defence of the U.S.A. and progress in
general. . . .*

"Professor Oberth was and is willing to move to the U.S.A. and
authorizes me again to make it known. . . . I ask you to let me be
present when you discuss with Professor Oberth and to bear the
expense for I am a refugee who lost everything" (List 1950).

But was no easy task to convince the army to employ Oberth
in the U.S. rocket program because the task at hand was the development of rocket technology and Oberth's genius lay in the creation
of new ideas. Wernher von Braun did succeed in getting the army
to employ Oberth and while at the Redstone Arsenal from 1955 to
1958, Oberth did theoretical analyses of the stability of satellite
orbits. He also did more detailed work on the space mirror (Ordway
and Sharpe 1979, pp. 378–9). In June 1957, Oberth produced the
report "An Estimate of the Flight Time and Accuracy for an Earth
to Moon Missile Plotted Against the Shut Off Velocity."

In March 1958, Oberth completed a report titled, "Problems
and Proposals Concerning the Interception of Satellites by Manned
Vehicles," which discusses the feasibility of destroying an orbital
satellite by missiles launched from the upper stages of a manned
rocket and guided to the target by the pilot. He faced the same
conundrum he did during the war at Peenemünde—he could not
gain access to his own work because he lacked security clearance!

A long-lasting contribution to space exploration during his brief
stay in America was the 1957 publication in English of his book
Man into Space, first published in Germany. There, he puts forth
the guidelines for a manned space program, now that the development of rockets had opened the door to the Space Age.

To prepare to send men into space, he advised, the prospective
astronauts must have available "methods for reproducing the conditions most likely to be met with," in space (Oberth 1957, p. 5).
Having considered and experimented with the possible biological

effects of near-zero gravity since his youth, he cautioned that "while aviation medicine could develop concurrently with aviation, space medicine must *precede* spaceflight. When we examine today's space-travel progress closely, we realize that there is not a moment to lose" (Oberth 1957, p. 7).

Using simplified graphics to make his concepts accessible to the nonspecialist, Oberth described the space station, space ferries, and other infrastructure prerequisite for manned space exploration. He assumed that the exploration of the Moon would not be a "one-shot" effort, but a sustained colonization program:

> I am always being approached by "inventors" who consider [the] space station superfluous and believe that spaceships can take off direct from Earth and make straight for other planets. This is not true.
>
> A flight to the Moon will be much simpler and cheaper if a space station is erected first (although this in itself will cost a vast amount of money), and if the spaceship is assembled there and then flies to the Moon from that starting point. Other planets cannot be reached with the means at present available in rocket engineering unless a space station is used [Oberth 1957, pp. 21–22].

Oberth stressed that the space station was an evolutionary concept, starting with an unmanned satellite, and growing to a more complex manned station. Its "principal purpose should be to make still more distant space travel simpler," functioning as a "filling station in space" (Oberth 1957, p. 61). But it also presents a unique, microgravity environment, and Oberth recommended that "this state of 'no gravity' or weightlessness be used for physical and medical experiments":

> Interesting experiments could be made on the growth of plants and Infusoria [minute organisms] under weightless conditions. Would plants become disconcerted by the absence of gravity, and what would be the result? The size of most plants is limited by the force of gravity. Would they grow to giant size? [Oberth 1957, pp. 63–65].

"All our scientific and technical knowledge is based on the existence of the force of gravity," Oberth said, so the station can investigate other physical phenomena, such as a candle flame (which was the subject of an experiment on a recent Space Shuttle mission), the behavior of liquids, and materials processing in space (Oberth 1957, p. 63).

Oberth then described the different types of space stations that should be constructed, the research with telescopes that can be carried out, the use of electric and nuclear propulsion for next-generation spacecraft, his space mirror orbiting the Earth, and his fantastic Moon car, which he expanded into a book two years later (Figure 8.6). He reported that "two thousand volunteers have already applied to me personally," to go into space. "I myself would willingly be the first to make such a trip," he said, "even if the chance of returning were only 50–50 (Oberth 1957, p. 80).

Oberth ended his informative excursion into the future asking:

And what would be the purpose of all this? For those who have never known the relentless urge to explore and discover, there is no answer. For those who have felt this urge, the answer is self-evident. For the latter there is no solution but to investigate every possible means of gaining knowledge of the universe [Oberth 1957, pp. 177–78].

Oberth's book *The Moon Car* was published after the success of the von Braun team's Explorer launch, that put the United States into space. The English translation by Willy Ley appeared in 1959, after Oberth had to return to Germany. "This book is dedicated to the great engineer and organizer Professor Dr. Wernher von Braun, who transformed the idea of space travel into reality. In appreciation and gratitude," Oberth wrote.

Oberth's design for this Moon car is a fantastically sized vehicle with the capability to hop over obstacles encountered on the surface of the Moon, as seen in Figure 8.7.

In 1959, when he reached the age of 65, Oberth was forced to retire from work for the U.S. government and he reluctantly returned to Germany, where he could collect a pension while continuing his study and work at home. His biographer Heinz Gartmann wrote: "the old castle in Feucht had almost become a place of pilgrimage. Whoever worked on rockets and came to Germany

FIGURE 8.6

HERMANN OBERTH'S SPACE PORT

Oberth's space station was truly a "grand design." This is his 1957 concept of a highly developed space station, to be used as a "springboard" for exploration of the Solar System. It includes an assembly shop and other facilities for such a purpose, and is also a scientific station, with a large telescope and experiment chambers to study the effects of variable gravities.

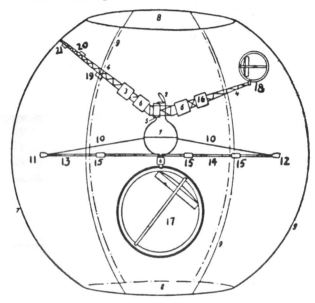

The springboard station or space port. (1) Assembly shop; (2) air lock; (3) reserve container; (4) Ross-Smith arm; (5) screen shielding air lock from sunlight; (6) refuse container; (7, 8, 9) wire to which watchdog bombs are attached; (10) tensioning wires; (11, 12) living quarters; (13, 14) connecting corridor; (15) chambers for experimenting with varying gravities; (16) food, water, and reserve air supply; (17, 18) observation telescope; (19, 20, 21) installations for special purposes.

Source: Hermann Oberth *Man into Space* (New York: Harper & Brothers, 1957).

FIGURE 8.7
OBERTH'S FABULOUS MOON CAR
The Moon Car which Hermann Oberth designed appears as an inverted vehicle,
with the bulk of the equipment on top, and a relatively small leg to the ground. The
entire vehicle was designed to be able to hop over uneven surfaces on the Moon,
and avoid canyons and crevices.

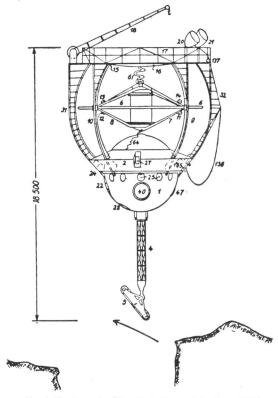

Source: Hermann Oberth *The Moon Car* (New York: Harper & Brothers, 1959).

visited Hermann Oberth. Publishers, editors, journalists, all came
to his door. . . . Many came only to know what the man looked like,
whose work . . . had so sharply influenced the history of technology
and perhaps the future history of the world" (Gartmann, 1955).

Hermann Oberth died in December 1989. Six months after
his death, in May 1990, Peenemünde veteran Konrad Dannenberg
published a paper in his memory. During his stay in Huntsville,
Dannenberg wrote, Oberth "made his greatest contributions by his
writings and his discussions with colleagues, by which he influenced

many members of the Rocket Team, myself included. He converted us into space enthusiasts and faithful believers in rocketry. This unobtrusive effort is in my opinion Hermann Oberth's greatest contribution to spaceflight" (Dannenberg 1990).

The effort to educate the public through the written word was carried on in Huntsville in the Rocket City Astronomical Association's magazine, *SPACE Journal*. Exemplary of what was offered was a series of articles by Ernst Stuhlinger on "Life on Other Stars." Stuhlinger, who was then the director of the Research Projects Office for the Army Ballistic Missile Agency in Huntsville, was born in 1913 in Germany. He holds a doctorate in physics from the University of Tübingen and he worked closely with Hans Geiger for seven years. At Peenemünde, he did guidance and control research.

In this series, Stuhlinger reviewed in detail the development of the atmosphere and other prerequisites for life forms on Earth. He proposed there are probably 100,000 planets in our Milky Way Galaxy with conditions similar to Earth. "This very question has been with mankind as long as there has been scientific thought," Stuhlinger wrote. "It will certainly remain not only the most intriguing question of all science, but also one of the most profound questions which can be asked by man" (Stuhlinger 1958, p. 22). Indeed, the program for the Search for Extraterrestrial Intelligence (SETI) today is a worldwide radio astronomy effort to continue the quest for the answer to the question: Is there life elsewhere in the universe?

As the Space Age came over the horizon with Sputnik, Edward Pendray, Willy Ley's colleague in the American Rocket Society, was already thinking about widespread applications of rockets. In the September 1957 issue of the rocket society's magazine, *Astronautics,* Pendray asked, somewhat impatiently, "When will rockets go commercial?" Pendray outlined 10 possible nonmilitary uses of rockets, which were presented with illustrations.

Pendray reported on the results of a 1947 survey taken for the Daniel and Florence Guggenheim Foundation (which funded the research of Robert Goddard) "of leaders of the then infant rocket and guided missile industry" on the future of the industry (Pendray 1957, p. 21). An overwhelming 83 percent "said they expected development within the decade of major peacetime nonmilitary industries based on rocket and jet propulsion." Although this had not yet happened by 1957, Pendray reports that the government-funded space industry had spent more than $1 billion in capital investment; employed at least 50,000 scientists, engineers, and technically trained personnel; and provided jobs for another 100,000 nontechnical workers, in 1,000 different companies, which provides a solid basis for a future commercial endeavor (Pendray 1957, p. 22).

"What principally appears to be lacking," Pendray wrote, "is some good, solid American daring, imagination and commercial enterprise." (Many would make the same argument today.) He listed 10 of possibly 24 nongovernment uses of rockets, including: the transport of mail and valuable, lightweight cargo via rocket; weather research; passenger rocket aircraft across the Atlantic, or transcontinental routes; spaceflight, including space research, a thirst for adventure, tourist curiosity, the possible colonization of the Moon and planets, and mining ventures; use of high-velocity jets produced by rocket engines for metal drilling, boring, and cutting; deep sea soundings using underwater rockets; photography, mapping, and exploring from medium altitudes; and rockets for spectacles, entertainment, and fireworks displays (Pendray 1957, p. 23).

In 1960, the only space program that had been approved by the Eisenhower administration was Project Mercury, for single-man orbital flights around the Earth. But as Willy Ley warned in a *Space World* magazine article titled "Getting Around—After We Get There," published that year, although the lunar landing might be 8–12 years away, "being ready ahead of time would do no harm but *not* being ready would be a catastrophe":

> A few weeks ago, I was sitting on the front steps of my house, looking at the full Moon and thinking about how to get around the lunarscape. . . . This is a situation wryly familiar to travelers of today: after the jet has whipped you across the continent in 4 hours and 40 minutes, you stand at the airport, screaming for a taxi. Only another 10 miles to go, but these 10 miles are almost harder to cover than the previous 2,500" [Ley 1960b, p. 57].

Ley then considered various proposals for traversing the lunar landscape, including the use of solar energy during the two-week lunar day; one by Wernher von Braun for powering a vehicle with a turbine driven by the decomposition of hydrogen peroxide, which would have to be supplied from Earth; using energy stored mechanically in a flywheel; using atomic power; and Hermann Oberth's Moon Car. Vehicles were also considered for use on Mars, where the presence of an atmosphere, though very thin, allows the possible use of blimps and other aerodynamic vehicles, in addition to land rovers.

In early 1961, before President Kennedy's announcement of the Apollo program, there was a very limited idea of what man could do in space. This was an interesting turn of events, because in the early prehistory of the space program it was assumed nearly everything would be done directly by men, including taking photographs and making observations, "largely because modern instrumentation didn't exist" (Ley 1961a, p. 21).

But, Ley wrote, "With the advent of guidance systems, telemetering, and television, the original idea of Man-in-Space was temporarily pushed into the background. . . . Carried away by their own accomplishments, some space planners even began to argue that there was no compelling need to put man into space." Ley argued to the contrary. "We now know that this reasoning was hasty at best and simply wrong in many cases," he wrote. "Certain unmanned satellite experiments which have failed miserably would not have gone wrong if a man had been aboard" (Ley 1961a, p. 22). This is even more true today, when, on every Space Shuttle science mission, the astronauts have had to "trouble-shoot" problems in experiments to save them from failure. "A manned satellite in orbit is not only a weather observing device, or a superlative astronomical observatory, or a monitor of possible enemy activities. It is also an inhabited 'house' in space. . . ." Ley continued. Ley discussed the Space Lab designed by the Martin company, which is similar in outline to the current space station designs, to make his point.

In March 1961, still before President Kennedy's Apollo announcement, Ley addressed the potential commercial applications of space technology in an article titled "Space Prospecting." "Almost exactly 30 years ago a German engineer and I were standing on the proving ground of the Verein für Raumschiffhart (Society for Space Travel) in Reinickendorf, Germany, watching the take-off of one of the early experimental liquid-fuel rockets," Ley began. The engineer asked Ley what would finally make money in rocketry. At that time, the answer he got back was "mail rockets, and Earth transportation" (Ley 1961b, p. 33). It is interesting looking back now, that neither of these two particular applications of rockets has proved to be commercially viable.

Ley then proposed that prospecting for space materials will be carried out from the lunar base. Asteroid mining will be of real value, he asserted, adding, "but don't try too hard to figure out what will be commercially viable in the future" (Ley 1961b, p. 52). "The commercial aspect of a certain voyage of 1492 was based on cheaper shipping of silks and spices from the Orient. Columbus could not foresee the immense flow of trade—including everything *but* silks and spices—that would come from the new world bonanza he had discovered" (Ley 1961b, p. 55).

Writing again in *Space World* in April 1961, Ley turned to answer questions posed to him, during a lecture series the preceding winter, about the uses of nuclear energy in space. Project Rover, he explained, was a project of the Atomic Energy Commission in the 1956–1957 period. But before Sputnik: "Project Rover suffered from the disease common to all scientific projects at the time—it was artificially starved by a tight-fisted and thoroughly unimaginative bureau of the budget. Rover feasibility studies virtually died of monetary malnutrition" (Ley 1061c, p. 20).

After Sputnik, $15 million was allocated for the construction of test facilities, and nuclear energy was being developed for use in the upper propulsion stage of the Saturn rocket. Nuclear-powered propulsion systems should be ready by 1965–1966, Ley reported. Nuclear propulsion "will boost our space program out of the Chemical Stone Ages into the Astronomical Age, speeding up the conquest of space vastly" (Ley 1961c, p. 54). As it turned out, for trips to the Moon it was found that the Saturn V engines could be upgraded sufficiently with liquid hydrogen upper stage propulsion systems and the Apollo program did not require nuclear propulsion.

It was well recognized, however, that nuclear propulsion would greatly enhance, and perhaps even be required to enable, manned missions to Mars. But when the manned Mars program was cancelled after Apollo, so was the nuclear propulsion program. It has only recently been resurrected, on a small scale.

Just months before Ley's untimely death in June 1969, *Events in Space* appeared. It is the first handbook, of all of the world's manned and unmanned satellite launches from 1957 to 1969. Ley did not live to see the Apollo 11 launch that landed the first men

Willy Ley was the single individual most responsible for rallying Americans throughout the 1950s to back a space program. He did this through the written word, radio and television, and personal appearances. Although he unfortunately died just a few weeks before the Apollo 11 spacecraft took the first astronauts to the Moon, his work helped lay the basis to make that flight possible.

National Air and Space Museum, Smithsonian Institution, A-4788D

on the Moon, but he reported with pleasure in this book that in *Frau im Mond,* "because of a dramatic requirement—the director wanted a full Moon in the sky during take-off—the flight path that Oberth calculated turned out to be the figure–8 flight path actually taken by Apollo 8." (Apollo 8 had circumnavigated the Moon for the first time in December 1968).

It was a sad moment for the Space Age when Willy Ley died on June 24, 1969, less than a month before the launch of Apollo 11. He had already purchased his plane ticket to fly down to Cape Canaveral. Lester del Ray wrote in an obituary:

It was largely Willy's work that killed the public antipathy to rockets after their use as a terror weapon [during the war] and began to make people dream of space again. When Kennedy proposed the race to the Moon he mentioned large sums required to finance it. ... Yet when public polls were taken

... the people were willing to support our space venture. ...
Somehow, through all his articles, Willy and those who were
converted by him had managed to convince half the nation [to
spend the money needed to go to the Moon] [del Ray 1969,
p. 156].

The affection and respect Ley's collaborators had for him is
exemplified by the fact that after he died, Chesley Bonestell publicized and supported the proposal of astronomer and long-time collaborator Robert S. Richardson, that a good-sized crater on the Moon
be named after Willy Ley.

Willy Ley had the rare ability to make the most difficult, and
to many, obscure, concepts in science accessible to the nontechnical
but interested public. He always looked at the present state of
science from the shoulders of the giants of the past, which then
informed his view of the future. In a December 1958 lecture at
the Franklin Institute in Philadelphia, Ley remarked, "It is easy to
prophesy the future because it is a future which began quite some
time ago" (Ley 1958c).

Wernher von Braun:
The Columbus
of Space

"We live in a democracy," [von Braun] used to say, "in which the will and the voice of people play a role. If you want to realize something as grand as space travel, you have got to win people to the idea. Being diplomatic is necessary, but it's not enough. You must be filled with the burning desire to see your idea come to life. You must have an absolute belief in the rightness of your cause and on your final success" [Stuhlinger and Ordway 1992 p. 173].

Wernher von Braun was a central figure in the successful American effort to put a man on the Moon. His burning desire to put mankind on the pathway to explore the universe kept him focused on that goal for more than four decades. His appreciation of the need to bring as many people as possible an understanding of and excitement about space travel led him in the late 1920s to help Hermann Oberth set up public exhibits on space travel in Germany, and throughout the 1960s to be the major public spokesman for space exploration.

From 1960 to 1970, von Braun directed the Marshall Space Flight Center in Huntsville, Alabama, where the Saturn V moon rocket was created. But his talents were not limited to masterful management or his ability to make complex concepts accessible to the common man. Wernher von Braun exercised an imagination that allowed him to look into the future and to instill his vision in others.

He could help solve the most detailed problem with a finicky rocket component and he could enrapture congressmen with testimony about the need for the Apollo program to be followed by the manned exploration of Mars. He was the most credible and sought-after spokesman for the space program during its period of greatest accomplishment because his own substantial contributions to it, as well as his ability to recruit others to the cause, flowed from a total and selfless commitment to a future he had already worked for 30 years to create.

On July 1, 1960, the George C. Marshall Space Flight Center in Huntsville officially came into being, when a group of 4,670 civil service employees, which had started a decade before as the "von Braun team," were transferred from the Army Ballistics Missile Agency (ABMA) to the newly created National Aeronautics and Space Administration (NASA).

Four months later, John F. Kennedy was elected President. By the spring, political events like the fiasco at the Bay of Pigs in Cuba had propelled the young and energetic new President to seek programs through which the United States could match the Soviets in a field of science and technology, and at the same time propel the stagnating U.S. economy forward. It was clear that space would be a major arena where the Soviets would test the mettle of the Free World. On April 12, 1961, Soviet cosmonaut Yuri Gagarin became the first man to orbit the Earth.

A few days after this feat, on April 20, President Kennedy ordered Vice President Lyndon Johnson to assess America's standing in the race for space. A JFK memorandum read: "In accordance with our conversation I would like for you as chairman of the Space Council to be in charge of making an overall survey of where we stand in space." A series of questions were posed, including,

Do we have a chance of beating the Soviets by putting a laboratory in space, or by a trip around the Moon, or by a rocket to land on the Moon, or by a rocket to go to the Moon and back with a man? Is there any other space program which promises dramatic results in which we could win?... How much additional would it cost?... Are we making maximum effort? Are we achieving necessary results?

In a reply forwarded to Kennedy by Johnson on April 29, von Braun stated that the Soviets had demonstrated a rocket "which can place 14,000 pounds of payload in orbit," compared to the 3,900-pound U.S. Mercury capsule to be launched on a Redstone rocket. With this booster capability, the Soviets can boost several astronauts into orbit simultaneously, perform an unmanned soft landing on the Moon, and hurl a substantial payload around the Moon to reenter the Earth's atmosphere, von Braun wrote.

But to land "*a man on the Moon and bring him back to Earth*" would require a rocket "*about 10 times as powerful*" as what the Soviets have so far demonstrated, von Braun asserted.

> We have a sporting chance of sending a three-man crew *around the Moon* ahead of the Soviets (1965/66) ... we have an excellent chance of beating the Soviets to the *first landing of a crew on the Moon* (including return capability, of course).
>
> With an all-out crash program I think we could accomplish this objective in 1967/68 ... [for] well over $1 billion for FY62, and ... the required increases for subsequent fiscal years may run twice as high or more. ...
>
> In my opinion, the most effective steps to improve our national stature in the space field, and to speed things up would be to identify a few (the fewer the better) goals in our space program as objectives of highest national priority, ... [and] put all other elements of our national space program on the "back burner. .." (For example: Let's land a man on the Moon in 1967 or 1968).

Less than one month later, on May 25, 1961, President John F. Kennedy would add some leeway to von Braun's timetable, committing the nation "to land a man on the Moon and return him safely to Earth" before the end of the decade of the 1960s. Kennedy's speech announcing the Apollo program would lead to the greatest peacetime mobilization of the scientific and engineering capabilities of any nation in history.

That von Braun was as good a politician as a technical adviser, was attested to by his colleague Hermann Koelle:

> Von Braun was closely involved in this decision process because Vice President Johnson was very friendly with von Braun. Through his election campaign, von Braun was invited by Johnson to give a speech to an electoral audience, and von

In his historic May 25, 1961 speech before a joint session of Congress, President John F. Kennedy committed the United States "to land a man on the Moon and return him safely to Earth." Wernher von Braun had suggested that as the goal for the civilian space program less than one month before.

Braun started, "Thanks to the greatest Texan ever, Lyndon Johnson." He had a very good line to Johnson and so he was involved. And he had the data. When von Braun said something, it was believable [Koelle 1992].

Dr. Brainerd Holmes, head of the NASA Office of Manned Space Flight during the Apollo program, commented on von Braun's prowess years later:

Without a doubt, the Germans had an influence on our decision to go to the Moon. . . . I think von Braun's letter [to Vice President Johnson] had a great influence on President Kennedy's decision. . . . There was just no one out there like von Braun. He was a unique personality, and he was the driving

force for the development of space travel and for going to the
Moon [Stuhlinger and Ordway 1992 p. 376].

How we would get to the Moon was one of the major questions
that had to be answered to get the Apollo program started.

Three principal modes were under consideration.

First was the direct mode. An even larger booster than the
Saturn (the Nova) would be necessary to carry men, fuel, materiel,
and equipment from the Earth directly to the surface of the Moon,
and return. This would be similar to the rocket portrayed in the
1929 film *The Woman in the Moon.* But it was determined that
such an enormous and complex booster could not be available in
time to meet Kennedy's timetable.

Second was the Earth-orbit rendezvous mode (EOR), favored
by the German leadership of the von Braun team. The EOR mode
would use at least two Saturn flights to bring spacecraft and astronauts to orbit, the lunar craft would be assembled there, and the
crew would then go to the surface of the Moon and back.

Finally there was the lunar-orbit rendezvous (LOR) mode. This
proposed to bring a smaller Apollo system to orbit with one Saturn
launch, fly to the Moon, leave one ship in orbit about the Moon,
land a small party on the surface, and have the lunar lander rendezvous with the mother ship for the return to Earth.

The Manned Spacecraft Center in Houston was wary of a rendezvous between two spacecraft that would take place in lunar
orbit 240,000 miles from Earth. The von Braun team also objected
to the lunar-orbit-rendezvous because of the "one-shot" nature of
the small mission. The next step after orbital rockets, they believed,
should be a space station that would be a refueling station, spacecraft
assembly and check-out facility, and multiuse Earth-observing post.

Von Braun recognized, however, that the successful completion
of the assigned lunar landing within the decade was more important
than the realization of the space station he had designed a decade
before. For that to be accomplished required compromise, give-
and-take, and a spirit of cooperation among competing NASA laboratories.

During a meeting at the Marshall Space Flight Center on June
7, 1962, with the NASA leadership from Washington, there were
six hours of presentations by the staff that were "markedly pro-
EOR" (Murray and Cox 1989, p. 139). Then, "to the surprise of most

of those present," including his own staff, von Braun announced that his staff now ranked the LOR first choice, "with the strong recommendation (to make up for the limited growth potential of this mode) to initiate, simultaneously, development of an unmanned, fully automatic, one-way logistics vehicle," which would expand the transport infrastructure, laying the basis for continued flights to the Moon (Logsdon 1971, p. 68).

"After much soul searching," both the Houston Manned Spacecraft Center and the Marshall Space Flight Center had come to favor the LOR mode, von Braun asserted. This "would give the Office of Manned Space Flight [in Washington] some additional assurance that our recommendations would not be too far from the truth" (Logsdon 1971, p. 69).

This agreement in NASA did not mean, however, that there was no opposition within the Kennedy administration. White House Science Adviser Dr. Jerome Wiesner had opposed the President's Apollo initiative from the beginning. When the program became a nationally announced *fait accompli,* he opposed the LOR mode chosen by NASA. According to historian John Logsdon, NASA Administrator James Webb threatened to resign if the President did not support NASA's decision (Logsdon 1971, p. 69). He did, and finally, by the end of 1962, America was on its way to the Moon.

Wernher von Braun understood the magnitude of the task at hand and the changes in American society required to meet it. Testifying before the Elliott Committee on Education and Labor of the House of Representatives on March 14, 1958, von Braun scored the lack of attention to science and math education and contrasted his own German education with the common fare in American schools.

"Youth can hardly be blamed for turning to the more glamorous attractions during school years," he said. "Scarcely a newspaper in this country does not boast of one or more sports pages; radio and television coverage of athletics is in like proportion. But do you see any science page, or mathematics page?" The previous month, von Braun had told a Chicago press conference:

What we are about to discover is whether a nation, who [sic] has rated its home run sluggers and its fullbacks above its scientists and philosophers, can meet the total competition of

NASA, Marshall Space Flight Center

Wernher von Braun had a continuing concern for the quality of education. He did not believe that a major space effort in Huntsville would be possible without an institution of higher learning to produce the next generation of scientists and engineers. He is pictured here helping to break ground for the University of Alabama Research Institute in Huntsville on December 20, 1962.

aggressive communism, and still preserve its way of life [von Braun 1958a, p. 5].

"Do Americans know enough to face this challenge?" a committee member asked. Von Braun answered:

May I put the emphasis not so much on the word "knowledge" but "capable of applying himself in several fields." In a new field like missiles, you are suddenly confronted with new

areas of science which . . . become important, where you cannot
possibly have a background, but if you have learned the techniques of getting into new fields, how to get the gist out of a
field that may be new to you, how to perform creative work
in this area, rather than just accumulating knowledge, you can
accomplish so much more.

Facing squarely the need to make "value judgments," von Braun
recommended that educators should

cut certain things out of the school curriculums that may be
less important than others. I think too much time in practically
all of the schools in the United States goes into things that you
might call social adjustment, boy-girl relationships in college,
and beauty care and automobile driving, and things like that,
and too little into hard learning like mathematics and physics
and chemistry, and so forth.

Von Braun expressed the strong belief that the drift toward
conformity in American culture and the distraction of the mass
media should be countered with a rigorous education that encour-
ages a young person to become a scientist who can be "left alone
to devote himself to a scientific project."

From the beginning of the Space Age, there was well-organized
opposition to this great project for mankind. These attacks on the
space program were developed by think tanks, left-leaning social
engineering organizations, and financial institutions. Filtered
through the mass media to the American public, the attacks became
a constant battering ram against the space agency. Uninformed "popular" opposition came from religious groups, social welfare and civil
rights activists, and scientists—all of whom should have been natural
allies in the exploration of the new frontier of space.

Soon after the launching of Sputnik, alarm bells went off for
the ideologues of the postindustrial society when the Institute for
Social Research released a study showing that four out of five respon-
dents believed the world was better off because of science (Freeman
1980, p. 34). Also alarming to this antiprogress faction was that a
section of American business could see the economic expansion
that would follow the take-off of the space program. "Hitching the
economy to the infinite" was the way the editors of *Fortune* maga-

zine phrased their economic optimism in 1962 (Freeman 1991, p. 57).

This worry was exacerbated as the Apollo program accelerated. By the mid 1960s, the London Tavistock Institute's journal, *Human Relations,* reported with horror that the space program was producing "redundant" and "supernumery" scientists and engineers. "There would soon be two scientists for every man, woman, and dog in the society," one report complained (Burdman 1980, p. 42).

Two months before the President's announcement of the Apollo program, the liberal think-tank Brookings Institution in Washington, D.C., published a report that advised that the space program

be concerned with the consequences of its own activities. ... The exploration of space requires vast investments of money, men and materials, and creative effort—investments which could be profitably applied also to other areas of human endeavor, and which may not be so applied if space activities overly attract the available resources [Freeman 1980, p. 33].

The often-repeated dictum that the space program was stealing resources from programs to fight poverty, rebuild the cities, cure diseases, and feed the hungry was itself invented to stop the development of the very technologies that had the potential to solve these problems!

Wernher von Braun took it upon himself to argue against the naysayers, explain the complex lunar mission and its benefits to the public, excite young people about their future in space. He also defended himself personally, as well as his German-born colleagues as a group, from those who saw the optimism and hope of the exploration of space as a threat to the established order.

For 10 years—from 1963–1973—Wernher von Braun contributed one article about space every month to the magazine *Popular Science,* explaining every possible aspect of space exploration to a wide audience. In 1961 alone, he made speeches on the importance of the space program before groups as diverse as the National Association of Real Estate Boards, the Society of Automotive Engineers, the Allied Trades of the Baking Industry, the Alabama State Legislature, the General Building Contractors Association, and dozens of other labor union, professional, business, citizen, and government groups.

The economic benefits of the new technologies created by the space program would be immense, von Braun explained. He anticipated the creation of remote sensing satellites to locate and help develop new resources and improve agriculture in the industrialized and developing nations; communications satellites to bring education to geographically remote and culturally isolated areas; and new materials, manufacturing techniques, and products that would revolutionize American and world standards of living.

Although Congress, on the whole, had applauded John F. Kennedy's lunar initiative, less than three months after his speech it cut $75 million from the $1.5 billion budget requested by NASA for fiscal year 1962. Von Braun scored this seemingly small cut, explaining that this would mean that NASA would not be able to hire 600 people who would have done the planning work "to find out where to spend the money more intelligently." He warned that there would be slippage in the Apollo schedule as the result of this reduction (Price 1961).

In addition to the battles in the halls of government, von Braun knew the fight had to be taken to the American people. In the 1960 edition of his novel, *First Men to the Moon,* he began by answering questions he has been most frequently asked. The first is: "Man's abode is the Earth. Are we not invading God's kingdom as we prepare for human travel through the universe?" (von Braun 1960a, p. 8).

Von Braun asked in reply:

Why should He object to our traveling from one planet of His kingdom to another? He instilled in our hearts the curiosity about the world around us, and He enabled us to acquire the scientific knowledge and technological capability to satisfy it. If God really wanted man to stay on Earth, I am certain He would have provided an impenetrable barrier and discouraged all our endeavors to cross it.

Readily admitting he was only a layman and that this is a "profound theological problem," von Braun responded to the question with quotes from a September 1956 statement of Pope Pius XII, who received a delegation of the International Astronautical Federation in Rome, during its 7th Congress:

The question of man's role in the Universe remained a question of religious interest throughout the space program. In this photograph, the Apollo 11 astronauts are meeting with Pope Paul VI at the Vatican in Rome on October 16, 1969, three months after their historic first landing on the Moon.

"The Lord, who has anchored an insatiable desire in man's heart, the desire for knowledge, had no intention of setting a limit to inquiry when He said 'Ye shall have dominion over the Earth' (*Gen.* 1, 28). It is all creation which He has entrusted to man and which He has given to the human mind to penetrate it and thus to recognize more and more the infinite greatness of its Creator.

"While up to now man has felt himself banned on Earth, so to speak, he has had to be satisfied with fragments of information which come from the universe, it appears now that the opportunity has come to put aside the barriers and arrive at new truths and new knowledge which God has given to the Earth in abundance" [von Braun 1960a, p. 8].

From the emerging civil rights movement, which was fighting for human dignity and economic opportunity for all citizens, came an uninformed response to the also-emerging civilian space program. On the eve of the launch of the Apollo 11 mission to the Moon in July 1969, the civil rights movement engaged in a dramatic near-head-on clash with the space program. As described by then-NASA Administrator Dr. Thomas Paine in an article in *21st Century Science & Technology* magazine, Reverend Ralph Abernathy organized a "March on Hunger" at the launch site at Cape Canaveral. Rev. Abernathy held a sign at the march which read, "$12 a day to feed an astronaut. We could feed a starving child for $8" (Paine 1989, p. 31).

Dr. Paine describes his meeting with Rev. Abernathy:

I said that he represented one of the major movements in America, and one of America's concerns. I pointed out that science, technology, and exploration—opening new lands— also was a very important part of the American heritage, and that the pioneers and the explorers had probably done more for the homeless and the hungry of the world than any amount of people who stayed home. I said that we were very proud of what we were doing, just as he was very proud of what he was doing.

Dr. Paine also pointed out that, even if the next morning's launch were cancelled, none of that money would go to poor people, and, indeed, that "it has been science and technology that has given the poor their only real relief. It hasn't been the distributing of alms that has made any dent."

The NASA administrator invited the marchers to sit in the viewing stand the next morning for the launch, while Rev. Abernathy "shifted his position," making clear that they were not there to "protest the Moon rocket at all . . . that on the contrary, they were very proud, as Americans, to be part of the great day that was going to dawn tomorrow."

It has been estimated that there were a million well-wishers at Cape Canaveral the morning of the Apollo 11 launch. There were 20,000 people in the grandstand, including 3,500 reporters and photographers from 56 nations (Freeman 1989, p. 18). Like everyone else, Dr. Paine reports, "the protesters shouted and cheered

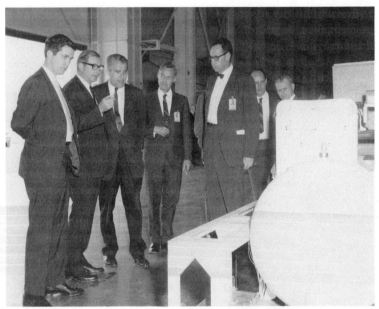

NASA, Marshall Space Flight Center

NASA chief Tom Paine remained one of the most optimistic promoters and supporters of space exploration even after he left the space program in 1970. Here he is seen to the left of Wernher von Braun, on a tour of Marshall Center facilities in April 1968.

and enjoyed it thoroughly, and I think they returned to their camp with a very strong feeling that [the Moon rocket] also carried their hopes for the future" (Paine 1989, p. 31). What more natural ally for an optimistic future than those most in need of new opportunities?

At the time that President Kennedy announced the Apollo program, the Soviet Union held an impressive lead, and all the "firsts" in the space race. As Wernher von Braun had noted in his 1961 memorandum to Kennedy, to land men on the Moon, a country would have to develop a rocket an order of magnitude larger than those that existed at the time. For the Soviets, this would turn out to be a challenge that they could not meet.

To win the race to the Moon, the U.S.S.R. decided to rely not only on its technical and managerial expertise, but also on psychological warfare to try to undermine and destabilize the aggressive American effort. To try to discredit the space program, the

Soviets chose as their number one target its most visible and eloquent spokesmen—Wernher von Braun.

The first systematic attempt to slander the German rocket scientists as "Nazis" came from the Soviet Union and its satellites in 1963. A well-known East German "muckraker," Julius Mader, wrote a biography of Wernher von Braun titled *Secret of Huntsville: The True Career of the Rocket Baron Wernher von Braun.* It was published by the East German military publishers Deutscher Militärverlag.

Mader was an entity known to Western intelligence agencies. He had made a career of exposing "Nazis" in the West German political establishment, concentrating in particular on the Western intelligence community. His numerous book titles in German include *Who's Who in the CIA* (1968), *No Longer Secret: The Development, System and Modus Operandi of the Imperialistic German Secret Service* (1969), *Neo-colonialist Practices of the Federal Republic of Germany in Relation to Namibia,* (1978), and *The CIA in Europe* (1982).

Mader's general strategy was to use the "Nazi" accusations to target individuals considered to be enemies of the German Democratic Republic and the Soviet Union. More generally his aim was to sow seeds of mistrust and suspicion against those responsible for the security of the Federal Republic of Germany. By the mid-1960s, there were left-wing groups active in West Germany that were used as "independent" institutions through which to funnel these slanders from the East to the West. In 1967, the East Germans republished Mader's 1963 book on von Braun. This occurred only two years before the lunar landing, and when the Soviets knew they could not beat the United States to the Moon. According to Dr. Walter Haüsserman, some people were also considering publishing the book in English but this project was dropped, probably because the rank propagandistic nature of the writing would have totally discredited it to a Western audience (Haüssermann 1992).

Mader's biography attempts to trace von Braun's "Nazi" roots to his "militaristic" Prussian background, in line with the propagandistic East German historiography of that period, that "Prussianism = militarism = Nazism." In reality, the greatest opposition to the rise of the Nazis had come from the stalwarts of the Wilhelmine state—the Prussian aristocracy. Von Braun's father resigned his post in the Bruning government when the Nazis took power in 1933.

Interspersed in Mader's narrative are numerous paeans to the

achievements of the Soviet Union in mastering rocket technology—
solely for peaceful purposes, of course. The rest of the book is a
combination of lies and half-truths, crafted to depict von Braun as
a war-mongering criminal, interested in space only for the purpose
of mass murder.

Mader fails to include any facts of von Braun's life that contradict his profile, including the fight between the German army and
the SS over control of the rocket program. He even infers that von
Braun might have been implicated in the murder of Klaus Riedel
in Peenemünde! Of course, Mader neglects to mention the fact that
both Riedel and von Braun were arrested by the Gestapo for talking
about spaceflight.

Space exploration in general plays a very small role in the
biography. Mader's chief interest is to "expose" von Braun's overrid-
ing obsession to develop a "cosmic weapons system," which is the
purpose attributed by Mader to the Apollo program. In particular,
Mader expresses dismay over the Redstone, the Honest John, the
Corporal, and the Nike—all missiles developed by the Germans in
America and deployed in Western Europe against a possible Soviet
attack.

In a 1963 article in the East German magazine *DDR im Wort
und Bild,* Mader wrote that "soon these new aggressive weapons
began appearing in the entire NATO area. The West German Bundeswehr threatens with them! They have been set up and armed in
Italy, in Turkey, in Greece, even in the Middle East, all around the
Socialist bloc" (Mader 1963a). This aggressive stance is compared
to the "peaceful uses of space" by the Kremlin.

Despite the background noise of opposition to the Apollo program from the Soviets and their propaganda outlets, however, the
Apollo program proceeded.

To Wernher von Braun's team in Huntsville fell the long-
awaited task of designing, developing, testing, and launching the
rocket that would take the first men to the Moon. On top of the
Saturn V booster sat the hopes and aspirations of mankind.

The Saturn V is most striking in its enormity. It was taller than
the Statue of Liberty, and composed of more than a million parts.
It was moved from the Vertical Assembly Building at Cape Canaveral
(the building with the greatest volume in the world) on a mobile
launch system, or "crawler," which is the largest thing that moves

NASA

The 363-foot tall Apollo 11 Saturn V rocket sits on the launch pad at Cape Canaveral three weeks before its launch. The Saturn V, which never had a failure, owed its success in substantial part to the managerial skill of project manager Arthur Rudolph.

on the Earth. Taken together, the Saturn V engines produced as much power as 85 Hoover Dams.

To create a rocket system that would have a 99 percent reliability, (only 1 in 100 flights would be expected to fail), required a meticulous attention to detail, extensive testing, stringent quality control, and new management techniques to coordinate and supervise more than 20,000 industrial contractors and 7,000 civil service employees. The job of project manager for the Saturn V rocket was given to one of von Braun's oldest and most capable associates, Arthur Rudolph. The management system developed for the Saturn program, which led to the development of a rocket that never suffered a flight failure, was crucial to the success of the entire Apollo program.

Von Braun's biographers relate that

> when von Braun spoke about management, he often cited Admiral Hyman Rickover, the father of the nuclear submarine program "When Rickover was asked, how in the world he had found the outstanding managers that had helped him with the construction of the Nautilus, he answered, " 'I don't hire managers; I employ damned good engineers. When I get to know them well enough, I make one of them a manager' " [Stuhlinger and Ordway 1992, p. 365].

Von Braun organized the Marshall Space Flight Center along the lines of the rocket research effort he headed at Peenemünde. A top-flight scientist or engineer was put in charge of each technical laboratory; each lab was responsible for a major aspect of space technology. These laboratories included guidance and control, aeroballistics, structures and materials, quality control, fabrication, testing, computers, and research.

For a project the size of the Saturn, however, some changes were necessary, and the project manager became primary. Rudolph reported directly to von Braun. The official NASA history of the Apollo/Saturn program relates that Arthur Rudolph's Program Control Center's

> success in tracking the myriad bits and pieces of Saturn vehicles impressed even NASA Administrator [James] Webb, who prided himself on managerial techniques and skills. Claiming that MSFC

NASA, Marshall Space Flight Center

One of the most dramatic events in the space program is the test-firing of large rocket engines. In this photograph, a first stage Saturn engine is being fired on a test stand. Since the end of the Saturn/Apollo program, these huge tests stands have been used for Shuttle main engine firing tests.

[Marshall Space Flight Center] was unusually thorough in its management may seem like a simplification. Given the diversity of the prime contractors and their armies of subcontractors and vendors, however, the clockwork efficiency and the reliability of the Saturn vehicles were remarkable. Meticulous attention to details, and keeping track of them, was a hallmark of MSFC [Bilstein 1980, p. 399].

The proof was in the final product: A total of 32 Saturn launches, including nine lunar missions; the first men to orbit the Moon; the first men to land there.

The NASA history reports that, "even after the Saturn V program was over, MSFC still received many requests from businesses and managers asking, 'how did you do it?' " The high esteem in which

Americans held the rocket scientists and engineers who landed men on the Moon has been reflected for years in the familiar admonition that for solving simple problems "you don't have to be a rocket scientist to. . . ."

The pride of Americans in the overall success of this great endeavor of their nation, the confidence in technological advancement it engendered, and the appreciation of the difficulty of that task is still expressed today. "If we could land a man on the Moon, then. . . ." we can surely solve any of the other problems facing society is another familiar saying today. What is required, the German space pioneers demonstrated, is a single-mindedness of purpose, the personal commitment of each man, and the national resources to accomplish the job.

More than two decades before he helped develop the Saturn V rocket for the Apollo program that would land men on the Moon, Wernher von Braun took advantage of the free time he had in the New Mexico desert while launching old V-2s, and wrote a fictional account of the first manned mission to Mars. The book's appendix contained all of the technical engineering details of how this mission could be performed, but von Braun used the form of a novel to paint his picture of what the future might hold and to voice his concerns and criticisms of the postwar society he observed from his new home in America.

It was not the first time von Braun had used the written word to give expression to an imagination which always kept him a few decades ahead of the engineers. At the age of 18, von Braun had written a short story called "Lunetta." In this piece, a group of explorers stranded at the North Pole is rescued by the crew of a rocket plane. They are taken to the space station Lunetta, where part of the station rotates to provide an artificial partial gravity for the health and comfort of the crew. A terrestrial observatory is equipped with telescopes for looking at the Earth, while an astronomical observatory is used to look out at the heavens. Although they are not anxious to leave, after a tour of Lunetta by the captain, the polar explorers board a rocket plane bound for Berlin, to return home.

Three years before von Braun's 1931 short story, his mentor Hermann Oberth had inserted a charming tale about a rocket flight around the Moon in the midst of his scholarly book *Ways to Space Flight*, doubtless giving encouragement to von Braun's imagination.

In 1958, after Sputnik had opened the door to the Space Age, von Braun published a longer fictional account of a lunar voyage in his book *First Men to the Moon*. The book is dedicated to his daughters, "Iris and Margrit who will live in a world in which flights to the Moon will be commonplace." In this story, which is generously sprinkled with American English slang expressions, von Braun's crew faces technical and equipment failures that require calm and measured responses. He describes the close coordination between the astronauts and the ground crew to troubleshoot problems, which later would be a crucial aspect of the Apollo flights.

Von Braun's astronauts describe in detail the surface of the Moon, talking into a tape recorder. "When they returned to Earth, these tapes would be searched by eager scientists for the answers to riddles man had asked since he first raised his eyes to the heavens" (von Braun 1960a, p. 56). The astronauts collect samples of rocks and dust for scientists to analyze on Earth and fire rockets onto the surface of the Moon to measure the resulting moonquakes.

A moment before the lunar lander is scheduled to start its engines for the voyage home, one of the explorers accidentally damages the air lock door, which must close in order for them to leave. On Earth, von Braun wrotes "millions of anxious listeners breathe lighter" when the problem is solved, and the crew lifts off the surface of the Moon to head home. On the way back they suffer a cabin leak from a small meteor hit and bad weather at the landing site in the Pacific Ocean, but they return to "a shouting, cheering mob" (von Braun 1960a, p. 91).

A trip to Mars, von Braun knew, would require orders of magnitude more complexity, precision, and resources than the relatively easy trip to the Moon.

The Moon is approximately 240,000 miles from Earth—a mere two-day trip. Mars, on the other hand, at its closest point to Earth is nearly 35 *million* miles away. And these relative positions of the Earth and Mars to each other at opposition occur approximately only once every two years, because it takes Mars nearly two Earth years to revolve around the Sun. Because Mars's orbit around the Sun is elliptical (the Earth's orbit is nearly circular), at opposition the distance between the Earth and Mars can be more than 60 million miles.

FIGURE 9.1
THE LEAST-ENERGY HOHMANN TRANSFER ORBIT TO MARS
In 1925, Walter Hohmann calculated the least-energy orbits that would transfer a
spacecraft from Earth to Mars orbit, assuming that only chemical rockets were
available. After a boost from Earth orbit, the spacecraft would coast unpowered the
rest of the trip. The most efficient mission is to leave Earth orbit (1) when Mars is
44 degrees ahead of Earth in its orbital path (2). When the spacecraft arrives after
a 250-day trip, both the spacecraft and Mars will be at point 3. At point 4, the
spacecraft would depart Mars and once again swing around more than two thirds
an Earth-orbit for a 250-day return trip.

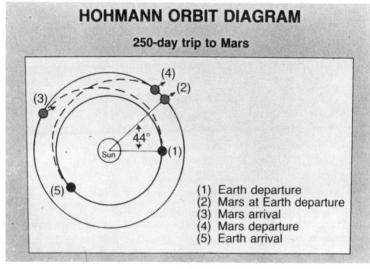

Source: Marsha Freeman, "Colonizing Mars: Moving Man into the Cosmos," *Fusion* (November
1985).

As seen in Figure 9.1, however, the distance travelers would
cover on a trip to Mars, if a least-energy path following a Keplerian
ellipse is followed, is not 35 million, but 735 million miles, requiring
260 days to coast on a ballistic trajectory after leaving Earth orbit.
The specific astronomical requirements for such a least-energy path,
which von Braun proposed in 1948, could be met with available
technology, and had been meticulously calculated by Dr. Walter
Hohmann in 1925.

Von Braun wrote in the 1953 introduction to the technical
appendix to *The Mars Project* that the development of "atomic
rocket drives" would "considerably simplify the problem, and I do
not propose to deny the possibility that nuclear energy may someday

propel space vessels. We must beware of using the word 'impossible' when we speak of technical developments. However ... all theories on the application of atomic energy to space ships are as yet purely speculative" (von Braun 1962, p. 2).

This will not be done by science fiction's "lone inventor," working in his basement on a Mars rocket, von Braun wrote:

> In 1492 Columbus knew less about the far Atlantic than we do about the heavens, yet he chose not to sail with a flotilla of less than three ships, and history tends to prove that he might never have returned to Spanish shores with his report of discoveries had he entrusted his fate to a single bottom. So it is with planetary exploration: It must be done on the grand scale [von Braun 1962, p. 2].

Each ship in the flotilla of 10 space vessels will be assembled at an Earth-orbital space station, von Braun specified. Using a suggestion made by Krafft Ehricke, von Braun's "neighbor" at the Fort Bliss Army Hospital where the Germans were housed in 1948, he proposed that only "three of the [ten] vessels will be equipped with 'landing boats' for descent to Mars's surface" (von Braun 1962, p. 3). In this way, the fuel for the Earth-return trip does not have to be landed on the surface of Mars but is stored in the vessels in orbit around Mars; a combination Earth-orbit-rendezvous, Mars-orbit-rendezvous mission mode.

Von Braun concludes his 1953 introduction to the published technical appendix of *The Mars Project*:

> There is scarcely any branch of science which has no bearing upon interplanetary flight, and this little booklet will have achieved its objective if it stimulates some of its readers to find, in their own particular specialties, contributions which may fill out one or more of the many gaps still existing in the scientific extrapolation of a voyage to a neighboring planet [von Braun 1962, p. 7.

In a letter to German colleague Hermann Koelle in June 1950, von Braun discusses the possibility of the book being published in Germany, and summarizes his approach:

The project is developed in the following manner: The whole
thing is a futuristic novel, based on solid technical facts. I have
consciously avoided utilizing any fantastic assumptions that
today could not be asserted with certainty (for example, nuclear propulsion). I have instead projected into the future technology which now exists and is well-known, and have investigated what can be accomplished with it. The result is an
expedition to Mars and back, with 70 people, supplied with
everything except the kitchen stove, including surface vehicles
with which they can shuttle about on Mars. . . . Everything is
done with chemical fuels . . . and not once do I introduce liquid
hydrogen, for which I don't have much use, as many other
authors do.

When he completed the novel in 1948, von Braun sent the
manuscript to 18 publishers. In his June 1950 letter, he reported
to Koelle:

The book has still not come out here. I am presently negotiat-
ing with the American Rocket Society and also some publishing
houses. The latter, however, want some things changed, which
I am not so happy about. Basically, they want me to drop all
the many scientific and technical details and build up the "story"
more, which admittedly is only a loose putty holding the whole
thing together. . . . My space friends urge me not to make any
such changes. It suits me better to publish the technical points
rather than a "best-seller," which is oriented too much to the
needs of New York subway riders.

Six months later von Braun reported that

for the time being I have spent several months corresponding
with some interested publishers. There I always run into difficulties because the publisher wants to water down the scientific
value of the book in favor of more suspense in the story itself.
"Who's interested in the atmosphere of Mars or the initial thrust
of a satellite ship? The story needs a woman!" —etc., etc. Most
of the suggestions are in this vein. . . . I have paid no attention
to these proposals, since that wasn't the goal I had in mind.
Two publishers (big companies!) wanted me to eliminate the

The cover of The Mars Project *by Wernher von Braun published by the University of Illinois Press in 1953. It has been recently reprinted with an introduction by Dr. Tom Paine. Only the technical appendix of the book has ever been published. The imaginative tale awaits publication.*

story entirely and instead present the technical material in the style of an "easily accessible technical presentation of the problems of space for laymen." First of all, I was too lazy after all the work I had put into it, and secondly, one couldn't present the organizational range of the problem as plastically in such a form [Von Braun 1950].

Although the American Rocket Society had decided to publish *The Mars Project,* von Braun reportes that the society needed to raise $15,000-$25,000 beforehand to cover publishing costs. They were apparently never successful in this, since the entire book has not been published to this day.

In 1950, the German publisher Otto Bechtle visited von Braun in Huntsville. He agreed to publish only the technical appendix of *The Mars Project* as a "mathematical proof of the feasibility of the

proposed interplanetary flight" (Ordway and Sharpe 1979, p. 361).
This appeared in 1952, and the next year, the University of Illinois
published an English translation. Excerpts of the novel appeared in
a series of 1960 articles in *This Week Magazine,* which provide a
glimpse of the imagination and critical thinking of Wernher von
Braun.

Von Braun prefaced the series of magazine articles on his novel
with the remarks:

Please understand that my story is fiction entirely—not a
prediction that we shall find such people and such technological marvels when we go to Mars. This conception is a scientist's
way of relaxing from the hard job of building the tools for the
exploration of outer space with rockets. It is also a means of
reminding myself—and others—that we should always keep
our minds open to new worlds and new wonders in the expanding conquest of our Universe [von Braun 1960b, p. 8].

The trip to Mars starts from the space station Lunetta. After a
260-day cruise, a crew of 12 transfers to the glider *Goddard,* leaving
the mother ship *Oberth* in Mars orbit. The glider then spirals down
to the surface through the thin Martian atmosphere. The explorers
find during their investigation of Mars that there is a civilization of
intelligent beings living underneath the surface of the planet.

The Earthmen are taken to a huge underground city, Ahla, the
capitol of Mars. It is built on 15 levels with a park capturing natural
sunlight nearest the surface and living quarters, subways, and power
plants and other infrastructure on lower levels. The Martians are a
technologically advanced civilization of 800 million inhabitants,
with all of the material comforts. But they lack a spirit of adventure.
Providing for the population through mass production has led to
standardization, producing "a soul-destroying equivalence of everything by which we live and a conformity that makes it very unappeal-
ing for a young Martian to become different or outstanding," one
young Martian laments (von Braun 1960c, p. 31).

At the end of the Earthmen's stay, the head of the Martian
Academy of Sciences gives a farewell address:

"Your voyage is indeed a great technological accomplishment that has made a profound impression on millions of Martians. .... Let me give you a word of warning and advice from
an old man.

"The history of this planet has taught us that idolatry of
our technical accomplishments constitutes the worst evil with
which we threaten our race and our civilization. Worshipping
those accomplishments renders man sterile and incapable of
meeting the demands of the future. If we worship scientific
achievement, we kill humility, and of humility alone can be
born any further progress, scientific or otherwise" [von Braun
1960c, pp. 23–4].

With this warning, the Martian unveils for the Earthmen and
other honored guests the fruit of the visit from Earth to his planet:

"I have the honor to report that inspired by your visit, Mars
has made its first venture into space. That light you see up
there is an artificial satellite that was launched only this after-
noon. When you Earthmen return to Mars, I can promise there
will a space station up there in orbit waiting to receive you"
[von Braun 1960c, pp. 23–4].

Considering the content of the story, it is not surprising that
no one would publish the novel. The science fiction being offered
to the American public in the 1940s was characterized not by
advanced extraterrestrial beings, but by banalized, depraved, war-
mongering, and even cannibalistic civilizations, more like *The First
Men in the Moon* of H.G. Wells than *From the Earth to the Moon*
by Jules Verne. While Wernher von Braun was writing *The Mars
Project,* science fiction author Ray Bradbury had just published his
depressing *Martian Chronicles.*
    Although he put his manuscript for *The Mars Project* aside,
Wernher von Braun never hesitated in his conviction that mankind
would one day go to Mars. In 1954, in the last article in a series
for *Collier's* magazine, titled "Can We Get to Mars," von Braun
proposes that it "will be a century or more before [man is] ready"
to go, but, he says, he is sure man will go to Mars (von Braun 1954b,
p. 23).
    In 1956, von Braun and Willy Ley wrote the book *The Explora-*

tion of Mars, illustrated by Chesley Bonestell. Here, the "grand scale" of von Braun's Mars mission is reduced to a more modest one, to consider what a real such space flight might entail. The authors propose that rather than a space spectacular, "the expedition to Mars should be considered the ultimate achievement of a gradual and often painful step-by-step development of manned spaceflight which may take decades to accomplish" (Ley and von Braun 1956, p. 97).

They pointed out that

technological prophecy spanning a time interval is handicapped by the rapid progress of the natural sciences and the likelihood of development of fundamentally new methods. It is entirely possible, for example, that within a decade or so successful tests with some sort of nuclear power system might be accomplished [Ley and von Braun 1956 p. 98].

However, maintaining the same approach of the original *Mars Project* to design a mission based on the best available technology, the authors stated: "If we can show how a Mars ship could conceivably be built on the basis of what we know now, we can safely deduce that actual designs of the future can only be superior." It is "probable," they write, "that the fundamental concept of subdividing an interplanetary expedition into an orbital supply operation, the interplanetary voyage proper, and a landing operation—each with separate vehicles—will still be adhered to." This concept, based on the most efficient use of a family of space vehicles, has indeed endured. It was fundamental to the Mars mission scenario developed by the National Commission on Space in 1985.

The authors explained that their study "may be considered a revision" of *The Mars Project.* The reduced mission involved a total propellant requirement of only 10 percent of the original scenario, involving half as many ferry supply missions to Earth orbit as the 950 projected in the earlier study. Looking now toward a mission that will be affordable, the authors explained that, "in order to keep the costs for the undertaking to a minimum, the expedition shall be limited to 12 men" (Ley and von Braun 1956, p. 108). Of those, nine will land on the surface of Mars, and spend 440 days exploring the Red Planet. One-way unmanned cargo ships will deliver supplies for the explorers.

FIGURE 9.2
TRANSFER OPERATION OF THE RELIEF SHIP
In this concept, the Mars ship remains in a 56,000-mile orbit without expending the energy to slow down to meet the space station. A relief vessel, using a transfer ellipse that intersects both the Mars ship and ferry orbits, is used to ferry crew members to the station. A similar scenario was put forward in 1986 by the National Commission on Space, headed by Tom Paine.

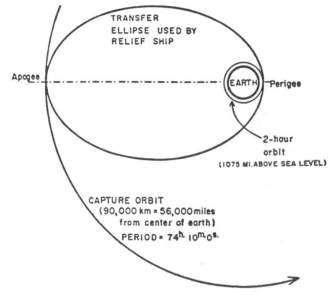

Source: Ley and von Braun, *The Exploration of Mars* (New York: The Viking Press. 1956).

To save fuel, von Braun and Ley proposed an unusual return scenario. Rather than decelerate to meet the space station in its 1,075-mile-high orbit of the Earth, the returning Mars ships will "settle in a very high circumterrestrial orbit of 56,000 miles' radius." They will be met by a "relief ship," which will ferry them to the station, from which they return to Earth, as described in Figure 9.2 (Ley and von Braun 1956, p. 127). They provided a lengthy bibliography at the end of the book, which traces the scientific history of theories and observations of Mars from the time of 17th century astronomer Johannes Kepler.

Planning for missions to Mars gained tremendous impetus after the announcement of the Apollo program, when it was clear that the technologies for manned spaceflight would be developed. In

June 1963, a symposium on the Exploration of Mars was held in Denver, Colorado, sponsored by the American Astronautical Society. More than 800 scientists and engineers attended, and papers were presented on every aspect of a manned Mars mission, from space vehicles to space medicine.

In his foreword to the proceedings of the conference, George Morgenthaler acknowledged that the predecessor to the current work was von Braun's "preliminary design study" in *The Mars Project* (Morgenthaler 1963, p. vi). But Mars mission studies no longer are in the realm of the fantastic, said Morgenthaler. "Much of the technology needed for the Mars trip will have been developed in earlier manned space programs," he reported, including the Saturn V rocket and studies of the physiological effect of space travel on humans.

Von Braun's colleagues Harry Ruppe and Ernst Steinhoff presented technical studies at the symposium. Other scientists, such as former colleague Krafft Ehricke, were also studying Mars missions through industry contracts with NASA.

For the celebration of Wernher von Braun's 50th birthday, his friends and colleagues produced a *Festschrift,* a collection of commemorative papers, to honor his achievements. In that volume, Ernst Steinhoff expands the paper he presented at the American Astronautical Society Symposium, proposing a comprehensive program to develop technologies for the self-sufficiency of the Mars explorers, making use of the local resources there.

In a 1965 article, von Braun inserts into his Mars scenario intermediate steps to colonization: By 1978 there could be a manned fly-by of Mars with a crew of three. By 1982, there could be a "stopover" mission with a short surface expedition by a crew of four, making use of nuclear propulsion systems. Some time later, there would be a semipermanent base established on Mars (von Braun 1965, p. 25).

But by 1965, the post-Apollo wind-down of the space program was already taking place. The work at the Marshall Space Flight Center on the Saturn V was nearing its completion. The NASA budget had reached its peak and had started to decline. Von Braun feared that the momentum of the Saturn/Apollo program would be lost. "It is interesting to note that the total cost of such a very ambitious-looking [trip to Mars] is in the same ballpark as what is being spent for Apollo," von Braun states to try to organize support for the next great leap into space (von Braun 1965, p. 34).

Wernher von Braun was acutely aware by the mid-1960s that the cultural outlook of the American population was changing.

The budget for NASA had been declining each year since 1965. In April 1968, von Braun testified before the Senate, scoring the cuts Congress was making in the space program. According to one newspaper account,

> Dr. von Braun warned yesterday that if the Nation bleeds the space program to feed social programs like the war-on-poverty it could wind up being a technological have-not Nation like Great Britain. Von Braun stated that the British built up welfare programs in the '50s while ignoring the burgeoning aerospace technology. Now, they don't have enough money to pay for their welfare programs [O'Toole 1968].

Von Braun defended the nuclear rocket program, which had been cut by the House from $60 to $12 million, stating that the new system could be ready to fly in 1976, knowing full well that if it were cancelled, a manned mission to Mars would be unlikely.

Beside the "war on poverty" which the Lyndon Johnson administration was funding in place of the space program, the government was enmired in a population war in Southeast Asia. In a speech before the American Society for Public Administration on March 20, 1968, von Braun reported that

> NASA's programs, like those of many other government agencies, are somewhat locked in by the need for austerity to reduce inflationary pressures on the economy, and the need to meet the demands on the budget of the Viet Nam conflict and other urgent national needs. The current space budget request certainly does not meet the nation's needs in space [von Braun 1968a].

Von Braun knew there was also a more fundamental issue involved in the attacks on the space program. By 1964, Robert M. Hutchins of the University of Chicago had promulgated his "Triple Revolution" theory, purporting that mankind had entered the "post-industrial society." In this new order, the "equitable distribution of dwindling resources" would replace the increase in the productive powers of labor and industry as the subject of economic activity.

This call for the end of economic growth intersected the growing disillusionment among young people with the Vietnam war, providing the basis for the "back-to-nature" ecology movement. The Vietnam-era drug counterculture portrayed high-technology research and development as the "enemy" of its plans for an "ecological utopia." Support was given to these movements in the U.S.A. and Great Britain by powerful financial interests. These interests feared that continued economic progress would transform former colonial countries just entering the industrial age into competitors on the international political scene. This was similar to the fear that Britain had of German economic competition before World War I, after World War II, and, more recently, after German reunification in 1989.

During the 1970s, the American public was brainwashed by a continuous assault on rationality and the idea of progress. Fear-mongering became a constant presence: "nuclear winter," "life-threatening" effects of DDT and other pesticides and chemicals, "ozone depletion," "global warming," and so on. The optimism of science and exploration was replaced by the irrational fear of virtually every human activity and invention.

Von Braun opened a speech before the Aviation and Space Writers on May 27, 1971 by discussing

a problem that disturbs me. . . . I speak of the climate of irrational hostility that seems to be growing in this country—especially among our college and university students—regarding science and technology.

We face a militant, highly emotional, even fanatical segment of the population which has seized upon a valid and good cause, but which will accept no facts, no reasoning that run counter to its own fixed ideology. . . . The anti-science/technology people are demanding that we pull the plug on modern civilization in the belief that somehow we shall all be the better off in a more primitive state.

But it isn't the young people, the students, who are really to blame for this attitude of hostility to science and technology. . . . They are simply misguided by certain social philosophers, cultural historians, and the like, whose teachings and published works provide only a very lopsided view of science and technology pictured as causing the downfall of man.

NASA, Marshall Space Flight Center

By the 1970s, Wernher von Braun was increasingly dismayed at the growing antiscience fervor in the United States. He could compare this turn against science to the excitement of the 1960s, when man was going into space and to the Moon. Here von Braun gives the Mercury astronauts a tour of the Fabrication Laboratory at the Restone Arsenal in 1959, where they examined Mercury/Redstone hardware. The Mercury capsule on top of the Redstone rocket took the first American, Alan Shepard, into space two years later.

Von Braun named "historian and philosopher" Lewis Mumford, who

> inveighs angrily and brilliantly against the "megamachine" of science and technology. . . . When Arnold Toynbee, equally famous as historian and philosopher, asks whether "space-manship folly" isn't also a crime because it wastes that "slender surplus product that man has succeeded in wringing out of nature within the past 5,000 years," he adds a moralistic fervor to the revolutionary spirit of the young. . . . The point Toynbee

wants to make is that spacemanship not only is a folly, it is also a crime against mankind.

The anti-science and anti-technology voices making blanket attacks on science and technology in the name of conservation, a clean environment, or improving the quality of human life, are doing the nation and all of us a great disservice. The problems they are rightly anxious and concerned about cannot be solved by a return-to-nature cult. That course leads only to disaster for multitudes of people.

Closely related to the general attacks on science and technology is the denigration of the space program among some persons.

Asserting his own view of the primacy of the individual, von Braun concluded that these social philosophers

have not yet learned to visualize mankind extending into the macrocosm, or for the spiritual need to do so. . . . Pragmatism is a valuable, stabilizing human characteristic; but without imagination we would not be human, and as long as man exercises this precious faculty, he will not long be imprisoned in the successive shells the pragmatists try to enclose him in [von Braun 1971b].

The depravity of the attacks on science, technology, and the space program reached new heights with the 1976 publication of *We Never Went to the Moon: America's $30 Billion Swindle.* Not only would there be no technological accomplishment in the future, this book asserts, but there were not any such accomplishments in the past! (Kaysing and Reid, 1976).

By the fall of 1968, NASA Administrator James Webb, who had tirelessly fought the battles to keep President Kennedy's Apollo promise, could see the handwriting on the wall. He resigned from office in October. An optimistic Tom Paine took the reins. But by the time the first men landed on the Moon on July 20, 1969, the embattled space program was fighting for its life.

Months before the first lunar landing, President Richard Nixon established a Space Task Group headed by Vice President Spiro Agnew to develop space policy recommendations for the post-Apollo period. In September, the Space Task Group presented its

MARS
INITIAL LANDING

UNITED
STATES

This depiction of an initial Mars landing in 1982 produced by the Marshall Space Flight Center was used as a graphic by Wernher von Braun in his 1969 presentation of an integrated space program for NASA to the task group formed by Vice President Spiro Agnew to formulate long-range post-Apollo goals for the space program. The astronauts are collecting samples to bring back to Earth. In orbit above is the planetary vehicle which does not land on the surface of Mars.

findings to the President, stating that "a manned Mars mission should be accepted as a long-range goal" and that the NASA budget should be increased to $6 billion.

The integrated space program for 1970 through 1990 presented by NASA to the Task Group consisted of space infrastructure to be built in the 1970s, centering around a 12-man space station, a reusable Earth-orbital shuttle, a multipurpose space tug, and a reusable interplanetary nuclear shuttle. Then, in the 1980s, the nation would be ready to set up a small lunar surface base, carry out an initial Mars landing, establish a lunar colony, and, finally, create a semipermanent Mars base (Figure 9.3).

The decisions on science policy were being dictated by other concerns, however. George Shultz's Office of Management and Budget reduced NASA's fiscal year 1970 budget request by $45 million,

FIGURE 9.3
VON BRAUN'S INTEGRATED SPACE PROGRAM, 1970–1990
In this comprehensive 20-year program, the Saturn rocket would remain the principal transportation vehicle while the reusable shuttle is being developed. By the end of the 1970s, space stations, a lunar outpost with six men, and a nuclear shuttle will have laid the technology basis for the manned Mars landing at the beginning of the 1980s. By today, there would be a temporary Mars base with a crew of 12, 48 men on the lunar surface, and 100 men in low-Earth orbit. Of this entire plan, only the Space Shuttle has been developed.

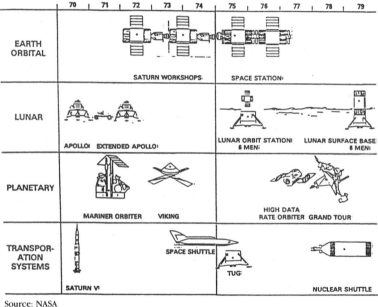

Source: NASA

even before the task group had issued its report. Between 1965 and 1971, the NASA budget would decline by more than 40 percent. Administrator Paine was committed to the full program and knew there was only one man who could possibly sell the Mars program to Congress and the nation—Wernher von Braun.

Paine, shared with James Webb, the previous NASA head, an appreciation for the special role of von Braun:

Almost 20 years later, [James] Webb recalled that during his time as Administrator in NASA management, Wernher von Braun was considerably more prominent than the NASA Direc-

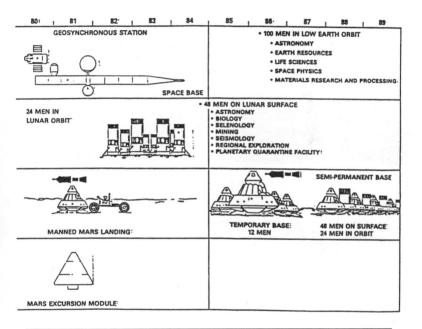

tor himself: "You shouldn't forget that von Braun was known as 'Mr. Spaceflight'. . . . He was convinced that the big rockets were the key to the next step—a flight to Mars. . . . Besides he was quite aware of the fact that he was a speaker who had a tremendous ability to captivate his audience. . . . He was well known to the public, whereas people like myself were not" [Stuhlinger and Ordway 1992, p. 374].

"I'm in the crossfire of mission planners, budget people, the general public, Congress, scientists, firms, and presidential advisers," Tom Paine said in 1970. In early 1970, Wernher von Braun left

On July 29, 1970 Dr. Paine announced to the press that he would be stepping down as NASA Administrator. He was hopeful that a Republican-appointed administrator would obtain a more open ear from the White House, and encouraged von Braun to stay to fight for the Mars program.

Huntsville, which had been his home for 20 years, to answer Paine's call for help. On March 1, he took up his new post as deputy associate administrator for planning at NASA:

> During an interview in 1985 Paine recalled some details of that period: "...as far as I remember, it [von Braun's transfer] was my idea. When I got him on the carpet, he was undecided. ... His first reaction was: 'I'll have to think about it.' But I had a fantastic ally: Maria. She wanted to move to Washington. She had been in the South long enough. ... I believe Maria—and she thought about the children—was of the opinion that a move to Washington would be in the family's interest" [Stuhlinger and Ordway 1992, p. 421–22].

Some of the Germans thought that von Braun's move to Washington was an effort on the part of Dr. Paine at NASA headquarters to lessen the German influence at the Marshall Space Flight Center. This is very unlikely. As Dr. Haüssermann, von Braun's colleague, remarked:

> Was this an intrigue to get [von Braun] away from Huntsville? I knew Dr. Paine too well. ... He had the honest opinion that he [could] help the country by bringing von Braun to Washington.
>
> He was a very, very clean, idealistic man. His personal modesty was unbelievable. Once I was down at the Cape [Canaveral] and was off [work] and could make one of these tours on the bus. I got on the bus and, sure enough, there was Doctor Paine on the same bus, sitting in the corner, just taking the tour, as I did. So I went to the bus driver, and said, "Please, make an announcement that Dr. Paine is here on the bus," and he did. We had a lot of fun there [Haüssermann 1992].

Von Braun had his work cut out for him in Washington. Across the nation the space program and the aerospace industry that depended upon it were in retreat. Since the lunar landing, tens of thousands of scientists, engineers, and highly skilled manufacturing workers had lost their jobs. This only fed the growing antiscience atmosphere in the country.

But the difficulties for the space program were only increased.

On July 28, 1970, five months after von Braun's transfer to headquarters, Paine announced his resignation from NASA and his intention to return to private life. Why?

"I was a Democrat, appointed by a Democratic President," Paine explained in a 1985 interview. "I believe Nixon kept me in my post because no Republican wanted the job—a couple months before the planned landing of a man on the Moon. ... Since everything worked well during the Moon landing, I was of the opinion that President Nixon really ought to appoint his own man. For if we had a NASA Administrator who felt allied with the President, the outlook for Wernher's visions would improve ... since I would not be able to achieve optimal cooperation, it would quite simply not have been fair, if I had remained" [Stuhlinger and Ordway 1992, p. 434].

While Wernher von Braun tried to fend off those in the Congress who would cancel manned spaceflight, the wrangling between the White House and the Office of Management and Budget over the same issue continued. Finally, President Nixon announced on January 5, 1971 that America would build a Space Shuttle. But that was all that was left for manned spaceflight from the ambitious program the Space Task Group had recommended, which would have landed Americans on Mars in 1983.

Determining that there was little more he could do in the space program, von Braun announced his resignation from NASA on May 26, 1972, and took a job in private industry. "Space without von Braun?" *The Washington Daily News* asked. "Inconceivable," it answered (Kirkman 1972b). Perceptive commentators warned that as went von Braun, so had gone the space program for more than a decade.

But Wernher von Braun never lost his faith that the American people and their elected representatives would come back to the adventure of space exploration in the future. Although suffering from cancer, which was to end his life on June 16, 1977, von Braun established the National Space Institute on July 15, 1975, to educate the public and rally support for space exploration. During a speech at its founding, von Braun stated, "it is in man's nature that he always wants to explore—to move on—to develop and advance.

"I also believe," von Braun said, "that the much heralded idea of the Earth as a limited planet is absolutely unacceptable . . . because for all eternity it would put a lid on man's natural growth." In truth, he said, we "have all the riches, mineral resources and energies of the Solar System at our disposal" (von Braun 1975).

While gravely ill, von Braun prepared a philosophical dissertation that was read to the synod of the Lutheran Church of America on October 29, 1976, in Philadelphia. The paper deals with issues of morality in science, and von Braun defends his viewpoint with a quote from Plato: "We can easily forgive a child who is afraid of the dark; the real tragedy of life is when men are afraid of the light."

Concerned about the attempts to straitjacket scientific advancement on ethical grounds, von Braun asks, "Is everything that is scientifically possible, permissible?" He warned that laws limiting scientific application should be established only after an area of possible abuse "of an otherwise promising and beneficial scientific discovery can be clearly identified and isolated. No judge would condemn a human embryo to death because it has the potential to become a criminal."

A large section of his dissertation considers what he terms "the most pressing problems of our generation": human survival and the severe economic problems of the majority of the world's peoples. Science can provide appropriate solutions, he asserted. He uses an example in which he was intimately involved: the NASA program to provide India with access to a communications satellite beaming educational programs to 2,500 remote villages, the "Teacher in the Sky" program. "We have no moral right to deny [education] to them," von Braun states:

Maybe the fact that I spent 20 years of my life in Huntsville has something to do with [this] conclusion. When I arrived there in 1950, the opinion was widespread among the predominantly white population of Huntsville that most black children were either not ready for first-class education, or that a general rise in their educational standards would only lead to trouble with job placements. Today, Huntsville has some of the finest integrated schools in the nation, and few, if any, of the predicted problems have arisen.

To those promoting the ideology of "zero growth" to curb the world's population, von Braun says pointedly that this idea

should be rejected as half-cocked and downright dangerous. ... The indiscriminate philosophy of "No Growth" makes no difference between the growth of population and growth as a means for continuing survival. We must reject this simplistic concept.

On the question of scientists and their relationship to God, von Braun asks:

What strange rationale makes some physicists accept the inconceivable electron as real while refusing to accept the reality of God on the grounds that they cannot conceive Him? One cannot be exposed to the law and order of the universe without concluding that there must be a Divine Intent behind

NASA, Marshall Space Flight Center

This photograph was the official portrait of Wernher von Braun when he was the director of the Marshall Space Flight Center. As director from 1960-1970, he oversaw the development of the Saturn V rocket that took men to the Moon. He "sold" America on the Apollo program, and helped plan out what should be the next decades' program for space exploration.

it all. Speaking for myself, I can only say that the grandeur of the cosmos serves only to confirm my belief in the certainty of a Creator. The better we understand the intricacies of the universe and all its harbors, the more reason we have found to marvel at God's creation.

The Universe revealed through scientific inquiry is the living witness that God is indeed at work. Understanding the nature of the creation provides a substantive basis for the faith by which we attempt to know the nature of the Creator [von Braun 1976].

Wernher von Braun could not have accomplished such extraordinary achievements in his lifetime had he not always held fast to the belief in the uniqueness of the individual.

In a eulogy at a memorial service at the National Cathedral on June 22, 1977, NASA Administrator James Fletcher fittingly said:

[von Braun] clung to what seemed an impossible dream for his entire life, despite pressures of politics, bureaucratic entanglements, war, loss of fortune or even, especially, personal criticism. . . . I sincerely hope that Wernher von Braun's passing shall be a reminder to all of us what one person can do to show the world the magnificent future which is in store for it, and the wonders that man is capable of performing.

Krafft Ehricke's Extraterrestrial Imperative

> Knowledge is tomorrow's most important tool. . . . Science is the most exciting life you can lead, because in performing research and making discoveries, there comes a realization that you have contributed to mankind—that you understand one more facet of the workings of nature which neither you nor anyone else ever understood before [Thomas 1960, p. 1].

Krafft A. Ehricke was one of the most remarkable men of this century. Following in the footsteps of the father of spaceflight, Hermann Oberth, he extended the science of astronautics to enable not only man's exploration of the Earth and Moon but his humanization of the Solar System. Like Wernher von Braun, he was a tireless promoter, lecturer, and public proponent of space exploration, willing to defend the truth, even when it was "unpopular." And like Willy Ley, Ehricke's breadth of knowledge spanned many fields of scientific endeavor, in addition to his lifelong study of space technology including the evolution of life and development of Earth's biosphere.

Ehricke saw man's colonization of space from the vantage point of evolution, locating the negentropic quality of life as the basis for solving the "crisis" in each historic period in the Earth's development. The Age of Space would, for the first time, allow the two-dimensional life of Earth to extend to three- and four-dimensional polyglobal civilizations.

For more than 40 years, Krafft Ehricke pursued all of his activities with a kindness and gentlemanliness often commented upon

National Air and Space Museum, Smithsonian Institution, 83-2823

Krafft A. Ehricke made major contributions to the science, technology, and philosophy of astronautics. He saw the negentropic quality of life, which is creative thinking in the human being, as the basis for solving every "crisis" throughout history.

by those who had the pleasure of knowing him. He left an indelible mark on the field of space science and technology, and his program for exploration is one mankind would do well to follow over the course of the 21st century.

Krafft Ehricke was born on March 24, 1917, in Berlin, Germany. At the age of 12, he saw the film *Woman in the Moon,* and was so fascinated with it that he saw it a dozen times. Ehricke termed Oberth's contribution to the film, "technological clairvoyance." The film excited Ehricke's imagination and set him on the path of his life's work. "When Christmas 1929 approached, Krafft presented his mother with a list—books on astronomy, flight mechanics, and propulsion" (Thomas 1960, p. 2).

Later, he heard about the activities of the Society for Space Travel in Berlin but, as he reported, he was only 14 years old and considered too young to participate. "I just stood around," he recalled. "I was terribly interested, but that was all [I was able to do]." So he applied himself to study and began designing spaceship models and writing articles for technical journals (Chapman 1960, p. 169).

Ehricke's parents were both dentists, and he made use of their equipment to conduct experiments to try to create materials to simulate the cracks and craters on the Moon. From the writings of Belgian physics Professor Joseph Antoine Plateau he learned how to "create a sphere in a fluid. By getting oil underneath the surface of the liquid, then using one of his mother's knitting needles, he was able to rotate the oil into a sphere. As it whirled, it split off moons, just as had our own Earth-Moon system in evolution" (Thomas 1960, p. 3).

Next, he acquired a telescope. "His first lecture on astronomy was delivered to a spellbound audience gathered in the waiting room of his mother's dental office. None who paid 10 cents to hear this youngster's remarks went away disappointed" (Thomas 1960 p. 4).

In 1938, Ehricke joined with Hans Kaiser in organizing the Society for Space Research in Germany and he wrote articles for its journal, *Space,* even through the war.

Ehricke attended the Technical University of Berlin, where he majored in aeronautical engineering. Among his teachers were Hans Geiger and Werner Karl Heisenberg. But his education was interrupted when he was drafted into the German Army in 1940. He was assigned to a tank unit in northern France. During the evacuation of Dunkirk, "a tank accidentally rolled over part of his body, breaking his leg in several places." He convalesced in Berlin, taking the opportunity to renew his studies (Chapman 1960, p. 170).

In the summer of 1941, Ehricke was sent to the Russian front as a commander of an armored unit. Luckily, in 1942, two patents he had filed on rocket technology brought him to the attention of army technical personnel and he was transferred to the rocket program at Peenemünde. "He learned later that the rest of his tank unit had been wiped out on the Russian front" (Chapman 1960, p. 170).

Ehricke later recalled:

Although I was assigned [at Peenemünde] as assistant to Dr. Walter Thiel, Director of Propulsion Development, I was not too eager to settle down in a plush office job. I am forever grateful to Dr. von Braun and Dr. Thiel that I did not have to. They gave me first the opportunity to work on the test stand with a monkey wrench, and in this manner I was able to acquaint myself thoroughly with the hardware on hand before theorizing on how to improve it. After all, that is the way they both started, so the benefits of such work were well illustrated.

In the last years I have observed young engineers starting right off as experts without having done honest design work on one single component or having once gotten their hands dirty on lowly hardware. I feel regrets for them, because they are deprived of a wonderful opportunity which will never return after they have grown in status and responsibility" [Thomas 1960, p. 7].

While at Peenemünde, Ehricke investigated the possibility of the use of nuclear energy for rocket propulsion for Dr. Thiel.

Ehricke was not in the original group of German specialists who came to the United States as part of Operation Paperclip in the final days of World War II, because his wife, Ingeborg, was somewhere in Berlin and he was not going to leave for America without finding her. "There was no transportation to get there—absolutely none," he told Shirley Thomas in 1960. "So he walked for 30 days to get from Bavaria to the capital," Thomas reports. He was quite relieved when he found Inge alive and well—"though, of course, living under most difficult conditions" (Thomas 1960, p. 8).

In December 1946, Ehricke was offered a contract to work in the United States. He joined the rest of the Paperclip group at Fort Bliss in 1947, and was given two principal assignments: to familiarize the military and industry personnel with the V-2 and to perform theoretical work (Thomas 1960, p. 9).

When the group of Germans was transferred to Huntsville, Alabama, he became chief of the Gas Dynamics Section at the Redstone Arsenal. Ehricke worked with ram jets and did heat transfer research, mainly on development of supersonic diffusers for high-speed ram jet engines (Thomas 1960, p. 10).

But Ehricke "grew restless with both the climate [in Huntsville] and von Braun's conservative engineering." When the army contracts for the Germans expired in 1952 and they were free to make a move, Ehricke, along with a number of others, moved to employment in the burgeoning defense/aerospace industry. Ehricke went to work at Bell Aircraft (Sloop 1978, p. 194). It would seem, too, that Wernher von Braun and Krafft Ehricke were too similar—in their boundless energy, restless creative spirit, and drive to accomplish—to have continued to work well together in a "team."

From the very dawn of the Space Age, Krafft Ehricke believed it was as important to develop a philosophical basis for this new era as it was to develop the technologies to bring it into being. "Astronautics is the science of operating in space and traveling to other worlds. The implications are such that it now becomes increasingly important to develop the philosophy, as well as the utilitarian aspects, of this new science," he wrote in 1957.

Though the practical aspects of astronautics had been under development for some time, Ehricke wrote,

the philosophy of astronautics is young and fertile. Its countless implications are far from exhausted. For this reason, the author, concerned for some 20 years with the study and advocacy of astronautics as a technical, as well as a cultural, mission, submits a few additional thoughts on this subject.

The concept of space travel carries with it enormous impact, because it challenges man on practically all fronts of his physical and spiritual existence. The idea of traveling to other celestial bodies reflects to the highest degree the independence and agility of the human mind. It lends ultimate dignity to man's technical and scientific endeavors. Above all, it touches on the philosophy of his very existence. As a result, the concept of space travel disregards national borders, refuses to recognize differences of historical or ethnological origin, and penetrates the fiber of one sociological or political creed as fast as that of the next.

Space travel holds perhaps the greatest general appeal for

our complex and divided world. ... If it can be done here, it can eventually be done in other segments of our life today, where man seems to be hopelessly and perpetually deadlocked. A feeling of enthusiasm and genuine interest seems to prevail among all those who deal with space flight and astronautics— school children learning about it, Congressmen allotting money for it, political leaders of the East and West praising their nation's contributions to its progress, and last, but not least, scientists and engineers blazing the trail toward its eventual accomplishment [Ehricke 1957, p. 26].

Ehricke summarized his philosophy of astronautics in three laws:

First Law. Nobody and nothing under the natural laws of this universe impose any limitations on man except man himself. Second Law. Not only the Earth, but the entire Solar System, and as much of the universe as he can reach under the laws of nature, are man's rightful field of activity. Third Law. By expanding through the universe, man fulfills his destiny as an element of life, endowed with the power of reason and the wisdom of the moral law within himself.

The first law is astronautics' challenge to man to write his declaration of independence from *a priori* thinking, from uncritically accepted conditions, in other words, from a past and principally different pre-technological world clinging to him. This can be done. The Declaration of Independence and the Constitution of this country prove it [Ehricke 1957, pp. 26–27].

After the development of life from the oceans, the expansion of life to the land, and the development of the mammal, Ehricke wrote,

the most versatile and perfect land animal. ... [human] life found itself stymied on the borders of space. There are no biological means where direct application would permit living beings to enter and cross space. It is intriguing to think that life may have answered this challenge by producing a new amphibian—man—whose restless mind reaches beyond the

confinements of his biological world. The human brain alone
is capable of utilizing certain superior qualities of inorganic
matter for entering space. ... It is a historical fact that man's
mind and spirit grow with the space in which he is allowed to
operate.

The importance of the second law can be measured by the
effect which the expansion of European man all over the Earth
had on the development of civilization. ... We today are merely
the shipbuilders for the men and women who will enter a new
era of discoveries and lay the foundations for those who will
come after them, those who will develop planetary technologies to create cosmic civilizations.

The third law specifies this anthropological character of
space operations. ... It [proclaims] man's natural right to explore and attempt to fertilize with human skill and wisdom all
those parts of the universe which he can reach, whether or
not they are inhabited by intelligent beings [Ehricke 1957, pp.
26–27].

"Realism of vision is needed," Ehricke believed:

We must be realistic, but there is a wrong kind of realism,
timid and static, which tells man to live for his existence alone
and not to rock the boat. The kind of realism we need is the
realism of vision—the realism of a Columbus, of our Constitution, of a Benjamin Franklin, of an Albert Einstein, of a Konstantin Tsiolkovsky, and of a Hermann Oberth [Ehricke 1957b,
p.27].

Thinking about the space program yet to come, in 1952 Ehricke
developed the ground-breaking idea of having two types of rocket
vehicles for manned space missions—one for the crew and a separate one for cargo. At the time, he was assistant project engineer
on long-range glide rocket studies at Bell Aircraft, working with
his former Peenemünde commander, Walter Dornberger. Ehricke
analyzed reusable winged orbiting craft, which led to the design of
the Air Force's Dynasoar (*Spaceflight* 1974, p. 437), and he calculated the specifications for winged orbital vehicles, which he saw
as the follow-ons to the winged A-4 test flown at Peenemünde.

In previous mission scenarios, it had always been assumed that the crew would carry with it all of the required equipment for its flight. But a manned spacecraft would include a winged return vehicle and life-support systems and would require safety provisions. With the addition of cargo aboard, the manned vehicle would be very heavy.

Cargo vehicles need none of these manned systems. If the two functions were separated, therefore, each vehicle could weigh less, and each design would be optimal for its specialized function. At Ehricke's suggestion, this concept of separating the men from the cargo was incorporated by Wernher von Braun in his design for *The Mars Project.*

In a 1954 paper, Ehricke proposed that a small ferry be used to transfer freight from an Earth-launched cargo carrier to the space station. Two years later, he improved his design and proposed the use of an unmanned supply ship that would be placed into orbit and unloaded directly, by a four-man crew through a series of space walks. The manned vehicle, he calculated, could take 1,200 pounds of payload, consisting mainly of the crew, its life support, and the winged return glide plane.

Each similarly sized cargo ship could take 1,200 pounds of payload, which could, for instance, provide food and water for 30 days. The purpose of the station, as Ehricke saw it, was to allow the beginning of a trip elsewhere. He proposed a third vehicle, which would be a larger cargo ship, with a payload capability of 11,000 pounds (Figure 10.1). These ships would leave their empty "propellant containers" (fuel tanks) in orbit as the building blocks for the space station. Constructing the station would require 47 such cargo flights. For lunar circumnavigation, he estimated that 50 flights of the cargo vehicles would be necessary to equip and fuel spaceships to the Moon.

Another specialized spacecraft was proposed by Ehricke in 1959, as the new Space Age opened the door to the Solar System. This was a "secondary vehicle" or "lifeboat rocket" to accompany a manned mission to Mars. Ehricke reports:

In 1947 to 1948, this author analyzed a number of missions to Mars by manned spacecraft in preparation for a novel. The desire for dramatic but factual events led him to consider more closely possible troubles, failures, and accidents of such a jour-

FIGURE 10.1
KRAFFT EHRICKE'S DESIGN FOR A CARGO SUPPLY SHIP
Krafft Ehricke determined that space transportation would be most efficient if specialized supply ships were designed to only carry cargo to complement specially designed manned spacecraft. Here is a schematic of the large 11,000-pound supply ship needed for construction of the space station.

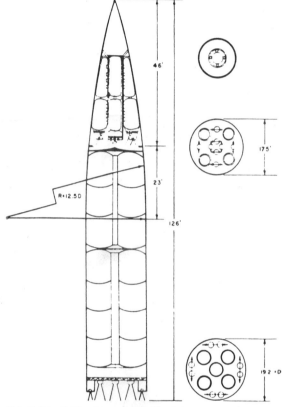

Source: Krafft A. Ehricke, "A New System for Satellite Orbits—Part 2," (*Jet Propulsion* Vol. 24, No. 6, November/December 1954).

ney, rather than to assume everything would go well [Ehricke 1960c, p. 505].

He decided that a "sister ship" was required for rescue in case of an accident. Space stations would have emergency crew return vehicles ready for launch at all times from the ground. But for trips millions of miles from Earth, only an accompanying vehicle would be useful. A rescue ship could be launched from Earth only if were nuclear-powered and could take a short route to the troubled Mars-bound vessel (Ehricke 1960c, p. 520).

As Ehricke later stated somewhat dramatically: "We want to avoid having to say, 'Well, that was just tough luck' and give the crews' families big insurance checks while their men slough around in some eccentric orbit between Mars and Jupiter. We want to get them back" (Grey and Grey 1962, p. 56).

Later, Ehricke extended this concept of a specialized family of vehicles to the sphere of unmanned planetary probes, proposing the development of "metaprobes" for exploration. Rather than send one or two large all-purpose spacecraft, a series of small Experiment Carriers could be deployed for a mission, each designed for a specific task. This would also permit many nations of the world to contribute to scientific exploration, he proposed to the representatives at the International Astronautical Federation in October 1968. A single Communications Link and Monitor spacecraft would monitor, direct, and interrogate the various Experiment Carriers and communicate their results to Earth (Ehricke 1968c).

As noted in earlier chapters, from the earliest days of the Space Age, there was contention in the space community over which fuels and propellants should be used in rockets. In 1947, Wernher von Braun asked Krafft Ehricke to check a report by Richard B. Canright of the Jet Propulsion Laboratory on the relative importance of exhaust velocity and propellant density for rockets of V-2 and larger sizes. Canright's analysis showed that for some large rockets, exhaust velocity (higher with hydrogen) was more important than fuel density (greater with petroleum-derivatives, or rocket fuel) and, therefore, liquid hydrogen would be superior for some applications.

Because cryogenic hydrogen had handling and materials problems, von Braun felt that kerosene-based chemical fuels would be best for easy handling in the military systems he was developing for the U.S. Army. But looking to the future, "Ehricke felt less restrained and hydrogen's potential remained prominent in his thinking" (Sloop 1978, p. 192).

In designing his mission for *The Mars Project,* von Braun had discounted the use of liquid hydrogen. "I don't like hydrogen. It's the devil's invention!" he had written to Hermann Koelle. "He was afraid of too many technical problems," Koelle explained. "The other alternative was to just build a somewhat bigger rocket, so he felt that it was easier to build bigger rockets than one with hydrogen" (Koelle 1992).

In an exhaustive study, Ehricke verified von Braun's contention that liquid hydrogen was not optimal for sub-orbital missiles, but he also confirmed Hermann Oberth's earlier conclusion that for the high-energy upper stages needed to send probes to the planets or men to the Moon, oxygen/hydrogen and comparable high-energy propellants were most attractive.

As Oberth and Tskiolkovsky had shown theoretically, to be most efficient, rockets should be constructed in stages. When one propulsion stage is exhausted, it is jettisoned, lowering the overall weight of the rocket. A second propulsion unit is then ignited on the second stage. The velocity of the rocket is the speed attained from the second stage added to the speed at the point of engine cutoff of the first stage. By adding stages, a higher final velocity is obtained.

In an article in the American Rocket Society's *Journal* in 1953, Ehricke made a detailed comparison of numerous combinations of chemical fuels and oxidizers, and the exhaust velocities for each set of propellants. He then determined the optimum range and applicability for each, including the velocity obtainable from working fluids with nuclear drives. He concluded that, for ascent from Earth, with final velocities of about 10,000 feet per second, a large number of chemical fuels are most efficient, such as the ones used in the rockets then under development. But for leaving Earth orbit, requiring a velocity between 10,000 to 20,000 feet per second, the density of the fuel becomes less important, and higher specific impulse propellants (with higher exhaust velocities) are preferred. For the even higher velocity requirements, such as circumnavigation of the Moon and interplanetary flights, working fluids such as hydrogen heated from a nuclear source become superior.

Hydrogen would be needed with liquid oxygen to open up cislunar space to man, and hydrogen also would also be the gateway to the Solar System, used with nuclear energy (Ehricke 1953).

"Centaur was the brainchild of Krafft Ehricke," the NASA history of the use of hydrogen reports:

> For nearly three decades, Ehricke had prepared himself for the Space Age; when it dawned with Sputnik, he was ready.

Within a month, he proposed a hydrogen-oxygen stage for use with the Atlas missile. Ehricke was able to move rapidly because previous work on the Atlas missile and the ideas of others [Tsiolkovsky and Oberth] about hydrogen-oxygen upper stages had laid the groundwork [Sloop 1978, p. 191].

In December 1957, General Dynamics Astronautics (incorporating Convair) submitted a proposal to the U.S. Air Force titled "A Satellite and Space Development Plan." It included a four-engine pressure-fed hydrogen-oxygen stage with each engine developing 7,000–7,500 pounds of thrust. The Air Force did not approve the proposal (Sloop 1978, pp. 194–5).

As soon as NASA was created, in July 1958, however, it established a committee to coordinate government plans for propulsion and launch vehicles. On August 29, the Pentagon's Advanced Research Projects Agency (ARPA) initiated the Centaur program for an Atlas upper stage (Sloop 1978, p. 195). In October, NASA Administrator Keith Glennan had the Centaur program transferred from ARPA to the civilian agency, to be used for both military and civilian purposes (Sloop 1978, p. 200).

The first rocket stage in the world to fly using liquid hydrogen and liquid oxygen propellants was the Centaur on top of an Atlas missile. Since then, liquid hydrogen technology has been used to take men to the Moon in the second and third stages of the Saturn V rocket and to send unmanned probes to virtually all of the planets. As Ehricke had seen in the 1950s, it would open the gateway to the Solar System.

Liquid hydrogen opened the gateway, but as Ehricke had shown in careful and exhaustive studies, nuclear energy—fission and then fusion—would be the preconditions for man to colonize the Solar System. Space historian Shirley Thomas relates that, even while Ehricke "crusaded" for the adoption of liquid hydrogen fuel, he was urging the next decisive progression, nuclear propulsion (Thomas 1960, p. 20).

In testimony before Congress in the 1950s, Ehricke stated:

This universe is run by nuclear energy. Space will be conquered only by manned nuclear powered vehicles. ... The chemical rocket engine is a carryover into the Space Age from the missile phase, just like the balloon helped bring about the air age. Like the balloon, the chemical rocket will retain

NASA, Marshall Space Flight Center

The liquid hydrogen Centaur upper stage has been the propulsion system used for many U.S. planetary probes and spacecraft. Here a Centaur upper stage sits atop a Titan vehicle. This Centaur sent the Viking spacecraft to Mars, where an orbiter and lander provided the first close-up view of the Red Planet.

indefinitely its usefulness for special applications. However, true astronautics and nuclear power are inseparably connected [Thomas 1960, p. 21].

Over the next 20 years, Ehricke would improve and expand his concepts for the use of nuclear energy in Earth orbit, cislunar space, on the Moon, and throughout the Solar System.

Another crucial concept for the development of space came under Ehricke's scrutiny in the 1950s. He objected to the proposal that a space station used as a point of departure into space and for other functions had to be one, massive structure.

Shirely Thomas reports that

> Ehricke deduced that this space station might be in a completely wrong plane [in relation to the destination planet] and would thus require great expenditure of power to change the flight vector of the departing vehicle to adjust for this error. This would be an even greater problem with vehicles returning to the space station after a probe into deep space; on a self-arbitrary orbit, which had neither the same inclination nor the same distance from the Earth as the orbiting station, the rendezvous would indeed be difficult [Thomas, 1960 p. 11].

Von Braun had proposed an enormous donut-shaped space station, with a crew of more than 50. In contrast, Ehricke proposed, in a paper delivered in 1954 at the Fifth International Astronautical Federation Congress at Innsbruck, that there first be smaller space stations, each optimized for different purposes (Thomas 1960, p. 11).

In late 1954, Ehricke left Bell Aircraft and joined Convair Astronautics in California. According to his wife, Ehricke had found the snowy winters in Buffalo, New York, too much of a reminder of the Russian front during the war, and they decided to move to a more moderate climate. Ehricke had hoped to continue his studies there and obtain a doctorate degree, but when he was hired to work on the burgeoning Air Force Atlas ICBM program, he could not find the time.

> At last he was next to a rocket vehicle which . . . was probably powerful enough to reach out toward the stars. . . . It did not take the German rocket expert long to show that the Atlas, with no extra stages mounted on its nose, was fully capable of casting a small payload into orbit around the Earth. Furthermore, Ehricke discovered, the missile could be made to project *itself* into a satellite orbit [Chapman 1960 p. 152].

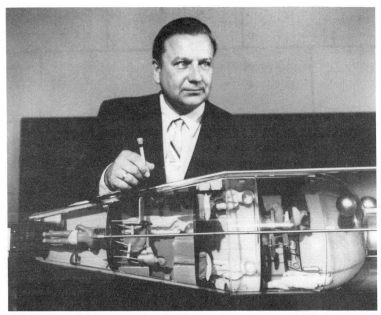

Convair photo 11403A, Courtesy National Air and Space Museum, Smithsonian Institution, 84-10330

In April 1958, Krafft Ehricke and Arthur Kantrowitz presented a proposal to a congressional committee for a four-man space station based on the Atlas missile. Here, in a photo taken a few days before the testimony, Ehricke is seen with a model of the space station.

"Literature contains projects envisioning gigantic satellites up to many million feet in volume," Ehricke wrote. "However, no functions have been suggested for such super-structures which could not be done equally well by much smaller satellites involving less than a half-dozen highly qualified people" (Ehricke 1959a, p. 157).

In the mid-1950s, Ehricke proposed that the first space station be built from empty Atlas rockets taken into orbit. "Very large inhabited satellites ... can be useful only in terms of industrial, medical, or recreational applications," Ehricke stated. But "in order for those to be useful, the problem of a comparatively inexpensive routine surface-to-orbit service must be solved first" (Ehricke 1959a, p. 157).

Krafft Ehricke and Dr. Arthur Kantrowitz, director of the Avco Research Laboratory, testified before the House Select Committee on Astronautics in April 1958 on a proposal for a four-man space station, based on the Atlas ICBM, to be placed in a 400-mile high orbit. It could be ready in five years, they stated, at a cost of $500 million. The joint Convair-Avco proposal was for a series of Minimum Manned Satellites (Clark 1958, pp. 26–28).

Seven Atlas rockets would deliver the primary structure, carry cargo, and transport the passenger ship carrying the first four crew members. A second passenger ship would carry a relief crew, and a nuclear auxiliary power plant would be brought up. The station would be assembled through a series of extravehicular activities by the crews. Return to Earth for the crews from the Atlas station would be in two-man gliders.

Physicist Arthur Kantrowitz was already well known in the space science community for having solved one of the most important problems in the young ICBM program—how to design a warhead so that it could sustain the heat of reentry. He had suggested in 1952 that shock tubes be used to simulate the environment of reentry in the laboratory and two years later, Air Force Gen. Bernard Schriever asked Kantrowitz to solve the problem. In addition to contributing to the success of the Atlas program, Kantrowitz designed one of the first supersonic wind tunnels in 1935, and he carried out pioneering research in aerodynamics, thermonuclear fusion, magnetohydrodynamics, and laser physics.

A report on the Convair station proposal in *The Washington Star,* December 29, 1958, described it as "the brainchild of Krafft Ehricke." Small rockets would rotate the station 2.5 times per minute providing some artificial gravity. It would have four levels and carry a water regeneration system. When the station was near completion, one cargo ship would bring the nuclear power plant.

By 1960, only in his early 40s, Krafft Ehricke had already made a name for himself in the spaceflight community. John Chapman, in his 1960 history of the Atlas missile, describes Ehricke as a

tireless, friendly, 42-year-old German, who became an American citizen in 1954. [He is] perhaps the leading exponent of spaceflight in the U.S. today. He talks spaceflight any time and anywhere—to students, generals, scientists, engineers, congressmen, television audiences, or to one person sitting with him in his office—always fluently and brilliantly, always with the same vibrant, boyish enthusiasm.

He captivates his listeners, with his sincerity of purpose, his seemingly boundless knowledge, and his animated delivery. An Air Force general was once so taken with an Ehricke discourse that he led Ehricke from a conference room to an airport— then held up a takeoff—all the while pumping him for more details. Constantly in demand for speeches, interviews, articles, and presentations, Ehricke faces a parade of visitors each day, often winds up talking to two of them at once [Chapman 1960, pp. 168–169].

A long series of calculations in the 1950s convinced Ehricke that another generally accepted approach for orbiting spacecraft could be made more efficient. Orbits of thousands of miles altitude were an unnecessary and expensive approach, he reasoned. Wernher von Braun, for example, had placed his space station in a two-hour orbit at more than 1,000 miles above the Earth. The 1957 discovery of the Van Allen radiation belt also made this altitude impractical for manned systems.

While thinking about the utility of various satellite orbits, in 1955 Ehricke introduced a novel concept of very, very low orbits. As opposed to the unpowered satellite that coasts in orbit, his satellite would be a powered orbiting vehicle, which he called a Satelloid. He explained that, for scientific investigations of the atmosphere, between the altitude that could be covered in aerodynamic gliders and that of a stably orbiting satellite, there was a region of 350,000 to 450,000 feet, which would be important to explore (Ehricke 1955).

Information from this region of the atmosphere, extending to the lower ionosphere, would be important for the development of reentry technology, needed for ICBMs as well as manned vehicles. This region he described as the "gate to the atmosphere," where aerodynamic forces begin to act on incoming vehicles. "Landing" a space vehicle, he explained, "means correct reentry into the atmosphere rather than touchdown on the landing field" (Ehricke 1956b).

This altitude had never been proposed previously for a satellite because the atmospheric drag would bring the satellite back to Earth before it completed even one orbit. Ehricke proposed that the Satelloid carry enough fuel to produce a small but continuous thrust to keep the vehicle at a 147.5 mile altitude. At that orbit, it would need only 1,000 pounds of propellant for 115 revolutions, for a stay-time of about a week.

To Krafft Ehricke, getting in to space was only the enabling technology for entirely new fields of science and exploration. In 1956, he made his first proposal for the use of space for the application of medicine and biology. In a lecture at the Franklin Institute in Philadelphia, he explained the concept of a "biosat," which would be used for the study of the effects of prolonged weightlessness, initially on plants and animals. The biosat would also test technologies for the preservation of liquid and solid foods in space, the maintenance of plant life, and spacecraft designs.

At some point, the biosat could test a closed-loop system in which the animals and plants were in "perfect symbiotic equilibrium," he said. In addition, the scientific research would be "devoted to the study of life itself and its manifold responses to different environmental conditions" (Ehricke 1956a, pp. 30, 33).

In 1966, with D. Newsom, a senior staff scientist in the Life Science Department of Convair, Ehricke put forward a comprehensive concept for the "Utilization of Space Environment for Therapeutic Purposes." The weightlessness of space and the possibility to vary the gravity level in orbit by rotating a spacecraft offered alleviative and curative possibilities, the authors proposed (Ehricke and Newsom 1966, p. 333).

Ehricke recounted:

> The senior author remembers to have read sometime in 1930 or 1931, when his then very youthful imagination was captured by early concepts of spaceflight, a summary of the biomedical "reasons" for the "impossibility" of space flight. . . . [spacefarers] will have a wide choice of death—by being crushed during the ascent, by freezing, by vomiting their guts out, or by being cremated [Ehricke and Newsom 1966, p. 334].

These fears having been discounted during successful manned orbital flights by the mid-1960s, Ehricke and Newsom explained that many of the "so-called unfavorable [biological changes during spaceflight] are so classified because they would be detrimental if the individual having reached a new equilibrium [in weightlessness] were suddenly transposed into a 1-gravity environment" (Ehricke

NASA, Johnson Space Center

It is well recognized today that the microgravity space environment provides important opportunities for research bearing on the treatment of disease, and the basic science of biology. Here, Space Shuttle mission specialist Dr. Rhea Seddon uses a baroreflex neck pressure chamber to collect data on cardiovascular deconditioning due to space flight. The photograph was taken in June 1991 during a special life sciences shuttle mission.

and Newsom 1966, p. 336). They assumed that astronauts will be given the opportunity to readjust gradually to 1-gravity before landing back on Earth in a variable-gravity rotating spacecraft.

Ehricke and Newsom proposed that the environment of weightlessness could be therapeutic, alleviating pathological conditions such as heart problems, hypertension, faulty muscle control and coordination, and pinched nerves and disks. Later on, an ambulance launch vehicle could transport persons with severe burns or spinal fractures up to this unique environment. They described an orbital hospital to treat injuries sustained in space as well as treat sick Earthlings (Ehricke and Newsom 1966, p. 346, 356).

In 1969, having outlined for the international space community the previous year the role of space for biomedical applications, Ehricke was asked to prepare a paper for the American Astronautical Society on space tourism: Why shouldn't space be fun? Ehricke defined space tourism as "the enjoyment of space." He also saw it as an important way to draw more people into participating in space (Ehricke 1967, p. 259, 261).

Seeing the Earth and the heavens from space will have a rejuvenating effect, Ehricke imagined, and will keep open the exploration of new frontiers for many. Global sightseeing, relaxation and rest, orbital excursions, sports, the entertainment of experimentation, and planetary and stellar observations are the activities he proposed for future space tourists (Ehricke 1967, p. 269). Ehricke suggested that for $80 per bed per night, one could vacation in orbit! A space zoo and botanic exhibitions would demonstrate the changes in biological systems in microgravity. Space walks, short excursions in "space boats," and new sports activities would be available. "World Rooms" of Venus and Mars would simulate the atmospheres and gravity conditions of these planets and allow tourists a look at other worlds (Ehricke 1967, p. 274).

"Men and women will be attracted by coming face to face with creation or the early origin of the universe and our Solar System in particular," Ehricke proposed. (Ehricke 1967, p. 265).

"Long before the Apollo program, when we were working on interplanetary probes in the early 1960s, there was already criticism of the space program," Ehricke stated in a presentation in New York in November 1981. "My concern over this mounting criticism and the lack of proper responses to it drove me to continue what I had started in the late 1950s—to develop a philosophy of space and of growth and of technology in general" (Ehricke 1982a, p. 20). "Early on it became clear that, beyond hardware specifics, nothing short of a comprehensive technological-economic-cultural-anthropological, in a word, a *global* approach would suffice" (Ehricke 1982b).

To provide this global view, during the 1960s, Ehricke developed the concept of *The Extraterrestrial Imperative,* and he wrote a yet-to-be-published book of that title. Its central concept is based on the "distinction between multiplication and growth." In developing this concept, Ehricke was very specific about his antagonists: "The *Limits to Growth* people see Earth as a life raft in hostile space. Hence, they see man's world as a closed system—restricted to Earth. I don't. Humanity's action world is no more closed than it is flat" (Maxwell 1974, p. 6).

Ehricke attacked the assumptions of the neo-Malthusian zero-growth movement:

> Meadows and Forrester ... in their book *The Limits to Growth,* compare the growth of mankind to the mindless and senseless multiplication of lilies in a pond. I never considered mankind a lily in a pond, senseless and mindless. . . . The *Global 2000 Report,* a warmed-over version of the original limits to growth nonsense, contains outright misinformation and, like its infamous predecessor, totally ignores the human capacity for limitless growth. Growth, in contrast to multiplication, is the increase in knowledge, in wisdom, in the capacity to grow in new ways [Ehricke 1982a, p. 20].

Before a rapt audience in November 1981, Ehricke described how Earth's biosphere has faced two Great Crises during its evolution. These were overcome, he said, through the development of photosynthesis, the ability for a plant to produce its own "resources," and the development of multicelled life that could make use of the new oxygen atmosphere which had been created by plants. In each Great Crisis, he stated, "life had only three choices: give up and perish, regress to a minimal state of existence, or advance and grow" (Ehricke 1982a, p. 21).

He made clear the consequences of choosing any but the third choice:

> In 1979, of all things in the Year of the Child of the United Nations, there were 12 million children who did not reach their first birthday. That's 50 percent more than all battle deaths in World War I, in four years. And that is an outrage to a species that calls itself civilized [Ehricke 1982a, p. 19].

Have we reached the end of what can be accomplished through scientific breakthroughs? Are we doomed to watch our world continually contract and become more "polluted" and miserable? "The naysers," Ehricke said,

> are the polluters of our future. They deny vital options to future generations. Everybody is running around saying we can't grow anymore. That will be a self-fulfilling prophecy unless someone stands up and says, "Oh yes we can!" Those who think we have reached the end of our tether live in an even more unreal world than those who in the last century advocated closing the patent offices because their mousey minds could not comprehend that there might be anything left to invent [Maxwell 1974, p. 10].

In a 1972 article in *The New York Times*, Ehricke turned on its head the environmentalists' description of the beautiful photographs of the full globe of the Earth taken by the Apollo astronauts as the "fragile" Earth that man was destroying. Ehricke told *The Times*, "viewing our Earth from space should make it obvious that the world into which we can now grow is no longer closed" (Ehricke 1972c).

> Earth is not merely a spaceship. It is a member of the Sun's convoy traversing the vast ocean of our Milky Way galaxy. We are separated from our sister ships by greater distances than our land surface is from the bottom of our oceans. But far more important than distance is the nature of the intervening medium.
>
> It is very fortuitous that we need only to traverse open space to reach our remote terrestrial resources. . . . Our companion worlds are underdeveloped. Earth is the only luxury passenger liner in a convoy of freighters loaded with resources. These resources are for us to use, after Earth has hatched us to the point where we have the intelligence and the means to gain partial independence from our planet [Ehricke 1971c, p. 24].

The "brave new world" of zero growth, Ehricke stressed, could not be foisted upon the world's peoples without establishing a set of "new value systems." What is at stake, Ehricke recognized, was not simply the space program, but the past 500 years' history of

FIGURE 10.2
THE EFFECTS OF SPACE ACTIVITIES
Krafft Ehricke never believed there were limits to human activity, and formulated
a number of charts, such as this one, to show how space activity furthers nearly all
human endeavors.

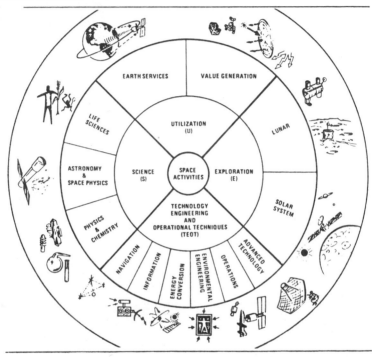

Source: Krafft A. Ehricke, "Space Applications for Earth-To-Low-Orbit Shuttle Vehicles," October
1970.

the development of civilization since the Renaissance. He defined
civilization as "a state of mental growth" (Ehricke 1972c).

The "new kind of disillusion" of the 1970s, he wrote, results
in a

> wave of pessimism that tends to undermine Man's confidence
> in a soaring future—and therewith in his nature which, some
> claim must be altered radically to conform with what is called
> insurmountable limitations. Confidence in a soaring future—
> spiritually as well as materially—is the essence of our techno-

scientific civilization and Western man's greatest message to mankind. Erosion of this confidence threatens the value system and weakens the drive on which our monumental accomplishments rest, ever since the dawn of the Renaissance.

And nowhere are the roots of the Renaissance spirit more deeply imbedded than in history's boldest social achievement, the United States of America [Ehricke 1971c, p. 18].

"For me," he states,

the development of the idea of space travel was always the most logical and most noble consequence of the Renaissance ideal, which again placed man in an organic and active relationship with his surrounding universe and which perceived in the synthesis of knowledge and capabilities its highest ideals. In that way was reestablished the connection with the noblest traditions of the ancient world. But in addition, something fundamentally new was added: experimentation and the objective methods of scientific research. The philosophical concept that was already present in embryo form in the ancient world, the foundation stone of Western civilization—that there can be one, and only one, truth, and that logical contradictions within a system are fundamentally false, and, therefore, an expression of imperfect knowledge and not some sort of magical influences—was cast into the forms of natural science.

The concepts of "limit" and "impossibility" were each relegated to two clearly distinct regions, namely the "limit" of our present state of knowledge and the "impossibility" of a process running counter to the well-understood laws of nature. With the breakthroughs of a Leonardo da Vinci, a Galileo and a Copernicus, of a Giordano Bruno, a Kepler and a Newton, there was concentrated a new intellectual energy of tremendous breadth. Its noblest characteristics were boldness of synthesis and fearlessness of perspective, steeled through a new disciplined way of thinking. In the end, everything culminated in the relativisation of "limits" and "impossibilities"—an intellectually creative achievement of the highest order. It forced a synthesis and provided, therefore, the luminous core of Renaissance thought. It has focused man's development for the next million years onto new paths, since it provided to man's thought and accomplishments, a cosmic dimension [Ehricke 1973 p. 196–197].

Ehricke could see the extension of the past into the present, as he recalled that

> as a very young man I formed my ideals in accordance with the spiritual inheritance of these giants. It became clear to me after I began to occupy myself with Hermann Oberth's work *The Rocket into Interplanetary Space,* having been stimulated to this through the film *Frau im Mond* in 1928–29, that I needn't look only at past centuries, but that I was the contemporary of a modern Leonardo da Vinci. Oberth's work reflects a boldness of synthesis, a fearlessness of perspective, that stood at the same level as the highest achievements of the Renaissance. In fact, Hermann Oberth's work is Renaissance material—timeless in the simple rigor and clear logic of the scientific thought that provided his syntheses and perspectives both with their austerity and their inspiration [Ehricke 1973, p. 197].

But how do we look at the future, from the standpoint of the past? "It is an extraordinary fact that we find ourselves at one of the very rare nodal points in an evolutionary history," Ehricke wrote in 1982, "in which the confluence of patient negentropic processes of eons accumulates a tremendous growth thrust potential whose acceptance and discharge will creatively play itself out over another eonic period." He includes a chart (Figure 10.3) with his short piece,

> worked out for my 1970 manuscript, "The Extraterrestrial Imperative," not publishable in the United States in the then prevailing atmosphere of no-growth and cultural pessimism. We have the freedom to make original choices, but the physical and evolutionary forces brought to bear by our choices are not subject to our discretion: That is where the dimension of responsibility comes in.
>
> Without the Open World of a limitless environment the mind dies. When the mind dies, all future will have become past [Ehricke 1982b].

"If God had wanted man to explore space," Krafft Ehricke often said, "He would have given him a Moon." With the Moon so close to Earth, the temptation will be too great for man to be "condemned to solitary confinement on one small planet," he stated optimistically (Ehricke 1974).

Throughout the 1970s, Ehricke worked on an extremely detailed study of the industrialization of the Moon. He saw Earth's companion as part of a two-planet system, which would create the "open world" of his Extraterrestrial Imperative in terms of resources, manufacturing, and products for other centers of civilization scattered throughout the Solar System. "Ours is a binary planetary system," he wrote in 1984. "There is no reason that only half of it should be inhabited, merely because life originated there.... Instead of searching for and speculating about life elsewhere," he counseled, "we will put it there" (Ehricke 1981a, p. 55). The book he completed on this subject, *The Seventh Continent: The Industrialization and Settlement of the Moon*, still awaits publication.

In it, Ehricke foresaw that five evolutionary stages, seen in Figure 10.4, each relying upon technological advances in energy production and use and space transportation systems, would lead to the establishment of Selenopolis, the capital city of a new lunar civilization.

In the first stage, detailed prospecting of the Moon would take place through the use of simple landers. So as not to be excluded from the "perpetually shadowed" regions of high lunar latitude and the polar regions, the landers would have the benefit of illumination from an orbiting Lunetta reflector. The idea of such an orbiting mirror was first proposed by Hermann Oberth in the 1920s and was updated and designed by Ehricke in great detail, for Earth applications, and later, for the Moon.

For Earth, the idea of space light is "to transmit solar radiation in a controlled manner to selected areas," Ehricke wrote. Lunetta systems in Earth-orbit are primarily for illumination (comparable to multiples of full moonlight in a cloudless sky) and Soletta systems are designed to deliver solar-level irradiation intensity to Earth.

Ehricke saw the primary applications for the Earth-orbital Lunetta in rural and developing nations to provide increased night light to extend the hours for productive activity, which could help reduce crop losses caused by inclement weather, increase the number of crops per year if conditions permit, and better utilize agricul-

FIGURE 10.3
THE CONSEQUENCES OF GROWTH VERSUS NO-GROWTH

Krafft Ehricke designed this chart in 1970 for his book, *The Extraterrestrial Imperative* which has never been published. Ehricke was attacking the prevailing cynicism by showing that a no-growth pathway would lead to a chauvinistic national outlook, stagnation and regression of progress, and geopolitical power politics. Eventually, the world would face ecological crises, mass starvation, wars, epidemics, and revolutions. Unfortunately, the no-growth pathway much of the world has indeed followed for the past 20 years has led to many of the consequences foreseen by Ehricke.

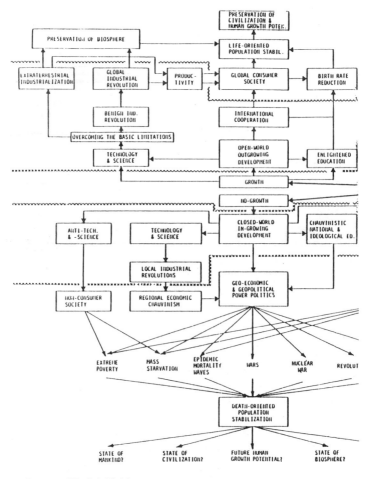

Source: Courtesy of Krafft A. Ehricke

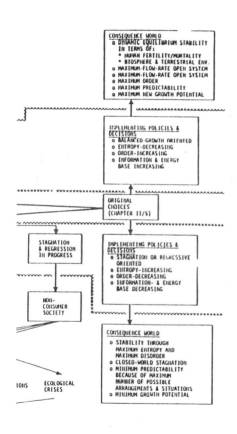

SPACE GLOBAL

FIGURE 10.4
THE FIVE STAGES OF LUNAR DEVELOPMENT
Krafft Ehricke proposed that the Moon be considered the seventh continent of the Earth. The development and exploitation of its resources would eliminate the notion that resources are finite. In the first two stages, Earth-Moon trade is in only one direction. By stage three, some lunar products are reaching the terrestrial market. By the fifth stage, industry on the Moon is not only self-sufficient and supplying Earth, but also is extending to supply new civilizations in other areas of the Solar System.

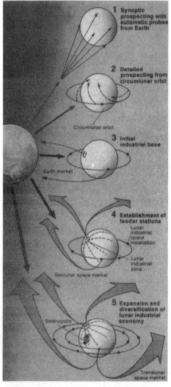

Source: Krafft A. Ehricke, "Industrializing the Moon," *Fusion* Vol. 6, No. 1, May-June 1984.

tural equipment and manpower. A Lunetta could also provide supplementary lighting for aid and rescue operations in disaster areas, urban regions at night, and enable industrial activities to be performed around the clock.

Soletta, providing man with a second Sun, would be designed for specific applications. These would include local weather modifi-

Krafft A. Ehricke

In this painting, Krafft Ehricke represents an Earth-orbital mirror attached to the Space Shuttle. It is reflecting the light from the Sun to an area which is in darkness on the Earth. Such a Lunetta would allow economic activity to take place on a 24-hour basis.

cation, a night "Sun" for electric power generation, in order to increase the rate of growth of biomass for agriculture, and mesoscale weather modification to prevent "prolonged dry, raining, or cold periods" and to irrigate dry areas (Ehricke 1981c, pp. 511–581).

For the first stage of lunar industrialization, a Lunetta would be used to aid in the prospecting for minerals. In the second stage, a Circumlunar Space Station (CLSS) would be added in orbit around the Moon. This would act as a "control and operations center for more sophisticated ground systems dispatched from Earth directly to the lunar surface," before permanent quarters were established on the lunar surface for men. In addition to the human habitat, the CLSS would also function as "an engineering and biological laboratory, experimenting with lunar materials delivered from different parts of the Moon by automated returners."

In stage three, a first-generation Central Lunar Processing Complex (CLPC) with a nuclear power station would be established, and industrialization would commence (Figure 10.5). The personnel to

FIGURE 10.5
MINING AND BENEFICIATION AT THE CLPC
In the third stage of lunar development, the processing of lunar raw materials at
the Central Lunar Processing Complex would include the use of nuclear-powered
electrolytic furnaces. The material would be mined (lower and upper right), brought
to the CLCP by conveyor belt, processed, and the product would be stored.

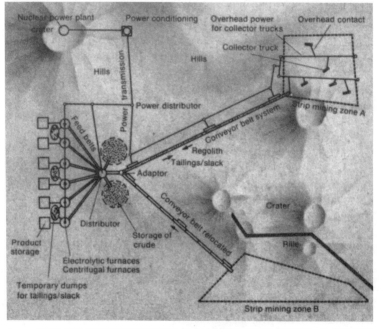

Source: Krafft A. Ehricke, "Industrializing the Moon," *Fusion* Part I. Vol. 5, No. 2, December
1981.

run the CLCP would be assigned to 9-to–12 month shifts to begin
the production of oxygen, silicon, aluminum, iron, glass, and other
materials. From these raw materials various processing technologies
would be developed to begin manufacturing.

Feeder stations would be established in stage four, "at places
that were identified at stages one and two as having a greater local
abundance of certain raw materials," similar to the development of
concentrations of industry near mineral reserves in the Midwest
industrial heartland of the U.S.A., or the Ruhr region of Germany.
The feeder stations would be largely unmanned, controlled and
operated from orbit in this stage. Materials collected in these "re-

mote mining operations" would be transported ballistically to receiver stations near the CLPC for processing.

Heat for materials processing technologies at the CLPC would include high-temperature nuclear reactors, nuclear-electric arc techniques, solar concentrator-heater ovens, underground atomic ovens stoked by small fission or fusion detonations, and high-temperature plasma directly from a fusion reactor.

In this stage, the lunar population would be increasing, laying the basis for stage five's development of Selenopolis. The city would be open-ended in design and would grow as the population and activities advance. "Enclosures of from 500 meters to several kilometers in width, and of 500 meters and more in height" would gradually expand across the lunar surface and beneath it, Ehricke wrote.

Selenopolis would replicate the diversity and specific nature of different climates on Earth. It would have cold winters, warm agricultural sections, and dry, subtropical, and semiarid climates. Such a new civilization can only be possible through the use of thermonuclear fusion as an energy source, Ehricke stated, while the smaller-scale industrial and habitation requirements of the previous stages can be met with advanced high-temperature nuclear fission and related technologies (Ehricke 1981a, pp. 21–31).

Producing fusion energy on the Moon would create a crucial new industry that would provide raw material for both the lunar and Earth-based fusion economies. Ehricke proposed that first-generation deuterium-tritium (D-T) fusion reactors on the Moon could be used to breed the rare isotope helium–3 for deuterium-helium fusion, a fusion reaction that is more difficult to create but produces a superior quality of energy. Unknown to Ehricke at that time was the fact that the deposition of material from the solar wind on the airless Moon has created a storehouse of natural helium–3 on the Moon, and over the past few years, proposals have been developed to mine this helium for use in fusion power plants (Freeman 1990, pp. 29–37).

Carefully studying the differences (and similarities) between the two worlds of the Earth and Moon, Ehricke created a new science, that of harenodynamics, for the lunar environment, to replace the aerodynamics required for air transportation on Earth. This "branch of spaceflight dynamics" Ehricke explains he proposes from the Latin *harenosus* meaning "sandy."

"Harenodynamics encompasses the dynamics of flow; boundary

Christopher Sloan

The slide lander, painted by Christopher Sloan, is based on a design by Krafft Ehricke. Ehricke invented the new science of harenodynamics to determine how the sand on the Moon could be used in place of aerodynamics and hydrodynamics on Earth. Demonstrated here is how to land a spacecraft when there is no air resistence to slow it down.

layer formation; and pressure, temperature, and gas (oxygen) release conditions in the boundary layer, at high speed flow of sand along harenodynamics brakes" on a new type of vehicle—the slide lander. The lunar plains, or maria, can be formed into suitable landing sites for these slide landers, which are designed to take advantage of the vacuum, low gravity, and sandy surface of the Moon (Ehricke 1981a, pp. 51–52).

A family of chemical, fission, and fusion-propelled cargo spacecraft would be needed for these successive stages of lunar industrialization to be both feasible and economical. While stage one can rely on the Space Shuttle and Shuttle-derived chemical propellant cargo carriers, a fleet of ships, which he dubs the "Diana Fleet," would be needed for a full-scale industrial economy, with increasingly less import from Earth and more export to Earth and other space-based destinations.

In stage two, a first-generation Geolunar Transport would use improved chemical heavy-lift launch vehicles, and clusters of Cen-

Christopher Sloan

Selenopolis was the name Krafft Ehricke gave to the city on the Moon which would become its capitol. On the right is a series of tokamak machines producing thermonuclear fusion power for the city, its transportation, and industry. Due to the lack of an atmosphere on the Moon, the superconducting magnets which resemble slices of an orange, can be left exposed.

taur liquid hydrogen rockets. The next stage requires a larger Geolunar Transport, supplied by a liquid oxygen from the lunar surface. A nuclear-electric geolunar freighter would be needed to transport cargo from lunar to Earth orbit, which in stage three could use lunar-mined sodium rather than rare hydrogen, as a propellant.

When the construction of Selenopolis begins the movement of mankind into a three-dimensional civilization, high-thrust "super freighters, capable of carrying several thousand tons of cargo," would be developed, relying on nuclear pulsed-power technology. The appropriate field of activity of pulsed drive and steady-state deuterium-Helium-3 fusion, Ehricke concluded, would be the heliocentric "ocean, reaching and making possible the economic exploitation of Mercurian, Martian, asteroidal, and particularly Jovian and Saturnian satellite resources, which the lunar experience will make possible" (Ehricke 1981a, p. 55).

Ehricke saw the development of polyglobal civilizations created by man not only on other celestial bodies but also in heliocentric orbits (becoming new "planets" revolving around the Sun). After the establishment of a production-intense Lunar Industrial Zone and an associated large orbiting Lunar Space Facility to utilize zero-gravity manufacturing based on lunar raw materials, Ehricke proposed that "it will become practical to build still larger systems, self-sufficient enough to seek their own heliocentric orbits—a 'Cellular Androsphere,' or 'Androcell' " (Ehricke 1974).

Civilization on the Earth is limited to the surface—to two dimensions. The development of the Moon, makes it possible for three dimensions to become the rightful field of human activity. With the concept of an Androcell, civilization is not limited to a stationary body or any particular location in the universe. "Once more or less independent, self-reproducing space communities are in existence, three-dimensional civilization will be fully developed," Ehricke wrote in 1975. "Interstellar operations are the theater of action on which civilization will grow into *four-dimensional proportions*. Whether transportation is relativistic or not, time as well as space are involved in this kind of civilization."

Krafft Ehricke gave his last presentation on his concept of lunar industrialization and the "birth of a polyglobal civilization" just weeks before he died, at a symposium on Lunar Bases and Space Activities of the 21st Century held in Washington, D.C., in October 1984. Ehricke received a standing ovation from hundreds of scientists, engineers, and industry and NASA representatives. For them, as Shirley Thomas had written nearly 25 years earlier, Krafft Ehricke was "the embodiment of his belief—the only limitations are those man places on himself, and the universe is man's rightful field of activity" (Thomas 1960, p. 22).

When Krafft Ehricke died on Dec. 11, 1984, after a battle with leukemia, reporter Keay Davidson of *The Los Angeles Times* described him as

a warm, witty man with impeccable manners. Ehricke was a popular lecturer who frequently appeared on San Diego radio and TV stations to discuss his ideas about colonizing the Moon and planets. He enthralled audiences with his plans for erecting low-gravity swimming pools on the Moon and for interstellar spaceships that would turn the galaxy into humanity's backyard.

Other obituaries were quite different in tone and content, however.

The January–February 1985 issue of *Martyrdom and Resistance*, which lists as its address and telephone that of the Anti-Defamation League of B'nai B'rith, makes the outrageous claim that, "the history of Ehricke, as well as his wife, reveals sympathetic and strong links with the Nazi party." Indeed, the article reports, only "death spared them of an impending revelation of their past by Charles R. Allen, Jr., the renowned journalist-lecturer on Nazi criminality and frequent contributor to *Martyrdom and Resistance*" (*Martyrdom and Resistance* 1985).

In the 1985 edition of his book, *Nazi War Criminals in America*, Charles Allen states that Ehricke, who was "an engineer in the Nazi V-rockets program, finished [his] career at the Dora-Nordhausen slave labor/rocket factory complex"—a complete fabrication of Allen. But that was not the worst of his "crimes," according to Allen, who wrote:

> Not widely known is the fact of Ehricke's membership in the Fusion Energy Foundation (FEF) and his listing on the editorial advisory board of FEF's official magazine, *Fusion*. The Fusion Energy Foundation is a well-known front group of the Lyndon H. LaRouche pro-fascist, anti-Semitic National Caucus of Labor Committees—a curious, turgid and mysteriously financed operation. . .(*Martyrdom and Resistance* 1985).

What most upsets Allen, however, is that "*Fusion* promotes nuclear energy plants and various concoctions of 'Star Wars' weaponry, including 'beam' weaponry." In addition, Allen quotes the *New Republic* that leaders of the LaRouche movement 'have conferred repeatedly with top [Reagan] Administration officials' and the CIA.

"Whatever the precise extent of the relationship between LaRouche's FEF and *Fusion* magazine on the one hand and Ehricke on the other, it remains the first demonstrated nexus between the American Far Right and the Paperclip scientists of Nazi Germany. Further in-depth investigations are required of this vital development" (Allen 1985, pp. 55–56).

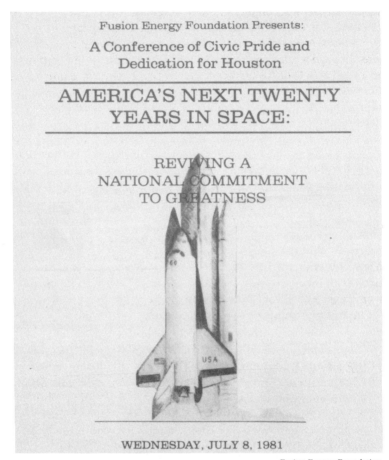

Fusion Energy Foundation Presents:

A Conference of Civic Pride and
Dedication for Houston

AMERICA'S NEXT TWENTY YEARS IN SPACE:

REVIVING A
NATIONAL COMMITMENT
TO GREATNESS

WEDNESDAY, JULY 8, 1981

Fusion Energy Foundation

Krafft Ehricke participated with the Fusion Energy Foundation in a conference to celebrate the first flight of the Space Shuttle in Houston on July 8, 1981. Along with Ehricke on the program was astronaut Dr. Claude Nicollier of the European Space Agency.

In fact, *Fusion* was a widely circulated science and technology magazine, which reached a peak circulation of more than 150,000. It promoted many otherwise "unpopular" causes, such as nuclear energy development, economic growth, a strong space program, beam weapon defense, and research on the frontiers of science. *Fusion* was shut down by the Justice Department in April 1987 under illegal proceedings of an "involuntary bankruptcy," which decision was overturned on appeal nearly two years later.

Ehricke's initial contact with the Fusion Energy Foundation was through a letter he wrote to the editor of *Fusion* in response to a 1981 article on fusion propulsion by Dr. Friedwardt Winterberg. On July 8, 1981, Ehricke accepted an invitation to speak at an FEF conference in Houston, "American's Next Twenty Years in Space," celebrating the first Space Shuttle launch.

Over the next three years, Ehricke authored two articles for *Fusion* on his program for lunar industrialization. He also went on a three-week tour in West Germany to lecture on these ideas, and was an inspiration and very patient intellectual resource for this author and other members of the *Fusion* staff.

The "Nazi" slander leveled against the German space pioneers, which has been revived periodically from the time they arrived in America, produced no concrete results until the 1980s, after the death of Wernher von Braun. In 1979, the Office of Special Investigations (OSI) was set up in the Department of Justice to investigate war crimes charges and secure indictments.

From its inception, the OSI has largely been a joint venture with Moscow. Collaboration with the Soviet procurator general had been initiated in 1976 by Henry Kissinger, ostensibly to investigate the refusal of the Soviets to allow Jews to emigrate to America. A campaign was launched in Congress by Elizabeth Holtzman, a New York Democrat, and Joshua Eilberg, a Pennsylvania Democrat, who complained that the Immigration and Naturalization Service had been "lax" in apprehending alleged war criminals who had entered the United States after the war.

By 1978, Holtzman, having attained a powerful position on the House Judiciary Committee, succeeded in having an amendment passed that allowed adjudicated Nazi persecutors to be deported to the Soviet Union. Their treatment there was to be of no concern to the United States. Under pressure from Holtzmann, Attorney General Griffin Bell agreed to set up a special department in the Criminal Division of the Justice Department that would be directly responsible for hunting such "war criminals" (Ashman and Wagman 1988, p. 188).

The heads of the newly created Office of Special Investigations, Walter Rockler and Alan Ryan, Jr., made a major effort to formalize relations with the Soviet procurator general's office, which together with the East German authorities, would become the prime source for "evidence" and witnesses against "war criminals." One of their first steps was to meet in Moscow with Russian Procurator General Roman Rudenko, the chief Soviet prosecutor at the Nuremberg trials (Ashman and Wagman 1988, p. 199). Rudenko had helped oversee Stalin's murder of 5 million Ukrainians through forced starvation in 1932–1933, and had played a major role in prosecuting Stalin's show trials of the 1930s. As a result of this "Moscow Agreement," as it was called, the OSI would deal directly with the Soviet procurator's office.

The U.S.A. would be able to ask Soviet citizens to testify in OSI cases. The Soviets also agreed to provide documentary evidence for the use of American prosecutors—much of which was cleverly manufactured. After the death of Rudenko, collaboration with the procurator general was through his successor, Aleksandr Rekunkov, in charge of the program of internal exile of Soviet dissidents and "refuseniks" (Ashman and Wagman 1988, p. 200).

Although the campaign to "hunt for Nazis" is most often portrayed as an initiative by Jewish organizations, and was indeed spearheaded in the United States by groups like the Anti-Defamation League, the prime movers were part of the same pro-Soviet network that had attacked Operation Paperclip in the late 1940s and Wernher von Braun in the 1960s.

One of the first people to compile lists of "suspected" war criminals was Charles R. Allen, Jr. In 1952, Allen authored a book titled *Concentration Camps U.S.A.,* in which he compared the imprisonment of U.S. communists under the McCarran Act to the Nazi death camp system. In 1963, the same year East German "journalist" Julius Mader published his attack on Wernher von Braun, Allen published a book called *Heusinger of the Fourth Reich.* Although it was an attack on the newly appointed chairman of the Permanent Military Committee of NATO, Gen. Adolf Ernst Heusinger, because he had been a member of the German General Staff during World War II, Allen's book was more specifically aimed at discrediting any military collaboration between the U.S.A. and West Germany, as well as German membership in NATO. General Heusinger was the inspector general of the West German Bundeswehr and the military adviser to Chancellor Konrad Adenauer.

But Allen's real motives for the attack all bore the stamp of Moscow: namely, "to generate a public debate" about "the arming

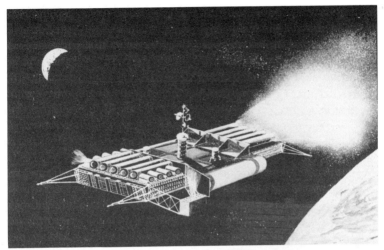

Krafft A. Ehricke

Krafft Ehricke devoted his life to the development of space exploration, and published articles about industrializing the Moon in Fusion *magazine. The concept seen in this painting by Ehricke is of a superfreighter, using lunar oxygen and lunar aluminum for fuel, en route between the Moon and the Earth. After his death Ehricke was slandered as a Nazi by the same antigrowth, pro-Soviet institutions that had led the attack on Arthur Rudolph.*

of West Germany, particularly with nuclear weapons either directly or indirectly; the role and validity of NATO and its direction in American foreign policy; the arms race; in short, the Cold War itself" (Allen 1963, p. 302). The Soviets were most worried about this new U.S.-West German relationship, which was strongly consolidated by President John F. Kennedy's warm reception on his trip to West Germany in 1961, while the Soviets were walling in the population of East Berlin.

In 1965, pro-Soviet propagandist Allen published his paeans to "homo sovieticus" in a travelogue, *Journey to the Soviet Trade Unions,* and in other works on the Soviet Union. In the 1960s, he became a senior editor of *The Nation* magazine, which Linda Hunt and others would utilize for their attacks on "NASA's Nazis."

Charles Allen published his first list of "war criminals" in 1963, in *Jewish Currents* magazine and in the Yiddish-language socialist paper, *Morning Freiheit,* although his "exposé" attracted little attention at the time (Brewda 1985). But when the OSI was formed in

1979, Allen became an adviser, publishing an expanded "list" in *Nazi War Criminals in America: The Basic Handbook*. Most interesting is the fact that in this 1981 "basic" book, Allen never even mentions Arthur Rudolph. It is the enlarged version of Allen's *Handbook* in 1985 that includes Arthur Rudolph for the first time, after he had already left the United States. This 1985 edition also mentions for the first time the recently deceased Krafft Ehricke, naming him as a Nazi for the "crime" of having published articles about industrializing the Moon in *Fusion* magazine!

From the beginning of the OSI's activities, various organizations and individuals raised the issue of "Soviet justice" coming to America. On August 20, 1984, at their 85th national convention in Chicago, the Veterans of Foreign Wars passed resolution 448, which requested President Ronald Reagan to investigate the affairs of the OSI, because the KGB had recently "furnished the OSI doctored tapes and so-called 'witnesses' and 'victims' " against those accused. Objections were also raised by the Joint Baltic American National Committee, the Captive Nations Committee, Ukrainian-Americans, and others.

The OSI also had its defenders, however: The Anti-Defamation League (ADL) of the B'nai B'rith did yeoman's service in propagandizing the "war criminal" issue. By June 1985, the American public was sufficiently angered over the cooperation between the Justice Department and the Soviets that the ADL decided to attack critics of the OSI's activities as "anti-Semites." The ADL even claimed that opponents of the OSI had been unable "to document a single instance, over the past 40 years of forged evidence or perjured testimony being obtained from the Soviet Union for use in Western trials of accused Nazi war criminals" (Anti-Defamation League 1985, p. 14). This self-serving claim ignored the fact that until 1979 the United States did not deem it suitable to accept *any* evidence from the Soviets at its face value.

The ADL's Fact-finding division collaborated directly with its Soviet counterparts. When East German Stasi agents in Sweden launched a disinformation campaign in 1986 against political activist Lyndon H. LaRouche, blaming him for the murder of Swedish Prime Minister Olof Palme, Irwin Suall, the head of the ADL's Fact-finding division, was the first to attempt to give credibility to this slander, traveling to Stockholm to fuel the campaign. In August 1992, former Stasi Colonel Dr. Herbert Brehmer revealed in an interview with the Swedish publication *Journalisten* the fact that this accusation against LaRouche's Swedish co-thinkers was manufactured for political cal reasons.

The same reliance on Soviet "evidence" was used when the OSI aimed at Arthur Rudolph. In a letter to the East German Ministry of Foreign Affairs dated July 15 1983, the U.S. embassy in Berlin, on behalf of the OSI, sought "the assistance of the authorities of the German Democratic Republic in obtaining evidence for the Rudolph case from appropriate archives, libraries and research institutions." Of particular merit, states the letter, were the archives of East German Professor Walter Bartel, who was characterized as "one of the world's foremost authorities on the history of the Mittelwerk." Bartel's archives had been utilized extensively by Julius Mader in his smear of von Braun in 1963 (Mader 1963, p. 300, 394).

In a 1984 interview with the Soviet German-language publication *Neue Zeit,* Mader charged Arthur Rudolph with war crimes. This interview with Mader and Walter Bartel was published in English shortly afterward in the Communist Party, U.S.A. newspaper, *The Daily World.* Other left-wing magazines, like *The Nation,* took up the hue-and-cry against "NASA'S Nazis," although often without revealing their sources.

This same "German scientists are Nazi" slander was employed after President Reagan's announcement of the Strategic Defense Initiative in March 1983 to make nuclear weapons "impotent and obsolete." Like the Apollo program, the SDI was seen by the Soviets as a threat to their ability to match the U.S. scientifically, technologically, militarily, and economically, even though the President had invited the Soviets to work jointly with the United States in this effort to protect the world from nuclear war.

One such effort to blunt the new beam weapon defense effort was by "peace activist" Jack Manno, who wrote in his book *Arming the Heavens* a year after the SDI announcement, that the program had a "Nazi legacy," because the U.S. rocket program found its roots in the work at Peenemünde and because the German-Americans had always warned of the hostile intentions of the Soviet Union (Manno 1984).

Also subject to direct Soviet attack immediately after President Reagan announced the Strategic Defense Initiative was political figure Lyndon LaRouche, Jr., who was the primary public spokesman for the beam weapons program. *Fusion* magazine, with which

EIRNS/Stuart Lewis

Seen here are Krafft Ehricke and the author just as he was about to give a presentation in New York in November 1981 following a three-week trip in Europe. Ehricke was horrified by the irrational antinuclear activists then on the rampage in West Germany. It reminded him of Germany in the 1930s, he said.

LaRouche was associated, was one of the chief sources of information on beam weapon technologies prior to the Reagan announcement. LaRouche had, in fact, conducted back-channel negotiations with the Soviets on a beam weapon defense program, at the behest of the Reagan administration. The Soviet press called for an investigation of LaRouche's finances, hoping that such a government witch-hunt would stop him and his colleagues from continuing to organize public support for the SDI.

This campaign was not limited to the United States. The left-wing opposition to the stationing of the Pershing II missiles in Germany and the announcement of the SDI prompted the radio station Westdeutscher Rundfunk to air a program called "Nazis without Swastikas" on November 30, 1983, taken from the characterization of the LaRouche movement by U.S. New Left scribbler Dennis King, who gave up his career as a peddler of student term papers for the more lucrative one of slandering LaRouche.

In an affidavit on January 18, 1984, for a legal suit against the radio station by the Fusion Energy Forum in West Germany, Ehricke stated: "in light of the large Jewish component of the FEF membership in Wiesbaden, as well as in New York, the charge of anti-Semitism is taken out of thin air; it possesses no basis in fact. . . . At no time has any anti-Semitic tendency ever been expressed."

As far as his own background and beliefs, Ehricke stated: "I personally have never, even in Hitler's time 'hitched my star to the wagon' of any anti-Semitic group. The tragic events that befell my own family under Hitler, which need not be gone into any further here, can be taken as proof. And I can prove that I have never belonged to any Nazi organization. . . . I did, however, belong to the German Army."

Later that same year, the father of spaceflight, Hermann Oberth, celebrated his 90th birthday. On November 30, there was an event to honor him in the city of Nürnberg, near his home in Feucht. When Oberth, his daughter, and other dignitaries arrived, they were greeted with a demonstration by a group of "punk rockers." Inside the hall, a disruption was carried out (before undercover police escorted the handcuffed protesters from the event), with shouts of "Nazi," and "war criminal" aimed at Oberth.

In the fall of 1981, Krafft Ehricke had a first-hand encounter with the irrational, antinuclear environmentalist Greens in Germany, while on a three-week speaking tour. When he returned from Europe, Ehricke told an audience in New York: "It is disconcerting to encounter the same shock troop kind of tactics, and the same kind of rallies with lots of emotional heat but little light of knowledge or reason, at the end of my life as I have seen as a young person in Berlin in 1929 to 1932." At Aachen University, the police had to be called to allow Ehricke's presentation to take place.

The youth of West Germany and other nations have unfortunately been greatly misled . . . today if a person even talks about space flight or nuclear energy, then the 'ecopaths' and cultural pessimists literally consider this to be an outright provocation that they will do their utmost to prevent. The sad thing, of course, is that these are people without hope, without goals. . . . They are the product not of an education in the classics, in the sciences, in technology, but of an education in hopelessness, in frustration [Ehricke 1982a, p. 19].

In 1956, Krafft Ehricke received the first Günther Löser Medal awarded by the International Astronautical Federation at its Congress in Rome for the paper he presented on the Satelloid the year before.

Krafft Ehricke spent his entire life looking for "limits" to man's activities and reported that he had found none.

He was recognized and honored throughout his life by his peers for his vision and comprehensive work in making space exploration a reality. In 1956, he was awarded the first Günther Löser Medal for presentation of the best paper at the Sixth International Aeronautical Federation Congress. In 1957, he received the Astronautics Award of the American Rocket Society, and an Honorary

Doctorate of Humane Letters from the National College of Education in Evanston, Ill. in 1961. In 1972, he received the I.B. Laskowitz Award from the New York Academy of Sciences for his concept of the Extraterrestrial Imperative, and two years later he was awarded the Golovine Award from the British Interplanetary Society.

While he was ill, Krista Ehricke Deer accepted the AIAA Goddard Astronautics Award in May 1984 for her father, given "for more than 40 years of practical and visionary contributions to astronautics."

Five months after his death, Krafft Ehricke was honored by hundreds of scientists, engineers, former colleagues, and international military and political figures at a memorial conference sponsored by two institutions to which he had made significant contributions during the last few years of his life—the Fusion Energy Foundation and the Schiller Institute. The Schiller Institute was founded in 1984 at the initiation of Helga Zepp-LaRouche to revive a strong American alliance with Germany and defeat the neo-Malthusian "Green" parties menacing Western Europe, through the return to classical culture, science, and economic development. Krafft Ehricke was a member of the Schiller Institute's international advisory board.

In his address to the Krafft Ehricke Memorial Conference, held June 15–16, 1985, in Virginia, Lyndon LaRouche discussed the importance of Ehricke's "enduring contribution to the future generations of global and interplanetary civilization." Locating his contributions within the framework that Ehricke himself relied upon, LaRouche stated that the German "pioneers of space drew upon one of the most precious contributions which German culture had already given to all mankind, the scientific heritage of Nicholas of Cusa, Johannes Kepler, Gottfried Liebniz, and Karl Gauss. . . . They have led all mankind along the only pathway by which we might reach the stars.

"In that effort," LaRouche continued,

our dear Krafft Ehricke served with notable distinction, to the degree that his name must be remembered most prominently by those who construct the first colonies on the Moon and Mars. He has helped in an important and practical degree, to make clear to humanity, that it has been the intent of the

Over the course of his entire life, Krafft Ehricke strove to see the present time become the Age of Reason. Although he was dismayed at the dramatic turn against science and rational thinking during the 1970s and early 1980s, he never became pessimistic or lost sight of the goal. Here are pictured the proceedings of the Krafft Ehricke Memorial Conference of June 1985.

Schiller Institute

Creator that mankind's destiny is to become mankind in the Universe. There, in the stars, lies mankind's entry into the long-awaited Age of Reason, when our species sheds at last the cultural residue of the beast [Schiller Institute 1985 pp. 27–28].

In her opening remarks to the same conference, Helga Zepp-LaRouche stated: "Krafft Ehricke himself was what I would call, on the basis of Friedrich Schiller, a beautiful soul. . . . He himself in his character and his personality represented the ideal of man Schiller was praising in his humanist ideal" (Schiller Institute 1985, p. 4).

Krafft Ehricke "was also convinced, and so am I," she continued,

that only through space travel, only when man lifts up his eyes away from the Earth, looks into the stars and actually thinks what his role can be, can he achieve what Schiller called the dignity of men. And only if we start to think about space, and the colonization of space, will the Age of Reason that the great humanists of European civilization were thinking of accomplishing be possible. That was the belief of Schiller, that was the belief of Krafft Ehricke: the fact that man is capable of reason, even under the most horrible condition of crisis. . . .

Krafft Ehricke absolutely deserves that people remember him. He was one of those individuals who represented a singularity that brought mankind a qualitative step further. I think we cannot honor him in a better way than trying to be like him [Schiller Institute 1985, pp. 10–11].

Epilogue

Where would we be today if we had adopted and followed the space exploration schedule put foward by the German space pioneers during the past 50 years?

If, after the Apollo program, the United States had implemented the integrated space program outlined by Wernher von Braun and others in 1969, today we would have a settlement on the Moon, with permanent occupants mining and manufacturing, using telescopes for research, and beginning to build the city, Selenopolis, that Krafft Ehricke envisioned.

Nuclear-propelled freighters would be servicing the growing colony on the Moon, the way trans-Atlantic ocean liners connected the old and new worlds on Earth. Simplified Earth-to-orbit transportation systems would have made space travel almost commonplace.

A decade ago the first explorers would have had landed on Mars. Taking advantage of the biannual opportunity when the relative orbital positions of the Earth and Mars allow the most efficient traverse, in 1993 the fifth Mars crew would be leaving Earth to deliver equipment and scientific instruments, as well as consumables, to the small Mars colony.

If fusion propulsion had been developed, tested, and available, manned missions to Mars would not be limited only to the most opportune planetary alignments but could leave more frequently, increasing the pace of colonization.

What about on Earth?

The peoples of this globe, were they able to employ the technologies developed through space exploration, would live very different lives than many do today.

A worldwide system of Earth-orbiting satellites and inexpensive ground receiver stations would make education, cultural programs, and basic medical information available to every citizen of every nation. Every farmer around the globe would have a constant picture of the state and health of his crops, an inventory of water reserves and resources, warning of catastrophic weather, and vastly increased agricultural productivity.

Perhaps by now Hermann Oberth and Krafft Ehricke's orbiting Lunetta and Soletta mirrors would be modifying the weather, extending the crop-growing season, preventing damage to crops through frost, and providing the light of multiple moons at night to otherwise dark towns and villages.

The fusion energy that would have been developed to take mankind to Mars would have opened an age of unlimited energy here on Earth. New methods of industrial production using highly energy dense lasers and other directed energy would have revolutionized man's work. Planetary engineering, necessary to terraform the Moon and Mars, would have been applied on Earth to make the deserts bloom and create the optimum conditions for growth, even in the most hostile environments on this planet.

Most important, the youth of all nations would have the intellectual tools to contribute to future progress. The outlook that man was not made to stay on this planet but to go out into the Universe to explore would have replaced the pessimism and despair of many today.

This was the goal of the German space pioneers—to make all worlds habitable, to disprove that there are limits to growth, and to open the Age of Reason. Although there have been decades of lost time, it is not too late.

Bibliography

ABMA, 1958. Presentation to NASA, December 15.

Akens, David S., and Satterfield, Paul H., 1962. "Historical Monograph: Army Ordnance Satellite Program." Huntsville: Marshall Space Flight Center.

Alder, Michael, 1971. "2-Star General Becomes Priest," *National Enquirer,* January 10.

Allen, Charles, R., 1963. *Heusinger of the Fourth Reich.* New York: Marzani & Munsell.

———, 1965. *Journey to the Soviet Trade Unions: An American Eye-Witness Report.* New York: Marzani & Munsell.

———, 1966. *Concentration Camps U.S.A.* New York: Marzani & Munsell.

———, 1981. "Nazi War Criminals in America: Facts ... Action, the Basic Handbook." Albany: Charles R. Allen, Jr. Productions.

———, 1985. *Nazi War Criminals in America: Facts ... Action, the Basic Handbook.* New York: Highgate House.

Anti-Defamation League of B'nai B'rith, 1985. *The Campaign Against the U.S. Justice Department's Prosecution of Suspected Nazi War Criminals.* Special Report. New York.

Ashman, Charles, and Wagman, Robert J., 1988. *The Nazi Hunters.* New York: Pharos Books.

Astronautik, 1976. "Professor Becker und die Raketentechnik," Vol. 13, No. 3, p. 80.

Aviation Week, 1959. "Ehricke Asks Single Space Chief," Vol. 71, No. 25, (December 21), p. 23.

Baar, James, 1960. "Medaris Retires with Blast at NASA," *Missiles and Rockets,* (February).

Baker, Michael, and Hughes, Kaylene, 1991. *Redstone Arsenal Complex Chronology, Part I.* Historical Division, U.S. Army Missile Command, Redstone Arsenal.

Baltimore Sun, 1958. "Medaris Says Army Works on Moon Shot," November 9.

———, 1960. "Missile Expert Is 'Not Mad At Anybody' As He Retires." February 23.

Barnard, Chester I., 1946. "Security Through the Sacrifice of Sovereignty," *Bulletin of the Atomic Scientists,* Vol. 2, No. 7 and 8, pp. 30–31.

Barth, Hans, ed., 1984. *Hermann Oberth: Briefwechsel.* Vol. 1 and 2. Bucharest: Kriterion Verlag.

———, 1991. *Hermann Oberth: Vater der Raumfahrt: Autorisierte Biographie.* Esslingen: Bechtle Verlag.

Bar-Zohar, Michel, 1967. *The Hunt for German Scientists.* New York: Hawthorn Books, Inc.

Bergaust, Erik, 1976. *Wernher von Braun.* Washington, D.C.; National Space Institute.

Bethe, Hans A., and Sack, H. S., 1947. "German Scientists in Army Employment," *Bulletin of the Atomic Scientists,* Vol. 3, No. 1 (January), pp. 65, 67.

Bilstein, Roger E., 1980. *Stages to Saturn: A Technological History of the Apollo/ Saturn Launch Vehicles.* Washington, D.C.: National Aeronautics and Space Administration.

Bower, Tom, 1987. *The Paperclip Conspiracy: The Hunt for Nazi Scientists.* Boston: Little, Brown and Company.

Bradbury, Ray, 1979. *The Martian Chronicles.* New York: Bantam Books.

Brewda, Joseph, 1985. "Disband the Office of Special Investigations! Soviet Catspaw Against American Science." *New Solidarity,* June 10.

Burdman, Mark, 1980. "The NATO Plan to Kill U.S. Science," *Fusion,* Vol. 3, No. 11 (September), pp. 41–47.

Busemann, Adolf, 1979. "An Interview with Adolf Busemann," *Fusion,* Vol. 5, No. 1 (October–November), pp. 33–41.

Carr, E.H., 1943. *International Relations Since the Peace Treaties.* London: Macmillan and Co., Limited.

Chapman, John L., 1960. *Atlas: The Story of a Missile.* New York: Harper & Brothers.

Clark, Evert, 1958. "Convair Plans Four-Man Space Station," *Aviation Week,* Vol. 68, No. 17 (April 28) pp. 26–28.

Chicago Tribune, 1958. "Gen. Medaris Predicts Moon Contact Soon," October 14.

Crater, Robert, 1969. "Von Braun Outlines Plans for Mars Trip," *The Knoxville News-Sentinel,* August 14.

Collier, Basil, 1965. *The Battle of the V-Weapons, 1944–45.* New York: William Morrow & Company.

Dannenberg, Konrad K., 1990. "In Memory of Hermann Oberth." Durand Lecture for Public Service, American Institute of Aeronautics and Astronautics Annual Meeting, May 1–3, 1990, Arlington, Virginia.

———, 1991."From Vahrenwald via the Moon to Dresden," *AIAA Student Journal,* Vol. 29, No. 1 (Spring) pp. 512.

———, 1992. Interview, (November 13), Huntsville.

Davidson, Keay, 1984. "Space Rocket Scientist Krafft Ehricke Dies at 67," *Los Angeles Times,* December 13.

Debus, Kurt H., 1973. "From the A–4 to Explorer 1." Seventh International History of Astronautics Symposium, 24th International Astronautical Congress, Baku, U.S.S.R., October 8, 1973.

DeVorkin, David H., 1992. *Science With a Vengeance.* New York: Springer Verlag.

del Rey, Lester, 1969. "Credo," *Galaxy Magazine,* (September) pp. 151–157.

Die Rakete, 1929. (October 15) p. 118.

Dietz, David, 1960. "Interplanetary Trips by '70 Are Predicted," *New York World-Telegram & Sun,* (June 25).

Dooling, Dave, 1977. "Japanese Film Crew Starts Work Here on Von Braun Life," *Huntsville Times,* February 15.

Dornberger, Walter, 1943 (English translation, 1945). "The Development of the Rocket Section of the Army Ordnance Office in the Years 1930–1943." Maryland: Foreign Document Evaluation Branch, Ordnance Research and Development Center, Abderdeen Proving Ground.

———, 1952. *V–2.* London: The Scientific Book Club.

———, 1958. "The Lessons of Peenemünde." *Astronautics,* (March), pp. 18, 20,58, 60.

Durant, Frederick C., 1960. Letter to Krafft Ehricke, May 26.
———, and James, George S., eds., 1974. *First Steps Toward Space*. Proceedings of the First and Second History Symposia of the International Academy of Astronautics. Washington, D.C.: Smithsonian Institution Press.
Ehricke, Krafft A., 1950. "The Peenemünde Rocket Center." *Rocketscience*, Part I, Vol. 4, No. 1 (March), pp. 17–22; Part II, Vol. 4. No 2. (June), pp. 31–35; Part III, Vol. 4. No. 3 (September), pp. 57–63; Part IV, Vol. 4, No. 4 (December), pp. 81–88.
———, 1951. "A Comparison of Rocket Propulsion at Constant Thrust and at Constant Acceleration." *Rocketscience*, Vol. 5, No. 3 (September), pp. 50–63.
———, 1953. "A Comparison of Propellants and Working Fluids for Rocket Propulsion," *Journal of the American Rocket Society*, Vol. 23, No. 5 (September–October), pp. 287–300.
———, 1954. "A New Supply System for Satellite Orbits," Part I, *Jet Propulsion*, Vol. 24, No. 5 (September–October), pp. 302–309; Part II, Vol. 24, No. 6 (November–December), pp. 365, 369–373.
———, 1955. "The Satelloid," presented at the American Rocket Society Fall Meeting, Los Angeles, September 18–21.
———, 1956a. "Astronautical and Space-Medical Research with Automatic Satellites," Monograph No. 2, *Earth Satellites as Research Vehicles*, Philadelphia: Journal of the Franklin Institute, (June), pp. 25–68.
———, 1956b. "Flight Mechanics of the Satelloid," *Aero Digest*, Vol. 73 (July), pp. 46–54.
———, 1957a. "Cislunar Orbits," in *Orbit Theory*, Proceedings of the Ninth Symposium in Applied Mathematics of the American Mathematical Society, New York, April 4–6, Birkhoff, Garret, and Langer, R.E. ed., Providence: American Mathematical Society.
———, 1957b. "The Anthropology of Astronautics," *Astronautics*, Vol. 2, No. 4 (November), pp. 26–27.
———, 1958a. "Our Philosophy of Space Missions," *Aero/Space Engineering*, Vol. 5, (May) pp. 38–43.
———, 1958b. "Space Flight," *Astronautics*, (November), pp. 46–48, 124–128.
———, 1958c. "Error Analysis of Single and Two-Force Field Spacecraft Orbits," in *Ten Steps Into Space. Monograph No. 6.*, Philadelphia: *Journal of the Franklin Institute*, (December), pp. 114–149.
———, 1959a. "Spacecraft and Spaceflight," in *Space Weapons: A Handbook of Military Astronautics*, editors of *Air Force*, New York: Frederick A. Praeger, pp. 144–162.
———, 1959b. "Interplanetary Probes: Three Problems," *Astronautics*, (January), pp. 20–22, 42, 44, 46.
———, 1960a. Letter to Frederick Durant, June 7.
———, 1960b. *Principles of Guided Missile Design*. Vol. 1. Princeton, New Jersey: D. Van Nostrand.
———, 1960c. "Rescue from Space by a Secondary Vehicle," in proceedings, *Second International Symposium on the Physics and Medicine of the Atmosphere and Space*, ed. Benson, Otis O. and Strughold, Hubertus. New York: John Wiley & Sons.
———, and Newsom, B.D., 1966. "Utilization of Space Environment for Therapeutic Purposes," in *Practical Space Applications*, ed. Kavanau, L.L., American Astronautical Society.
———, 1967. "Space Tourism," in *Commercial Utilization of Space*. ed. Gilmer, J. Ray, et al., American Astronautical Society.
———, 1968a. "Synoptic Comparison of Advanced Propulsion Systems for Maneu-

vering Operations Associated With Several Employment Modes in Geolunar Space," presented to the 5th Symposium on Advanced Propulsion Concepts, Chicago, April 8–10.

———, 1968b. "A Strategic Approach to Interplanetary Flight," presented at the Fourth International Symposium on Bioastronautics and the Exploration of Space, San Antonio, June 1968.

———, 1968c. "The Metaprobe—A Concept for Regional Exploration of the Solar System and a Means to Develop International Teamwork in Space Research." Presented at the 19th Congress of the International Astronautical Federation, New York, October 13–19.

———, 1969. "Man, Resources, and Planets," in, *Organizing Space Activities for World Needs*. ed., Steinhoff, Ernst. New York: Pergamon Press.

———, 1970. "Space Applications for Earth-To-Low-Orbit Shuttle Vehicles." Presented to the Space Institute of the University of Tennessee, Tullahoma, October.

———, 1971a. "Our Commitment to Space," *Spaceflight*, Vol. 13, No. 3 (March), p. 82.

———, 1971b. "Planning Space Stations for Long Range Utilization of Space for Earthians," presented to the von Karman Institute for Fluid Dynamics, Brussels, September.

———, 1971c. "Extraterrestrial Imperative," *Bulletin of the Atomic Scientists*, (November), pp. 18–26.

———, 1972a. "Astrogenic Environments: The Effect of Stellar Spectral Classes on the Evolutionary Pace of Life," *Spaceflight*, Vol. 14, No. 1 (January) pp. 2–14.

———, 1972b. Testimony before the Manned Space Flight subcommittee of the House Committee on Science and Astronautics, March 8.

——-, 1972c. "The Extraterrestrial Imperative," *New York Times*, March 31, p. C29.

———, 1973. "Professor Oberth's Vierte Prämisse und das Raumzeitalter," *Astronautik* Vol. 10, No. 3, pp. 196–199.

———, 1974. "Space Stations—Tool of New Growth in An Open World." Invited lecture at the 25th International Astronautical Congress, Amsterdam, October.

———, 1975. "A Long-Range Perspective and Some Fundamental Aspects of Interstellar Evolution," *Journal of the British Interplanetary Society*, Vol. 28, pp. 713–734.

———, 1978. Interview with Frank Winter, (June 30).

———, 1981a. "Industrializing the Moon: The First Step into a New Open World," Part I. *Fusion* Vol 5, No. 2 (December), pp. 21–31. Part II, *Fusion*. Vol. 6, No. 1 (May–June 1984), pp. 46–55.

———, 1981b. *New Growth in an Open World: The Threshold of the First Cosmopolitan Millennium*. La Jolla, California: Space Global. (August).

———, 1981c. "Contributions of Space Reflector Technology to Food Production, Local Weather Manipulation and Energy Supply, 1985–2020," *Journal of the British Interplanetary Society*, Vol. 34, No. 12. (December), pp. 511–518.

———, 1982a. "The Extraterrestrial Imperative: Why Mankind Must Colonize Space," *Fusion*, Vol. 5, No. 6 (December), pp. 18–24.

———, 1982b. *Collected Works of K.A. Ehricke*, preface. La Jolla, California: Space Global. SG-OW-9ET-4182.

———, 1984a. "Harenodynamic Cooling: The Use of Lunar Sand as Cooling Medium," *Acta Astronautica*, Vol. 11, No. 6, pp. 319–327.

———, 1984b. Affidavit to the Westdeutschen Rundfunk, January 18.

Elder, John, 1991. "The Experience of Hermann Oberth," presented at the 42nd Congress of the International Astronautical Federation, October 5–11, Montreal, Canada.

Emme, Eugene M., ed., 1964. *The History of Rocket Technology*. Detroit: Wayne State University.

Engelmann, Joachinm, 1990. *V-2: Dawn of the Rocket Age*. West Chester, Pennsylvania: Schiffer Publishing.

Engle, Rolf, 1931. "The Historical Development of Rocket Technology." Unpublished.

Fisher, Marc, 1992. "Germany Cancels V-2 Launch Fete," *Washington Post*, September 29.

Fletcher, James C., 1976. Letter to President Gerald Ford, December 23.

Folberth, Otto, 1930. "Hermann Oberth," *Klingsor*, Vol. 7, No. 2 (February) pp. 41–45.

Folkart, Burt A., 1990. "Maj. Gen. John Bruce Medaris; Head of Unmanned Space Unit," *Los Angeles Times*, July 16.

Franklin, Thomas, 1987. *An American in Exile: The Story of Arthur Rudolph*. Huntsville: Christopher Kaylor Company.

Freeman, Marsha, 1980. "The NASA Story: The Fight for America's Future," *Fusion*, Vol. 3, No. 11 (September), pp. 25–40.

———, 1982. "Will the Republicans Make the Same Mistake Again?" *New Solidarity*, December 30.

———, 1985. "Colonizing Mars: Moving Man into the Cosmos," *Fusion*, Vol. 7, No. 6 (November–December) pp. 18–28.

———, 1989a. "The Apollo Legacy: Return America to Leadership in Space," *21st Century Science & Technology*, Vol. 2, No. 3 (May–June), pp. 18–32.

———, 1989b. "Medaris: The Man Who Put America into Space," *Executive Intelligence Review*, Vol. 16, No. 33 (August 18) pp. 16–21.

———, 1990. "Mining Helium on the Moon to Power the Earth," *21st Century Science & Technology*, Vol. 3, No. 3 (Summer), pp. 29–37.

———, 1991. "Sending Man into Space Is the Key to Economic Growth," *21st Century Science & Technology*, Vol. 4, No. 2 (Summer), pp. 55–63.

Fusion Energy Foundation, 1983. *Beam Defense: The Alternative to Nuclear Destruction*. Fallbrook, California: Aero Publishing, Inc.

Gartmann, Heinz, 1955. *Träumer, Forscher, Konstrukteure; das Abenteuer de Weltraumfahrt*. Düsseldorf: Econ-Verlag. (English translation by John Chambless).

———, 1956. *The Men Behind the Space Rockets*. New York: David McKay.

General Dynamics, 1985. "The Atlas Launch Vehicle: How It Boosted America Into the Space Age," San Diego.

General Electric Company, 1952. "Final Report, Project Hermes V-2 Missile Program," September.

Generales, Constantine D.J., 1963. "Selected Events Leading to Development of Space Medicine," *New York State Journal of Medicine*, Vol. 63, No. 9 (May 1) p. 1303.

———, 1977. Letter to the editor, *New York State Journal of Medicine*, (November) pp. 2174–2175.

Gimball, John, 1990. "German Scientists, United States Denazification Policy, and the 'Paperclip Conspiracy,'" *The International History Review*, Vol. 12, No. 3 (August) pp. 441–465.

Goodman, Walter, 1987. "'The Nazi Connection' on 'Frontline,'" *New York Times*, February 24.

Goran, Morris, 1967. *The Story of Fritz Haber*. Norman: University of Oklahoma Press.

Goudsmit, Samuel, 1947. Letter to the Editor. *Bulletin of the Atomic Scientists*, Vol. 3, No. 1 (January), pp. 64, 67.

Grey, Jerry, and Grey, Vivian, eds., 1962. *Space Flight Report to the Nation*. New York: Basic Books.

Guenzel, Karl Wenzel, 1988. *Die Fliegenden Fluessigkeitsraketen—Raketenpionier Klaus Riedel.* Holzminden: Guenzel, Huepke & Sohn.

Hahn, Frank, 1993. "General Kurt von Schleicher's Proposal For Infrastructure Projects in Germany," *New Federalist,* Vol. 7, No. 2, January 11, p. 5.

Hall, R. Cargill, 1964. "Early U.S. Satellite Proposals," in Emme, *The History of Rocket Technology.* Detroit: Wayne State University, pp. 67–93.

Hartl, Hans, 1958. *Hermann Oberth: Vorkämpfer der Weltraumfahrt.* Hanover: Theodore Oppermann Verlag.

Haüssermann, Walter., 1992. Interview, (November 12), Huntsville.

Henry, Frank, 1958. "America's Mr. Missile," *Baltimore Sun,* November 9.

Herald-Times-Reporter (Manitowoc-Two Rivers, Wisconsin). 1977. "Von Braun's Surrender is Recalled by Jackson," August 22.

Heitmann, Jan, 1991. "The Peenemünde Rocket Centre," *After the Battle,* No. 74 (November), pp. 1–25.

Henke, Uwe Parpart, 1986. "The Question of Scientific Method: How the Riemannian Approach Allowed the Development of Supersonic Flight," *Fusion,* Vol. 8, No. 1 (January–February), pp. 39–49.

Hermann, Rudolph, 1963. "Evaporative Film Cooling for Hypersonic Reentry Vehicles," in *Astronautical Engineering and Science: From Peenemünde to Planetary Science,* edited by Stuhlinger, et al.; New York: McGraw-Hill Book Company, pp. 261–279.

———, 1981. "The Supersonic Wind Tunnels at Peenemünde and Kochel and Their Contributions to the Aerodynamics of Rocket-Powered Vehicles," presented at the 32nd Congress of the International Astronautical Federation, Rome. September 11.

Hines, William, 1959. "Space Expert Sees Man Exploring Stars," *Washington Star,* January 25.

———, 1960. "Space Effort Splintered, Medaris Tells House," *Washington Star,* February 18.

Höhne, Heinz, 1969. *The Order of the Death's Head.* New York: Ballantine Books.

Hochmuth, Milton, 1985. Letter to Senator Sam Nunn, April 25.

Houston Chronicle, 1971. "Von Braun Asks Hike in Science Education," January 26.

Hughes, Kaylene, 1990. *Redstone Arsenal's Pioneering Efforts in Space.* Redstone Arsenal, U.S. Army Missile Command.

Hunt, Linda, 1985. "U.S. Coverup of Nazi Scientists," *Bulletin of the Atomic Scientists,* Vol. 41, No. 4 (April), pp. 16–24.

———, 1991. *Secret Agenda.* New York: St. Martin's Press.

Huzel, Dieter K., 1962. *Peenemünde to Canaveral.* New Jersey: Prentice-Hall, Inc.

———, 1975. "Why Peenemünde?" Unpublished.

Irving, David, 1965. *The Mare's Nest.* Boston: Little, Brown and Company.

———, 1967. *The German Atomic Bomb.* New York: Simon and Schuster.

Joubert, Philip del la Ferte, 1957. *Rocket.* New York: Philosophical Library.

Kaiser, Hans, 1949a. "The Spirit of Astronautics in Germany in the Last 15 Years," *Journal of the British Interplanetary Society,* Vol. 8, No. 2 (March), pp. 49–51.

———, 1949b. "The Peenemünde Rocket Projects," *Rocketscience,* Vol. 3, No. 4 (December), pp. 92–93.

Kansas City Times, 1972. "And Wernher von Braun Moves On," June 2.

Kanter, Katherine, 1993. "How British Elites Thwarted the German Resistance," *Executive Intelligence Review,* Vol. 20, No. 5 (January 29), pp. 54–57.

Kaysing, Bill, and Reid, Randy, 1976. *We Never Went to the Moon: America's Thirty Billion Dollar Swindle!* Fountain Valley: Eden Press.

348

HOW WE GOT TO THE MOON

Kennedy, Gregory P., 1983. *Vengeance Weapon 2: The V-2 Guided Missile.* Washington, D.C.: Smithsonian Institution Press.

Kennedy, John F., 1961. Memorandum to Lyndon Johnson, April 20.

Kiker, Edward, B., 1992. "United States Army Involvement in Lunar Exploration." Center for Space Policy and Law Annual Symposium, February 21.

Kirkman, Don, 1972a. "Von Braun Hopes to Fly in Space Shuttle," *Houston Post,* April 4.

———, 1972b. "Space Without Dr. von Braun?" *Washington Daily News,* May 27.

Klee, Ernst, and Merk, Otto, 1965. *The Birth of the Missile: The Secrets of Peenemünde.* New York: E.P. Dutton & Company, Inc.

Klemperer, Wolfgang B., 1945. "Survey of Facilities in Germany for Development of Guided Missiles. Part I." Alsos Mission, October 2.

Koelle, Heinz Hermann, 1992. Interview, (December 11), Berlin.

Lasby, Clarence G., 1975. *Project Paperclip: German Scientists and the Cold War.* New York: Atheneum.

Ley, Willy, 1926. *Die Fahrt ins Weltall.* Leipzig: Hochmeister & Thal.

———, 1928. *Die Möglichkeit der Weltraumfahrt: Allgemeinverständliche Beiträge zum Raumschiffahrtsproblem.* Leipzig: Hochmeister & Thal.

———, 1931. Letters to G. Edward Pendray, October 6 and November 2.

———, 1932a. Letter to Hermann Oberth, May 25.

———, 1932b. Letter to G. Edward Pendray, June 30.

———, 1934. Letter to G. Edward Pendray, May 15.

———, 1935a. Letter to G. Edward Pendray, January 30.

———, 1935b. "Rockets," *Popular Flying,* (November) pp. 422–425, 461.

———, 1936. "Some Practical Aspects of Rocketeering," *Aviation,* Vol. 35 (November), pp. 18–20.

———, 1937a. "Eight Days in the Story of Rocketry," *Thrilling Wonder Stories,* Vol. 10. No. 3 (December) pp. 56–64.

———, 1937b. "The Dawn of the Conquest of Space," *Astounding Stories,* Vol. 19 (March) pp. 104–110.

———, 1937c. "Visitors from the Void," *Astounding Stories,* Vol. 19 (May) pp. 91–98.

———, 1940a. "Stations in Space," *Amazing Stories,* Vol. 14, No. 2 (February) pp. 122–124.

———, 1940b. "What's Wrong with Rockets." *Amazing Stories,* Vol. 14, No. 3 (March), pp. 39–40, 49, 145.

———, 1940c. "The Balloon Hoax," *Fantastic Adventures,* Vol. 2 (March) pp. 29–30.

———, 1940d. "Calling All Martians!" *Thrilling Wonder Stories,* Vol. 18, No. 2 (November) pp. 34–39.

———, 1943. "The End of the Rocket Society," No. 6 (August), pp. 64–78; Part 2, Vol. 32, No. 1 (September), pp. 58–75.

———, 1944. "Charting Highways to the Stars," *Travel,* Vol. 23, No. 4 (August) pp. 5–9, 30.

———, 1945. "V–2—Rocket Cargo Ships," *Astounding Science Fiction,* Vol. 35, No. 3, (May), pp. 100–122.

———, 1950. *The Conquest of Space.* New York: The Viking Press.

———, 1953. "Space Travel: Science Fiction and Science Fact," *Publishers' Weekly,* Vol. 164, No. 17 (October 24) p. 1742.

———, and von Braun, Wernher, 1956. *The Exploration of Mars.* New York: The Viking Press.

———, 1957a. *Rockets, Missiles, and Space Travel.* New York: The Viking Press.

————, 1957b. *Willy Ley's For Your Information: On Earth and in the Sky.* New York: Ace Books, Inc.

————, 1958a. "Goal of Missile Race—Space 'Superiority,' " *New York Mirror,* January 5.

————, 1958b. "Will Time Drag for Spacemen?" *New York Mirror,* January 19.

————, 1958c. "The Long History of Space Travel," in, *Ten Steps Into Space,* Monograph No. 6. Lancaster: The Franklin Institute.

————, 1958d. *Space Travel.* Poughkeepsie: Guild Press, Inc.

————, 1960a. "Travel by Rocket," *Science World,* Vol. 7, No. 8, (May 18) pp. 10–12.

————, 1960b. "Getting Around—When We Get There," *Space World,* Vol. 1, No. 4 (November) pp. 27, 57–61.

————, 1961a. "Living in Orbit," *Space World,* Vol. 1, No. 5 (January) pp. 21–23, 55–58.

————, 1961b. "Space Prospecting," *Space World,* Vol. 1, No. 6 (March) pp. 32–33, 52–55.

————, 1961c. "Project Rover," *Space World,* Vol. 1, No. 7 (April) pp. 2–23, 54.

————, 1965. "Manned Space Flight, Prediction and Reality," speech before the New York Section of the American Astronautical Society, May 26, Bethpage, New York.

————, 1969. *Events in Space.* New York: David McKay Company.

List, Willy, 1950. Letter to Commander-in-Chief of the U.S.A. Military Forces in Germany, August 21.

Logsdon, John M., 1970. *The Decision to Go to the Moon.* Cambridge: MIT Press.

————, 1971. "Selecting the Way to the Moon: The Choice of the Lunar Orbital Rendezvous Mode," *Aerospace Historian,* Vol. 18, No. 2 (June) pp. 63–70.

A Lunar Exploration Program Based Upon Saturn-Boosted Systems. Report No. DV-TR-2-60, February. Army Ballistic Missile Agency, Redstone Arsenal.

MacGregor, Ellen, 1951. *Miss Pickerell Goes to Mars.* New York: McGraw Hill.

Mader, Julius, 1963a. "Die Karriere des Wernher von Braun," *DDR im Wort und Bild,* No. 7.

————, 1963b. *Geheimnis von Huntsville: Die wahre Karriere des Raketbarons Wernher von Braun.* Berlin: Deutscher Militärverlag.

————, 1984. "Einer vom Unternehmen 'Paperclip,' " *Neue Zeit,* No. 49, pp. 18–21.

Manno, Jack, 1984. *Arming the Heavens.* New York: Dodd, Mead & Company.

Marianoff, Dimitri, 1944. *Einstein, An Intimate Study of a Great Man.* New York: Doubleday, Doran & Company, Inc.

Marshall Star, "Young French Boy Bids Farewell to Dr. W. von Braun," June 14.

Martyrdom and Resistance, 1985. "Krafft Ehricke, Scientist, Dies: Reveals Links with Nazi Party." Vol. 11, No. 3, (January–February).

Max-Planck-Gesellschaft, 1988. "Mit der Regener-Tonne Beginnt die Weltraumforschung," press release, November 24.

Maxwell, A.E., 1974. "Ehricke Space Garden," *Intellectual Digest,* Vol. 4, No. 10, (June) pp. 6, 8, 10.

Medaris, John B., 1956. "Army Ballistic Missile Agency," *Army Information Digest,* Vol. 11, No. 12 (December), pp. 54–61.

————, 1960. *Countdown to Decision.* New York: G.P. Putnam's Sons.

"Meet the Press," 1959. November 29.

Mendell, W.W., ed, 1985. *Lunar Bases and Space Activities of the 21st Century.* Houston: The Lunar and Planetary Institute.

Miller, Ron and Durant, Frederick C., 1983. *Worlds Beyond: The Art of Chesley Bonestell.* Norfolk: The Donning Company.

Morgenthaler, George, W., ed., 1963. *Exploration of Mars,* Proceedings of the Symposium on the Exploration of Mars, June 6–7, American Astronautical Society, Denver, Colorado.

Morse, Richard S., 1960. Letter to the editor. *Aviation Week,* (October 24) p. 118.

Moskowitz, Sam, 1966. "The Willy Ley Story," *Worlds of Tomorrow,* Vol. 3 No. 7 (May) pp. 30–42.

Murray, Charles, and Cox, Catherine Bly, 1989. *Apollo: The Race to the Moon.* New York: Simon and Schuster.

National Aeronautics and Space Administration, 1970. "Dr. Von Braun NASA Planning Head," January 27 press release.

———, 1985. *Marshall Space Flight Center, 1960–1985.* Report 25M–1285.

Neufeld, Michael J., 1990. "Weimar Culture and Futuristic Technology: The Rocket and Spaceflight Fad in Germany, 1923–1933," *Technology and Culture,* Vol. 31, No. 4 (October) pp. 725–752.

New York Times, 1967. "Maj. Gen. Holger Toftoy Dies; Leader in U.S. Rocket Program," April 20.

———, 1969. "Willie Ley, 62, Prolific Writer on Scientific Subjects, Is Dead," June 25.

———, 1970. "End of von Braun Era Feared By 'Spacemen' of Huntsville, February 1.

Oberg, James E., 1981. *Red Star in Orbit.* New York: Random House.

Oberth, Hermann, 1923. *Die Rakete zu den Planetenrämen.* Munich: R. Oldenbourg.

———, 1928. Letter to Fritz von Opel, May 2.

———, 1929. *Wege zur Raumschiffahrt.* Munich-Berlin: R. Oldenbourg. [Page citations in the text are for the English translation, *Ways to Spaceflight,* Report NASA TT F–622, January 1972.]

———, 1948. Letter to Willy Ley, December 24, in Barth, 1984, Vol. 1, p. 152.

———, 1957. *Man Into Space: New Projects for Rocket and Space Travel.* New York: Harper & Brothers.

———, 1958. *Problems and Proposals Concerning the Interception of Satellites by Manned Vehicles.* Report ABMA-DV–3, March 3, Army Ballistic Missile Agency, Redstone Arsenal.

———, 1959. *The Moon Car.* New York: Harper & Brothers.

———, 1967. "Autobiography," in *The Coming of the Space Age.* edited by Arthur Clarke. New York: Meredith Press.

———, 1974. "My Contributions to Astronautics," in *First Steps Toward Space,* edited by Frederick C. Durant and George James, Washington, D.C.: Smithsonian Institution Press.

O'Neill, Robert J., 1968. *The German Army and the Nazi Party.* London: Corgi Books.

Ordway, Frederick I. and Sharpe, Mitchell R., 1979. *The Rocket Team.* New York: Thomas Y. Crowell, Publishers.

———, and Liebermann, Randy, eds., 1992. *Blueprint for Space: Science Fiction to Science Fact.* Washington, D.C.: Smithsonian Institution Press.

———, and Sharpe, Mitchell R., and Wakeford, Ronald C., 1988. "Project Horizon: An Early Study of a Lunar Outpost," *Acta Astronautica,* Vol. 17, No. 10, pp. 1105–1121.

O'Toole, Thomas, 1968. "Von Braun Warns on Space Cuts," *Washington Post,* May 1.

Paine, Thomas O., 1989. "We Are Also Americans," *21st Century Science & Technology,* Vol. 2, No. 3 (May–June) pp. 30–31.

Päch, Susanne, 1980. "Fifty Years of Activity in Rocketry and Space Flight: Rolf Engel," *Spaceflight,* Vol. 22 (June 6) pp. 231–236.

Pearson, Drew, and Anderson, Jack, 1959. "Wernher von Braun: Columbus of Space," *True Magazine*, Vol. 40, No. 261 (February) pp. 18–29.

"Peenemünde East Through the Eyes of 500 Detained at Garmisch," 1945. Unpublished document in the NASA History Office, Washington, D.C.

Pendray, G. Edward, 1934. "What's in the Rocket?" *Scientific American*, Vol. 151, No. 1 (July) pp. 10–12.

———, 1940. "Rocket Power From Atoms?" *Astronautics*, No. 45 (April) pp. 912.

———, 1955. "The First Quarter Century of the American Rocket Society," *Jet Propulsion*, Vol. 25, No 11 (November) pp. 586–593.

———, 1957. "When Will Rockets Go Commercial?" *Astronautics*, (September) pp. 20–23, 68.

Price, Bem, 1961. "U.S. Has a Chance to Win Moon Race," *New York Paper*, September.

Project Horizon: "A U.S. Army Study for the Establishment of a Lunar Military Outpost," 1959. U.S. Army Ordnance Missile Command, Redstone Arsenal, Alabama, (June 8) 4 volumes.

Raether, Manfred J., 1958. *Applications of Thermonuclear Reactions to Rocket Propulsion*, Report DSP-TN–12–58, Army Ballistic Missile Agency, November 26.

Reid, Constance, 1986. *Hilbert-Courant*. New York: Springer-Verlag.

Reisig, Gerhard, 1992. Interview, (November 11), Huntsville.

Rogers, Georgia Ann, 1977. "Von Braun Hailed as 'Child of God,' " *Huntsville News*, June 25.

Rogers, Warren, Jr., 1960. "Switch to Nuclear Rockets Called Way to Outdo Russians," *New York Herald Tribune*. February 17.

Roth-Oberth, Erna, 1992. Interview, (December 8), Feucht.

Rublowsky, John, 1961. "Tough-Talking General," *Space World*, Vol. 1, No. 6, (March) pp. 21, 55–57.

Rudolph, Arthur, 1992. Interview, (December 14), Hamburg.

Ruppe, Harry, 1992. Interview, (December 9), Munich.

Ryan, Cornelius, ed., 1952. *Across the Space Frontier*. London: Sidgwick and Jackson Limited.

———, ed., 1953. *Man on the Moon*. London: Sidgwick and Jackson Limited.

Saegesser, Lee D., 1977. "U.S. Satellite Proposals, 1945–49," *Spaceflight*, Vol. 19, No. 4 (April) pp. 132–137.

Saturn System Study, 1959. Report DSP-TM1-59, March 13, Army Ballistic Missile Agency, Redstone Arsenal.

Schiller Institute, 1985. *Colonize Space! Open the Age of Reason*. New York: New Benjamin Franklin House Publishing Company, Inc.

Schmidt, William E., 1992. "Suffer Germans Gladly? Not These East Enders," *New York Times*, October 2.

Schriever, Bernard, 1961. "Forward," in Thomas, Shirley, *Men of Space*. Vol. 3, pp. vii–ix.

Schulze, H.A., 1965. "Technical Data on the Development of the A4/V-2." Huntsville: Marshall Space Flight Center, February 25.

Sharpe, Terry H., and von Tiesenhausen, Georg, 1969. *Integrated Space Program—1970–1990*. Report IN-PO-SA-69-4, Marshall Space Flight Center, December 10.

Shirer, William, L., 1960. *The Rise and Fall of the Third Reich*. New York: Simon and Schuster.

Shurkin, Joel, N., 1977. "Wernher von Braun, 65, Space Pioneer, is Dead," *Philadelphia Inquirer*, June 18.

Simpson, Christopher, 1988. *Blowback: America's Recruitment of Nazis and its Effect on the Cold War*. New York: Weidenfeld & Nicolson.

Sloop, John L., 1978. *Liquid Hydrogen As A Propulsion Fuel.* Report SP–4404. Washington, D.C.: National Aeronautics and Space Administration.

Speer, Albert, 1970. *Inside the Third Reich.* New York: Avon Books.

Spaceflight, 1974. "Krafft Ehricke to Receive Golovine Award." Vol. 16, No. 11 (November) p. 437.

Storch, Franz, 1969. "Hermann Oberth und die Frau im Mond," *Neue Literatur,* Vol. 20, No. 9.

Stubno, William J., 1980. *The Impact of the von Braun Board of Directors on the American Space Program.* Masters Thesis, University of Alabama in Huntsville.

Stuhlinger, Ernst, 1958. "Life on Other Stars," *Space Journal,* Vol. 1, No. 3 (Summer) pp. 21–30.

———, ed., et al., 1963 *Astronautical Engineering and Science: From Peenemünde to Planetary Science,* New York: McGraw-Hill Book Company.

———, 1976a. "Dr. Wernher von Braun Biography," in *The Eagle Has Returned,* ed. Steinhoff, Ernst A. Vol. 43, San Diego: American Astronautical Society.

———, 1976b. "Hermann Oberth Biography," in *The Eagle Has Returned,* ed. Steinhoff, Ernst A. Vol. 43, San Diego: American Astronautical Society.

———, and Ordway, Frederick I., 1992. *Wernher von Braun—Aufbruch in den Weltraum.* Esslingen-München: Bechtle Verlag.

Tennenbaum, Jonathan, 1991a. "How Nuclear Fission Was Really Discovered," *21st Century Science & Technology,* Vol. 4, No 1 (Spring) pp. 30–37.

———, 1991b. "Fission and the Breakthrough of Women in Fundamental Scientific Research," *21st Century Science & Technology,* Vol. 4, No. 1 (Spring), pp. 26–29.

Thomas, Shirley, 1960. *Men of Space.* Vol. 1. Philadelphia: Chilton Company.

———, 1961a. *Men of Space.* Vol. 2. Philadelphia: Chilton Company.

———, 1961b. *Men of Space.* Vol. 3. Philadelphia: Chilton Company.

Veterans of Foreign Wars, 1984. Resolution No. 448, August 20.

von Braun, Wernher, 1931. "Lunetta." Unpublished.

———, 1945. "Survey of the Development of Liquid Rockets in Germany and Their Future Prospects," in "Report on Certain Phases of War Research in Germany," by Fritz Zwicky, Pasadena: Aerojet Engineering Corporation, October 1.

———, 1950. Letter to H.H. Koelle, November 4.

———, 1951. Letter to Willy Ley, December 30.

———, 1952. "Why I Chose America," *The American Magazine,* Vol. 154 (July) pp. 15, 111–115.

———, 1954a. Letter to Willy Ley, April 30.

———, 1954b. "Can We Get to Mars?" *Collier's,* Vol. 133, No. 9 (April 30) pp. 22–28.

———, 1956. "Reminiscences of German Rocketry," *Journal of the British Interplanetary Society,* Vol. 15, No. 3 (May–June), pp. 125–145.

———, 1958a. "The Acid Test," *Space Journal,* Vol. 1, No. 3 (Summer) pp. 31–36.

———, and Stuhlinger, Ernst, and Koelle, H.H., 1958b. "ABMA Presentation to the National Aeronautics and Space Administration," December 15. Report No. D-TN1–59, Army Ballistic Missile Agency, Redstone Arsenal.

———, 1959a. "Im Dienste einer Welterschütternde Idee," *Suddeutsche Zeitung,* (January 17–18).

———, 1959b. Congressional Testimony before the Joint Hearings, Preparedness Investigating Subcommittee on the Committee on Armed Services and the Committee on Aeronautical and Space Sciences, United States Senate, January 29 and 30.

———, 1960a. *First Men to the Moon.* New York: Holt, Rinehart, and Winston.

———, 1960b. "Life on Mars," *This Week Magazine,* (April 14) pp. 813, 28–29.

———, 1960c. "Underground in the City of Ahla!" *This Week Magazine*, (May 1) pp. 28–33.

———, 1960d. "The Terrible Secret of Mars," *This Week Magazine*, (May 8) pp. 18–25.

———, 1961a. "First Men to the Moon," *Reader's Digest*, Vol. 78, No. 465 (January) pp. 174–192.

———, 1961b. Memorandum to Lyndon Johnson, April 20.

———, 1961c. Memorandum to Lyndon Johnson, June 20.

———, 1962. *The Mars Project.* Urbana: University of Illinois Press.

———, 1963. Memorandum to James E. Webb, July 31.

———, 1964. "The Redstone, Jupiter, and Juno," in Emme, *The History of Rocket Technology.* Detroit: Wayne State University, pp. 107–121.

———, 1965. "The Next 20 Years of Interplanetary Exploration," *Astronautics and Aeronautics*, Vol. 3, No. 11 (November) pp. 24–34.

———, 1967. "Marshall Center in Transition," *Sperryscope*, (Second Quarter) p. 913.

———, 1968a. "The Space Program: Ally of Social Progress," speech before the American Society for Public Administration, Washington, D.C., March 20.

———, 1968b. "Has U.S. Settled for No. 2 in Space?" *U.S. News & World Report*, (October 14) pp. 74–76.

———, 1968c. "What It's Like to Be Weightless," *Popular Science*, Vol. 193, No. 6 (December) pp. 80–82.

———, 1969a. "Will Mighty Magnets Protect Voyagers to Planets?" *Popular Science*, Vol. 194, No. 1 (January) pp. 98–100, 198.

———, 1969b. Presentation to the Space Task Group on Manned Mars Landing, August 4.

———, 1970. "We Also Build on Failures." *Congressional Record*, May 18.

———, 1971a. Statement before the House Committee on Science and Astronautics, March 3.

———, 1971b. Speech before the Washington Chapter, Aviation and Space Writers, May 27.

———, 1972. "How We'll Team Up With the Russians in Space," *Popular Science*, Vol. 201, No. 2 (August) pp. 76–78, 118.

———, 1974. Letter to Frederick C. Durant, November 8.

———, 1975. *Congressional Record*, July 25.

———, 1976. Presentation to the Synod of the Luthern Church of America, October 26.

von Karman, Theodore, with Lee Edson, 1967. *The Wind and Beyond, Theodore von Karman: Pioneer in Aviation and Pathfinder in Space.* Boston: Little, Brown & Company.

Walters, Helen, 1962. *Hermann Oberth: Father of Space Travel.* New York: Macmillan.

Washington Post, 1960. "Missileman Von Braun Doesn't Explode at Rocket," June 22.

———, 1966. "Von Braun Plans Polar Project," December 22.

———, 1969. "Von Braun's War Foe 'Thankful' He Failed,' " July 22.

Washington Star, 1958. "Men in Space Station Held Possibility." December 20.

———, 1960. " 'Higher Up' Is Blamed for U.S. Space Delay," August 28.

Weeks, Betty, 1958. Letter to Frederick Durant, April 23.

Williams, Beryl, and Epstein, Samuel, 1955. *The Rocket Pioneers.* New York: Julian Messner.

Winter, Frank, 1983 *Prelude to the Space Age, The Rocket Societies: 1924–1940.* Washington, D.C.: Smithsonian Institution Press.

————, 1990. *Rockets into Space.* Cambridge: Harvard University Press.

Witkin, Richard, 1961. "Speed Nike Zeus, Medaris Pleads," *New York Times,* September 21.

Zoike, Helmut, M., 1978. Letter to Frank Winter, December 26.

Zwicky, Fritz, 1945. *Report on Certain Phases of War Research in Germany.* Pasadena: Aerojet Engineering Corp.

Index

About the Author

Marsha Freeman is an associate editor of *21st Century Science & Technology* magazine, and the former Washington editor of *Fusion* magazine. She has been a science writer for fifteen years and has authored hundreds of articles on various aspects of space exploration, including space science, technology, history, biology, the Soviet and Japanese space programs, and space policy. Ms. Freeman has also written on a wide variety of advanced technologies, including nuclear and fusion energy, magnetically levitated transportation, magnetohydrodynamics, and superconductivity.

She has been a witness before the U.S. Congress on questions of science policy, and is cited in *Who's Who in American Women.* Ms. Freeman is an elected member of the National Association of Science Writers and the Aviation/Space Writers Association.